*For Aradhna, who made it happen*

# CONTENTS

# Acknowledgements

First and foremost, for coming up with the idea for the adventure and helping me see it through, as well as for her love, trust and considerable editorial skills, I have to thank my partner Aradhna Tayal. For additional support during the trip, as well as their unending championing of my crazy pursuits and my writing, I'm indebted to my parents Ian and Kath Boyter. Dad especially showed me that it's okay to swap the drafty and cramped interior of a Mazda Bongo for a five-star Romanian hotel, if you absolutely have to. Prem and Mridula Tayal are also to be especially thanked for the former's endless supply of unusual tools and the latter's endless supply of delicious food, in addition to their unflagging support.

Thanks to David James for helping us with our website and for the live mapping of my meanderings, as well as coming out to visit us and support Aradhna, not once but twice (clearly a glutton for punishment). Sarah Bond also kindly joined us to cross the border into Bulgaria and was my only running companion throughout, which was much appreciated. Aradhna's friend's relatives, the energetic Eagles (Buff and Hugh) showed us just how much fun vanlife could be (albeit in their hotel on wheels) as well as bringing me Scottish treats and helping Aradhna with geographic tips and morale boosting cheerleading. Roxy was rendered inhabitable with the tireless assistance of Jennifer and Chris Manley, who helped Aradhna and I with last minute wiring, engine-tuning and upholstering our sylish cushions.

To those we met along the way, we shall not forget your kindness: Cornelia and Winfried Miller, the Sonnleitner family, Hakki Sarialioğlu and kin – Hawaiian massage, fresh bread baked over a campfire, the trials and tribulations of Istanbulspor football team – we could never have anticipated these would enrich our trip as well as your boundless hospitality and generosity. Moritz and others helped jump-start us (both our vehicle and our spirit). Joka and Björn (plus their pack) showed us we are not alone in our nomadic tendencies. Mary from the Chalons-sur-Marne campsite was Aradhna's first interview subject and kindly donated tokens for our first much-needed clothing wash. And to those we met whose names we never got – a mighty thank you.

Gratitude is due also to the legion of followers back home, keeping us motivated and donating vital gifts in the run-up to our departure for France. Your support kept our show on, and sometimes well off, the road.

For believing in the book from the very start and ensuring I gave it everything I could, much gratitude is due to my non-fiction agent, Nick Walters at David Luxton Associates. David Burrill and Ross Jamieson at Great Northern books helped shape my wanderings into something resembling coherence. My father (a man of many talents) designed the wonderful cover, along with David.

I remain grateful to my colleagues at the Hurley Group and NHS Practitioner Health for agreeing my six-month sabbatical and for coping without me during my gallivanting.

Finally, I'd like to thank the citizens of Europe, who still prove that a complex network of different peoples, cultures, races, religions and languages can still feel unified, share in the same goals and aspire to greater kindness, despite the tide of separatism that threatens to sink our island.

# Introduction by Aradhna Tayal

What an adventure we had. A genuine real-life adventure. Swap Timmy the dog for Roxy the campervan, the smugglers' island for the whole of Europe and ginger beer for Irn Bru. Not many people have an experience like this, ever. How do I even begin to look back on everything we achieved and experienced?

It started with finding my perfect partner in crime: a bonkers dreamer with boundless imagination, overflowing with more ideas than you could fit into a lifetime. Match that with my unquenchable thirst for travel and romantic notions of a European escapade. Sprinkle in Gavin's tireless endurance and my practical producer's head. An adventure is born.

I never meant for it to happen! I was swept along in the excitement when Gavin's previous book, *Downhill from Here* was released. As Gavin did the rounds of interviews and book launches, we spent endless hours pondering, "What next?" I was fascinated by the premise, but I was adamant that nothing was going to drag me into the lonely wilderness of the Appalachian Trail! Gavin has this way of saying something enough times that it sort of becomes a thing without anyone ever noticing. When the Orient Express first popped into my head, I felt that jolt of excitement. Most people might then either smile wistfully at a pipe dream, or even start saving for the train ride. What did we do? We bought a bunch of maps, built a home in a car (with zero previous automotive or DIY skills), jacked in our jobs and booked a ferry to France.

I, along with anyone who had ever met me, was utterly bemused by my decision to live in a campervan – I have, after all, always hated camping! I was excited about living in our little home on wheels, that we had spent six months painstakingly and lovingly making. I was nervous about the practical side of it – our bathroom consisted of a bucket, trowel and sponge – but I felt oddly confident in figuring it out with Gavin by my side. Choosing to travel in a campervan had started as a practical choice since there was just no way we could afford to pay for hotels for the duration, as Gavin had done during *Downhill from Here*. It turned out to be a very key part of the journey, for me in particular, as it was up to me to look after Roxy, our campervan, to keep her running, clean and well-stocked. She was my closest and often only companion, as Gavin was off out on a trail somewhere through most of the day, every day for three and a half months.

It really is lovely living in a campervan. You get a new view every day, you've always got everything you need with you because your home is always with you, and you realise how few physical things you actually need to live. It's fun and satisfying to find that perfect hidden spot to spend the night, usually wild camping by a forest, or next to a river or lake we can swim in. We felt resourceful and wholesome, learning to use minimal water to reduce waste and making the effort to buy fewer food products in unnecessary plastic packaging, as we were fastidious about carrying all our rubbish with us until we found a recycling bank. We found ourselves becoming more flexible, in body due to reaching and stretching around the van, and in mind through figuring out new ways to live together under these extraordinary circumstances.

Living in a van is also quite hard work, especially in one as small as Roxy, who started life as an eight-seater car. To drive, all objects need to be secured in the back. Then every time you stop, there's the vanlife dance: every morning, every lunchtime, every pick-up, every night, every single day. My clothes box: passenger seat. Gavin's boxes: driver seat. Bucket and wellies: passenger footwell. Laptop and camera: driver footwell. Running bag and gear: dashboard. There's a very specific order for any task; you can't rush vanlife! It's also something that I mostly carried out alone.

Gavin and I set off on this journey together, but we each very much had our own adventures and experiences in isolation. His was centred on running and his own endurance. Mine involved driving across the continent, navigating only vaguely charted routes, figuring out different currencies, laws, driving regulations, languages, shops and the rest, all whilst keeping the three of us (Roxy included) alive and in good spirits. People ask me what I did with all my spare time while Gavin was out running. With attending to him and to Roxy, including topping up the diesel, gas and drinking water, there wasn't a huge amount of free time left.

For anyone who is new to sport, as I was, I cannot emphasise enough the importance and burden – yes, burden – of the support team, or individual in my case. I was woefully ignorant and unprepared for the immense challenge of catering to someone's every need, especially when said person is your partner and is really whiney and demanding when they're tired, which is ALL of the time if they're running twenty or more miles every day. I was there to coax him out in the morning when his muscles were stiff and the van was cosy, to help with planning out the route for the day, to restock his gels, snacks and water, to buy and prepare lunch and dinner for him, to massage aching calves, to wash disgusting clothes when we couldn't find a laundrette, to be on call to meet him unexpectedly when he was flagging, to supply hot water for tea and a shower (aka bucket bath), and to be his friend when he needed a chat and a cuddle.

The hardest thing I battled with was loneliness. I'm used to seeing friends frequently and thrive off social interaction. I am definitely an extrovert to Gavin's introvert. Where he loved spending hours and hours in his own thoughts all day, I keenly waited for the end of each day, for his company and conversation, though I often had to fight with his phone for his attention. When we set off, I expected that I would spend my days cycling to cute markets and cafés – the only difference between me and Amelie would be my lack of basket! Instead I was stranded in the cold and deserted countryside with the added insult of driving through Champagne out of season when the only thing open was a pharmacy. I came to rely on messages and calls from friends back home, and was especially grateful to the visitors we welcomed along the way – Buff and Hugh, David (twice) and Sarah. One particular moment I recall was sitting in Roxy by the side of a farm in Romania, on the phone to my friend Liz whilst waiting for Gavin in the midst of a thunder storm. There were fierce lightning bolts striking down in the fields just to my right and there were stormy black clouds up ahead. With my friend's voice wrapping around me like a cosy blanket, a potentially frightening time turned into a fond memory that I now cherish.

Through my isolation, I all the more greatly embraced those chance meetings with new friends we made along the way. In particular: the moment that Cornelia Miller stepped out of the bushes and into the icy Lake Chiemsee against a blazing sunset over the Alps; and the moment that Maria Sonnleitner looked up from planting carrots to smile at me as Roxy and I trespassed onto her parents' farm, lost in Austria. I found immense warmth and generosity in the chance encounters I had along the whole journey. There's the French campsite manager sneaking us free laundry tokens, the German father taking time away from his family at Easter to bring us beer and shortbread, the Romanian grandma laughing with me as she taught me how to use an archaic water pump, the Bulgarian homeowner climbing a ladder up the tree in his garden to pick fresh cherries for us and, of course, the Turkish businessman who opened his home and heart to us. I hope that they all know how much their kindness and friendship meant to me.

I did also take time to try and explore the surrounding areas when I could, and Gavin tried to encourage me in this as much as he could. One sunny day when Gavin left me at Riedlingen, Germany, where we had our first encounter with the Danube, I decided to follow suit and cycle along the river all the way to an abbey, that had been recommended to me, roughly 12km away. The ride there was beautiful and Zwiefalter Münster was absolutely stunning. However, I got a little sidetracked when, just next door, I noticed Zwiefalter Klosterbräu, the brewery of the beer we had been enjoying recently (we always tried to sample the local brew as we travelled). I asked for a small taster of each of their four beers on tap. Over a pint later (oopsie), I thought I'd better be on my way but wanted to buy some treats for Gavin and over-enthusiastically ended up with seven 500ml bottles which I then had to try and stuff into my handbag and carry whilst cycling the 12km back to Roxy. By then, the weather had turned and I found myself in tears, trying to cycle into strong winds and stinging raindrops. I somehow managed it with all beer bottles intact, albeit forty-five minutes late to pick up a soaking and shivering Gavin. Thank goodness I'd picked up a Pilsner for him!

Gavin and I each have a lifetime of memories from this insane, wondrous, incredible adventure. It changed us in unexpected and delightful ways, which I'm still resolving in my own life back in the "real" world. During difficult times where undercurrents of division, racism and xenophobia are too often seen creeping into modern society, I am heartened by the humanity I witnessed across the breadth of this remarkable continent. It was fascinating and frequently humbling to see how the landscape, culture and economies of Europe change as you travel from west to east. I am proud and grateful to have experienced Europe and lived within it in a way that few people do, all the while with the safety and security afforded to those clutching a British passport.

I'd like to take a final moment to give a special mention to Romania and the Transalpina, which I missed traversing. Gavin's dad,

Ian, took over support and companionship duties for two weeks when I flew back to the UK to care for my grandma while my parents were away. It was heartbreaking at the time to leave Gavin, Roxy and our adventure, and to miss out on the long-anticipated journey through the Carpathians. I'm now incredibly grateful to Ian and Gavin for making it possible for me to come and spend that valuable time with Naniji, who passed away a year later. I hope to visit the Transalpina another time soon and complete the journey at last.

I hope you enjoy reading about our adventure, and that it inspires you in your own endeavours.

*Aradhna looking very French*

# Forwards

Some of mankind's greatest acts of philanthropy have had their genesis in boredom. Numerous creative breakthroughs have emerged out of ennui too. Or as Kierkegaard put it, "The gods were bored, therefore they created human beings". For Aradhna and me, the inspiration for Summer 2018's epic journey came from an exceptionally tedious wait for a line of fans to snake their way towards the legendary US ultrarunner Dean Karnazes[1] in Waterstones bookshop, Piccadilly.

A few days previously, I'd launched my own book *Downhill from Here*[2] in the same room, a thrilling and terrifying experience. Now I was going to meet the man who first inspired me to consider running extraordinary distances, ask him to sign my copy of his latest book *The Road to Sparta*[3] and present him with a copy of my own. I wasn't the bored one, that's for sure.

Unfortunately, since I was at the back of the line, my girlfriend Aradhna had to wait patiently while I inched my way forward and met the very charming Dean (who thrilled me by asking me to sign my own book for him). This took the better part of half an hour, which left her mind to wander. She was running a sort of thought experiment in her head, along the lines of, "Where would I be prepared to go if asked to support Gavin on another crazily long run?"[4] I'd already mentioned my enthusiasm to follow in the footsteps of Scott Jurek and run the 2,800-mile-long Appalachian Trail from Georgia to Maine. Aradhna wasn't so keen – spending around 90 days in a campervan in backwoods America lacked the requisite romance.

Aradhna had enjoyed reading about my last adventure, running the length of Britain. If we were to do something affordable yet epic it would probably lie within Europe. My thought process when choosing my first adventure had been, "What's the longest trail I could run in the UK? Why not all of it?" Could the same logic be applied to Europe? Exactly how big is Europe anyway? It made sense to run west to east; might it be possible to somehow cross the continent entirely? A quick glance at a map on her phone told Aradhna that from the westernmost

---

1    Author of *Ultramarathon Man* (Allen & Unwin, 2017) about his early running exploits, and a key inspiration for my own.

2    *Downhill from Here*, Sandstone Press, 2017.

3    *The Road to Sparta*, Allen & Unwin, 2018.

4    In September-October 2017 I ran 1174 miles from John O'Groats to Land's End, taking scenic and mountainous routes wherever possible. *Downhill from Here* describes that adventure.

point on the French coast to the easternmost point in Turkey was approximately 4600km – that was probably excessive.

Then she remembered the Orient Express, the first pan-European railway service, which opened in 1883 and took well-heeled passengers from Paris to Constantinople (as it was known then to Europeans). Now wouldn't that be a journey? Could it be undertaken in a matter of a few months on foot? A quick bit of Googling revealed that it would be no Sunday stroll (around 2300 miles, or 3701km by runnable routes), but also that it wasn't as daunting a distance as she'd first assumed. Certainly, the mileage was challenging – almost twice what I'd run in my JOG-LE[1]. Back in 2015 I'd managed 1174 miles (1889km) in 48 days, including a few days off for injury. At the same rate, 3-3½ months might be possible for a pan-European adventure.

What particularly appealed were the station stops on the Orient line:

*Paris – Strasbourg – Munich – Vienna – Budapest – Bucharest – Istanbul*

These read like a roll-call of romantic adventure. While I was running, Aradhna could be strolling the boulevards of Paris, checking out Viennese architecture or burrowing into the souks of Istanbul. I'd later have to remind her that there might be one or two support duties to perform amidst the sightseeing, but the general notion was sound – an experience to cherish for both of us. Aradhna developed a plan to create a documentary film about the notion of home, interviewing locals we met along the way, which would further fascinate her while I plodded ever eastwards.

By the time I had my photo taken with Dean and was able to return the compliment of a signed book, Aradhna had contrived my next adventure. As we downed the last of our complimentary wine, she outlined her idea. All I had to do was say yes. I listened with an eyebrow poised for scepticism but never used it. It was just too brilliant an adventure to refuse. By the time I left the bookshop, my girlfriend had mapped out the summer of 2018 for us both and I decided to throw myself into the scheme with gusto.

\*\*\*

In 1966, the year of Swinging London, flower power and free love, Ford released its Falcon and Bronco, Jaguar launched its XJ13 and

---

1  Common abbreviation for John O'Groats to Land's End. For ease of reference, JOGLE (without the hyphen) will be used from now on.

Jensen produced a car with the fantastic name of Interceptor. Mazda created ... the Bongo. In fact, it's worse than that. As well as it's proud "Ecosse" badge, surrounded by EU stars (which we loved), my sister's vehicle wore a sticker reading "Bongo Friendee". This was the vehicle Fiona was trying to sell us.

"Look, you can reverse the seats, fold them down, slide them around..." she said, ably demonstrating how the six seats in the back of the minibus-sized vehicle could be transformed into an uncomfortable-looking bed. My sceptical eyebrow twitched. This was the Young family's runaround, not a cosy campervan. Sure, it boasted a "pop-top" or AFT (basically an electronically raiseable roof-tent) and additional cupholders, but it was no Winnebago.

I was visiting my family in Edinburgh with Aradhna in the summer of 2017, just after our decision to "run the Orient". We'd mentioned our plan, to variously incredulous and excited friends, parents and siblings and had added, almost as a footnote, that we might buy a campervan. My sister has become a talented salesperson and saw an immediate opening. She was selling their Mazda Bongo, now that her three kids were all gangly youths. Fiona and husband Niall had already spoken to a local dealer who had his eye on the vehicle and was offering a reasonable cash payment. They wanted a quick sale to use the money to part-fund a new car purchase. They were hoping to use this new car to pull a much fancier caravan – an upgrade from the cramped Bongo. It seemed a win-win, to the Youngs at least.

Aradhna and I weren't so sure. We found it hard to imagine this compact vehicle as our home on wheels. For one thing, it was no wider than a standard saloon car, although it was a fair bit longer. To stand up in the interior, you had to raise the wedge-shaped roof compartment. There might be room for a sink, cooker, fridge and miniature wardrobe but there certainly wouldn't be room for a shower or a toilet.

On the other hand, a quick bit of research on the internet revealed that pre-converted Bongos were on the market for far more money than my sister was asking. Even allowing for buying pre-fabricated cabinets and a "rock and roll"[1] bed, we'd still save a lot of money on any comparable vehicle. Our web browsing also revealed the hidden world of "vanlife" and a whole community of people who live "off-grid" in self-converted vans. "Digital nomads", they called themselves, although I preferred the term "techno-hippies". Aradhna's friend Sally pointed out that Instagram was full of adventurous young couples

---

1    A sofa-bed that slides flat for sleeping. Its nickname oversells the glamour of this mechanism.

fashioning themselves campervans and posing in front of incredible scenery (yoga on the roof at dawn was a common theme). While we weren't quite up for adopting a clickbait lifestyle, we were encouraged to discover that self-builds were not uncommon.

Assuming we bought the Bongo, we could pay a conversion company to fit out our campervan, at no little expense – approximately twice to three times what we would pay for the vehicle. Alternatively, we could save a little more cash by purchasing pre-fabricated kits and installing the kitchen, wardrobe and sofa-bed ourselves. Finally, we could just create the interior entirely from scratch. Aradhna's friend Sally drew her attention to a strange new world of campervan self-conversion, with Instagram accounts, blogs and social media followers. If others were doing it, why couldn't we? Wasn't there a step-by-step guide to pretty much any task you could think of on YouTube?

The fact that neither Aradhna nor I had any DIY experience whatsoever didn't seem to us an insurmountable problem. Perhaps it would even be fun. We weren't going to have long to mull the decision over – Fiona wanted an answer within 24 hours as the dealer she'd previously spoken to was standing by.

Slightly giddy from speculation and with the need to decide quickly, we threw caution to the wind and bought our campervan-to-be, making my sister very happy indeed. Her much-loved people carrier (the family had named him Buddy and Fiona even possessed an "I love my Bongo" mug) had found a new set of adoptive parents. Fiona would even have visitation rights!

Driving Roxy back down to London (she didn't feel like a "Buddy", so we renamed her, inspired by the first CD we played in her[1]) Aradhna and I looked at one another in mild panic. What had just happened? We had gone to visit family and had apparently bought a van. We decided that this was no mere accident of fate. Roxy was destined to be our transport, our home, our refuge.

The daunting project ahead was to handcraft a home on wheels we'd be inhabiting for over a third of a year, while planning and executing a 2,300-mile run across all of Europe. Sometimes it's best not to examine a challenge from every angle, second-guessing your own abilities.

Sometimes, to paraphrase the popular song, you must head out on

---

1    *More than This – The Best of Bryan Ferry and Roxy Music.*

the highway and face whatever comes your way[1].

***

When we drove Roxy down to London, we parked up around the corner from Aradhna's parents in New Malden. We didn't want them to see the vehicle we had purchased for two reasons. Firstly, it was Prem's (Aradhna's father's) birthday and we didn't want him to think we'd bought Roxy as some sort of perverse gift. Secondly, we had yet to ask them a big favour – could we park Roxy on their driveway for six months while we worked on her? Aradhna and I lived in a third-floor apartment with severe local parking restrictions and no access to Prem's Aladdin's cave of a garage and its multiplexity of tools and useful things. Although initially baffled as to why we had bought a campervan, the folks agreed with our plan and let us park Roxy in front of their house. Over the next six months we would be regular visitors to New Malden, amusing the neighbours with our ad hoc DIY skills (me chiselling using the front doorstep as a work bench) and trial and error approach to carpentry.

We were a little hampered by only being able to visit on occasional weekends, as work and life pressures absorbed much of our time. As the days shortened through autumn and winter, it became difficult to work on Roxy's interior, since she wouldn't fit in the garage and we had no outdoor working lights. Nevertheless, we squeezed in as many hours as we could.

First, we ripped out the rear chairs, carpets and seating rails as well as the plastic siding. After much sanding, soaping and rust-removal, we had a pristine (and surprisingly spacious) blank canvas to work with. The next job was to insulate Roxy and create a wooden base upon which to lay our Victorian patterned vinyl flooring (we decided to go bold and bright for Roxy's look; we didn't want anything about her to be dull). A Korean couple's videos[2] proved especially helpful here, showing us how to use existing boltholes where we had removed the chairs and rails to fasten down some wooden batons, into which we could then screw the plywood floor (over a double layer of peel-and-stick insulation). It took longer than we'd hoped (several weeks) but we ended up with a secure, insulated and pristine surface upon which to build our living space.

I remembered the day I "discovered" (via the modern miracle

---

1    "Born to be Wild" – Steppenwolf (1968).
2    https://www.youtube.com/channel/UCiqeAszKCXygIwOzYVLJysg

that is Google) the lap joint, a simple, square U-shape cut into two pieces of wood, allowing them to intersect at right angles. It was a beautifully simple and elegant solution to the problem of how to create rigid frames from wooden struts. My grandfather was a "joiner" (as we say in Scotland) and I wanted to honour his profession by cutting no corners. I got a piece of graph paper and doodled the first of many schematics for a piece of furniture built from intersecting struts. The fact that my first sketch resulted in something literally impossible, a crazed M.C. Escher optical illusion, did not faze me. After much heated "discussion" with Aradhna, I also decided that it ought to be securely bolted to Roxy's side (using the leftover rear seatbelt boltholes) so that it wouldn't rattle about and break loose in transit. This I feel was one of my few sensible decisions in the whole project.

I could bore you with the full DIY saga, but I won't. As winter began to bite, we chiselled, insulated, wired and plumbed our way towards a viable interior for Roxy. Sub-zero temperatures would often numb my fingers to the point of uselessness, but Mridula, Aradhna's mum, would always be nearby with a plate of tasty and filling Indian food (and bottomless cups of chai). We became the sort of people who eagerly set off for their local B&Q at 8am, in search of MDF. I particularly enjoyed the game of wondering out aloud, "If only I had something like X..." (where X is an obscure tool or oddly-shaped screw) only to see Prem scurrying off to the back of the garage and invariably returning with several versions of X, often patinated with a layer of dust, but perfectly suited to the task at hand.

We had friends come to help us too – Jen helped Aradhna with the electrical soldering (as a jeweller, she was particularly adept at this) and also created beautiful upholstered cushions for the sofa-bed. Her boyfriend Chris, something of a petrolhead with a pristine collection of shiny tools, helped us with the wiring of our leisure battery (a secondary power source for our water pump, lights, etc), power and USB sockets, as well as listing at great length the checks and repairs we might consider before driving our 20-year-old vehicle 10,000 miles across Europe and back. Aradhna's tech-savvy friend David helped us create a website to use for our blog and interactive map of my progress during the run.

At Christmas we were able to show Fiona and Niall what we had done to their beloved Buddy so far, although the cabinets were still a skeleton structure. It's fair to say that my family was dumbfounded by my newfound carpentry skills, although they had obviously not been present for all the swearing, chisel injuries, accidentally broken struts and dubious health and safety practices that had led to Roxy's refit. I told them that just because my childhood tendency had been to take things apart (sometimes by mistake), that didn't mean I couldn't construct something to a plan. They kept their scepticism in check.

Rapidly running out of time as our intended departure date of 8th March approached, I finished work (having been given a six-month sabbatical from the NHS mental health organisation where I was an administrator) and devoted myself, along with Aradhna, to completing the build. We painted cabinet doors (some of which Prem and Mridula repainted after I made a rookie, wrong-undercoat error), fitting LED strip-lighting and a dimmer switch, plumbed in a sink, electronically activated tap and waste water tank, connected a portable camping stove to a secreted gas cylinder and figured out some elegant (and not so elegant) storage solutions.

In February, we took the nearly-complete Roxy for a test run to a campsite at Crowborough in East Sussex. Predictably freezing cold, we nevertheless enjoyed our weekend testing out the cooking and sleeping facilities and meeting a couple in the local pub who had travelled extensively by campervan in Australia. We began to feel we were part of a "vanlife" community and, most importantly, we realised that *we could do this*.

By the beginning of March, with calloused and numb hands, we stood back to admire the (almost) finished product. Incredibly, Roxy looked reasonably convincing as a home, her woodwork shining a brilliant white under the soft yellow glow of the interior lighting, patterned vinyl floor working surprisingly well alongside the similarly-themed upholstery.

To be honest, we had both surprised ourselves with our level of DIY competence, and we felt this boded well. Surely compared to the seven-month struggle to create a campervan from a people carrier, merely living in her would be easy.

Naïveté is of course one of the essential qualities of any adventurer.

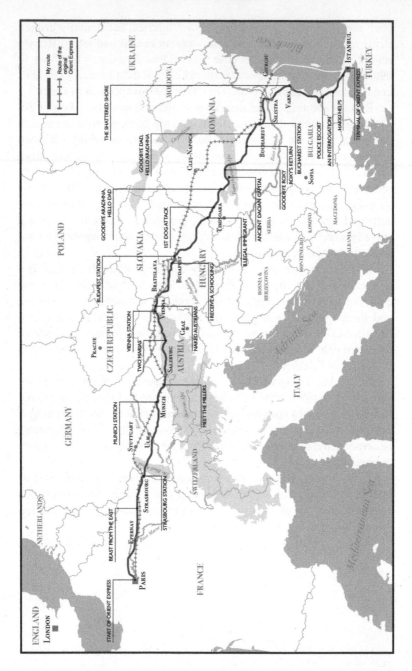

# Chapter 0: A Long-Kept Secret

I've been lying to my girlfriend for months. I've been making excuses to absent myself at inopportune moments. I'm sure Aradhna finds it hugely frustrating, given how much preparation and training I should be doing for our pan-European adventure.

Today I've told her that, after work, I'll be going to meet my friend Indy to see a movie. I've chosen a film I'm sure Aradhna will never want to see, so that I can lie about how good it was without being caught out[1]. Instead of heading to the cinema, I'm going to meet a woman in Shoreditch. I've had several clandestine meetings with Emma over the last few months but this one is special. Emma has something for me.

Jewellery designer Emma Madden's workshop is tucked away in a red-brick mews of small businesses in a largely residential area a fifteen-minute walk from Old Street. It always seems to be raining when I meet Emma but I don't care. I'm too excited. Emma shakes my hand and goes to fetch a small jewellery box. I open it with trepidation.

A sapphire gleams within, round-cut and two-coloured (pale blue and grey). It is set atop a square gold base with diagonals criss-crossing underneath. Two small diamonds balance the composition, set into the 18-carat gold band on either side of the main stone. I designed it myself, with Emma's help and advice. Then Emma made it a reality. I watch glimmers of light reflecting back at me from the shiny new engagement ring, it feels somehow far from real. Am I really about to do this?

For weeks Aradhna and I have been joking that this trip will really prove the strength of our relationship. If we can survive for months on end rattling around together in a small metal box, crossing unfamiliar territories, away from our networks of friends and family, won't we have proven that we're meant to be life partners?

Although it's frightening and challenging, as it surely ought to be,

---

1     Quite possibly *John Wick 2*. Aradhna had previously not reacted well when she agreed to watch an action movie and I played her the first *John Wick* movie, which begins, uncompromisingly, with puppy murder.

my plan is exciting too. I'm going to wait until we reach Istanbul, then arrange something special, choose my moment and ask Aradhna to marry me.

Some couples discuss such plans in detail, demystifying the process and removing the delicious, terrifying frisson of surprise. I've heard some even choose the ring together in advance. I feel I know my partner well enough to say for certain that neither of us wants a prosaic, pre-planned proposal.

Whatever happens, as I leave Emma's workshop that wet February evening, I feel assured that tradition will be satisfied and I will retain the element of surprise.

Now where the hell will I hide the damn thing?

# PART ONE: OLD EUROPE

(France/Germany/Austria)

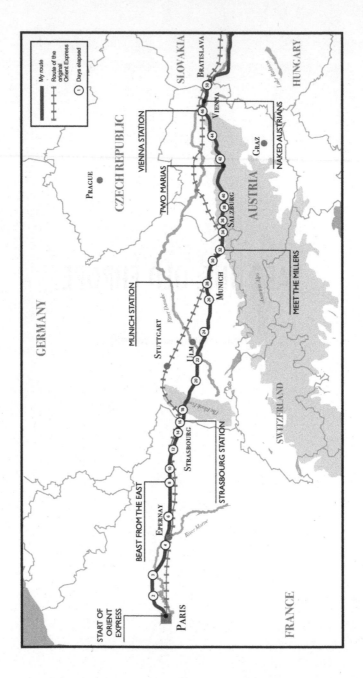

# Chapter 1: The Drowned Forest

*T-Minus 3 Days*

Now that it's finally happening, it's beginning to dawn on us just what we've let ourselves in for. I'll be running through eight European countries, all but one of which (France) I've never visited before. I speak very little French and no other languages apart from English; Aradhna fares a little better in Latinate languages but is far from fluent.

We haven't taken a holiday together that lasted more than a few days and we have just committed to over five months of adventure[1], whilst living in a metal box just three cubic metres in volume.

Aradhna has to secure a safe place to sleep, enough water to drink, electricity when required, diesel for our engine, food (including many thousands of calories for me daily), a way of washing our clothes as well as looking after my needs, whilst navigating, updating social media and somehow keeping her regular work ticking over too.

I have committed to run over 3000km, crossing seven international border checkpoints, over 180 rivers and 16,500 metres of ascent through forest, mountains, plains and major cities. I have no idea if I can run my aimed-for 40-50km a day for around 100 days. We have no plans for dealing with injuries other than throwing ourselves at the mercy of local healthcare facilities (we both have EHIC cards and travel insurance at the ready).

Friends may intermittently visit us but we will largely be on our own, relying entirely upon each other. This will necessitate a huge investment of trust in one another and will require patience, forbearance and (presumably) the ability to count to ten several times a day.

It gradually hits home – we might be in Paris, one of Europe's most romantic and exciting cities, but this is no holiday. This is base camp.

\*\*\*

---

1   Including a lazy drive back to Calais via countries unfamiliar, including Greece, Albania, Montenegro, Bosnia & Herzegovina, Croatia and Luxembourg.

With all the drama of buying, creating and testing Roxy, I have almost completely forgotten to train.

That's not entirely true, although it feels that way as I huff my way around the Bois de Vincennes park, along with seemingly dozens of other runners, on the afternoon of the 10th March 2018, the eve of day one of our adventure. I certainly don't feel like an "endurance athlete" (as I was once hilariously described). My training has consisted of running about 35-40 miles per week, including several runs over 15 miles long, plus entering a few ultra races and trail marathons. I ran the Cotswolds 24 Hour race for the third consecutive year (disappointingly managing only 96 miles, where I had managed over 100 previously), the Dark Star River marathon (actually 28 miles long) and the Beachy Head Marathon (very hilly!). I performed well at these events and felt reasonably fit, but I can't say I followed a focused and detailed training regime.

From running the length of Britain, I know that I'll get leaner and fitter as the weeks wear on and I just hope the first few days won't exhaust or cripple me. On the previous challenge I had aimed for an unrealistic forty miles and managed roughly a marathon per day. This time my target will be approximately thirty miles per day (48km). I know I'll probably fall short of that, given some of the terrain I'll face, but I always think it's good to aim high.

\*\*\*

8th March 2018: Aradhna and I arrive in Paris in the evening, battling traffic and exhaustion to find a suitable parking space by the side of the quiet park on the outskirts of town, and situated in the general direction I'll be running three days later. For two days we wake to the percussive tapping of woodpeckers and get used to the rhythm of life in a van. This proves deceptively easy, but then we haven't yet embarked on the adventure proper. Things will no doubt become considerably more challenging once I begin my run and Aradhna has to fend for herself in foreign and unknown parts.

\*\*\*

On the evening of 10th March we meet up with the parents in a nice hotel overlooking the Gare de l'Est, where we'll all be staying that night. It is only the second time our families have met and I feel a little nervous and jittery, knowing what I'll be embarking upon the following day, but the meal, at a local and recommended Indian restaurant, goes well and the calories are most welcome. Aradhna grips my hand under the table. Our adventure together is about to start and we are relieved that our families are supporting us so avidly.

***

### Day 1

The following morning at a little before 10am, I stand shivering in late winter sunlight outside the station, while the families position me like a mannequin for the obligatory "setting off" photos. This is it – over the top. There's no going back now.

After hugging my family and Aradhna, I trot off around the station and out of sight, which is good because moments later I am straddling and swinging absurdly on a park gate I assumed was locked, only to find it's actually open. Feeling idiotic as I clamber off the gate, I jog along cobbled lanes alongside the canal at Quai de Valmy and make for the famous Père Lachaise cemetery.

My original plan had been to run between the famous graves (I like the idea of "turning right at Oscar Wilde and left at Jim Morrison") but a firm wave of the hand from two gendarmes guarding the entrance warns me off. Suddenly I realise it's hardly respectful to go jogging through a graveyard in Lycra. A lesson is learnt. Not everywhere on my intended route will be appropriate or even possible to run.

Fortunately, it's easy enough to get back on track as I slide through the sleepy boulevards on this crisp, bright Sunday morning. I feel a surge of optimism fill me. I've always had a powerful imagination but also the ability to assume that fate will prove kind in my adventures and that I will generally be okay. In the weeks to come, my optimism and sunny outlook may be increasingly tested. For now, however, I run in spring sunlight and am glad.

Soon I am heading for the Bois de Vincennes again where we have planned to briefly reconvene at Roxy (my parents have not seen her since the refit was completed). It has taken me around 45 minutes to run the 8km[1] so far and I make it back to the van in advance of Aradhna and the four parents. They arrive about thirty minutes later and we give our folks the guided tour as well as ensuring I have enough food and nutrition for the twenty miles I still have to run. I

---

[1]    Since this is a book about running in Europe, it would seem fitting to use metric measurements of distance. Also, it feels more impressive to me to say I was attempting to run 3400km, rather than 2113 miles.

deflect parental concern as much as possible and set off cheerily again, my father filming me on his phone.

Soon I've located Paris's other river, the Marne, and am following a pedestrian trail along its pretty, winding banks. I feel good and am enjoying the sights and sounds of a very different Paris, more akin to a riverside village complete with ornately wood-beamed cottages, each of which is different to its neighbour. I pass a sandstone sculpture of a reclining nude woman and follow a loop of the river down towards La Varenne Saint Hilaire. Shortly thereafter, I make my first navigational error.

I have been relying on Google Maps to get me through the maze of city streets and out into the country and it has suggested a route through a large park-like area at Ormesson-sur-Marne. However, when I get to the small town and find a route down to the "park" it turns out to be a vast country estate and château[1], walled, gated and very much out of bounds. Google doesn't know the difference between a country lane and a private road. There's nothing to do but backtrack and circle the estate, a detour of around three kilometres. From now on, I will have to modify my assumption that technology will always prove my friend. The detour adds arduous kilometres.

Still, this is day one, and so far my energy seems boundless, although I suspect much of this is pure adrenalin. I'm running from Paris to Istanbul! Every so often, I have to mentally catch myself and actively recall that bizarre fact. As far as I am aware, nobody has done this. It's unprecedented – a true adventure. Thoughts like these will help me in my darkest moments, the first of which isn't long in coming.

***

Heading south out of Noiseau I arrive at an entrance to the first of several forests I've planned to run through. Before starting the trip, I decided to run as many off-road routes as possible, partly because running endlessly on tarmac is tough on the feet and legs but mostly because it would just be prettier.

The Fôret Domaniale de Notre Dame is only a small wood of roughly 230km². Its quiet rows of trees and straight gravel paths beckon me away from the tarmac. I quickly realise that it must have rained or snowed heavily recently as the woods on either side of the

---

1    The castle currently standing on the estate has largely been in occupation by the same family (the Le Fevres d'Ormesson) since 1598.

main path are waterlogged, deep pools reflecting skeletal trees. The traffic noise falls gradually away behind me and pale green butterflies flit alongside.

I make good progress and quickly arrive at the junction of eight separate paths in the centre of the forest. I begin to see other people – families out for a stroll, cyclists and dog walkers. This place is evidently a popular getaway for Parisians. Taking a narrower route towards the southern extent of the forest, I suddenly arrive at a bit of a dead end – ahead of me lies an immense mirror, the woods entirely flooded. Several hundred yards behind me, a group of elderly walkers with Alpine poles progress towards the obstacle. I find a possible exit point by leaping over a small stream and head off on a perpendicular path. I hope the Alpine walkers prove agile enough to follow my lead.

\*\*\*

Fatigue finally catching up with me, I run down a steep footpath alongside a golf course, hoping to cross a busy road at its foot. I am thwarted by a high chain-link fence and have to backtrack to the golf course entrance and run surreptitiously across the grass. In my native Scotland, walkers have right of way across all golf courses; I suspect this is not the case in France. Here I am already trespassing, on day one.

I make it across the greens, duck behind a row of oak trees and find a hedge with big enough gaps for me to squeeze through. Scratched and grimy, I run back down to the main road to call Aradhna and arrange a lift. I have no idea how to progress from here tomorrow, but for now, feet aching and wet from my time in the Drowned Forest, I am ready to call it a day. I have run 40km and am happy with that.

\*\*\*

That night we park up at a different entrance to the forest and Aradhna cooks her first meal in Roxy – a tasty and filling pasta. Cooking always makes Aradhna happy and I'm glad she's able to make us both something nutritious and delicious despite the cramped "kitchen" and limited implements. Her multi-coloured and labelled spice box will fast become a key element of her culinary success.

Later on, I need to go to the loo for something more substantial than a pee, so I grit my teeth, grab a small garden trowel and head torch and set off to dig a hole. Having completed my business, I bury both product and paper and fill in the hole, satisfied that I'm being as environmentally friendly as possible. It's surprisingly easy and provides instant relief. Although I feel happy that this one problem with living in a van has been solved, it will prove several days before Aradhna crosses this Rubicon.

She does, however, attempt a pee under the protection of the shower tent, only to have it blow over as a horse and carriage is ambling past. Fortunately, Aradhna acts fast and narrowly escapes mooning some day-tripping French family.

*** 

At the start of day two I insist we start as close to our finish point as possible, so we return to the golf course. Unfortunately, the grand gate to the palatial estate is firmly shut, so we find our way to a car park by a nearby cemetery and I run along a small service road to the rear entrance to the course. This is open – I venture briefly inside to gawp at the château-like clubhouse before turning tail and running back the way I'd come. Although it irks me a little that the map of my run will have a hundred-yard gap in it, I realise this is trivial in the grand scheme of things and press on.

The morning of the second day proves overcast and chilly, ideal running weather as I pass through another small forest, an industrial park and the outskirts of La Queue-en-Brie. My plan is to traverse the much larger Fôret Domaniale d'Armainvilliers, which proves altogether quieter, darker and spookier than yesterday's wood. I zig-zag along increasingly grassy and muddy footpaths with not a soul in sight until the waterlogged course I'm following ends abruptly at yet another fence and padlocked gate. The fence extends for many kilometres in both directions. Beyond the perimeter, I can see a well-maintained estate, rows of pristine trees and a sliver of the Étang d'Armainvilliers southern reservoir. Once again, my mapping systems (and my lack of forward-planning, if I'm honest) have let me down. A gloom settles over me – I can't believe I've gone so wrong, so quickly. And this is comfortable, familiar France – what if this happens in the wilds of the Austrian Alps or the forests of Bulgaria?

*** 

After plodding disconsolately around in shin-high mud, plagued by insects for half an hour, I concede that the estate is of significant size and that continuing to follow the trackless perimeter fence south would be futile. I turn north and make it back onto proper paths ... but not for long.

This time my route peters out into a veritable bog of standing water, tuffets of grass and fallen tree trunks. My progress slows to a squelchy meander along what seems like miles of untrodden forest. There is a lot of swearing. I doubt anyone except a keen entomologist or bryologist[1] has set boot (or wader) in this region for many months. A quick look at my phone and Garmin device[2] reveals that I must either find a way between the two reservoirs to the north-east or, worst-case scenario, skirt around the top of both lakes. The notion of a paved roadway suddenly seems utterly idyllic.

Much swearing and exhaustion later, I emerge onto a path with actual signposts, albeit weather-worn ones, and head east along the top of the Étang de Vincennes, then cut down to my planned route via the village of Favières. In total, the unwanted detour adds around 8km and costs me a couple of hours. However, I am now in open farmland and can settle into a proper running stride again. It's a setback, not a defeat.

From my previous running adventure, I know that a rate of around 8-9kph allows me to keep running for six to eight hours per day, but this is very dependent on my overall level of fatigue and the terrain. At worst, my pace might drop to around the speed of a fast walk. I don't really see the point of running slower than a brisk hiker could manage, so I keep the pace, at the very least, above walking speed at all times.

\*\*\*

At Neufmoutiers-en-Brie[3], as it begins to rain, Aradhna makes me a filling late lunch of pasta and cheese on toast and I press on along quiet rural roads lined with mistletoe (pom-pom trees, we call them). As the rain stops, a rainbow forms in the early evening light, a beautiful sight with which to end the day. Also welcome is the sight of Aradhna on her bike, ready to accompany me the last couple of kilometres to Hautefeuille. We find another forest to park outside (they always seem to have space for a few cars) and settle in for the night. We are

---

1    One who studies mosses and liverwort.
2    A device for recording location and communicating this via satellite via an interactive mapping site. It can also be used to send emails anywhere on the planet with a clear line of sight with the satellite network.
3    The village place-names made it very clear that we were in the Brie region, a fact that would make Aradhna, a soft cheese enthusiast, very happy.

rewarded with a glorious sunset, the sky on fire with red and orange backlit clouds.

***

Aradhna feels a little down – she isn't enjoying simply driving to the prearranged lunch spot and hanging around for hours while I am waylaid by geography. I tentatively suggest she might be a little more selfish with her time after I leave each morning. I can give her sufficient notice of where and when to meet me. She should be able to find time to explore, either in Roxy or by bike. Of course, I am naïve – Aradhna has a lot of administrative tasks to keep her busy – but I hope she'll manage to carve out a little time for herself.

Before we set off on this trip we talked extensively about this not being my solo voyage but rather a shared adventure across Europe. In addition, Aradhna wanted to make her film about "home", interviewing interesting people we met along the way. That project was her baby and would have nothing to do with my running. I sincerely hope she'll manage to get some good footage and fulfil her own creative needs as we progress.

***

Day three brings yet another forest our way. This time, feeling fragile from my misadventures the previous day, I stick to a small road that runs through the edge of it and emerge by the tiny village of Pommeuse. Climbing through the backstreets of that hilly town, I manage to infuriate at least a dozen dogs and I escape to the sound of them all complaining at once. I begin to realise that the word "chemin" denotes not so much a road but a footpath which may or may not be accessible to motor vehicles. I actively seek these now, as they usually prove light on traffic and often picturesque.

The day begins overcast and a little chilly but improves once I reach the town of Coulommiers, where I pause briefly in a park to watch some stately swans strut past me, apparently unimpressed. My legs are feeling stiff but I am in no significant pain; so far, so good, I think. Things get trickier when I try to take what I assume is a quiet road out of town only to find it's a popular local cut-through for drivers. I have not quite become used to running alongside busy traffic and spend a lot of time darting onto grassy verges to avoid cars and trucks blasting past me along the narrow, winding lanes.

Eventually I reach Saint-Siméon and the Grand Morin River and reservoir to the east of the village, where I meet Aradhna for lunch. She is a little frustrated by the toilets at the reservoir being closed and later there is further frustration when the local fromagerie's café proves shut too – no local brie for Aradhna. Fortunately, a local directs her to some public loos and decent enough supermarket cheese provides some consolation.

*** 

It occurs to me, dear reader, that I've made a simple assumption that may be unjustified. I've assumed that, like me, you see the value in running, day after day, for months, across an entire continent, rather than doing something normal like simply taking a really long holiday. Perhaps I ought to elucidate why, for me, this adventure seemed essential to my – even to our – emotional well-being.

In 2015 I ran from John O'Groats to Land's End, in part simply because I was bored (with job, a lack of creative fulfilment and a moribund love life). Digging deeper, I think I was having something of a midlife crisis, seeking meaning through adventure, because real excitement (and someone to share it with) was missing from my life. I needed to prove my self-worth. If I did something that impressed me, perhaps I'd become more impressive to others and doors would open that had previously seemed bolted shut.

What I found was a sense of peace and gratitude for having the kind of life and support network that allow me to push myself beyond my previously assumed limits and write a book about it (and an as-yet-incomplete film).

Three years passed, I met my intended life-partner and finally entered a life of responsibility and comparative convention. However, in my core, a restless flame still burned. I'd caught the adventure bug and wanted to test my mettle with an even-greater challenge. The deep psychology of this adventure is something hard to fathom, but I know I wanted to share this new adventure with Aradhna and prove that my first multi-day run wasn't just a once-in-a-lifetime fluke. This is what I do now, I thought, I run really long distances and then write about it, for the enjoyment of others. And why not? There are worse things I could be doing.

***

After lunch, the creeping fatigue begins to get to me. Straight, flat roads through endless farmland offer little to divert my tired brain away from thoughts of stopping. Avenues lined with pristine and identical trees are almost too symmetrical to feel real. The fields are ploughed in perfect lines, as if combed by a pedant. I need something to happen, something to bring respite from the repetition.

Over lunch I experience a bit of an enthusiasm slump; Aradhna persuades me to continue. After all, if I wimp out now on day three, how will I ever make it to day 100? I plod on, glad to have battled my weakness of will with my girlfriend's help, although still dealing with a creeping fatigue. Eventually I reach the village of Nogent-l'Artaud, where we stop for the night.

We decide to head for a campsite since I have now exhausted the paltry supply of running clothes I brought (we keep used, sweaty gear in a plastic tub with an airtight lid we dubbed the "isolation box", for reasons best left to the imagination). I need to do some washing and access to a proper shower would be much appreciated.

As well as going to the loo, showering is the other big quandary of living in a small van. In Sussex, we tried one of those black plastic bags with a shower head attached that you hang in direct sunlight until the water inside is warm, but unfortunately it leaked through two large holes. We abandoned it in favour of buying a pop-up shower tent (six foot in height with a four-foot-square floor area, yet capable of folding up into a circular bag about 18 inches in diameter). I fill a bucket with hot water and surreptitiously take a sponge, towel and shower gel into the tent. It works remarkably well and not once during the trip does anyone question what our oddly shaped tent is for. That said, a conventional shower is still far preferable, particularly in sub-zero temperatures.

Unfortunately, the campsite turns out to have no washing machine so I spend a fun half hour hand-washing my disgusting laundry in a toilet block sink.

\*\*\*

I have a reunion with the river Marne on 14th March as I cross the bridge at Nogent and begin to follow a footpath along its north bank. I say footpath but it's largely two deep runnels made by farm vehicles and local riverbank dwellers' cars. Fortunately, the weather stays dry and my mood lifts as I watch the gently-flowing river drifting east. I will have no navigational issues for several days, since our plan is to follow the river into the heart of the Champagne region. We are both excited about the possibility of having a tasting at a local vineyard, although the tourist season is still a couple of months away. The notion of running through Champagne without having a glass or two seems inconceivable[1].

My fatigue seems to have lifted a little too. I always find it amazing how mental attitude can quickly affect physical performance, especially in ultrarunning, where sheer bloody-mindedness drives you on once your energy reserves run low. As I run, a deep peace descends; I see no walkers, joggers or cyclists on the footpath and the only signs of human habitation I pass are occasional homes whose fenced gardens back onto the path. I pass an inviting boat dock idiosyncratically decorated with the Jolly Roger[2], which feels like the owner is sending somewhat mixed messages. A series of locks and tidal barriers keep the Marne's waters smooth and glassy. I pause by a small semi-derelict dock to grab a snack of nuts and dried fruit. A noise by my side alerts me to the presence of an inquisitive swan. I have no idea if swans can eat fruit and nuts but throw a few in the water and my feathered companion eagerly gobbles them up. I feed the swan two more handfuls and go on my way.

Lunch proper takes place at Château Thierry. Roxy is parked near the river, my damp running clothes hanging off her on all sides, drying in the cool sunlight. It is just warm enough for Aradhna and I to enjoy an al fresco meal, including some local bread and cheese. We sit on a bench and watch the river glide by. An elderly local man taps his beret in passing and wishes us *bon appétit!* Could there be anything more French?

As ever, getting started again is challenging, as I trot past massive factories on the southern side of the river, then run out into open farmland. Although it isn't the most direct route by which to head east, we have decided that a few days following the river will be good for us both.

Although I pass cryptic signs for river users, I don't see a single boat all day. There are more swans, ducks, black herons, cormorants and possibly even a grebe (my birding skills are limited at best). Pale blue wildflowers dot the verges, an early indicator of approaching spring. More evidence of severe winter weather is presented by fallen trees

---

1    There are 465 champagne growers in the region, according to www.champagne.fr – we felt certain we could visit at least one of them!

2    The skull and crossbones flag of piracy, dating back to the early eighteenth century and designed to invoke fear in the crew of any ship facing down a pirate vessel.

which my tired legs struggle to hop over. I occasionally pass a hillside village, small houses and stone churches set against a backdrop of vineyards stretching up the sunlit slopes. Chartèves is the last of these villages before the arching green metal bridge at Jaulgonne, where I finally decide to stop for the day.

We are already beginning to find our feet in the van, and are settling into a daily routine. After finishing running each day, I erect our pop-up shower tent and have a bucket bath (hot water from the kettle mixed with cold from our water tank). Aradhna then feeds me some snacks and we collaborate on dinner (my contribution is generally the washing up). In the evenings we sit outside with a glass of wine or watch an episode or two of the box sets a friend has provided for us on a portable drive.

When it's time to sleep we have the choice of upstairs or downstairs. The Mazda Bongo has an electronic roof which lifts up at the front to create a wedge-like tent which is surprisingly roomy. You access this through a trapdoor and the sides are made of durable canvas, with an outer layer of netting so that you have the option of sleeping with maximum ventilation and minimum insects.

Downstairs, a fold-out bed suffices, considerably narrower but warmer, more comfortable and certainly more surreptitious. There are curtains to pull down for privacy and a plastic cover to put over Roxy's windscreen to block out the light. With the roof down, we are just an anonymous grey van.

Sleep usually comes swiftly and, in the morning, the sun edges in around curtains and seeps through the canvas, coaxing us awake. It is a life of simplicity and routine.

\*\*\*

On the evening of the 14th March, Aradhna and I take a short walk around the village of Jaulgonne, looking for a bar, but finding nothing but a pharmacy still open for business. We settle for the bottled beer we have already stashed in Roxy's coolbox and settle down for the night. Being lifelong "townies" Aradhna and I haven't quite acclimatised to the slower pace of life in rural France; we will have plenty of opportunity to learn – it will be 350km until we reach our first port of call – Strasbourg.

\*\*\*

The following day we drive round to the bridge to begin my running. I am wearing my new trail shoes which might help me today since a fine rain is falling and the footpaths will be muddy. It's only when I meet up with Aradhna later that I remember that I left my other shoes under the van the night before and never mentioned this salient fact. Of course, Aradhna drove off in Roxy, leaving them behind. It is my fault entirely but it's hugely frustrating, nevertheless. Aradhna wants to drive back to see if we could find them but I know the shoes will be gone; no doubt the property of an opportunistic local. Besides, we have champagne to seek out.

Necessity notwithstanding, I am glad to be wearing the trail shoes, since it rains endlessly as I skirt the edges of fields lined with more "pom-pom trees". Cypresses form stately rows and the tiny villages are interspersed with increasing numbers of vineyards, where the occasional employee can be seen pruning or tying up the vines. The river is glassy smooth as a thin mist lies over the soaking wet landscape. Then – unexpected but strangely welcome – a sign of life! A long, wide barge chugs downstream, big enough that a saloon car sits parked halfway along its length.

Alongside a larger vineyard, a tarmac service road takes over for a while and I run gingerly through the puddles, aware that my trail shoes are not best suited to road surfaces. I am also acutely aware of my eternal weakness – my right knee – which tends to hurt a little more in cold weather. To keep it in line, I have forced a tight support tube over my knee. I have Ehlers-Danlos Syndrome[1], a rare but largely benign collagen deficiency which causes elastic skin and hypermobility in certain joints. It can be problematic for a runner when his knees want to rotate in a range of unhelpful directions!

A kilometre or so along the service road, someone has painted a giant yellow heart on the road containing the cryptic inscription "Fred 1996". A declaration of love? Memorial to a family member? Elaborate tag from a self-regarding Frenchman? It will remain a mystery.

The town of Châtillon-sur-Marne crouches prettily on the hillside beyond the fields as the rain becomes more and more persistent. Although I've packed a waterproof jacket and several pairs of leggings, I am soon cold and soaked through as I take shelter under a small road bridge and try to wipe my smartphone dry enough to be able to send a progress report. Nothing is truly waterproof if you run in the rain all day.

---

1    https://en.wikipedia.org/wiki/Ehlers-Danlos_syndromes

Soon a tight hamstring joins the small gang of body parts clamouring for me to stop running. I refuse to concede just yet as it is my intention to manage at least 32-35km per day and I have learnt from previous long-distance running the vital difference between a niggle that can be ignored and an incipient serious injury. Still, I have promised Aradhna that we'll try to tour a vineyard, and this gives me a legitimate excuse to call a halt to that day's run. The thought of wine spurs me on to a late spurt of speed – I cover the last 10km in 45 minutes.

At Damery, the river splits into a bow shape, the straight edge a canal lined with mistletoe and dwarf trees whose twigs bear the nubs of spring buds trying to burst through. Perhaps this incessant rain will help. I meet Aradhna and, following a debriefing regarding my missing footwear, have a quick "bucket bath" before changing for our impromptu vineyard visit. Unfortunately, although the town boasts several wine growers, none are open for a surprise visit from two accidental tourists. It is still distinctly off-season; things won't pick up in the region until the beginning of May.

We are both coming down with a serious case of "the glums" and something must be done. Both of us have, at times, struggled with depression, my most serious episode requiring a clinical intervention when I was 26. In the close quarters of Roxy, everything is magnified and it's easy for a foul mood to become contagious. We have to work even harder than we might back home to keep our spirits up and support one another in escaping the doldrums. There must and shall be champagne.

*****

Aradhna and I decide to shake off the gloom with a wine tasting session at the nearby regional capital of Épernay. If we can't visit a working vineyard, we can certainly find a specialist champagne bar. We explore the huge *cave* at Comme C, its arches laden with dusty bottles, and order a tasting flight of six local champagnes and a vegetarian sharing platter. This is the life!

Fairly tipsy, we return to the stadium car park where we have stashed Roxy only to find some officials closing the gate and politely asking us to leave. Knowing we are probably over the limit, we drive exceptionally carefully to the nearby parking spot they directed us to – where Roxy is dwarfed by huge white campervans on either side. These are of the kind with huge quiff-like protrusions over the driver's cab, containing bunks. I dub them "Elvises" because of their "hairstyles" and am grateful we're driving something a little stealthier and more manoeuvrable. Relieved that we have found a safe, legal camping spot without mishap, we drop quickly off into a wine-sodden sleep.

**KILOMETRES TRAVELLED: 181;**
**KILOMETRES REMAINING: 3217**

# Chapter 2: Chasing Coypus

## Day 6

In 1883, the Orient Express's elite passengers (paying the modern-day equivalent of €1,750 each) dressed to impress and the train's staff were no less well turned-out, in sharp suits, knee breeches, polished shoes and gloves. Nothing was less than immaculate, and few concessions were made to the dirt and grime of long-distance train travel.

By contrast, our own clothing reserves on our pan-European crossing consist of one 50-litre plastic box each and no more than three pairs of shoes (which had to include wellies and flip flops!)

A clothes shopping trip isn't the way I'd wanted to start day six, but my road shoes must be replaced, so a trip to Épernay's Decathlon sports store becomes a necessary evil. Fortunately, I emerge with a suitable and reasonably priced pair, as well as some running shorts and a high-vis top. We buy ourselves some croissants to enjoy with a late brunch. I don't get running until 12pm but at least I'm doing so in a brand-new pair of luminous yellow Mizunos.

I am rather ambivalent when it comes to running shoes and have no brand loyalty. I've worn everything – Mizunos, Asics, Adidas, Brooks, Nike, Saucony ... I can't say I've noticed anything superlative about any specific make of footwear. What I haven't tried is "barefoot running", either literally or in something minimal like Vibram FiveFingers (basically rubber gloves for the feet)[1]. My only real rule is that if the shoes are good, they won't hurt you and you won't get hurt. And as for the supposed 500-mile limit recommended for any pair of shoes, I tend to find my shoes only really get properly comfortable after about 300 miles! I'm unlikely to cast them aside a few weeks later. I buy a mid-price pair and tend to wear them into the ground and only get rid of them once my feet, ankles and calves tell me they are no longer receiving the right kind of support. Please don't take this strategy as a tip – it's just my idiosyncrasy (and if I'm honest, laziness). What you wear on your feet is very much up to you and the

---

1    For more on this, see Christopher McDougall's book *Born to Run* (Profile Books, 2010).

feet know best.

*\*\**

Today my feet are reasonably happy. Although it's a grey day, it is dry underfoot and my legs feel rested and capable.

I continue to follow the Marne's sinuous curves as far as Cumières, where the first of a series of canals running parallel to the river begins. These man-made waterways are incredibly straight and cut hundreds of kilometres from the distance one would have to travel by river alone, given the Marne's intricate loops and deviations.

Cumières also features a series of metal silhouette sculptures demonstrating stages in the wine-making process, some incorporating real elements like a hand-turned wine press. I stop to photograph the first of many European "insect hotels" – what looks like a bird box is open at front and back and filled with a variety of different materials including hollow tubes, sticks and leaves to encourage flying and crawling residents.

Cherry blossom blooms along the canal bank as the sun emerges eventually from thick cumulus clouds. I run through the pleasantly-named town of Magenta and am stopped in my tracks at Mareuil-sur-Ay by the apparition of a grand country house mirrored in the still water. One might turn a photograph upside down; the viewer would be none the wiser.

The running is straightforward and enjoyable as the temperature becomes more ambient – it feels like spring has decided to make an early showing. We take a late lunch at Tours-sur-Marne and decide that I should carry on running until around 6:30pm, to make up for time lost in our emergency shopping trip that morning.

*\*\**

The latter stage of the day's running is bleaker, straighter and a lot less fun than the earlier session. I have the shovel with me as I desperately need to go to the loo. Unfortunately, the wiry underbrush and lack of leaves provide no cover for covert squatting. I wait until I am in the middle of a very long, straight section of the canal, with maximum visibility in both directions so that I can "abandon shit" if necessary. When I'm sure the coast is clear, I dig my hole and drop my shorts, hoping that a speedy cyclist won't catch me in the act. Fortunately, I get away with it and cover my traces.

A couple of gigantic barges complete with onboard cars slide slowly down the canal as I reach the town of Saint-Martin-sur-le-Pré, exhausted and dehydrated, having forgotten to refill my backpack at lunchtime[1]. The run ends in a rainy and un-picturesque industrial zone, highly unsuitable for spending the night. We decide to repair to a nearby campsite.

\*\*\*

At the site at Chalôns-en-Champagne, we meet site superintendent Mary and, after a gentle prompt from me, Aradhna asks if she could interview Mary for her film. She is kind enough to give us free washing machine tokens and a generous discount, once we tell her about our adventure. Despite being in her early twenties, Mary has travelled a lot and lived abroad and proves a keen and interesting interviewee the following morning. At last Aradhna has her first "talking head" in the can and has something to build upon. This makes her begin to feel she is more than just my support driver and dutifully supportive girlfriend in this endeavour. The trip should have much to offer her too, if she takes what opportunities present themselves.

\*\*\*

We sleep late on 17th March and call an admin morning. As well as the interview with Mary to conduct, I have a pile of A4 maps to laminate and store in our master folder. Although arduous, this allows me to take individual maps out to run with. Being total stationery geeks, we've brought a laminator with us and make the most of the electrical hook-up available at the campsite. We are nothing if not resourceful.

Possibly due to the constant icy precipitation, I see scarcely anyone as I make my way along the canal through Châlons and out into the fields once more. Everything seems oddly melancholy, including the graffiti. By one bridge, the portrait of a young boy in a baseball cap bears the legend "R.I.P. Lucas". Under another, Tristan has proclaimed his love for Melissa but the declaration looks oddly perfunctory. Perhaps he has yet to meet his Isolde.

At Sarry, I ignore warning signs, enter a construction site (unmanned as it's a Sunday) and cross a bridge over an unfinished motorway, its empty vastness a perfect backdrop for the endless drizzle.

---

1    I carry with me a CamelBak pack containing a reservoir that holds up to two litres of water. Unfortunately, two litres of H2O is fairly heavy, so I tend not to fill it more than 2/3 full at any time. For a full running kit list, see Appendix I.

My route has finally taken me away from the Marne and its accompanying canals and out into farmland. The temperature plummets and rain quickly cools to a slanting sleet, which always seems to be aimed directly into my face. I feel one side of my head growing numb as I battle the elements. A row of electricity pylons hums and crackles above me as I reach the top of a hill to survey an unchanging landscape of fields and villages. I struggle to keep my spirits up. The farms grow so vast and open that I am left without cover from the brutal wind, crossing tiny farm tracks between ploughed fields. I lose my way and consult my Garmin to seek the best direction to find shelter. I am simply too cold to keep running, shivering in wet and ineffectual layers of Lycra and nylon.

As I run, I find my mind wandering, doing its best to distract me from the horrible conditions. I have been leaping over long, swollen earthworms on the road and I spend minutes calculating the life expectancy of a six-inch worm travelling at a normal invertebrate speed across an averagely busy farm road. These and other delirious thought processes keep me going as my bare arms begin to experience a deep pain from the cold, something I've not experienced before. I'd be hard-pressed to explain the appeal of running to anyone who might have asked at this point (but of course nobody but me is mad enough to be outdoors today).

It's almost impossible to see through the rain and I am unable to get my smartphone's touchscreen to work so that I can send Aradhna a Mayday message. I make for a nearby copse of scrawny trees and manage to get just enough cover to wipe the water from my phone and call for a pick-up. There's no answer, but I leave a message asking Aradhna to meet me at the nearby hamlet of Marson. I make good speed there and stand shivering under a bus shelter in what seems a ghost town, the residents no doubt safely ensconced somewhere cosy and dry.

When Aradhna arrives twenty minutes later, I am in a foul mood. I lie in the roof tent, swaddled in blankets, a hot water bottle cradled in my arms, until I thaw out. I have not enjoyed the morning's run at all and find myself unable to raise even a modicum of enthusiasm for continuing the adventure.

"I can't go back out there. It's Baltic – I can feel it in my bones."

Aradhna sighs. "Why don't you just dry out, rest for a bit and then maybe you'll feel…"

"I really won't – it's utter hell out there," I moan.

Aradhna begins to use "positive reinforcement" to egg me on, handing sweets up into the roof compartment as a prelude to encouraging me back out into the cold and damp.

"Just a few miles more," my better half cajoles.

I'm told I let out a childlike whine at the very suggestion of it.

"Look," she continues patiently. "You've got thousands of miles to run still. If you let a little rain get to you…"

She's got a point. Still, despite my better half's entreaties, I'm far from keen to venture out again. Once more Aradhna, in her guise as coach, delivers a pep talk, assuring me that "just a few more km" will suffice to make the day worthwhile. Battling lethargy and defeatism I come to accept that if I can't raise the willpower to head out into the rain again, it throws real doubt on my ability to stand the course and make it all the way to Istanbul. I take off my dry civvies and put on a fresh set of running gear, then set off once more, Aradhna sticking close by in Roxy, cheerleading from the verge.

\*\*\*

Having warmed up and with food in my belly and Aradhna's encouragement, the afternoon's session is quite manageable, and I make it 10km to the town of Le Fresne without further complaint. There I am greeted by Roxy, parked in a muddy field by the side of the road near a scary flowerpot man who appears to be some kind of village mascot. When we try to drive away, Roxy's rear wheels spin futilely on the muddy grass and it's clear she's stuck. There's nothing for it but for me to get out and push. After several attempts, we manage to manoeuvre her onto a drier bit of grass and she skids onto the roadway, liberally spraying me from head to foot with a jet of liquid mud. It's in my eyes, nose, mouth and I'm comically striped from neck to groin. Aradhna cracks up at my ridiculous appearance and I give up my grumpiness at this indignity and join her. In a sense, it's the perfect end to a difficult day.

\*\*\*

After half an hour of hunting, we cross a small bridge over a stream and find a hidden spot between a small wood and a farmer's field. The rain is still falling intermittently and is turning to sleet but we settle into our familiar evening routine and think little of it. I even brave the icy temperatures to have a bucket bath without the pop-up tent, hoping that no intrepid locals chance upon my nakedness.

\*\*\*

I have no idea that olive oil could freeze until I wake on the morning on the 18th March and notice a thick, opaque liquid in the plastic bottle by the sill. Our breath has frozen into a layer of ice on the inside of the windows and the temperature in the van remains sub-zero. Our night's sleep has been challenging to say the least – we wrapped ourselves in the thin duvet we'd brought plus two blankets and most of our clothes. I yank open the side door of the van with some difficulty and look out into a pristine white wilderness of snow.

During the night about three inches has fallen, soft and silent, shrouding everything. My breath clouds before me as I tramp out across the snow, into what later turns out to be someone's garden, to find a suitable al fresco loo (a hole dug beneath a bush). A little later, as we both struggle to warm up inside our van, two well wrapped-up parents walk by pulling a small child on a sled. We wave hello as we put the kettle on, as much for warmth as for our morning cuppa. It is even more difficult than usual to get Aradhna to open her eyes and embrace the day as we realise that there is a limit to the effectiveness of campervan insulation. Still, there isn't quite enough snow on the ground to stop me from running. I put on the trail shoes and as many layers as I can, plus gloves and a woolly hat.

Back on the farm roads, it seems a very different environment than the previous day, the fields blanketed in white or dotted with blobs of snow revealing spring shoots underneath. An oddly spectral powdered snow blows across the more exposed roads, floating like low-lying smoke. The landscape is starkly pretty under its winter coat, although now and then the pervasive stink of manure hits me, heady and inescapable.

At the village of Bussy-le-Repos wooden-beamed farm buildings are brightly painted and shuttered against the cold. A sign points to a town with the eerie name of Possesse; I run the other way. Nearby, a tall pyramidal monument surmounted by a cross commemorates ... something (I couldn't find a plaque). Further on a car lies horrifically crumpled in a ditch, the accident site still cordoned off with police tape. Everything seems redolent with mortality, the snow a decorative shroud over the underlying truth – that all things must pass away.

Shaking off the morbid thoughts, I press on, crossing the regional border from Marne into Meuse. The roads are quiet and the villages silent and as uninhabited as the first act of a rural horror film. I use music to drive me on, my hands tucked into the sleeves of my jacket, since my only pair of gloves are wet from yesterday's rain – another oversight.

Laheycourt proves unusually pretty with its red-painted lion-faced water pumps built into huge stone columns and smart wooden-beamed homes with square, unfenced front gardens. Something about the mood of the place reminds me of a Western frontier town (with me the mysterious stranger riding into town on Shanks's pony[1]). Like most French towns, it displays a prominent First World War memorial, a stark reminder of the horrible battles that took place in this region.

Further on, at Villotte-devant-Louppy, a shaggy miniature pony crops the grass beneath the snow, seemingly unperturbed by the weather. This town has a demonstrative water pump of its own, surmounted by a recumbent bull. Not so very long ago, this "parish pump" would have been a social hub for the village, in a less complacent age when nobody took their utilities for granted. French villages often boast communal lavoirs (spring-fed clothes washing pools, often covered to protect those doing their laundry from the elements) and these obsolete features are usually well-maintained, a living link with the past. Other common man-made features of the landscape, quite foreign to this sceptical Scot, are the roadside shrines and crosses, a constant reminder to wanderers not to stray from the righteous path. I take heed.

***

For our evening hideaway, Aradhna finds a route into a wood near Lisle-en-Barrois, which we dub the "enchanted forest" as we look up to see the icy branches fringing a pristine network of stars. The effect is quite magical, a soothing balm for weary travellers, and it's extremely quiet at night. We catch up on any sleep we have been missing, hidden away in this realm of icy silence.

The following morning, I venture back out into the snow.

If anything, it's even icier than the previous day. Britain is suffering under an unusually cold late winter spell dubbed the "Beast from the East"[2], a polar vortex bringing snow from Siberia into Europe. France is feeling the sting from this huge weather cycle too. The wind

---

1    Nothing to do with a person called Shank, the expression derives from an old word for the lower legs.

2    https://en.wikipedia.org/wiki/2018_Great_Britain_and_Ireland_cold_wave

is bitterly chilly, lowering my body temperature yet further as I run wrapped in six layers of clothing – two t-shirts, a running jacket, waterproof and high-vis vest. As I struggle on to Les Hauts-de-Chée and Raival, desolate trees like gnarled claws line the roads. At the latter town, the gates to the château are firmly shut; everything and everyone in hiding, bar the odd cautious motorist, who give this lunatic runner a wide berth. I carry on to Nicey-sur-Aire, the temperature at least numbing away any aches I might normally have felt in my joints.

A forlorn maypole stands like an abandoned totem in a field outside Nicey and then a giant trash-ball sculpture appears at the entrance to a wooded section of road. Around five metres in diameter and seemingly contrived from bits and pieces of metal found at fly-tipping sites, the artwork by Maarten Vanden Eynde[1] is undeniably diverting but I don't tarry long.

Soon I begin to climb into the Forêt Domaniale de Les-Koeurs, where there are vantage points from which to view the snowy landscape. The road then arcs sharply down, around a bend decorated with a cross dedicated to "Jennifer", who has clearly been unfortunate on the dangerous bend. I'm untroubled by speeding traffic as I reach Kœur-la-Petite (having passed through La Grande) and meet Aradhna, who's managed to ask two local men for help filling our water tank. We have lunch and confer over routes. The traffic through the town and on to Sampigny looks unpleasant so I choose an alternative route over the hills via forest paths and for once get away with it. Scraps of blue sky are visible as I break the treeline and run down to the town and then on to Mécrin.

There I meet up with Aradhna once more. She wants to cycle with me to the camping spot she has found and assures me that it's nearby. The playing fields south of Mécrin are flooded and partially frosted with snow and, as the sky dims to a burnished bronze, the effect is eerily magical. Aradhna's reasonable pace and the scenic distraction keep me going for a full 3km to Pont-sur-Meuse, although I take issue with her definition of "nearby". The sunset is livid and the small park adjacent to houses proves an excellent rest stop. That said, I suffer a restless night with some kidney pain, possibly from dehydration. In the cold weather I am drinking less than I should. I have to remember to look after myself; I can't just delegate that responsibility to my indefatigable partner.

---

1    His website can be found here and details many large-scale and fascinating works: http://www.maartenvandeneynde.com

***

Tempers are frayed in Roxy the follow morning after several cold days with no respite in sight. To make matters worse, the pump supplying our tap is broken (possibly due to ice forming inside it), meaning that we have to fill an array of containers with water from the main tank and avoid stumbling over them – space, as ever, is at a premium. I hope the running portion of the day will prove less stressful than the irritating morning routine.

Fortunately, I get lucky with the trail I follow – a hill path which runs alongside frozen fields then ducks into forest. The ice in the soil makes it easier to run across what would otherwise have been thick mud. Heading from pretty forest back onto farmland, the terrain begins to undulate, and I climb a hill path on the outskirts of a military compound. At its summit, I think I see smoke until I realise that it is steam rising from an immense pile of manure being heaped up by diggers. The smell is astonishing, almost chewable.

There are some indications of a coming thaw – more visible crops in the fields as the sun emerges, bringing the temperature up. Whilst running through a peaceful forest, I spot two beaver-like rodents, about the size of a domestic rabbit, swimming along a waterlogged ditch and then scurrying up a bank. I later discover these are coypu, a non-native species once brought to France for their fur, now rife in waterlogged forest regions, and something of a scourge to native vegetation.

In the early afternoon, I reach a hungry and bored Aradhna at the village of Broussey-Raulecourt. My girlfriend promptly forgets her frustration when I somehow manage to pour a whole kettleful of boiling water down my leg.

My screams can probably be heard from the distant hills.

**KILOMETRES TRAVELLED: 369;**
**KILOMETRES REMAINING: 3029**

# Tips for Multi-Day Runners – 1. Planning

Planning your adventure begins from the day you identify your project. Make sure whatever you choose is a good fit in terms of what you want to get out of it, the time you have available, your financial and other resources and, crucially, your own abilities. Admittedly, when you embark on your first adventure run, you may not know your limitations – discovering them becomes the point of the whole exercise.

## BUDGET
We found it helpful to make multiple budgets, for best- and worst-case scenarios. What can you lose, to keep costs low? What are your absolute must-haves, those items which are non-negotiable? Once you've done this, you'll have both a target for fundraising and a lower limit, below which the project becomes untenable.

## MAPPING AND RESEARCHING
Start doing this from day one. Partly because it's a lengthy and complex process and getting a head start on it will make you safer and more successful, but also because the psychological effect of getting to grips with the terrain will keep you motivated and excited through the long months of planning as well as those arduous training sessions.

## PRESSING THE START BUTTON
My adventure running buddy, Chris Thrall, who recently completed his own JOGLE run[1], unsupported and sleeping each night in a tent, has an unexpected piece of advice. He said that sometimes it's best to throw caution to the wind and go public as soon as you've decided to undertake the adventure. Shout about it to as many people as possible. It will help engage your friends to support you, help build a public profile, should you be fundraising or seeking a sponsor, and vitally, it will make sure you commit!

---

[1]    http://christhrall.com/blog/?p=695

# Chapter 3: Into the Void

My screams might have awoken the entire village, yet nobody comes to investigate.

Aradhna thrusts a bottle of cold water into my hands and I immediately pour it over my leggings, soaking my left thigh where most of the scalding water has landed. The pain quickly dims to a manageable level as I peel off the tights and am relieved to find that none of the skin comes with them. We decide that I can't risk running immediately after the injury, as a livid red weal begins to rise on my skin. Today, the universe has found a way to force me to take it easy. I push a cold compress against the injured area as we drive to the nearest campsite, a "capitainerie" at the riverside town of Pont-à-Mousson, some 30km away.

***

The town is pretty, large enough to feature a gothic cathedral, and we locate our parking spot with relative ease. As we're finishing early for the day, we decide to treat ourselves to the use of a washing machine and showers. The capitainerie is a mooring spot on the banks of the Moselle River where the residents of pleasure boats and campervans alike can avail themselves of basic facilities. There are a few electrical hook-ups and limited access to fresh water, but the rooms housing the showers and washing machine are about to be locked for the night so we grab two beers and almost barricade ourselves into the laundry room until our load is done. Unfortunately, we're confused about how to operate the drier and have to abandon the operation with armfuls of clean but soaking wet garments. The manager kindly allows us time to shower before the cleaners finish up and lock the building.

After hanging up the laundry as best we can, we've had enough of the chores and opt to eat out in the attached restaurant. After ten days on the road, it is our first meal out and does not disappoint, particularly the delicious crème brûlée and local red wine. Our aches and worries are soon put behind us as we walk back to the van, for once not shivering in an arctic breeze.

*\*\**

## Day 11

With Roxy still draped in drying laundry, the 21st March delivers useful sunshine and I start my run a little later than might have been wise. Nevertheless, I'm soon making good progress through the forests of the Parc Naturel Régional de Lorraine, under pleasantly sunny skies and without much pain from my scalded thigh, wrapped in a protective bandage under my leggings. The forest is livid with evergreens and moss and a few small deer sprint skittishly away from my approach.

Unfortunately, Google Maps lets me down once more, the trail it has indicated quickly degrading into evident disuse and ending at a barbed wire fence. Beyond the barrier, green fields and reedy ponds lie between me and the road with which I'd hoped to intersect. This time I decide a bit of judicious trespassing is in order. I cross the fence by means of a fallen tree that has pushed the wire down enough for me to hop over. Quickly skirting the field and jumping a drainage ditch with only partial success (result – one wet foot), I use the reeds for cover and pass a couple of duck-hunters' hides, which are fortunately unoccupied. Quietly, I slip through a farm unnoticed and emerge into the village of Minorville, which seems a strangely self-deprecating name.

Unlike their British counterparts, French villages are often adjacent to local farms, rather than set apart from them. It is not unusual to see combine harvesters parked outside the local church or cow barns attached to terraced housing. I like this – it is as if the French, noted gourmands, see no reason to hide the mechanisms for food production away from where they live and cook their meals. I also notice that the town halls in these villages always seem to fly both the French and European Union flag. At least in its public face, France remains a proud member of the EU.

Heading off into sunlit fields again, two saltires, presumably made by withered contrails, emblazon the sky – an encouraging sign, I decide (as a Scot). Rising into gentle hills, I see the southern plateau spread out beneath me. We plan to head further east before turning south at the confluence of the Moselle and Meurthe rivers (I begin to wonder whether all French rivers begin with M). I run past a junior riding party – a line of kids trotting along the ridge on ponies – and manage to take the correct path through a tangled forest, emerging at Rogéville. The afternoon session passes without incident and I reach a main road to see signs for Nancy and Metz. The former will be our first major city on the route. When I reach Saizerais with its impressive war memorial, the sun is already beginning its final descent. We find the path I'll take the following day, a narrow trail leading into the forest, and go to park up. The campervan app Park4Night proves vital once more, directing us to a quiet lakeside haven for the night. The clear evening skies do not prepare us for what is to follow.

*** 

Snow! Heavy, thick flakes in a constant stream. They float down onto Roxy's windscreen and drift down the glass, collecting at the bottom. Outside our protective bubble, snow is rapidly covering the roadways and trails, but it feels like a freak flurry, rather than a lasting storm.

Expecting it to blow over, we drive back to my start point and I record a piece for social media about venturing out into the inclement weather. In fact, I really enjoy running in snow. So long as my footwear has enough grip, it's not too deep and provided I am well wrapped up, snow running can be very soothing. In my customary six layers, I head out into the white-out. Minutes later, I am running along a perfect white corridor, surrounded by trees draped in the fluffiest, stickiest snow, yet still displaying some of their autumn colours. A few inches of snow have fallen and mine are the only footsteps in sight, stretching out behind me into nothingness. Ahead, the world becomes a misty impression of a landscape, a view Monet would have cherished. I manage to take one photograph I'm proud of that encapsulates the stillness and the dangerously calming void ahead.

I say dangerous, because landmarks are obscured in heavy snow. Fortunately, I know exactly where I'm going and easily follow the three horizontal yellow stripes of a national footpath. These trail-markers are pinned to trees at regular intervals and prove all but unmissable. I don't feel cold at all. The beautiful and peculiar stillness is made even more surreal by the sight of a sign affixed to some bushes proclaiming the "Model Club de L'Avant Garde". A little further on, the plot thickens – two large covered wooden stands face one another across a snowy field, rows of empty seats awaiting spectators. The effect is surreal – a white void as the subject of dozens of fascinated but invisible voyeurs.

A bit of judicious web browsing ends the mystery. The field belongs to a model car racing club (with model boat and plane divisions too), which has been in existence since 1977. I'd hoped the "avant-garde" part of their name might suggest that they raced remote controlled lobsters and urinals but disappointingly, this appears not to be the case.

I enjoy looking back through the blizzard and seeing the trail of footprints vanishing into undifferentiated whiteness. I take down my hood because I want to better hear the silence, without the rustling of fabric against my ears. As I mount the hill and begin to descend, the snowfall lightens and I emerge from the trees into another strange environment – a sports and recreation ground called "Pompey Adventures", concrete table tennis tables stark against the snow, only the crows at play.

I run down a steep, curving road as the snow becomes sleet at a lower, warmer altitude. By the time I reach the small town of Pompey, icy rain has replaced the eerie comfort of snow altogether and it's hard to believe what I'd experienced just twenty minutes ago. I run to the banks of the Moselle and find a trail heading east, and then turn off onto a canal towpath, past accomplished graffiti and industrial buildings. In a complex maze of canals and river tributaries, I quickly lose my way and, as is my wont, decide to forge on ahead through tangled undergrowth and up a "desire path" to suburban roads lined with big box outlets and petrol stations. Like a rabbit emerging onto the side of a motorway, I am perplexed and a little afraid as I dash over the tarmac, under an arcing overpass and locate another scrap of trail leading me back to the town of Champigneulles and the canal once more.

***

A shack made from reclaimed wood and polythene sheeting stands by the side of an especially quiet stretch of canal as I plod through the unending rain. The makeshift dwelling makes me appreciate the warmth and comparative comfort of Roxy, waiting somewhere in Nancy, the city I'm approaching. My hiatus from the world of brick and mortar homes is at least temporary and voluntary; the poor soul who calls this miserable hovel home is far less fortunate.

Barges moored on the canal are the only evidence that anyone uses this waterway; it is too wet for even the most resolute of fishermen as I reach the city outskirts. My right knee has begun to ache worryingly and I have had enough of running in the rain. We decide to call it a day and head for a hardware store to buy a replacement water pump (although we won't get around to fitting it for several days).

At Nancy, we book an Airbnb apartment in the old town and find ourselves in an oddly palatial yet cosy suite with old master paintings, enormous Japanese vases and the all-important hot shower and double bed. We explore a bit of the city by night, huddled under an umbrella and ducking into a pizza place for comfort food. After two weeks of sleeping in Roxy, it feels wonderful and strange to have so much space, warmth and convenience in our accommodation. Hot water on tap, a bed you can spread out in. Somehow it also feels a little like cheating too – should an adventure include moments of luxury? We conclude that it should.

In the morning Aradhna decides to see a bit more of Nancy (this time without the rain) by cycling from the flat to our start position, while I drive. Unfortunately, she evidently cycles over a piece of broken glass and ends up pushing the bike, with a flat rear tyre, the last few hundred metres, while I wait by the canal, worried. I mount the bike onto Roxy and add fixing it to my to-do list. Today I have to deviate from the waterways and pass through the suburb of Tomblaine to the south-east of the city to find farmland and quiet roads again.

Passing a water tower, painted pale blue and decorated with images of birds, I skirt an epic crucified Jesus shrine and find the Forêt Communale de Pulnoy, the trail low-key but marked with a red diamond. Mud is everywhere; sticking to my trail shoes and making me slip around on ineffectual soles. Finally, the horse tracks lead me to the village of Cerville which boasts several huge natural gas storage sites, appearing on the land as mysterious stepped terraces and cordoned-off wells with pipes protruding from the earth, surmounted with valves and gauges. I am unable to research what I see whilst I run, of course; such mysteries are always solved in hindsight[1].

At the end of the Cerville natural gas facility, an unofficial route alongside a swollen stream leads me into waterlogged fields where herons and ducks flee at the sound of my squelching footsteps. My knee appreciates the soft terrain, although the mud reduces me to a slow galumph. I throw my backpack across a drainage ditch and follow it with a mighty, but only partially successful leap.

I return to roads near Buissoncourt. As a wayfinding resource, my mobile phone is proving highly erratic. I cross a grassy field, the only track being a slightly paler stripe of grass indicating that, at some point

---

1   https://www.storengy.fr/en/our-sites/cerville-trois-fontaines-labbaye

in the last decade, a jeep might have passed that way. Nevertheless, this "road" leads me in the right direction, whereas at Courbesseaux the next marked trail vanishes into a dense wood, depositing me at another padlocked and seemingly ancient fence.

At Valhey I spot my first cows (they featured extensively in my John O'Groats to Land's End adventure) and run past ploughed fields of red earth to a village steeped in wartime history – Bathelémont. On this site, on 3rd November 1917, the first three American casualties of World War I occurred. The American "doughboys" of the 1st U.S. Division were ambushed in their trenches at 3am by German forces and killed – a corporal and two privates. Bathelémont honours their memory with an impressive monument, miniature graveyard and placard explaining what happened. The town also features a preserved German WWI bunker and an ancient fountain (the spring now marked as non-potable). A small covered visitor display elucidates the village's history.

I find Bathelémont the most interesting village I've run through so far, but the light is fading fast and so am I. Worried by my slow progress and aching knee, Aradhna has already texted to warn me of a fearsome hill ahead; fortunately, it proves quite manageable and I end the day with a credible 40km under the belt. I find my girlfriend waiting by the side of the road near the Parroy reservoir, where she has found a lovely and peaceful spot to spend the night.

It is important to us, and to the success of the project in general, that we both feel we are getting something from each day. Although we are journeying together across Europe in a campervan, this is no holiday. On vacation you cherry-pick the places you see and stay; Aradhna will have to travel with me through the nondescript places as well as the beautiful and fascinating ones. This trip will last several months; it's vital that my partner (in both senses) feels more than merely a support driver. She needs to be my co-adventurer, as well as my constant companion. As we shall see, this is a tall order.

\*\*\*

We wake to find a layer of mist floating on the placid water of the Étang, although it clears by the time I set off once more, this time along the canal that runs alongside the reservoir. It turns out to be the Canal de la Marne au Rhin (Est), which as its name suggests, links the Marne and Rhine rivers. In theory, I could follow this all the way to Strasbourg. In practice, however, this would involve a great many sinuous curves and bends and add dozens of kilometres to my journey. It might also prove rather dull. I decide to stick to it for the time being, looking forward to a day of easy navigation.

The sun is gently warming as I make steady progress and my knee, for now, keeps quiet. My bandaged burn prickles only a little and everything is going well until I find myself with an unexpected companion.

A black Labrador comes bounding down the towpath, tongue lolling, seemingly keen to make friends. He nuzzles my side as I slow to a jog to avoid leading him too far from his owner. Unfortunately, no owner appears; the dog keeps pace with me for about half a kilometre before I realise we might have a problem. My canine friend sports a leather collar which bears no identifying information. He seems agitated and keeps leaping off to bark at cars passing on a nearby road. I get the feeling he is looking for someone in these cars – someone familiar. Could he have been abandoned? Or perhaps he's just lost? Minutes pass and I sit down on the verge trying not to be slobbered on by my excitable companion.

I have stopped between villages, a little way west from a road which passes over the canal and near some farmhouses. It has brightened to a gloriously sunny day and, had I not my greater mission to attend to, it might be perfectly pleasant to run with the Labrador. That said, I don't want to be accused of dog-napping by a worried Frenchman, but nor can I wait here for much longer without losing valuable time.

I call Aradhna and tentatively suggest she drive over to meet me at a nearby village. She can stay with the dog until help comes, probably in the form of the local animal rescue service. She isn't keen, having been in the middle of a much-needed call to a friend, which she had to cut short when she saw me repeatedly calling. I've seemingly found a way to cut into one of her few moments of downtime.

She suggests I call the relevant authorities to see what they can do. I telephone the SPA (Société pour le Protection des Animaux). The man who answers the phone speaks very little English and my French is rudimentary at best, but I manage to explain my situation after ten minutes of lexical confusion. His nonplussed suggestion is simply to call the local police. Not terribly helpful, I think.

I am about to do as he suggests when I realise the mystery Labrador has vanished. While I was talking to the SPA I'd noticed another apparently stray dog come racing along the canal. The animals greeted one another with the customary sniffs and started play-fighting and running around one another. While my back was turned, finishing my rescue call, the canine pals evidently made off together.

I feel somewhat put out, given all the efforts I've made but I decide to meet Aradhna at the next village and sate my raging hunger in compensation. She laughs at my woeful story as she prepares a picnic for us both, including a sneaky half-glass of red wine. We make the most of the sunshine and eat our canal-side lunch together. It will not be my last encounter with stray dogs.

\*\*\*

Apart from a few cyclists, some dog-walkers firmly attached to their animals and a couple of barges, I run in solitude all afternoon. On the map I notice that the canal appears to pass through a couple of reservoirs at Réchicourt-le-Château and Gondrexange. At Réchicourt the watercourse runs on a raised causeway with reedy banks on either side. I watch white herons take wing and flotillas of ducks gliding across the calm waters of the reservoir. The dam at the reservoir's eastern extent contains a lock, allowing boats to descend or climb the 15.5 metres between sections of canal.

Even more dramatically, approaching Gondrexange, the canal slices directly through the reservoir at the same level, narrow banks rising on either side to keep the waterways distinct. I climb to run along the top of one of these dykes, my shadow stretching out before me. I've been maintaining good speed to make up for the hour or so lost in my futile canine rescue attempt.

The sun is low in the sky behind me as I race to the town of Gondrexange and head under the A4 road to leave the canal.

I pass wooden homes that suddenly take on a Germanic appearance with protruding eaves and steeply angled gables containing front doors. I am entering the Alsace region, an area that once belonged to the German Hapsburg Empire and had been a disputed territory for over 300 years, up until the end of the Second World War. It remains semi-autonomous from the rest of France in a few legal regards and the Alsatian language is now being promoted in local schools as crucial to the maintenance of the region's unique cultural identity.

\*\*\*

Aradhna texts to suggest I meet her at the village of Neufmoulin. I fail to read the message until I've run through the town and am exhaustedly crawling uphill towards the next village. I meet Aradhna in a lay-by that might have been suitable for a surreptitious night's sleep, were it not for the presence of a possibly abandoned car and an unworkably steep incline. We drive on into the pretty town of Lorquin but find nothing viable until night falls, whereupon we creep into a quiet field. The landowner, who lives nearby, sees us park up and comes to check up on us. He graciously allows us to stay for the night once we make it clear we are alone and moving on in the morning. Like Blanche DuBois[1], we have come to rely on the kindness of strangers.

\*\*\*

## Day 15

Today begins with the now familiar sight of a beaded layer of ice frozen to the inside of Roxy's windows. Fortunately, the weather warms up as we return to the lay-by. I feel every degree of the incline as Aradhna films me plodding uphill, trying to put on a brave face for the cameras, despite an intense fatigue. Beyond Lorquin, the road out of town proves incredibly busy. I leap out of the way of a white Porsche, moving at least 100mph, and vow to find a safer alternative.

One significant difference between this adventure and my JOGLE is the lack of clear long-distance off-road routes. There are many short bits of trail to follow but nothing especially significant, necessitating a lot of improvisation and route-tweaking. At the end of each day I mark my actual route in black ink on our laminated maps and it seldom matches the pink lines of intention I scrawled across Europe several weeks ago.

Still, plans are rarely immutable, especially in long-distance running. In two weeks, we have covered over 530km (more than 330 miles) and although I am still far from my target of 48 kilometres a day[2], I'm happy with progress so far and don't feel I've failed to give all I have to the run.

## KILOMETRES TRAVELLED: 538;
## KILOMETRES REMAINING: 2860

---

1     It should ne noted that Blanche is in the process of being committed to a sanatorium when she makes her famous pronouncement in Tennessee Williams' *A Streetcar Named Desire*.

2     I was averaging around 35km per day at this point.

# Chapter 4: Valley of the Three Fountains

More than two weeks into the adventure, I have still not tired of my own company during each day's run. I've always been a bit of a loner, if not actively antisocial.

During my training, however, I did a few of my long Sunday training runs in the company of various strangers. I'd begun to host running tours of north London – urban trail-running, if you will – for Airbnb's new Experiences offshoot. I ran with teachers, shopkeepers, academics and even one competitive company director, who almost ran me into the ground (until I rallied in the last few miles). I'd meet my clients at the Castle climbing centre in Haringay and lead them around the Woodberry reservoirs, past kayakers and waterfowl, up the 17th-century "New River"[1], then through Finsbury Park and along the Parkland Walk, a repurposed railway path. The run then took in a loop of Highgate Wood, an ancient forest listed in the Domesday Book, then an ascent of the Bishop's Avenue, flanked by some of the most opulent properties in London[2] and culminated in an off-road circuit of Hampstead Heath and a final sprint up Parliament Hill to admire the view. It was nice to show my fellow runners that it's possible to have a scenic trail run, even in 21st-century London, if you stitch together some of the city's many green routes and spaces.

In this current project, however, I am quite alone as I run, with plenty of time to think. Too much time, perhaps. At least I have Aradhna to help me make sense of it all; she injects much-needed common sense and is especially good at route-finding. On 25th March, we decide that I'll take the Rue des Vosges / D41 south-east out of Lorquin, then zig-zag through the mountains to Strasbourg. A quiet road marked "Cubolot" seems more promising than the D41 as I pass houses whose lawns are decorated with flat wooden cartoons of

---

1    It's neither a river nor new, being a man-made watercourse completed in 1609 under engineer Sir Hugh Myddleton and carrying 24 million gallons of water into London from Hertfordshire. A real feat of engineering, it drops just 8 metres over its 20-mile length, as it winds around the contour lines.

2    Including Heath Hall, built by William Lyle (of Tate & Lyle renown), and recently sold for £25 million, a fraction of its original asking price.

bunnies, ducks, painted eggs and other paraphernalia of Easter. I have entirely forgotten the season. It seems the Alsatians take Easter very seriously indeed.

My surroundings take on a very different feel; this is very much a place that revolves around wood. The houses are intricately constructed with ornately carved balconies and eaves in the German style, sometimes coupled with French windows. Piles of wood lie seasoning under crude roadside shelters. Old barns loom with a slightly sinister, ramshackle charm. I pass few people in the chilly, bright morning until I rejoin the main road near Vasperwiller. An old station house has been converted into a private home there, but it still displays the old sign, clock and sundry other indicators of its past life.

The road winds through the valley and I take to a cycle path and then a short trail (the Saar *wanderweg*) whose signage promises Abreschviller. Soon I reach the little town and skirt its southern extent. I pass an old hand pump and text Aradhna, who is ever on the lookout for water refills for Roxy's tank. However, she has found alternative means. A sports hall and outdoor swimming area seem very Germanic and a narrow-gauge railway, though not currently in operation, provides a handy line to follow off into a wooded trail.

The geology of this region has changed from the rolling hills and plains of central France – large rocky outcrops dominate, half-hidden in thick green moss. The trail, marked with a logo like an Austrian flag turned through 90 degrees, leads through pine forest and up a rocky hillside past foresters' cabins and a small shrine carved into the rock, complete with miniature Virgin Mary statuette and potted plants. A village called Grand-Soldat boasts a stream of crystal-clear water and narrow-gauge station situated in an ornate log cabin. I cross a little wooden bridge and run along a shady path above the stream. Pyramids of cut and marked logs indicate we are in a forestry region as I climb to 545m and a clearing called the Col de Brechpunkt. Place-names are beginning to sound distinctly German now, as we progress deeper into Alsace.

***

The forest path keeps climbing and I pass nobody as I run slowly up red clay paths into the trees. The air chills. Icicles and small patches of snow are still in evidence. My fatigue tends to lift in environments like these, where I can stretch out and run without fear of traffic and with beautiful mountain views over limitless forest all around me. I reach a roadway streaked with snow and free from traffic. In the few moments when I have a mobile signal I am able to check for messages from Aradhna. One such text informs me that she is waiting in the town of Wangenbourg-Engenthal. My phone battery is running low and I'm concerned about my slowing progress as I pause to gulp down a glucose gel and some nuts and raisins.

Meanwhile, Aradhna is worried. Getting no response from me, and with no opportunity to reconvene at lunchtime, she realises how dangerous this situation could become. The lack of phone reception makes it difficult for her to follow my progress on the Garmin website. She drives Roxy up steep roads covered with black ice in the general direction I'm heading, hoping to encounter me on the road.

I manage to send Aradhna a message using my Garmin device, reassuring her that I will head for Wangenbourg but I remain uncertain how long this will take. Weakness of will is causing me to find any excuse to pause in my running – to take photos, eat or drink or check my progress. There is a multiplicity of trail-markers, but none seems to be directing me towards Wangenbourg. Just as I'm beginning to despair of finding the correct route, a couple in their fifties march by using hiking poles. I ask if they have come from Wangenbourg and they assure me that they have. That said, I don't know when they left the village and it is now almost 5pm. I'd better get a move on.

Aradhna has given up trying to coincide with me and, frustrated by having no mobile signal, she drives back down to Wangenbourg in time to pick up my message. Finally, she is able to relax, but the accumulated stress has taken its toll. She decides to ask our friend David to put an interactive map of my progress on our blog. This will mean that she's not the only one following my progress. In a sense, the burden will be shared and she can also call a friend to check where I am, rather than using up her data allowance surfing the internet on her phone.

Somewhere up in the mountains, I go into emergency mode, where my legs take over and my desire to rest up takes a back seat. Once more I reach a trail junction and a cluster of markers. Fortunately, a sign points towards "Wangenbourg", accompanied by the now familiar red and white logo. Separately, a blue "W" symbol indicates the way I've come. I follow the first marker, reluctant as ever to backtrack.

The trail is covered in an inch of snow; I struggle not to slip and fall on the downhills. Then, high up on a section that looks more like a goat-path than a national trail, a spectacular view opens up. Mist-swathed hills and a patchwork of forest and fields lie below me. I allow myself to pause and breathe it all in. After all, if you can't stop now and then when faced with such a panorama, what's the point of it all? I get a spike of reception and text Aradhna to tell her I am making slow but steady progress.

As afternoon turns to early evening, a little town emerges between the distant trees – surely Wangenbourg. As much as the snow will allow, I speed up and totter down to the tarmac once more, cutting down some steps past an old fountain. I locate Aradhna and Roxy and slump onto a bench to admire the view. From the little car park, the town is spread out below us, wooden houses arranged without plan or grid amongst a network of tiny roads. The town is overlooked by its ruined 13th-century castle, perched upon a rocky outcrop. We find our rest stop by a children's playground only a few hundred metres from the castle and decide to treat ourselves to dinner in a nearby restaurant.

As I sit eating a traditional tarte flambée and drinking local beer, I ask Aradhna if she was worried about me, given the nature of the trail and my comparative silence for many hours. She admits that she had been concerned and had spent most of the day without phone reception, parked on a treacherous mountain road hoping that I'd appear from a trailhead.

Although it had been a difficult day for Aradhna, she had been reassured by my texts when they finally did arrive. I vowed to check in more regularly when out on such remote routes.

I've just finished my large rectangular tarte when, bizarrely, another identical tarte arrives (as Aradhna had warned that it might). Apparently, I have inadvertently ordered my meal in two instalments (a common way to serve the quickly-cooling dish). I readjust the parameters of my appetite and forge on. Half an hour later, both of us feeling pleasantly stuffed, Aradhna and I walk back to our little home on wheels. It has been a challenging but rewarding day, with more of the same terrain to follow.

***

Monday 26th March starts sluggishly. I feel utterly lethargic and simply don't want to get out there into the frosty morning air and run. My legs feel leaden and sleep has seemingly not renewed my energy reserves. However, I can't let the adventure stumble at the first sign of hills – there will be many more to come, including the Austrian Alps and the Carpathians. To fail here would be to admit that, at 47, I'm just not up to the task. This I will not allow.

I was 44 when I ran the length of Britain, but that challenge had been easier in several ways. Firstly, I had been able to follow established trails for at least 65% of the way. Secondly, it had taken 48 days – seven weeks – not the three months plus we'd earmarked for Running the Orient. Thirdly, we'd rested up each night in comfortable bed and breakfasts, not an unheated van where everything has to be replaced, renewed, cleaned, fixed or moved around at regular intervals. Fourthly, the only language barrier I'd faced in 2015 had been strong regional English accents. Finally, I knew many of the places through which I'd run. This time round, everything is new and unknown.

I suppose the stresses listed above, plus my growing fatigue on a foundation of very little training, make for a wavering sense of motivation. It's all so bloody difficult!

Realising how pathetic this train of thought is, I force myself into my running clothes, ably abetted by Aradhna's refusal to let me slack off. I know I'll probably enjoy running once I am on the trail again and so it proves.

*** 

I begin by circling the castle, spiralling around the rocky crag upon which it stands into the valley below. A carpet of anachronistic autumn leaves belies the season, as I climb the opposite side of the valley and reach the Pont du Brocard at 375 metres. A tarmac road carries me through forestry plantations and past a lonely cottage at Cosswiller, a single inquisitive horse staring at me from its field. Ahead, according to Google Maps, lies the Valley of the Three Fountains. I pass the first of these adjacent to a small and ancient reservoir – a natural spring piped through a stone marked "1897". Cupping my hands, I swallow a few refreshing mouthfuls then rest a little further on for a quick lunch of nuts and dried fruit.

I leave the road for a forest trail and spot deer flitting between the trees while the green canopy above me is alive with birdsong. Fallen trees speak of recent storms but nothing but a gentle breeze penetrates the trees all around me. Emerging onto a gravel roadway, I see a derelict house standing in a nearby clearing, a red-painted graffiti face glowering from a bricked-up window. The spooky vibe of the place is diminished a little by a dog-walker throwing sticks for his red setter in the adjacent field.

The trail hairpins back on itself as it follows the contour lines and I pursue yellow cross trail-markers down to Wasselonne, despite seeing the town's name on none of the signs I'd passed. Two men with Alsatians (I wonder if the breed was indigenous to the region)[1] stop to stare at my exhausted figure loping across their pasture. The trail has opened out above the town. I have an encouraging view of Wasselonne spread out in the valley below. Soon I am jogging through small backstreets and reach a red sandstone church oddly reminiscent of buildings in Glasgow. Aradhna has trouble locating me so, after a brief pause on a bench, I run around the corner to a little square of shops and café where she has located that rare jewel – a laundrette.

***

## Day 17

Given my fatigue and the numerous administrative tasks and repairs we'd put off, we declare an admin day on the morning of the 27th March. I have now been running for 16 days in succession, the longest consecutive streak in my life. My legs are feeling the cumulative effect of this exertion. Plus, we have numerous chores to fulfil. As well as the errant water pump to replace, we have Aradhna's flat bicycle tyre and the doors of the coolbox to fix (they keep falling off) plus motor oil to source as Roxy is getting unadvisedly low on lubricant. Watched over by an inquisitive stork, nesting on a nearby telephone pole, we set about the tasks in hand.

Replacing the water pump is a little frustrating, requiring some fiddly rewiring and me furiously sanding down the sides of the pump since it turns out to be a couple of millimetres too wide for the neck of our water tank (stupidly I hadn't checked before we bought it). Having successfully inserted the new pump we discover that the fault lies somewhere else in the electrical system. Unable to solve the problem, we abandon the task and I set about finding and repairing the punctures in Aradhna's bicycle tyre. There's a tiny piece of glass between inner tube and tyre which has pierced the rubber in five separate places. A patch won't fix it; a replacement will be required.

A trip to a local LeClerc provides oil, superglue and a spare inner tube (not to mention delicious French cakes and coffee). We head back to Roxy for round two. With some difficulty (and a helpful YouTube video, I fit the new inner tube and inflate Aradhna's tyre successfully.

---

1    It is, and the breed is now properly known as German Shepherd, since they were bred to aid shepherds in the region. After the First World War, the dogs were renamed "Alsatian" as it was believed that an association with anything explicitly German might make them less popular.

I then glue sawn-in-half clothes pegs to the coolbox to act as stops for the doors, so they no longer fall off. Meanwhile Aradhna takes five phone calls vital to her work as a project manager and film producer.

A little disappointed that we've not had time to visit any of the plentiful local vineyards, we relax that evening secure in the knowledge that we put in a good day's work whilst resting my legs. The next day should see me reach Strasbourg but with 30km still to run, I'll need all the rest I can get.

\*\*\*

There is no good reason for my late start the next day. I am malingering. A toilet-stop and second breakfast in a local supermarket probably don't help. Nevertheless, I feel well-rested and confident I can make up the mileage. A dry but overcast morning sees me out of Wasselonne and along the road to Marlenheim, which impresses with its colourfully painted houses and shops, intricately patterned with wooden beams and decorated with flowers, rabbits and other Easter iconography. Beyond the town lie hills lined with fruit trees, furled netting ready to shelter the vines once pollinated. I feel a little odd running along what are clearly tractor paths across the middle of farms but take the lack of fencing or warning signs as encouragement. I am almost caught having a pee in some bushes by a woman riding by on a small tractor but manage to zip up and flee in time.

At Furdenheim, the sky greys over, promising rain. Cherry and apple blossom are in full bloom along the side of the road and a little way past Achenheim's impressive canalside *lavorie*, I spy a footpath that should take me all the way to Strasbourg. Willows tickle the water's surface and cute lockside cottages hide behind the trees as I nod my hellos to variously bemused or grumpy French people out walking their dogs or heading to lunch.

Blocks of housing are interspersed with farms, even quite close to the outskirts of Strasbourg, the country gently blending into the city. I follow a red diamond pinned to the trees (trails find me even when I fail to find them). I cross a small bridge onto the Rue des Capuchins and find myself suddenly in definitive suburbs. Something marked on the map as a Roman road leads me straight into the heart of the city. People throng the glistening, wet streets and I pass open doorways smelling of aniseed (a bar) and scorched steel (a garage). A left turn later I am on the Rue de Nancy in search of the Gare de Strasbourg and our first official stop on the Orient Line. I feel the familiar end-of-race adrenalin flood me as I speed up and race on strong, fast legs to the gleaming glass curve of Strasbourg station. The rain is incessant as I look at the time on my phone: 3:55pm. I have run 27.7km in under 4 hours and it feels very good indeed. I take a few quick photos of an array of European flags and call my girlfriend. I want us both to celebrate the milestone together. A few minutes later, she arrives.

Aradhna has managed to find a questionably legal place to park Roxy so we can grab a few damp but triumphant photos for the Facebook page and blog. Then we go to find our Airbnb hideaway. An exhausting trek with far too much luggage later, we are resting in a small but modern apartment right in the cobbled heart of the old town, a stone's throw from the cathedral.

***

A pancake breakfast the following morning makes up in part for the few hours' editing work I have to do at the apartment. Aradhna is understandably itchy to explore the town so I cut the session short and we head out into a fine drizzle which quickly clears up. Around a few cobbled corners we encounter the incredible cathedral with its intricate carved exterior and legendary astronomical clock. A close friend, Sara, wrote an entertaining and informative article about the city for a travel magazine[1] and, Christine, one of Aradhna's friends (and producer of one of my in-development film projects) was born in Strasbourg, so we know what to look for next – the Place Marcel Gayot. There we sit watching the life of the city while sipping local beers. With pleasing symmetry, an elderly man leans out from his high window, people-watching tourists like us.

Next, we head to the area nicknamed "Petit France", an area of quaint, brightly-painted wooden houses, narrow lanes and canals. On the way there we see a man cycling with a guitar case under one arm, a tiny dog peeping out from a wicker basket over the handlebars. A little later a young woman storms past, displaying impressive abdominal muscles beneath a bulging sports bra whilst raising and lowering a huge truck tyre above her head.

In the evening, also following Sara's recommendation, we repair to the *weinstub* Fink Stuebel, where we eat an enormous three-course meal including the local speciality, spätzle, a sort of soft, fluffy egg noodle. We down a bottle of a local pinot noir while I work on my veal vol-au-vent with extra copper pot of veal chunks. This is on top

---

1    Sara Lodge, "A Glass of Alsace", *Weekly Standard*, 28th January 2018.

of the cakes we'd eaten earlier in the day on what seemed a necessary patisserie visit. Alsace knows how to feed its visitors.

Back in the hotel, we both feel bloated and more than a little uncomfortable and getting to sleep on our inflated bellies proves a challenge. Still, we have loved our compact day of sightseeing in this historic yet anything but insular European city[1].

**KILOMETRES TRAVELLED: 599;**
**KILOMETRES REMAINING: 2799**

---

1    Along with Brussels and Luxembourg City, Strasbourg is one of the key European Union administrative centres and therefore attracts thousands of diplomatic visitors in addition to its international tourists. It is well worth a visit.

# Chapter 5: Beware of the Frogs

*Day 20*

I'm not the most travelled of people. At age 48 I still have not seen any of America apart from New York, LA and San Francisco and have not been to South America at all. All I know of the vast continent of Africa is Egypt (which felt more Middle Eastern to the ignorant teenager I'd been when I visited). India is a mystery to me, South-East Asia a mythical place of Vietnam War movies and Japanese Manga.

Even within Europe the furthest I've travelled was a few days' location scouting for a putative film project in Lithuania. I've never been to Greece or Germany, let alone Eastern Europe. The reasons for my lack of travel are abundant but include parlous finances in my youth, family and school holidays which were inevitably UK-based (apart from a few jazz festivals my dad played at in Ascona in Switzerland) and I suppose a general lack of the wanderlust that seemed to fill my contemporaries. My journeying has largely been internal – I think of myself as a great explorer of the internal landscapes of the imagination. I did my travelling through words, writing science fiction stories, thriller scripts and movies about vampires and Roman legionnaires in AD107.

Thus it is especially hard for me to believe that by the end of day 20, we have travelled entirely across France and into Germany. This feels like a more significant border crossing than Scotland into England had been during my previous adventure. As Aradhna cycles with me past the cathedral and out of town along suburban streets, we both feel the import of the day ahead. With only minor difficulties we navigate to the banks of the Rhine, pass a cruise boat with the bizarre name of Amadeus Brilliant and head for the bridge over to Kehl. First, we cross a series of small tributaries and skirt the port, where container ships are being loaded with colourful metal boxes by giant cranes.

I stop for a photograph on the far side of the bridge, the slate-grey waters of the mighty Rhine sliding under a glowering sky. A few more steps and I'll be in Germany. One country down, seven to go. It is as easy to cross into Deutschland as it is to cross the Thames footbridge back home – no border guards, no fuss. This is part of what Europe means to us – free passage, unification and a recognition that borders are arbitrary and changeable.

\*\*\*

Aradhna kisses me goodbye and, once over the Rhine, I immediately run the wrong way. To clarify, I head in a planned direction, but the curving, concrete A-road with its hurtling traffic proves un-runnable. Instead, I divert along a flood protection dam whose long arc stretches several miles south, continually frustrating me by taking me under bridges with no means of ascending to the roads above. Eventually, I find a side road heading away from the dam and through the amusingly-titled town of Kork.

From there I find myself on quietish roads leading through farmland. Daffodils are in evidence along the verges. I cross an autobahn east of Legelshurst and am glad I've found quieter roads, although many of the cars that pass me seem to be doing autobahn speeds. Things improve a little as, making my route up as I go along, I skirt yet more vineyards. Rain has started falling and clearly has no intention of stopping; fortunately, neither have I. I run through impressive smallholdings featuring rows of semi-cylindrical tents protecting vegetables, the rain creating white noise on the plastic sheeting.

Stadelhofen is a pretty town with a gushing river running through it. Haslach boasts a mysterious white-walled institute, like something from the *X-Files*. Beyond the thin silver birches are the unmistakable outlines of hills. They rise around me almost surreptitiously, their flanks lined with pristine rows of vines, as if the land had been combed. At Oberkirch, a carved statue of a woodsman seems to guard the way ahead. The road is darkly Germanic, mossy and very still with only the unending percussion of rain on leaves and my wet footsteps. I realise very quickly why this region had earned its name – the *Schwarzwald*, or Black Forest. Night-time here will be very dark indeed.

Nevertheless, I am happy running in woodland, dark and dripping though it may be. As a child, I grew up exploring local woodlands in Edinburgh with my family. When training in North London, a favoured route takes me up to Highgate Wood. A circuit is just under a mile and takes me past a Victorian drinking fountain, a mysterious forest house, playing fields and some prehistoric earthworks (which admittedly resemble nothing more than a ditch). I breathe deeply and oxygenated air fills my lungs. I belt down steep slopes and leap over logs, slide through black mud and kick my way through a carpet of leaves. This is my happy place.

\*\*\*

I turn through ninety degrees once more to follow a forestry cut-through up a steep, muddy bank. At the road above, a wooden cabin stands open as a rest-stop for forest users. I keep going. The darkness lifts as I emerge from the forest fringe into a white and misty afternoon. The golden flesh of logs split for firewood is ample evidence of a human presence, but I see no-one as I gaze along a green valley towards hints of human habitation – puffs of woodsmoke and glimpses of roofs.

Glistening green meadows and veils of mist make a fairytale landscape of the approach to the town of Kappelrodeck. I exchange vineyards for fields and track for tarmac once more. Huge guest houses promise large and refreshing steins of beer as my imagination runs wild. A magnificent sunset framed by an almost hallucinogenic rainbow ends my day in style.

\*\*\*

The weather seems to have rained itself out the following day and the river Murg[1] sparkles under a blue sky scattered with white clouds. I climb high above the valley via painfully steep hillside paths that strain my quads and hamstrings. Things go a little awry outside the village of Seebach. I spy a trail seemingly leading into the forested hillside and head over a tiny wooden bridge across the stream, only to find the path vanishes amongst the trees. Predictably, my attempts to find my way lead me further astray, into a forest as mossy and tangled as something from the imagination of Peter Jackson or Guillermo del Toro. A stream tumbles through long grasses and around chaotically piled rocks and tree stumps.

I fight with the terrain for some time, with rising levels of frustration and anger (and wet feet) until I emerge onto a well-maintained forest path lined with piles of cut logs. I have been having momentary flashbacks to the disastrous events of 5th September 2015, when I became dangerously lost for five hours in the Scottish Highlands and eventually had to swim a forty-foot-wide river. It is with immense

---

1　Its name caused some amusement, being the Hindi word for chicken.

relief that I find myself running once more along a wide gravel path that winds gradually up the mountainside.

\*\*\*

I pass one of many wooden hides, this one perched twenty feet up a ladder, with a view down a wooded hillside. I decide to take a short break there. It proves remarkably peaceful amongst the pine branches and I imagine what it would be like spotting a deer through the trees and levelling a telescopic sight, then pulling the trigger. I know I'd never be able to do such a thing, but it's also true that I'd gladly eat a venison burger (particularly after a long day's running). Is this squeamishness just weakness of character or is my non-vegetarianism a species of hypocrisy?[1] Getting down the ladder proves trickier than getting up into the hide.

\*\*\*

I climb ever-higher, towards Baiersbronn, finding the paths quickly snow-filled in places. My feet occasionally break through a hard crust and plunge me into knee-deep, icy snow, making running on these drifts tricky. The trail takes me out onto a high tarmac road, where an out-of-season ski resort is evident – silent ski lifts and a steep grassy slope stand testament to a lively winter season now past. Still, groups of hikers are in evidence and the car park is half-full. Two mountain bikers pass me at speed, turning off the road at a trailhead. An old stone marker indicates Obertal, which is the direction in which I should be heading, so I follow the cyclists, who are soon out of sight on the spookily quiet trail.

There must have been a storm here in recent days – young trees lie stretched across the path or tilt precipitously overhead as I speed up to run under them. An old fountain, mysteriously dated 1922–1934 offers no water, its pipe possibly frozen solid. A brown river slides away to my left and something about it reminds me of Colinton Dell, a shady footpath by the Water of Leith in Edinburgh. Once again, I feel very at home here.

One of my favourite places to run has always been the area around my parents' house. As well as the Dell, you could run up Torphin Hill and through an ex-golf course, now reclaimed by nature, past

---

1   My partner is a vegetarian, but I am not. We cook vegetarian food at home but when we order in, or eat in a restaurant, I sometimes choose a meat or fish option. It seems to work.

the Tiphereth[1] residential camp for adults with autism and learning disabilities, and on up to the first of several reservoirs, beneath gorse- and heather-speckled hillsides. A typical five-mile run might then lead me past fields of grazing horses, down the Poet's Glen, once walked by "weaver poet" James Thomson[2], then home past author J.K. Rowling's[3] huge gymkhana and estate and under the City Bypass to finish. I always feel a deep sense of coming home whenever I return to Edinburgh. Running amongst its hills, shady riverbanks and woods has ingrained in me an affinity for familiar landscapes that make foreign places less foreign.

*\*\**

At Obertal I run through a small, pretty park then take a tiny riverside trail out towards Mitteltal (the place names were rather literal – upper valley and middle valley). The houses become grand lodges, often with carved wooden balconies on multiple floors, whitewashed with wood stores and low hanging eaves. Obertal boasts a huge timber yard and it does seem that every building, from home to barn to factory, is built almost entirely from wood. Baiersbronn finally appears and I jog up steep roads to the top of the town and look down upon a sunlit valley. Further forest trails, well-surfaced and level, speed me quickly onwards.

At lunch, which we take al fresco by the side of a sparkling stream, we decide that I'll run until 6:30pm and try to reach Schopfloch. With 21km to run, this promises to be a tall order. We're finding my persistently late starts are pushing the end of each running day closer and closer to sunset, making our evenings rushed and unrelaxing. I've taken it upon myself to upload an album of photos to the Facebook page each evening and probably spend a little too much time selecting, editing and captioning them. Aradhna is doing most of the cooking in Roxy and I do the washing up. With blog writing, route planning and various other administrative tasks to fit in before bedtime, this doesn't leave any time to relax together, unless I start running at a sensible time. Three weeks of this schedule is taking its toll on our moods and we find ourselves becoming short-tempered with one another and rarely getting to sleep before midnight. I'm worried that this hothouse test of our relationship is on the verge of failing, and we are less than a third of the way through it.

---

1    www.tiphereth.org.uk
2    Late 18th / early 19th century author of *Poems, Chiefly in the Scottish Dialect* (Leith, 1819), who lived in nearby Currie.
3    Author of a popular series of books about a boy wizard, plus scion of a merchandising empire.

\*\*\*

The forest gives way to a gentle valley leading down to Freudenstadt, the picturesque houses overlooked by a valley-spanning railway bridge. Further narrow trails take every ounce of energy I have left as I manage to reach Schopfloch, predictably as the sun begins to set. Aradhna imagines I will emerge from a forest route but I have taken to the roads and we convene, prosaically, at a Volkswagen showroom by the side of a major road. The weird apparition of a rabbit-shaped cloud illuminated in orange light floats overhead. Despite having both seen the frankly terrifying film *Watership Down*[1], we decided to take it as a good omen.

\*\*\*

That night, as we rest in a quiet spot by the edge of a forest, I reflect on the day's running. Around 60% of it has felt sluggish, with me regularly dropping into what I call second gear (first gear is a fast walk), when I could have been maintaining 5.5 minutes per kilometre. I've found that if I catch myself slipping into second gear, I can easily make a conscious effort to speed up. I wonder why my pace is becoming so lethargic. Is this fatigue or even boredom? Germany has certainly proved picturesque and very runnable so far, with only a few small navigational issues to deal with, but there has been no risk element, no fearsome mountain path to scale or bog to cross. At the end of my third week, is it all becoming just a bit too nice?

\*\*\*

Rain helps remove much of the niceness of the following morning's 10:30am start (early for me, believe it or not). Rain turning rapidly to something between sleet and snow. My cold fingers struggle to lace up my shoes as I sit at the edge of the van rethinking my attitude to things being nice. However, the icy deluge improves my speed significantly as I make it to the attractive town of Dettlingen, with its impressively ornate sign. I find I run faster when it's cold and the temperature helps numb any muscular aches that develop.

The road out of Dettlingen quickly becomes impossible to run – narrow, blind bends with traffic hurling past, throwing up spray. I see what looks like a forest trail heading uphill, parallel to the road, but

---

1    The 1978 animated film's sequence featuring a ghostly black rabbit drifting over twilit fields to the sound of Art Garfunkel singing "Bright Eyes" remains one of the more disturbing memories from my childhood. Look it up online and you'll see what I mean!

it quickly becomes a muddy catastrophe leading me in entirely the wrong direction. I have to scramble down a leafy, 45-degree slope to get back onto the lethal road once more. I run the corners as fast as possible, hoping that drivers have their lights on and their attention on the road. The villages of Diessen and Horb come and go and then a wide valley opens out with, thankfully, a muddy path running in tandem with the tarmac. Red triangular signs on the nearby road warn of the terrifying danger of … frogs?! What can this mean?

A little later, following a trail into a scrap of woodland by the side of a stream, I look down to see the puddles are full of frogspawn. Clusters of frogs' eggs stare up at me like tiny eyeballs, thousands upon thousands of them. Once these all hatch, I can well imagine a plague of frogs becoming a menace on wet roads.

The path peters out once more – clearly it's a forestry access route rather than a public footpath. To continue, I'll have to get back into the flat grassy valley on the other side of the stream. I use a thin limb as a sort of banister to pull myself through the surprisingly fast-flowing current. Icy water chills my feet and legs but doesn't bother me unduly as I find my pace. A little later I see a barrier ahead and duck under it to discover I've been running on private land – again.

\*\*\*

Groups of mossy, gnarly trees dot the valley, with rain-rotten barns here and there. A tyre swing rotates forlornly amongst the branches. This is evidently a very moist place. Then, a little later, a minor miracle occurs – the sun glances out between veils of grey cloud, throwing silvery light down onto the tiny farm road I've found. I take a legitimate trail at the valley's head and reach the town of Sulz am Neckar where I run alongside a train track, wondering if the Orient Express ever came this way. Eagles can be seen wheeling overhead as I head out into fields once more, regaining the road just west of Haigerloch.

\*\*\*

Aradhna and I have recently discussed what she should do during the long wait for me to reach our designated lunch location. She expressed a desire to fill her days, quite reasonably, with something more interesting than shopping at the local Lidl, doing the laundry or waiting in a lay-by in the rain. Aradhna discovers there is an impressive local *schloss* worth visiting and not too far away – the Hohenzollern Castle.

I've been keeping her abreast of my progress and, given the undulating terrain and generally slow pace, my overambitious estimate of 1:30pm has slipped by one and then two hours. In other words, she has plenty of time to go exploring, she decides, seething with frustration after yet another text from me readjusting my estimate.

After an exhaustively steep walk up the hill from which it protrudes, Aradhna finds the castle dramatic and fascinating. Her efforts are rewarded with impressive 360-degree views from the Disneyesque Bavarian palace with its conical towers and elegant rooms. As required, she puts giant slippers over her shoes to walk on the elaborate parquet flooring and admire the interiors.

Meanwhile, I am belting along a dangerously narrow bit of main road outside Stetten, admiring an industrial plant and plodding on towards Owingen. Once there, I slump down on a bench in a little garden adjoining a church. It's cold and I am hungry, so I devour what little I have with me (nuts and dried fruit, glucose gel and some sweets) and wait.

Aradhna arrives forty-five minutes later, irritated by all my timing revisions. I am more than a little grumpy too, having waited so long; tempers are frayed. We find a nearby lay-by in which to have lunch – food is often the solution to our angst.

Given all the rain, Aradhna sensibly follows the European habit of having the headlights on in daylight. Unfortunately, she forgets to switch them off. When we try to drive back to Owingen after lunch, the ignition produces a wheeze and a clunking sound and then nothing. The mistake is quite unlike Aradhna, who is usually very good at remembering everything, but it was bound to happen to one of us eventually. We are in trouble. There is nobody around and, in fact, we haven't seen anyone out and about for an hour. We are reminded how fragile our plans are if any one detail is neglected.

\*\*\*

Miraculously, a car draws up at the lay-by and a red-headed man in his late thirties and an East Asian woman get out to swap seats.

Aradhna springs into action, running over shouting a suddenly-remembered phrase in German:

"*Entschuldigen sie, bitte!*[1]"

and asking for a jump start, which Moritz, a local giving his au pair a driving lesson, is happy to provide. It turns out that not so very long

---

1   "Excuse me, please!"

ago, Moritz cycled from Stuttgart to Barcelona; as a kindred spirit, he appreciates our tales of adventure. With much gratitude we wave him goodbye and I embark on my short second session that day. I made it as far as Steinhofen, where a surprise is waiting for me.

As I run into the outskirts of the town, I pass a large stables complex, with attached restaurant and then, a little way beyond it, there's a graveyard with some parking spaces outside. We have discovered that graveyard car parks are great places for surreptitious wild camping – they are seldom manned or gated and parking is free. There's Roxy, and a little way off, Aradhna is apparently interviewing someone for her film. I do a bit of a double-take – it's Moritz. It transpires that he has taken it upon himself to go looking for us, wanting to be of some service. Driving generally south and east, he saw our unmistakable vehicle and came over to wish us well and bring us some gifts for the road – a canister of camping gas (ours has run out but this is unfortunately the wrong kind), two local beers and even some Walkers Scottish shortbread, a souvenir from a recent holiday. We are very touched and Aradhna gets a great interview for her "Home" film.

Later that evening, our moods lifted by the kindness of our roadside saviour (we dubbed him St Moritz), Aradhna and I decide to dine in the stables restaurant and solve the fuel problem the next day. As would happen frequently on this adventure, the kindness of strangers has helped salve whatever niggling irritations were building up. We toast Moritz and are renewed by our tasty pizzas (the one meal it is impossible to cook in our van) and Pilsners.

***

Easter Monday begins with a surreptitious visit to a building site portaloo (we are once again grateful for Germans' reluctance to put fences around things). As I run away from Steinhofen and the attached town of Bisingen, I can see the schloss Aradhna had visited glowering on the horizon to my left. It's a shame I won't pass closer to it, but at least I can admire its silhouette and aim to get it behind me before lunch.

I find what looks like a promising, albeit steep and muddy, forest road, lined with cut tree trunks but with no sign of foresters on this public holiday. As I'd planned to run on roads, I haven't worn my trail shoes and progress is slippery and challenging, particularly when I have to cross a mini-ravine to get from one path to another (Google Maps shows two footpaths with a 200m gap between them – now I know why). A weasel scurries out of my way as I tramp through its habitat. The second path takes me to the edge of a pond where some questionable-looking German men are gathered; possibly fishing, possibly deciding where to dump the bodies. I give them a wide berth and leap over logs to dig deeper into the trees.

After struggling through the gloomy wood for an hour or so I climb up onto a B-road and emerge into a bright, sunlit day. A little later, I find a gravel path leading out into a wide, green valley. There are German families out enjoying an Easter Monday walk or cycle ride and my route looks suddenly a lot more civilized.

Then comes a large country park with well-signposted wooded trails and again I can run freely once more. The trees carry signposts to the nearest villages and nesting boxes for birds. The paths are all named – I take one called "Schwandelweg". I feel a simple happiness come over me amongst the trees – this is what I signed up for. I am able to follow a marked cycle route towards Neufra, a pretty village nestling in a valley, through which winds a gurgling stream.

*\*\**

Watched over by some squat carved stone figures holding crosses, Roxy and Aradhna greet me by the local church (if in doubt, we always meet by the village church in unfamiliar towns). After a late lunch, we debate how far I should try to run. I have already been on my feet for five hours and am dog tired. At Gammertingen, I give in to my body's cries of fatigue. We head to a local campsite to avail ourselves of the facilities, including cooking a meal in their communal kitchen.

The following morning, I am still fatigued and we both decide that a late start would not be unwelcome. For one thing, there is admin to do – a gas cylinder to source (the campsite has one), laundry and dishes to wash, water to refill. But mostly, what we both need is a bit of relaxation. It's a sunny day so we drape Roxy in wet clothes and make ourselves a filling brunch.

I start running around 3pm, refreshed and with renewed legs. I've eaten my customary granola with fresh fruit plus scrambled egg on toast, a brioche, a toasted cheese sandwich and sweets. With the large bowl of pasta I downed the previous evening, I am well refuelled.

*\*\**

Cooking in the van brings its own set of challenges. It can get excessively hot and humid with both rings on, even with the windows open. We put the roof up so that Aradhna can stand up to stir the pasta or rice dishes that are our staples. Very occasionally, we lift the stove outside and put it on a portable table to cook. We have no oven, so everything must either be cooked on the hob or grilled (and the grill has trouble with anything more challenging than cheese on toast).

Still, it is remarkable what we've managed to create already – omelettes, pastas, risottos, soup, stir fries and vegetarian chilli, lunch wraps and curries. I know that cooking makes Aradhna happy and reinforces the feeling of home that is all-important when you are nomadic. In the entire trip, we probably eat out a dozen times.

\*\*\*

As I enter the forest once more, snowdrops are in evidence on the mossy banks, their flowers like miniature lampshades, white with green tips. I pass a small wooden hut whose dark interior contains a bright green glowing light source. I do not investigate – some things are meant to remain mysterious.

At Kettenacker, I stop to photograph a tiny roadside chapel, before heading out onto dusty trails once more. For a while I leapfrog two young kids cycling slowly home from school and stopping here and there to mess about along the way (just as I used to – I was once two hours late getting home because a friend and I paused to play with toy cars on a muddy embankment). He does a "wheelie", she cycles with "no hands". Eventually, I leave them behind – the girl offers a shy "Allo!" as I pass.

I run towards the forest fringe. An impressively large tree stands at the junction of two forking paths, as if guarding the way. After some difficulty in navigating, I find the right path, making good speed. I am enjoying the spring bounty in evidence all around – clumps of clover and wild strawberries (which are delicious), catkins on the trees, wildflowers in abundance. The path becomes a rocky gully, high outcrops of white, flinty rock protruding from the greenery on either side. The trees begin to crowd over me; a rather comedic sign depicting a man with a fallen branch on his head warns of the attendant dangers.

The ravine is a beautiful and much-needed diversion from the endless repetition of village, farm and forest. A little way along its length, a well appears, its mouth covered by a metal lid which can be slid aside to reveal a layer of protective glass. I peer into the gloom, imagining something peering back. Perhaps the glass is there to keep something from getting out, rather than to stop wayward kids from falling in? I shiver and slide the metal covering back.

Meanwhile, Aradhna has been exploring and making her own exciting discoveries. Deciding to stick to the Danube for a little longer, she cycles north from Riedlingen to Zwiefalten, having been told by friends that the latter's ornate Münster is well worth a visit. And so it proves, set in a pretty garden, its interior painted with celestial frescoes and decorated with baroque gold details in every corner. Even more enticing is the town's brewery, which makes the delicious beers we've been enjoying for several days. In the taproom Aradhna samples a variety of their products, trying (and almost succeeding) to stay on the right side of sobriety. Before she knows quite what has happened, or how, she finds herself wobbling back to Roxy carrying seven beers in her handbag and coat pockets. A strong headwind, with an accompaniment of horizontal rain, makes the journey back unnecessarily challenging.

\*\*\*

While Aradhna is battling the elements, I am running ever-faster, fully lost in my surroundings and in the simple joy of running. One of my favourite London routes is the Thames towpath between Hammersmith and Kingston. I love its peacefulness in early morning or (more commonly for me) late evening and feel at peace following that green artery through the city. The ravine provides a similar pleasure for an hour or so, before it releases me into the bottom of a wide, verdant valley.

After a while another forest trail appears on my right, leading gently uphill. A little further into the trees my path is blocked by a large red-lettered canvas sign stretched between the trees:

*HALT! BAUMFALLINGEN!*

I Google and came up with "Stop! Tree-felling!" This is problematic since my route onward to Riedlingen inevitably takes me through this sizeable chunk of forest. I listen intently and, hearing no buzz of chainsaws, decide to take a chance. I duck under the sign and belt through the trees as fast as my legs will carry me. Bursting out of the treeline a few minutes later, and ducking under a similar sign, I realise I've gotten away with it. Trespassing is becoming a way of life.

I pass a father and son roaring illegally by on a quad bike then blast down to Pflummern, experiencing the thrill of "rocket legs" for perhaps the first time in the run. This is my name for that blissful state of effortless speed that can suddenly overtake a runner. I seldom know where it comes from but never question it; when it happens, the smart runner takes full advantage.

Nearing Riedlingen, I pass a fenced-off area containing a herd of very tame-looking deer, perhaps destined for venison. Those nearest the fence appear to be munching pieces of sliced bread. One gives me a quizzical look as it gulps down its sandwich.

I run the last 5km into Riedlingen in under 24 minutes, having decided to run as fast as I possibly can, since it seems I have energy to spare. I encounter the legendary Danube (aka Donau), as it slides gracefully between smart whitewashed buildings, their many-windowed gables facing the river. We will rejoin this legendary waterway several times along the journey, like re-encountering a constant friend after a period of absence. A series of colourful stork statues decorate the waterside as I negotiate a route through the busy town to the car park where Aradhna and Roxy are waiting.

We'd planned to sleep in the car park but some youths appear with beers, joints and loud music, so we beat a hasty retreat to a quiet picnic spot just out of town.

\*\*\*

I begin to regret my overzealous turn of speed the following morning as the fatigue returns. The route out of town is confusing and I am almost killed sprinting over a dual carriageway which seems to have no convenient crossing points. I crawl past stonemasons and factories as I head towards Unlingen. By the side of the road I spot another of the now familiar "Blumen" stalls. The image of a red-faced German springs to mind, escaping from a domestic argument, driving furiously around at 130kph before screeching to a halt by one of these stalls to buy a peace offering for his hard-suffering wife. I can't decide whether the scenario is touching or ridiculous.

Outside Unlingen, there is a feast of oddities to keep my wandering mind active – a pyramid of posters advertising a country banjo-picker, some "outsider art" comprised of offcuts of wood daubed with colourful abstract patterns, a pair of camels – yes, camels – lazily munching their breakfast and eyeing the passing runner with suspicion, as if I am the one who doesn't belong.

I begin to see rows of snow-capped mountains to the south, distant yet dauntingly high. I feel a pang of jealousy – why am I not running amongst stupendous peaks? Momentary geographical confusion makes me think the range of mountains might be Switzerland. In reality, of course, I am looking at the Alps that flank the German-Austrian border. I fervently hope these mountains will not run out before I reach Austria. As ever, I have to be careful what I wish for.

As the sun climbs high into a cloudless sky, I reach Uttenweiler and use my few remaining Euros to buy a pint of chocolate milk, which I down on a bench by a touching allegorical sculpture of a mother and daughter. I can almost feel the sugary, fatty goodness circulating around my innards, enriching my energy levels.

A trail-marker denotes the Oberschwäbischer Pilgerweg and encourages me onwards. Any route suitable for robed monks will suit this ultrarunner nicely. Vividly green hills and dairy farms abound. One farm has found a novel solution to allow its chickens free range between henhouse and fenced-off pasture – the barn literally stretches over the gravel roadway, forming a thin bridge over which the chickens hop.

Outside Attenweiler I catch my first glimpse of edelweiss, the verges dotted with little white star-shaped blooms. Immediately, the famous song (as featured in *The Sound of Music* and bizarrely as an alarm tone on my father's digital watch) becomes a persistent earworm. It dissipates only when a crack of gunfire rings out and a group of startled deer race across my path in the muddy forest. I hope no short-sighted hunters will set their sights on me as I quicken my pace to get out of the trees.

At Schemmerhofen an incredible pillow of ominous grey clouds forms over pristine rows of plastic-wrapped vegetables as I limp on to Schemmerberg and grind to an exhausted halt.

***

Aradhna has proven as ingenious as ever and had already spotted a quiet road between two small reservoirs where we can pull off and park. During the night we are briefly shadowed by a mysterious SUV whose engine growls menacingly, although nobody emerges. After a while, the mystery visitor moves on and we breathe a sigh of relief and slip off back to sleep.

**KILOMETRES TRAVELLED: 808;**
**KILOMETRES REMAINING: 2590**

# Tips for Multi-Day Runners – 2. Training

If I'm absolutely honest, I probably didn't train as much for this project as I did for my first epic run (the JOGLE). This is in part because the experience of knowing how my body would adapt as I began daily long-distance running gave me the confidence that it would cope. However, it was also because my time was very limited during the lead-up to this adventure. Here, therefore, are my general principles and tips for learning to run multi-day, back-to-back long runs.

*GET OFF THE ROAD*
Try as much as possible to train on different terrains. Unless your intended adventure is explicitly about sticking to the tarmac, you'll be fitter and happier if you mix some trail-running in with your road work. Make sure you do some hill sessions too – either long runs over undulating routes or short fast repetitions uphill followed by steady jogs down to recover.

*BACK-TO-BACK*
Get to the point where you can run 35km on Saturday and another 20km the following day. If you do this as often as possible, your legs will get used to everyday aches and pains and you will build resistance as you increase your stamina and cardiovascular fitness. Don't, however, overdo it and risk injuring yourself before you even start your journey. Above all – taper! You need a good base of rested muscles when you set off.

*DAY AND NIGHT*
Get used to running long distances at different times of day or night, so that you can both learn your own body's natural preferences and become mentally stronger at times when you feel sluggish. Get a head torch and run on a trail after dark – it can be a lot of fun (take a fully charged phone plus money or travel cards).

*BOOK SOME RACES*
Get some ultra races under your belt. If you've done marathons, start with a 50-miler, then 100km and perhaps even try 100 miles or a 24-

hour race. Having these mini-goals in the calendar helps focus your training and is a huge confidence booster. Don't obsess over times or mileage, however, just try to enjoy it. Talk about your adventure to the like-minded crazies you're running with – they will offer encouragement and remind you what an incredible adventure you're about to have.

*HAVE FUN*

Most of all, make sure you are running in the most varied, interesting and beautiful places you can. Going on holiday? Business trip? Pack your running gear. Remember that you don't need to run fast (unless you are training to beat someone's record) but you do need to run long.

# Chapter 6: Bavarian Biergartens

While the passengers on the inaugural Orient Express to Istanbul had to contend with over 250 hours of incarceration as they travelled, they at least had moving countryside vistas to feast upon, whilst comfortably housed in what was intended to resemble a luxury hotel.

Roxy is anything but a deluxe conveyance and my own vistas are changing far too slowly for my liking, especially when fatigue begins to erode my resilience. However, if I am becoming bored and restless, I only have myself to blame. I plotted this route, after all.

It's not to say that the Bavarian villages I'm passing through lack charm. Take wells and fountains, to cite one small example. Kirchhaslach's ornate well is decorated with Easter garlands and many brightly-painted eggs. Furbuch's water source is surmounted with a brilliantly burnished copper basin. Civic pride is in evidence everywhere I look.

Rather, it's as if I'd decided to run from John O'Groats to Land's End only to find myself in an unending Cotswolds of gently rolling hills and picture postcard villages. That previous adventure was defined by its hardships and wild scenery as much as the quieter, quainter stretches. After a few days of this Bavarian cuteness, I crave extremity. The mountains are coming closer; between me and the peaks lies Munich. I will have to be patient.

## Day 26

Pfaffenhausen provides some quirky diversion – a bierhaus sports a tiny pink spaceship on its roof, possibly pinched from a fairground ride. In the local stonemason's yard I spy leaping dolphins and somnolent snails. I feel more like the latter than the former as I plod out into open country once more.

A hint of wildness presents itself in the form of an immense meadow at Salgen, through which tumbles an icy tributary of the river Mindel. The endless pastureland is cut in half by the trail I follow, curving past immense sun-bleached tree stumps and rows of fledgling

Christmas trees. The sky is a pale blue bowl around which the sun's fiery marble rolls.

I head past ambling walkers towards Tussenhausen, making for Turkheim and the running day's end. Aradhna joins me on her bicycle as we pass a reservoir and impromptu nature reserve made from an abandoned quarry. Spidery shrubs form ideal shelters for nesting waterfowl. Aradhna comments lightheartedly on my slowness and I try not to take offence. The kilometres are taking their toll. When I run under the yellow-painted arch of Turkheim and reach Roxy, we have covered around 750km in 27 days.

\*\*\*

On 7th April, I set off from the Ludwugstor building (now a museum) at Turkheim, Aradhna relaxing with a coffee in the sunshine of the outdoor café. I stave off pangs of jealousy as I negotiate the wooden tables and duck back under the yellow arch to take a convenient cycle path over the tumbling river Wertach towards Buchloe.

A timber-framed warehouse is going up at the fringes of the small town and I pause to admire the craftsmanship, impressed that even functional, industrial buildings get a traditional build in this part of Germany. Woodcraft of a more hobbyist kind (though still impressive) is evident in a back garden over which towered an immense cream cheese factory. A garden shed has been built cartoonishly crooked like a cabin conjured from a Grimm fairytale.

Running in sparkling sunlight I photograph brilliantly red fire hydrants and humming power lines, the azure sky and brilliant light reawakening my joy in photography for its own sake. I've carried it since childhood and still remember my first bit of nature photography – a photo I took on a box Brownie camera, lying on my back in Edinburgh's Royal Botanic Gardens and looking up at the cherry blossom set against a similarly blue sky.

Each village I pass through sports its own epic maypole (or *maibaum*), white-painted and decorated with "branches" depicting local crafts, industries and professions. These are a focal point of civic pride in Germany as well as friendly competition between neighbouring villages. There have even been cases of towns stealing their neighbours' poles in the dead of night, although these days they are very securely bolted down or imprisoned in concrete bases[1]. They

---

1    Some maypole thieves are evidently more ambitious than others, as this article reveals: https://www.thelocal.de/20170412/thieves-rewarded-with-beer-after-stealing-munichs-maypole

often tower thirty or forty feet into the air, their height limited only by the length of tree trunk available.

I soon approach Landsberg, in an altogether more positive mood than recent days. The patterning of ploughed fields and green pastures give way to tarmac roads, colourfully striped with red cycle lanes and brightly-painted houses. By the river at Landsberg, where swans glide in the still crescent above the weir's edge, I am greeted by a recumbent Poseidon. The statue bears an uncanny resemblance to Leonard Nimoy and appears as quizzically implacable as his most famous onscreen role.

Long, colourful townhouses, decorated with trompe l'oeil window pediments, lead me inexorably towards a flight of steps that carry me panting and aching up to the ruins of a 13th-century castle[1]. I run around remnants of the town walls and find a major road leading towards Munich.

Unfortunately, Google sees fit to send me along a narrow A-road, which runs alongside the autobahn and has a similarly terrifying speed limit (or lack of it). After a few miles of this, I manage to locate a turn-off under the autobahn and follow a cycle path between road and woodland, a much less fraught route to run. I stop for a brief rest and fuel stop, munching nuts and cranberries as I sit with my back to a tree, legs stretched out in the dry leaves.

Heading away from the traffic towards a small town, I pass a large white-walled factory or scientific facility which squats like something sinister beyond the ploughed fields. I spot Roxy a moment later, driving up a gently curving road in the distance. Evidently Aradhna has not seen me, so I race off in pursuit, catching up with her at Eresing, where we have lunch.

\*\*\*

We spot a large lake on the map – Ammersee – and aim to make it there before sunset. The Alps' jagged backdrop urges me on and my lungs and legs feel strong. A lot of German walkers and cyclists pass me by as I crest gentle hills on roads and cycle paths. One woman walks a tiny dog that seems determined to carry an immense stick ten times its size in its mouth. A father and daughter slice by me on rollerblades. Cyclists especially are in evidence – tourers with heavy panniers and sunglassed racers in colourful Lycra.

---

1    The town has a certain notoriety too, containing the prison where an incarcerated Adolf Hitler wrote *Mein Kampf*, as well as having been the locus of the Hitler Youth movement.

Still going strong, I reach Eching am Ammersee and find a bustling playground for well-heeled Germans. A pristine lake gleams in the late afternoon sunlight, flanked by expensive houses, distant mountains surrounding its southern extent. Hundreds of sunbathers, cyclists, picnickers and walkers roam the northern shore at Stegen, Aradhna and I amongst them. We stop to sit with our toes in the water and clink our beer bottles. Then we record a video message for a friend of mine getting married in Australia and paddle in the still icy water (nobody is swimming). Moments of downtime like this, where we genuinely have nothing urgent to attend to, are becoming few and far between, and are precious.

As we consider our next move, paddleboarders, yachts and ferries variously drift or chug their way across the placid water, alongside ducks and coots. An absurdly low-slung Lamborghini idles by, growling like a frustrated bear as the driver creeps amongst a sea of pedestrians. Summer must be madness here, we decide.

Unfortunately, the campsite we find proves half-shut and unattended, its toilets locked, despite the presence of several other campervans. We avail ourselves of some free water and flee to a hidden lay-by off a local B-road.

***

The following day begins once more in brilliant sunlight at the lake. My route takes me away from the water, through a car park, across a field and then along an endless cycle path which undulates and meanders its way towards Munich once more. Bicycles whip by; this seems a common long-distance route for touring cyclists. As well as the usual skimpy racers, two long, orange pod-bikes blast by, their recumbent pilots waving cheerily from the bean-shaped fibreglass vehicles, only their heads and hands visible.

This path carries me painlessly on for six miles before depositing me once more at the side of a major A-road, this one much quieter than yesterday's route, thankfully. Munich lies around 35km to the east. The distance ought to be quite achievable, providing no calamities ensue.

***

I locate a long-distance cycle path, named the "Kreisradwanderweg" and follow it past livid green fields and then, in vivid contrast, find myself skirting huge industrial plants and cutting (probably unwisely) through a dusty quarry site towards Neugilching, where I am greeted by pretty floral displays and some sort of container park for asylum seekers. Germany is proving a land of many contrasts. The container park is one of the few residences I've seen with a fence around it, although it looks quite climbable. And at least this small enclave of refugees is integrated into the community, rather than being hidden away at its fringes, fenced and forgotten.

My route next takes me around some small ponds at Krailling and off through suburban sprawl at Planegg, amusingly twinned with England's Didcot (and others). From this point on it's a slog along suburban streets towards Munich proper. The first sign for Marienplatz appears 4.6km from the city centre, directing me past offices and brightly-coloured townhouses.

Although I'm relieved to be reaching Munich with such ease, the Hauptbahnhof proves disappointingly bland. Some confusion in our research means we are uncertain which Munich station hosted the Orient Express in its heyday; my plan is to visit both, just in case.

I set off from the nondescript central station towards the Ostbahnhof, passing the ornate Mariensäule with its endless, sky-scraping ornamentation. In the Marienplatz, I pause briefly to photograph a glass harmonica player, his hands gliding over water-filled wine stems, creating an eerie soundtrack to my high-speed tourism. The city centre is vibrant and bustling and I have to exercise all of my proprioception to avoid collisions.

Then it hits me – I am in Munich! The beer-lover's Mecca, although we are six months from Oktoberfest. It's all too easy to begin taking for granted the many towns and cities I'll pass through, given the sheer number of them (over 750, I estimate) but this is a place to savour on a cold winter's afternoon. I wish I could stop and enjoy it, but time is pressing.

To make matters a little more challenging, my phone's battery abruptly dies, leaving me with only the Garmin to navigate with. Uh-oh.

Although stations don't appear to be named on the Garmin's maps, I pick an impressive-looking confluence of train lines and head for that. My hunch pays off, fortunately. A golden glow lights up the horizon as I cross the river Isar and locate the Ostbahnhof. Its drab exterior does not much improve on the Central Station's dour functionality, but I meet Aradhna and we take the required selfies. We have reached our second station stop on the Orient Line and there's much to celebrate.

***

Our Munich day off starts well, with homemade pancakes and a wander round the Englishergarten, the picturesque park to the north of the city we've camped at overnight. I even down a stein of beer, the huge glass as big as my head. We have planned to spend tonight at another Airbnb flat, having had good experiences in Nancy and Strasbourg. Alas it is not to be.

When we arrive late at the rental flat, following an epic drive through dense traffic, we find the owner (himself a tenant, we expect) tumbling out of bed to greet us. That is, he seems to have got out of the very bed we are going to sleep in. The flat boasts "dust bunnies", pubic hairs, a mouldy fridge, the world's largest collection of returnable beer bottles and a dense stink of stale tobacco. Being the polite Brits that we are, we accept our host's only set of keys (he stresses their importance several times) and let reality sink in before we decide there is no way we are staying here. The flat has all the ambience of a superficially tidied crime scene. A lengthy call to Airbnb later, and after sending evidentiary photos to their admin team, we get a full refund and return gratefully to Roxy … only to discover my running shoes have been stolen.

In the interest of full disclosure, I should admit that I realise I left my shoes to air under the van as we were on the way to the rental flat. However, by this point, we are already so late that we decide to let fate choose whether I get my Mizunos back. Fate evidently decrees that a local homeless man requires footwear more than I do (possibly true). Cursing my stupidity, we decide a trip to a local sports shop will become part of our relaxing day off. I find one in the centre of town and, following a spot of emergency kit washing in a bucket of soapy water, we jump on a local bus.

Fortune smiles, for once, when the manager of the running shop, Ivo, turns out to be a keen long-distance runner himself. When we tell him what we were attempting, he gives me a significant discount on my new Nike shoes, throwing in a free technical t-shirt for good measure. Ivo wishes us well and sends us on our way, encouraged by his enthusiasm and energy.[1]

A little while later, we meet up with Aradhna's old friend Dave, an Englishman who married a German and relocated to Munich a couple of years ago. He takes us to a local biergarten as evening dims to night-

---

1    Runner's Point, on Sendlinger Strasse.

time. We help ourselves to heaped plates of food and steins of lager. Although I found the multiple ticketing system for ordering food and drink somewhat baffling (order at one counter, collect at another, pay at a third), the sausages are delicious and much-appreciated. Aradhna tucks into potato dumplings in a mushroom sauce, which taste better than they look. Later, we move to a nearby restaurant for apple strudel and coffee.

We round the evening off with a nocturnal stroll around the Mariensäule, which is prettily illuminated, and take some photos. Against all odds, we've salvaged a pleasant evening from a frustrating day.

*** 

## Day 31

On 10th April I stand admiring my new shoes outside the Ostbahnhof, kiss Aradhna goodbye and trot off along the very long, straight 304 road. As ever, leaving the city means passing through concentric circles of varying land use – shops and offices become lower-rent apartment blocks and small houses before retail parks and industrial estates take over. I feel oddly cheered to pass a Mini showroom, amongst the glass boxes stuffed with Audis and Volkswagens. Eventually, a cluster of small shops and cafés announces the arrival of the suburbs. Surprisingly, one suburban street seems to lead straight into the forest. Germany continues to impress with its laissez-faire attitude to fencing.

I take brief respite from my fast dash from the city on a bench on the other side of the woods. The new running shoes are performing well and I've made good speed so far. I have the lure of the Alps to urge me on, so don't tarry long.

We'd revised our route to loop slightly south and take in some of the gentler peaks and passes, heading for Salzburg. The thought cheers and encourages me; I have become a little bored of gently rolling hills and decorous farmland. I want something more rugged and invigorating.

Approaching Harthausen, I am greeted by a limp Union Jack, sharing a flagpole on this windless day with an equally listless German flag. The reason for this display of unity remains a mystery but the town also features an impressive WWI statue. A stone soldier stoops to comfort a helmetless compatriot; the effect is melancholy and regretful. Perhaps bonds with Britain were forged on the battlefields here. Harthausen also boasts a large, fenced enclosure of farmed deer, munching moist grass amongst a series of sculptures of WWI biplanes. I have no time to investigate the incongruity of it all. I run on.

At Hoch Holz, a forest of skinny pine trees towers above me. Alongside the trail, I pass what I assume would be another grisly roadside crucifixion. Instead a plaque commemorates a chubby and evidently much-loved local, one Herbert Rodig[1]. The trails follow gentle inclines, gaps between the trees offering occasional glimpses of stunning Alpine ranges. Now I can enjoy these brief views with anticipation, knowing I will soon be amongst the mountains.

Minutes later I've left the forest for circuitous roads once more and am dashing for my life around blind curves, heading for Moosach, where we stop for lunch outside a Catholic centre (we surreptitiously use their loos, counting it an act of Christian charity).

My target for the afternoon is Aßling, but the final undulations of the plain north of the Alps carry me through many small villages en route – Pullenhofen, Alxing, Obereichhofen, Lorenzenberg and finally Aßling as the light begins to dim.

We decide to shoot a clip of me running down into the town and drive to a convenient side street to park Roxy. As we pull up, a local train rattles by on tracks hidden by trees. The railway becomes visible behind a grassy field a little way off. My dad has been urging Aradhna to film a shot of me running alongside a train; I think the idea's a little bit corny. We decide we could have fun with it here though.

Looking down the rails (there are, as ever, no fences) we can see a local station platform about 1/4 mile away. We wait for a train to pull up there and then I hover just off-camera, poised and ready. When the train starts up again, I tear alongside it, my deadpan expression collapsing into laughter as I pretend to race the train. Three takes later (services are frequent) we have one "in the can" and head off to do something sensible, like make camp.

Our campsite is a long drive away but a shower is much-needed, even if that shower is coin operated and a kindly German has to gift us the necessary change. The following day we decide to start running late, given the disappointments of our Munich day off. We have yet more washing to do (my bucket wash had been an emergency measure for just a few key items of kit). We also relax, my legs appreciating the extra few hours of inactivity.

Then, at 3pm, I set off from Aßling, heading for a place our tourist

---

1    About whom the internet is apparently entirely ignorant.

map has underlined as interesting, a town with the unpromising name of Rott.

Huge barn-like houses dot the hills, a very Bavarian style of architecture featuring large ornate balconies and deeply-slanting eaves, everything carved in sumptuously varnished wood or whitewashed. Perhaps wisely, I avoid a diversion to the village of Anger and make good speed over the 10km to Rott, passing small farms with goats and chickens, then crossing the train tracks once more. There's even a chocolate factory and I consider a visit to the attached shop for a present for Aradhna. However, the chances of it not melting to a messy gloop with my body heat are slim.

The mountains now stand out in sharp relief to my right and, encouragingly, ahead of me. My afternoon target is Amerang, whose name is homophonous to the set up of an especially questionable Scottish joke[1]. Entering a wooded region, I am encouraged by the sight of a vintage VW campervan. Evidently we aren't the only surreptitious sleepers around.

I cross the river Inn at Griestatt, with its impressive Herculean statues holding stone blocks aloft and guarding the bridge. On the outskirts of the next town some local wag has erected a cluster of signposts marking the kilometres to places as far flung as Auckland, Singapore and Meerufenfushi. No Istanbul, sadly (I work it out later as 2867km, which terrifies me).

I hare off onto a trail once more, following Google Maps' suggestion and the fabled blue dot. So far on this trip, this strategy has served me well, most of the time. During my length-of-Britain run, I found my phone had little or no reception much of the time. So far, Europe has proven far more accommodating with its telecom networks. That said, Google does have some fairly generous ideas about what constitutes a footpath. I soon find myself wandering aimlessly along the side of a small river, looking in vain for a bridge and finding that the fabled blue dot seems determined to lead me around in circles.

Eventually, a tiny rickety bridge carries me over the water and sends me across a field whose "footpath" is evident only in the vaguest stripes of shoe-flattened grass. Eventually a strip of gravel appears and I race past an elderly couple who smile and say something I can only respond to with a laugh (having zero German).

\*\*\*

---

1    "Is that a cake you're holding or a meringue?" "No, you're right. It's a cake." An accent helps.

Schonstett's maypole is the most impressive yet, a veritable skyscraper with carved figurines depicting farmers, bakers and firemen. I keep plodding on and the day ends at Amerang with a hill, which I decide I feel fit enough to run (amazing how the thought of a sit down, hot food and a bucket bath can inspire an ultrarunner). It has been a shortish day (just 26km travelled) and my legs have been aching constantly, but tomorrow will be better. Tomorrow is always better.

***

Public toilets are very much a British obsession. At least, the provision, at every public gathering place, of free public loos, seems more of a given in the UK than in the rest of Europe (or so I found). Amerang surprises and delights me with its charge-free, unisex, disability-friendly convenience, and I avail myself of this unexpected service wholeheartedly.

In vanlife, toilet facilities are a godsend; the alternative entails scurrying into the underbrush with a trowel and a primal fear of being found out.

Setting off with the call of nature satisfyingly answered puts me in a good mood on 13th April. A series of pleasantly quiet forest roads and paths across meadows sprinkled with yellow and purple wildflowers carry me effortlessly ever-closer towards the Alps and Austria. At the oddly English-sounding Altersham I pass a garden that boasts its own mini observatory, a three-metre white dome protruding from the lawn like a giant mushroom.

A few kilometres later I reach the tiny village of Pavolding and am surprised to find a working water wheel, rotating slowly in a gurgling stream. Nearby stands the first of three impressively large bronze sculptures by Heinrich Kirchner, a mid-twentieth-century sculptor born in the village. Symbolic and figurative, the bronze figures are emblematic of a Germanic rural romanticism, yet mysterious and pagan too. The best of them is "Erde Mutter", a swollen-bellied mother offering her baby to the sky (joyfully, not as a sacrifice). I run on, pleased to have discovered these surprising works.

***

Seebruck is my lunchtime destination. I stop early in the day, but only because the silvery lake with its backdrop of snowy peaks, seems like somewhere Aradhna would love and in that moment of arriving at the water's edge I miss her company. It's a commonly recurring sensation – the feeling of chancing upon a moment of beauty or strangeness that has to be shared, yet can't be. It is a sensation than increases my feelings of loneliness, and Aradhna's too.

I call my partner and she drives over from where she's been waiting, a little east of my location. Aradhna's feeling quite relaxed – she has enjoyed an hour or so by the lake at Prien am Chiemsee and has met a paddleboarder who runs a local food van together with his Thai wife. Aradhna reckons the couple would make excellent interviewees for her documentary and has made a loose arrangement to meet them at the van later on.

Following our car park picnic, I lope off at my usual post-meal funereal pace. A footpath alongside the lake takes me past an idyllic bench viewpoint, whose temptation I avoid, then over fields and towards the town of Chieming. I'll skirt the lake's north-eastern shore and then forge south east in the direction of the border and Salzburg. Some extraordinarily beautiful running (and reasonably brisk too) brings me to Traunstein by early evening, past guest houses with bucolic painted scenes on their pastel-painted gables, ornate calligraphy often spelling out the name of the families within.

\*\*\*

We drive to Prien as fast as is feasible to interview Aradhna's paddleboarder and his Thai wife at their food van, but arrive about 20 minutes after it closes. In part this is because we stop at a service station for a pee stop and discover it has showers too. The opportunity seems too good to pass up but adds fifteen minutes to our journey. Time is our most precious commodity and we feel guilty squandering it.

We can see no sign of them at the nearby flats and Aradhna draws a blank at every door she tries. Maybe they live elsewhere and just park their van here (as we do back in London with Roxy). It's not going to happen.

Aradhna is already feeling that she's been missing opportunities to obtain interviews through being too busy or too shy to talk to locals. Having just missed this chance to get something interesting in the can, my partner's mood darkens.

As I mentioned, my girlfriend and I are both prone to bleak moods and introspection. I find running helps stave off my darker moments, and I'm getting plenty of peripatetic therapy on this adventure. As a very sociable person, left to her own devices, Aradhna is finding it harder to keep her spirits up. Quite reasonably, she misses convivial company and I am often too exhausted to be much fun on an evening. Making her film allows Aradhna to feel she has something for herself, an activity that doesn't revolve around me and my needs. Now it seems that even that project is failing to deliver. I wish I could help her.

We return to the lakeside, following a Park4Night lead to locate a picnic spot for the night. A spectacular sunset is in progress so we walk through the trees to the water's edge. A bench is artfully positioned in front of the gently lapping waters and although the sun is setting somewhere behind us, we embrace and watch a golden light illuminate the waterfowl.

"It'll be fine," I say, somewhat limply. "You'll see."

I couldn't have known how prophetic my words would prove.

**KILOMETRES TRAVELLED: 1072;**
**KILOMETRES REMAINING: 2326**

# Chapter 7: The Hills are Alive

It is 9am and a hearty, middle-aged German woman is slapping me viciously across the back of the knees. The pain is excruciating. She does this nine times, until tears spring to my eyes. I'm told it's for my own good; I'm having trouble believing this.

It started innocently enough, although unexpectedly, the previous evening as we sat on our bench by the lakeside. The evening by Chiemsee had taken a turn for the melancholy, when something happened to shake us out of it.

A woman in her fifties, with bobbed auburn hair and comfortable, bohemian clothes, emerges between the trees, from the direction of the pretty cottage we have seen at the water's edge. After nodding hello to us, she takes off her shoes and wades into the water. Aradhna, wanting the distraction of conversation with the newcomer, asks:

"How is the water?"

"It's very cold. Refreshing though," replies the woman, with a curious smile.

Cornelia turns out to be a fascinating individual, living with her husband Winfried over the winter at the house on Chiemsee, but spending much of her time in the mountains at Oberstdorf, near the Austrian border, or much further afield – in Hawaii. It transpires that she is a masseuse and physical therapist specialising in Hawaiian treatments, having gone there on holiday and fallen in love with the place. We talk for a while about the lake and how peaceful it is (and refreshingly cold on the feet) and then, very casually, Cornelia invites us to join her and Winfried for a glass of wine in their garden. We gratefully accept and spend a very pleasant hour or two in their company talking about travel, running, adventures and our shared conviction of the importance of living life to the full.

Winfried's English is a little more basic than Cornelia's but he has a very jovial, humorous personality and the couple prove very enjoyable company. A deep sense of conviviality and relaxation descends, exactly what we both need after the trials and disappointments of the day. Our hosts insist that we repark Roxy in their back garden for safety, and we gladly take them up on this offer, as well as using their shower and toilet facilities (vanlifers never pass up such an opportunity).

***

The following morning we join Cornelia and Winfried for breakfast. I have agreed to get up early to cycle with Winfried a half mile or so to the local "bio" shop to buy fresh bread. My aching thighs struggle to keep up with Winfried's brisk pace but I enjoy the ride along quiet lanes, clutching my bagels, seeded bread and some goji berries to sprinkle on our cereal.

We combine resources and lay out a tasty spread – bread, homemade jam, goat's cheese and Gouda, banana and raspberries. Cornelia puts on some Hawaiian music and I recognise a song I'd heard years ago on a compilation, "The Beauty of Mauna Kea" by Keola Beamer and George Winston. The song, sung in a lilting alto, floats out into the warm morning air and forms a perfect accompaniment to our breakfast. Then, as we are grudgingly getting ready to go, the Millers shower us with gifts – local beers, foot salts and herbal face masks. Cornelia's final gift is the aforementioned back-of-the-legs thwacking. I express doubt that this will help the ache in my hamstring, but for the rest of the running day, amazingly, I feel no pain, from that part of my legs at least.

***

Refreshed by our encounter with our new German friends, we embark on day 32 with renewed vigour. Under a sky filled with lumpy grey-white clouds, I run stiff-legged along a footpath following the river Traun and turn off onto a cycle path accompanying a B-road through pleasant green valleys. With uncharacteristic brevity, nearby villages are called things like "Au", "Eck" and "Ed". Is there a tax on syllables in this part of Germany?

Soon the cycle path comes to an abrupt end and I divert north through the village of Surtal and find local single-track roads and footpaths free from the stress of speeding BMWs. Disappointed not to be passing through the town of Nutz, I am spurred onto greater speed by the mountains ahead – so close now I can see the drifts of snow filling their sharp upper slopes.

Soon I arrive at a main road junction and sit for a moment looking at a sign promising "just" 20km more to run to Salzburg. That morning, Aradhna packed me a lunch, since we decided my daily mileage was still a little too low (closer to 35km rather than the hoped for 45km per day) and so I couldn't stop for a proper meal. Not stopping will certainly help but it will be a lonelier journey, without that bit of contact halfway through the running day.

That said, Aradhna would say (and I'd agree) that I tend to be far from sociable at lunchtime. We'd joke that I'd often be a shambling zombie demanding "Drink!" like the disreputable elder priest in *Father Ted*. I'd then slump down into a chair with a thousand-yard stare, before stuffing my face with as much finger food as possible (see Appendix III for a typical day's nutrition). Eventually, perhaps after 20 minutes, I'd begin to be able to utter actual sentences. I'd not be fascinating company, even at my best – cumulative fatigue and the knowledge that I still had half a day's running ahead of me would rob me of my sparkle. I also had a tendency to malinger on bad days – if I was in too much pain or if it was raining heavily. Suddenly having an extra cup of tea would seem vitally important. Aradhna would do her best to keep me on mission and send me on my way, but there's only so much you can prod a recalcitrant ultrarunner. Ultimately, if I didn't find a deep resource of willpower from somewhere, I'd never have left that fold-up canvas chair.

All of which goes to explain why giving me a packed lunch and saying, "I'll see you at Salzburg," was very much the best strategy for today.

After prising myself off the bench, I pass through the towns of Ufering (the addition of an "S" and another "f" would make this place name highly apposite for much of my adventure) and Straß [1], pushing on through a growing lethargy, counting off the small picturesque villages without much enthusiasm.

Suddenly I emerge from my funk onto a riverbank, a footpath leading off to left and right. On the far bank I can see pale yellow- and white-painted barns with sloping tiled roofs, behind them a curtain of dark mountains. The river Saalach separates Germany and Austria and, once I cross the gently, flowing river I'd be in my third country and heading into the historic city of Salzburg. My mood immediately brightens. That said, I know Austria only from the romanticised vision presented in *The Sound of Music*, which my sister Fiona had loved so much as a child that she owned the soundtrack and played it with

---

1   A hamlet that should ideally be twinned with Somerset's town named Street.

irritating frequency (I've since grown to appreciate the film more as the masterpiece it certainly is).

The river's quiet majesty has been dammed and channelled by an epic weir with art deco curves like something from Fritz Lang's *Metropolis*. To my left, the near-invisible border is rendered very real by a group of German police cars and officers doing stop and searches of vehicles entering Germany. No such barrier exists in the direction I am heading, however. I am expecting proudly flying red and white flags, but there's nothing to confirm my entry into Austria but a smallish sign saying "Salzburg", past which stream an endless slew of trucks and tourists in liveried coaches.

As I cross the water I squint into the dazzling sunlight and see, beyond the weir, a massive fortress, the Hohensalzburg, gleaming on a rocky plug with snowy peaks arrayed behind. Suddenly I feel that I really am in Austria and that dramatic mountain passes and trails will soon be mine. For today, however, all I have to do is negotiate the ubiquitously bland city suburbs and find Roxy.

This I eventually do, after much urban orienteering, wrong turns and confusion. Somewhere near the university halls of residence, Aradhna has found a quiet road with a brownfield site and open fields on one side and terraced housing on the other. It isn't beautiful but we decide to set aside an extra day to see Salzburg in all its finery. Functional will do for now.

\*\*\*

The following day, as I go for my morning "movement" (behind a mound of earth stacked for eventual landscaping) my furtive evacuation is surreally soundtracked by a male singer soloing beautifully in Hindi. Unfortunately, he stops by the time I wake Aradhna, who might have identified the song. It seems the hills (or spoil heaps) of Salzburg really are alive with the sound of music.

Another surprise comes in the form of a brisk knock on the door a little later, as we are preparing our morning meal. Aradhna smiles knowingly as she slides the side of the van open to reveal the Millers, who have driven all the way from Chiemsee to join us for breakfast. Although we feel a little guilty that we've chosen a less than idyllic picnic spot we get the foldable camp chairs out and pass a pleasant hour in the warm morning light with our guests. I receive a second knee-whacking (nineteen blows this time – I couldn't think of a polite way to decline) to help me on my way and we said our goodbyes, promising to visit Cornelia and Winfried in their summer home in Oberstdorf, on our return journey.

***

The 35th day of our adventure is a "bonus" day off. We'd always planned to reward ourselves with one full day off from running (and supporting running) in each of the Orient Express towns along the way. Salzburg isn't an Orient station. However, given its celebrated status, we feel it would be rude and bizarre just to tear through the city and out the other side. Munich was a difficult disappointment in many ways. Salzburg will refresh our souls, we hope.

And so it proves. We begin with a meandering walk up to Hohensalzburg Castle via the impressive Kapitelplatz, with its giant golden globe sculpture[1] and street musicians. The castle itself is as grand and ancient as we'd hoped, commanding awe-inspiring views of the city on all sides. Thrown into sharp relief by piercing sunlight, the mountains to the south-east appear hyperreal and daunting – will I really be amongst their jagged, snowy slopes soon?

The castle's Golden Hall with its gilt-dotted painted rafters and spiralling stone columns is especially impressive. There's even a macabre marionette museum, where we push a button to release a sinisterly-laughing puppet skull.

Passing an age-old bakery powered by a waterwheel, we find a café and enjoy cakes and wine on a sunlit terrace. Then later, at the Schloss Hellbrunn, Aradhna is delighted to discover the actual gazebo that features in the "I am 16, going on 17" number in *The Sound of Music*, gifted to the city by the film's production team. Much posing for photographs follows. In the formal gardens of the *schloss* we watch carp glide in the rather murky ponds before throwing caution to the winds and returning to the city centre for yet more cake (accompanied by a Pilsner this time).

What such days off do for me, as a long-distance runner, is twofold. Firstly, they provide "active recovery". I'm still stretching my legs and exercising aching muscles, but I'm doing so at walking pace. Secondly, they induce a little useful guilt – devoting a day to nothing but pleasure tends to make me begin the next running day with something to prove.

---

1    An enigmatic nine-metre-tall sculpture by German artist Stephan Balkenhol (2007). The globe rests on an ornate wrought-iron stand and is surmounted by a lifesize "everyman figure" looking straight ahead.

Most vitally of all, they keep our relationship on an even keel, allowing us to devote time to one another, without the distraction of route-finding or running support. If you need to sustain a supported run for months on end, whilst living in a van with one other person, you'd better make time for some unadulterated fun along the way. And I am keenly aware of the secret I have stored away in Roxy's darkest recesses, and what it may mean for our future.

*** 

## Day 36

Fun firmly over, I start running on 15th April alongside a river and straight up into the slopes, finding a scenic *wanderweg* to take me into the Alps. I am excited about the prospect of doing battle with the mountains, as I trot energetically up a winding trail past stepped, man-made waterfalls. Meltwater flows in this region are often managed this way, important in an area that evidently gets a lot of precipitation.

From Guggenthal, I take an ever-more glorious path into the mountains. One spectacular valley at Ebenau stretches out before me; in the foreground an old mill's waterwheel rotates slowly in a gushing sluice. The scene is perfect – the Alps of my imagination in microcosm.

The many green pastures on these foothills are marked with odd totems – posies of flowers, leaves and catkins suspended on long sticks. A country tradition in celebration of springtime? I take photographic evidence and run on. Climbing a winding, wooded B-road I come across several posters and photographs plastered to trees, telling a cautionary tale of two teenage girls who (I guess) perished on the roadside. Every idyll has its rude interruption.

At Faistenau, hills finally become mountains and extreme gradients on the forestry trails reduce me frequently to a walk. Fuschl features a pretty lake and pale-yellow plastered buildings with heavy, shady eaves. Soon I reach a crossroads (metaphorical and literal). I could follow the main road to St Gilgen or take to the mountain trails instead. The latter route approximately doubles the distance and difficulty but really, it is no choice at all. Trails beat tarmac every time; I head into the trees on a 13km route.

The path takes me up and up into the mountains proper, following splashing, impossibly icy streams that gurgle in every valley. Soon, pink tufts of heather decorate the coarse grasses, reminding me of

Highland ways in Scotland.

At Marienkopf I notice a tiny path leading to the summit of one of the peaks and temptation overcomes me. Five minutes of scrambling later, I stand on top of a rocky pinnacle, with a spectacular 360-degree panorama of mountains, forests, lakes and tiny settlements laid out before me. The godlike perch is decorated, as most would be, with a metal cross, but this roost also sports a metal box containing a climbers' log book and pencils. I scribble a message as I drink in the views, then go on my way.

The white bells of hellebores and sprinklings of melting snow tell me how high I am climbing. A little later, the snow scattering becomes a quarter-mile-long drift, fully covering the path, traipsed across by the many walkers who have left deep footprints in evidence. I galumph on, hoping that things won't worsen. I would stop briefly to eat, but it is mid-afternoon now and St Gilgen is still several kilometres away.

Eventually, exposed and icy paths give way to muddy, leaf-strewn descents, as I duck under partially fallen trees and leap logs which lie across the trail. Getting surprisingly good reception, I call Aradhna to change our plan to meet at the amusingly-named village of Au. I'll push on as far as St Gilgen and see where things stand.

*** 

We are soon to be visited by the Eagles, the uncle and aunt of one of Aradhna's friends, their surname fitting, given the altitudes we are now reaching. Hugh and Buff Eagle are keen campervan enthusiasts in their sixties. We'll travel in convoy for a few days as they continue a six-week-long journey around Europe. Aradhna meets them at Au, near the lake (Mondsee). The couple wave cheerily in unison from the doorway of their campervan as planned (I am still out in the mountains). Over a cup of tea, Hugh and Buff gain some insight into the fraught nature of adventure-running support navigation, as Aradhna wrestles with Google, her satnav and paper maps, in an attempt to locate the best spot to pick me up later.

*** 

Meanwhile, I am negotiating a tricky descent. Concealed rocks and tree-roots under the leaves quickly increase the ache and unsteadiness in my legs. However, knowing that visitors await my arrival helps me rally as I plummet down the rocky mountainside and out onto green meadows once more. Ahead of me lies the shimmering mirror of Wolfgangsee, wooden decks and swimming platforms inviting nobody in yet, as winter's chill still pervades the alpine air.

\*\*\*

I follow pavement and hiker-worn desire paths around the lake and past the villages of Brunnwinkl and Winkl towards a smaller lake – Krottensee – where Aradhna has identified somewhere we might stop for the night. The final stretch is a run downhill at full tilt as Roxy and the Eagles' white van pursue me to a quiet lay-by surrounded on three sides by forest. Then, breathless but pleased that I've ended the day with a sprint, I meet our jovial visitors and am happy to accept their offer of a shower and meal (they have a wet room, no less).

\*\*\*

That evening, four of us sit in the convivial surroundings of their Fiat van dining on macaroni cheese (Aradhna's favourite) and sharing tales of life on the road. It is wonderful to spend time with two other grown adults who feel that living in a small metal box for months on end is a rational and fun thing to do. Although the weather outside is becoming grey and drizzly as afternoon light fades into evening gloom, our moods are ebullient. I am now in the thick of the mountains I'd craved and Aradhna has company.

The Eagles have kindly brought us a care package of matches, gas lighters for our stove, Scottish oatcakes and Irn Bru[1]. Not your ordinary adventurer's shopping list, but vital to our own idiosyncratic needs.

\*\*\*

The night passes a little less restfully than we'd hoped with heavy rain and frequently-stopping trucks spoiling the peace and quiet. The following day begins in mist and drizzle, which quickly clears as I continue down the winding valley. By 10:30am sunlight has reasserted dominance as I locate a trailhead and begin my stiff-legged ascent. I stop to photograph a sunbathing black and orange salamander and my phone rings.

---

1    As well as a fantastic runner's pick-me-up, Irn Bru is also my go-to hangover cure. It beats a raw egg and spinach smoothie any day.

***

It is a worried-sounding Aradhna. "Gavin, do you have the van keys?" she asks, doubtfully. This is evidently a long shot. I vigorously deny the possibility before checking a backpack pocket and finding two sets of Roxy keys – mine and Aradhna's. Oops.

Having climbed determinedly a kilometre or so up the mountainside, I now have to race back down to meet Hugh and Aradhna (Buff remains in our lay-by to guard Roxy) and shamefacedly hand over the extra keys. I then turn tail and climb the mountain for a second time, adding around 2km to my daily slog.

Halfway up the winding trail, I pause by a well-positioned bench to take in a staggering view of today's lake – Mondsee – mirroring the surrounding mountains with astonishing clarity.

The terrain quickly becomes barren and rocky, with crashing waterfalls plunging down the slopes to break the tyranny of stone and scrubby pine. I am able to circumvent some of the long, winding loops with pedestrian cut-throughs that angle more directly up the mountainside. High cliffs tower above me and, as ever, I run alone and see no-one.

I pass a geometrically straight cut in the plantation to my left and spot the eerily quiet mechanism of a ski-lift stretching up the steep slope, waiting out the warm seasons until it can grind into action once more. I run on, eventually plunging down the grassy slope of another piste to an empty resort complete with cabins, wildlife walks and signposts to slopes of varying difficulty. Inevitably, I begin to climb again.

From a high vantage point above the silvery lake I can make out two tiny metallic blocks – Roxy and the Eagles' vehicle resting in a quiet car park. I leap and clamber over fallen logs and scattered piles of leaves as I make my eager descent. A little later, on aching legs, I make it out onto the wooded shore of Langbathsee, finally passing two other runners completing a loop in the opposite direction. Then comes a familiar face, under a familiar yellow bicycle helmet – Aradhna has decided to cycle round the lake too. I wave cheerily, but decline to turn round and take a full circuit with her – I have the finish line in sight and when that blessed moment takes hold, nothing will persuade me to run some more. I hope she won't be too disappointed. Later, she tells me that she was. Once again, I'd missed a key opportunity to share a moment together. Why do I keep doing this?

Reaching the lake, I decide to give into temptation and take the plunge. Stripping off my outer layers, I grab my shower gel and a towel and stride into the icy water in just my Lycra undershorts. Needless to say, the temperature is unforgivingly cold, the lake filled with recent meltwater from deep winter drifts. A few moments thrashing about is all I can stand, but the relief it brings my aching muscles and joints is immense.

As part of my training for my previous adventure, I took part in a study at Middlesex University's Sports Science Lab. The aim was to compare and contrast three different kinds of post-marathon recovery treatment. A sample of runners were asked to run a measured marathon distance around the University grounds at their Hendon facility, then take one of three recovery treatments. The first was to consume a concentrate made from cherries, the second to walk for four minutes around a cryogenic chamber set to -85 degrees Celsius[1].

The third method, which I experienced, was a six-degree ice bath, in which I had to stay submerged up to the waist for 10 minutes. Although singularly effective, this treatment produced a shockwave of extraordinary agony and remains probably the single most painful experience I've ever had.

Langbathsee's waters are nowhere like as cold, but are almost as effective, numbing the residual ache and revitalising my senses. I quickly soap and rinse myself, swim around a bit and tiptoe out. From now on I will take every opportunity to dip my tired limbs.

## KILOMETRES TRAVELLED: 1191;
## KILOMETRES REMAINING: 2207

---

1   To put this into context, that's less than 5 degrees warmer than the coldest temperature ever recorded on earth, and athletes spend time in these chambers almost entirely naked. I think I'd stick with the cherries! Journal of Geophysical Research, VOL. 114, D24102, doi:10.1029/2009JD012104, 2009: http://nora.nerc.ac.uk/id/eprint/9656/1/jgrd15635.pdf

# Tips for Multi-Day Runners - 3. Kit

Multi-day adventurers think long and hard about this one. In Sean Conway's book about his own JOGLE[1], he describes going to the extent of chopping his toothbrush in two to lighten his load a little bit more. You don't have to go to such extremes if you're supported, but do think long and hard about what you need and what you can do without. A general rule of thumb is that if something is best described as "nice to have" you probably don't need it and you won't have time to use it anyway!

**Essential kit**
(For a full list of what I used on this adventure, see Appendix I)

*GPS tracker / communicator* – I wouldn't be without one of these now, plus ample chargers and sufficient credit. It might be the single most expensive item of kit you'll buy but it could literally save your life. For extra effectiveness, get one that uses one of the satellite networks (for example, Iridium or Thuraya) – you will literally be able to text or email your support driver even if you're deep in the Amazon jungle or the Antarctic.

*Sufficient clothes* – it's a bit of a no-brainer this one, ·but you will get through a LOT of running gear and having to wash it every other night will be a massive pain in your posterior. Running in wet or smelly clothing, or with inadequate protection from rain, cold or direct sunshine will demoralise you more than almost anything else you'll encounter.

*Water bladder* – consider using a backpack with an internal reservoir for water and a drinking tube, in preference to bottles. They hold much more, distribute the weight evenly and deliver hydration whenever you need it without requiring you to stop or risk losing a drop through splashing. Do remember to refill them at every opportunity!

*Phones* – I'd advise two. A "vanilla" one which is good for nothing

---

1   *Running Britain*, Sean Conway (Mortimer Lion Publishing, 2018).

but calls and texts (and consequently the battery lasts for days) and another one for navigation / photography. Additional battery chargers are a godsend too. You might even try a fold-out solar charger (I haven't but others swear by them).

*Snacks and electrolytes*. Running on empty is dangerous and no fun at all. At best it will slow you down and ruin your day. At worst it will kill you. Maintain your fluid intake, salt levels (drop a tablet or two in your water bladder) and keep topping up your sugar and carbohydrate levels. The diet can wait!

*Paper maps* – Google Maps is mostly fine. GPS trackers often come with detailed mapping software, but it is rarely very user-friendly and relies on you having battery power and a GPS signal. Sometimes nothing can beat a good trail map (make sure you get or create laminated maps where possible) and a compass. Having this back-up could be the lifeline that gets you out of a thorny situation.

# Chapter 8: Two More Marias

*Day 38*

That evening the Eagles again treat us to a home-cooked meal of quiche, asparagus and local beers. Apart from a late night visitation from what sounds like a group of Italians, the night passes peacefully and the morning of 17th April rewards us with a glorious sunrise. By ten o'clock the car park has filled with a coachload of Chinese tourists who are fascinated by our campervan and not at all shy about peering inside. We humour their inquisitiveness and I take this as a signal that I should be on my way.

Today will see me taking to the roads once more, heading for Ebensee. My legs are stiff and inflexible and I hobble the first few kilometres, heading downstream along a small river with regular stepped weirs. I wave cheerily at a couple of quantity surveyors as I waddle past. They seem to be enjoying the late spring sunshine as much as I am.

Ebensee is a picture-postcard town on yet another mountain lake – Traunsee. The river feeding the lake is lined with blossoming cherry trees and light green leaves adorn the deciduous trees along the lakeside. I head for a trail marked on local maps, popular with walkers and starting at the nearby village of Rindbach. Finding my way through a maze of backstreets and decorous homes, I locate the trailhead and run up a wide path lined with pine needles and dappled in sunlight.

Signposts offer a diversion via some narrow waterfalls, which I take, always keen to spice my daily run with variety. The cataract is impressive, thousands of gallons of water plummeting off the high mountain, squeezed between sharp planes of rock. I trot up steep steps to the top and take some photos before rejoining the main walking route.

The path is easy to navigate – flat, blasted from the mountainside and bolstered in places with concrete abutments. Though the incline is gentle, my legs are deadened and every step feels effortful. My pace drops to a slow jog as the heat of the day rises towards noon.

Soon the path splits into three, only one of these ways marked on Google Maps. Which is correct? There's nothing for it but to guess and, as expected, my first attempt leads me astray, requiring 500 metres of backtracking. I take a short break to eat a snack and dip my feet in the brutally cold stream, something that somehow manages to be soothing and agonising simultaneously. Later, having found the correct trail, I pass a perfect natural rock basin in the river. Had I time, I might have bathed, but I am already worried about my slow pace and the consequences of not making it off the mountainside before dark. Although I have a silver foil emergency "survival bag" with me, I really don't want to have to use it.

Three years previously, I was in a similarly worrisome situation and could even have died. On 5th March 2015[1], after five and a half hours of stumbling blindly through the Scottish Highlands, I eventually had to swim a deep, gushing river as twilight began to turn the lights out on my misadventure. I then walked shivering for miles along a country lane, while no cars passed me. I had no idea how I'd get back to my panic-stricken father (and support driver) and if it wasn't for the kindly assistance of an elderly lady who drove me ten miles to the nearest town, I might have perished from hypothermia. This was not an experience I was looking to repeat in 2018.

A kilometre further up the mountain, I no longer have a problem with heat causing fatigue. The temperature has cooled enough to keep drifts of snow from melting; one such obstacle now stretches for half a kilometre before me. Encouragingly, there are already a line of deep footprints in the crusty snow which has drifted up to two-feet deep in places, so I follow my mysterious predecessor and make it to the other side without mishap.

The verges are brightened by blue, star-shaped gentians and vibrantly green spring growth decorates the young trees. I still can't raise a decent pace from my aching limbs and rely heavily upon trail-markers (the Austrian flag) to reassure me that this is a sensible route as the path I've chosen narrows. I am aiming for a place called Habernau but the signs for that seem to stop, replaced by others offering Almtal or Almsee instead. I know my legs don't have that much left in them, so I call Aradhna and ask her to meet me at Habernau anyway, hoping I'll (literally) stumble upon it.

The way ahead, a vaguely discernible dirt line cutting through

---

1    As recounted in *Downhill from Here* pp 58-67.

preserved layers of autumn leaves, winds in and out of fallen trees and boulders, challenging my dwindling energy reserves yet further. I start using my hands to push down my thighs on ascents and then grab a branch as a walking staff (I name it Gandalf). The spoor of deer is in evidence, as well as hidden puddles of meltwater under the leaves. Signs for the unlikely sounding Cumberland Wild Park appear now – I call Aradhna and she dutifully packs up once more and heads there.

Half an hour later the path turns once more and seems to be heading for Habernau after all. I make another embarrassing call. To her credit, Aradhna does not lose her cool when, for the second time, she repacks the van and heads (with the Eagles who, by now, must think me an entirely incompetent orienteer) back to Habernau.

When we finally coincide, I am utterly spent and can't face any more mountains. We find an official parking place off a lakeside road and Aradhna and I go for a short walk, finding a local inn whose restaurant is closed and a scenic chair-swing affording a spectacular view of the peaks surrounding us. Aradhna swings in the basket chair, enjoying a rare reprieve from her trials.

\*\*\*

The sun rises on 18th April behind a thick bank of fog, creating the eerie illusion that it is a misplaced stage light, its billions of lumens vastly diminished by the grey-white veil that surrounds us. The road is quiet and only a few ducks and swans stir the placid lake's surface. The effect is mesmerising and strange and we all take many photographs. I feel immediately happier, my energy levels renewed.

The mist clears after an hour or so, as we sit out enjoying a delicious second breakfast of homemade pancakes. I then help Aradhna film an interview with our caravan friends, seated together under a blazingly blue sky.

All of this means I don't start running until 3pm but my legs appreciate the extended break. I find the elusive Habernau and continue up a sunlit forest trail flanked with immense rocky outcrops, to which trees tenaciously cling. Sparkling rivulets of water cascade down the stony sides of the mountain and colourful lizards and basking salamanders scuttle out of my way.

The Eagles are leaving us today but our friend David is arriving on a local train midway through tomorrow afternoon. David will be the first brave soul to live with us in the van, taking the upstairs "suite" for three days (and braving the elements beyond its canvas sides).

Aradhna is looking forward to having some company and perhaps some help with the physical and navigational challenges that form an inescapable part of her support duties.

***

Pale blue flowers dot the verges as the forest path lifts high into the mountains. I come to a large hunting lodge, shut up for the season and decorated with lines of impressive yet sinister antlers. Outside, a stream has been diverted through a pipe into a trough made from a hollowed-out log, a common site in the region. I can imagine packs of hunting dogs lapping eagerly between forages.

I quickly realise that the forest path I've found is, once again, not taking me the way I need to go; such routes seldom do. They tend to spiral up and around the peaks, allowing logging vehicles to access the higher slopes. They don't curve sinuously between the mountains, unlike the (frequently dangerous) roads down below.

Fortunately, my Garmin saves me again, allowing me to march up muddy slopes landscaped by loggers, then pick my way down leaf-deep slopes to find a different road. Just as I am getting my bearings, a sound stops me in my tracks … a distant pattering of hooves, perhaps dozens of them. I squint between the trees off to the south. There are deer trotting between the trees – not dozens of them, however – hundreds.

The herd streams seemingly endlessly along the slopes opposite where I stand frozen in place. They are heading in the same direction, with urgency – perhaps evading early huntsmen (maybe the season has started after all) or driven on by vehicles. Whatever the reason for the procession, there are a great many red deer doing what I should be doing; namely, heading east. I don't care – this is a sight worth stopping to watch, a once-in-a-lifetime glimpse of the kind of immense herd the ancient European forests must once have played host to, in a time when they were less circumscribed and shaped by man.

Within the herd I think I can even identify several responsible adult animals, drifting at the perimeters, ensuring that nobody is left behind and adolescents don't dawdle. At the back come the older, greyer, slower animals. I briefly wonder if there are wolves here, but discount the possibility. Men with guns and Land Rovers are foe enough in these protected woods.

When the deer finally pass, a breathtaking sight I feel privileged to have witnessed, I take the road heading south-east. A Land Rover stops in passing and (brazening out the encounter, having no idea if I am trespassing on private land) I ask the gent inside if I am going the right way for Steyrling. He doesn't seem fazed by or disapproving of my presence and confirms that I am on the right track.

Feeling the ache of four and a half hours of constant mountain-running in my legs, I am very grateful to find signs of human habitation. I jog past some impressive houses, midway between aristocratic mansions and giant barns in the Austrian style. Further on, I cross a blue tumbling river in spate via a small footbridge and emerge onto a road. Signs behind me indicate that I'd somehow stumbled through someone's private estate, although I have no recollection of climbing fences or opening illicit gates. Wherever I am, it isn't quite Steyrling, but I am utterly spent. Today's adventures will stop here.

Exhausted, I call Aradhna and redirect her once more to collect me (she hides her frustration remarkably well). I'd run a little over 32km and have nothing left in the tank. While there is still enough light to find a parking spot, we perch on a patch of ground by the side of a river. Aradhna later tells me I sleep so soundly that I entirely miss the massive logging truck that comes to collect a nearby stack of tree trunks in the small hours.

\*\*\*

## Day 40

The morning brings another sparkling day, as I race to get to Steyrling proper before David arrives on his morning train. Aradhna has driven on ahead and while I am passing through the pretty town, our new visitor steps off a train at the tiniest station any of us have ever seen. Apparently the train conductor asked David twice if he was certain he was getting off at the right place.

Meanwhile, I follow a cycle route under the main road, past a lemon-yellow hillside schloss and on to a road junction marked with a plaque dedicated to local 19th-century doctor and poet Josef Moser. Crossing the road at a gallop, I find another, quieter path parallel to an A-road and sprinkled with wildflowers and fluttering butterflies.

The sun fairly bakes me all morning. At 28 degrees[1] it is the hottest day yet and I gulp down free stream water from springs as well as the somewhat brackish, warm stuff in my backpack.

---

1    I'm trying to stick to consistent measures. It's a weirdly British tendency to exaggerate weather extremes by reporting cold temperatures in negative degrees Celsius but hot ones in Fahrenheit. 28°C is 82.4°F.

At Mölln I run across a narrow bridge over an impressive gorge before diverting from the road into beautiful green meadows. I've never seen so many dandelions in one place, their vibrant yellow stippling the grass as if sprayed on.

A few kilometres into the valley I pass a tepee-like skeletal structure. It resembles a gibbet or medieval torture device. An immense rock hangs suspended from a wooden support.

Rather than having some sinister purpose, a nearby plaque explains its far more wholesome use. Apparently groups of young school kids are brought here and given an impressive demonstration of the value of teamwork, first being asked to pull on the rope individually or in pairs to raise the stone from its sandy bed. Inevitably, they fail to lift the boulder at first. Then, the whole team pulls on the rope, tug-of-war-style, to achieve the task. The simple pragmatism of this teaching tool seems to me very Austrian.

*** 

Aradhna has been in touch, confirming that she has picked up David and they will be waiting for me at a village called Breitenau. The cycle path I am following runs high above the main road below and takes me across another spectacular bridge over the aquamarine Steyr river, which snakes off through the forest to the south. Breitenau's decoratively painted firehouse appears to my left (Austrians and Germans express a great deal of pride in their local fire services), featuring an illustration of a heroically giant fireman pouring water on a blazing toy house. The village itself is tiny and the church where I'd expected to meet the others for lunch comes and goes with no sign of them. I haven't seen Roxy pass me on the road either and begin to wonder if they've got lost.

I stop to call Aradhna and she insists that they are definitely parked by the church in Breitenau. This is somewhat baffling, as I've just run through the tiny village entirely.

More perplexingly, the map seems to show the road I am on as Breitenau, a nearby mountain is called Breitenau and there is a town to the south-east named Innerbreitenau. I decide to make for the latter.

Finally, some homesteads appear, a patch of manicured green and Roxy parked aside the local church. I feel immense relief as well as my usual fatigue, but force a smile and offer an apologetically sweaty handshake as David emerges from behind the van to greet me with a beaming smile. He has been helping Aradhna prepare my usual picnic-style lunchtime feast and I hope my appreciation is evident. We are especially happy to have David with us. As well as being exceptionally resourceful and helpful, he is one of Aradhna's very best friends and will help carry the very evident burden of supporting me.

Aradhna has already had a talk with me about trying to appear more upbeat and less demanding. It's a reasonable criticism. I might not feel like being chatty, but the least I can do is remain civil, even if my body just wants to eat and recline.

Around 90 minutes later, sated and having completed around 27km in the morning, I set off to try to top 40km by the end of the day. Google shows the route ahead as a tangle of zig-zagging forest trails which often end abruptly (possibly at the top of a mountain). Linking these together as I head east will be a challenge. Sticking to the roads isn't an option, however. They will take me too far south and there is also the fact that Austrians (and Germans) seem determined to drive as fast as humanly possible in any given situation. It is as if drivers deem it their patriotic duty to prove the superiority of their Mercedes, BMWs, Volkswagens and Audis over all other vehicles by driving them at blinding speeds.

There is also the small matter of realising that my bowel, bladder and stomach are all entirely full, something I recognised before lunch, but failed to do anything about. Not that going to the toilet would have been easy, in a small village with no open cafés or public conveniences. Heading for the hills is now a biological necessity; I pack the trowel and some loo paper and hobble off.

I quickly locate the trail, which soon begins its inevitable climb into the hills. I answer the call of nature as soon as I can, which brings a relief that borders on transcendence. Everything is going well, bar my pace, which is plodding, until the trail I am on simply vanishes, the gravel path stopping as if the engineers and digging machines that had sliced it from the mountainside had stopped for a tea break one day and never returned. Piles of fallen branches and thick vegetation prevent me from continuing. I consult my Garmin, looking for a parallel route. There is one, less than a kilometre away. Just one problem presents itself – I'll have to climb directly up the slope to my left, an incline of roughly 40°.

I spot a wooden ladder on the side of the hill and climb ten feet up a rocky face to find a small path leading to a hide suspended above the treeline. Unfortunately, the path does not then lead on anywhere, but I take this sign of human habitation as encouragement and begin to scramble up the slope. At times, I have to clamber over fallen tree trunks and pull on saplings to manhandle my way up the incline, which seems to be getting close to 60° in places. There is the real possibility of falling backwards and tumbling down to the path below, snagging myself on multiple briars as I fall.

I make for a curious wooden box, about a foot across and affixed to a tree stump. The front of it lies open, like a puppet theatre (if such things still exist). In the middle of the "stage" is a chunk of rose quartz about the size of a human head. The pink mineral sparkles in the afternoon sunlight. What weird talisman is this? Nothing is written nearby to explain the puzzle.

It will remain a mystery until many months later, when Cornelia Miller reveals that rose quartz is supposedly a healing mineral, lowering stress and tension in the heart. I decide to park my scepticism on hearing this. The silicon dioxide crystal does prove auspicious in a way – directing me up the slope, over the top of the forested hillside and down the other side to another trail. I feel immense gratitude and follow the new route past hides hidden high in the pines and glimpses of a perfect mountain vista – forested slopes lit by the slanting afternoon sunlight. Long shadows throw dark stripes over the path as I head back down into the valley.

*\*\**

It is 5:30pm when I check in with Aradhna on a final meeting point for the day. She tells me they have found a perfect spot by the river Reichramingbach. I make good speed, with this end in sight, emerging from the forest onto a small road bridge over the river. A wide loop of river cradles a slow-moving pool of blue-green water, in which two people wade, perhaps unwisely given the chilling temperature. I do a double-take – it's Aradhna and David, trouser legs rolled up, beers in hand, laughing at the terrifying cold. I wave and run to join them, finding the water soothing but painfully icy.

The nearby picnic spot comes with its own toilets, a great facility, albeit comprised of wooden seats suspended over vast holes in the ground. We cook a tasty dinner and look up at the stars. Occasional comets streak across the speckled blackness overhead – actual shooting stars.

Having someone else with us reminds us how fortunate Aradhna and I are to be able to change our horizons every evening and witness moments of absolute silence and clarity like this. David's awestruck attitude to the alpine surroundings reawakens our own enthusiasm. We must not let this trip become work; it should remain an adventure.

\*\*\*

The following morning sees me running north along the river bank, heading for the town of Reichraming. It doesn't seem quite right to be heading north, but by this point in our journey I've accepted that direct routes will be few and far between. I'd rather take a scenic diversion than a boring and dangerous A-road. Unlike on my JOGLE, this route has no "record" to measure my progress against (and inevitably fall short of). By default, I'll be the record holder for running the Orient Express route from Paris to Istanbul and that will do.

Soon I pass a few riverside homes and a bend in the road at which someone has pinned up a bedsheet on which is written the following:

*Man sieht's Claudia an aber sie gibt's wirkli scho 40 jahre lang egal ob rockig, punkig, sozial, sie is grenzgenial!!!*[1]

Clearly, someone is a major fan of birthday girl Claudia. Further on a small church bears a painted declaration:

*Herr! Erbarme dich unser nach der Menge deiner Erbarmnisse.* (Lord, have mercy on us, as you are all-merciful).

Were I a religious man, I would concur with this sentiment. Let today be as painless and as sublime as yesterday. I follow the R7 cycle route, one of many such long-distance routes in the country (the Austrians are keen cyclists). It winds alongside the river, through the valley and I run baked by a relentless sun under a deep blue sky, marked only by drifting contrails.

Reichraming soon appears, a kids' play park boasting an endearingly ramshackle wooden treehouse with metal slide and rope-bridge walkways. Children brought up here must be spoilt in the best possible way, having such idyllic environs to explore. The town's red-tiled roofs, whitewashed buildings and square church steeple are perfectly mirrored in the still green river as I run along the opposite bank under blossoming cherry and apple trees.

I take a route which climbs up the southern slopes and looks down upon the valley through which a railway runs, alongside the road. My B-road rollercoasters up and down, crossing the railway and river in places. After Grossraming, the road grows quieter and more farmsteads appear. Some inquisitive goats come to inspect me during

---

1    [sic] Roughly translated: You won't believe Claudia is 40! No matter whether into punk, rock or socialising, she is cutting edge!

one pause to get my bearings. I am heading for Weyer Markt, as its name suggests, a noted centre of commerce dating back to the Middle Ages.

An impressive weir with a covered wooden bridge greets me as I run into the town, looking for Aradhna and David. Civic pride is in evidence with ornate fountains, statues and pretty municipal buildings. I find my companions by a drinking water fountain and gladly fill my backpack (they have filled Roxy's tank and we wash the lunch dishes; in vanlife you cannot miss an opportunity to get the chores done).

*\*\**

After lunch, it's back to the roads, dodging crazy drivers and realising what all the CDs hanging from the bushes are for – additional reflectors at night to mark the edge of the road. I am briefly diverted by the sight of several men abseiling down a steep rock face beyond the road on the other side of the valley. Evidently some rocks have fallen into the road and the dangling workers are making the cliff safe again. A long line of frustrated drivers waits as the men clear the road.

The river I am now following is the Ybbs and the route I am running is evidently recommended for cyclists and day trippers as being both picturesque and historical – many such tourists are in evidence. I am running east again now and making good progress, free from problematic navigation and moving over easy terrain. My only source of anxiety is the less then generous drivers who skim past me at 100kph. I compose a rude ditty as I run, in which these drivers admit that their superpowered cars substitute for something lacking in their manhoods. The lyrics are laced with comforting obscenities. Singing it in my head allows me to remain sanguine rather than stressed-out.

Outside Hollenstein a field full of immense solar panels stands as evidence that today's weather is far from unusual in the region. I manage a good pace down to the town, partly to get the hell out of the traffic. I find myself chasing after Roxy, effectively flagging her down into a lay-by. We quickly realise the road through the town is too busy to stop at, since we need to raise Roxy's roof for David to sleep in, which always gives us away as illicit overnight campers.

We head up a small road into the hills and quickly get ourselves lost, ending up in a quietly beautiful high valley on a gravel roadway which crosses a farm, the route ahead marked by a "Private" sign. The road might be private but according to our maps it does seem to link up with larger roads at the valley's end. Could we continue anyway?

Aradhna spots a young girl planting vegetables beside the farmhouse and hops out to talk to her. Twenty minutes later, when she had not yet returned and seems deep in conversation, I turn to David.

"I'll bet you she's going to return with a spot for us to park for the night."

He nods. "You're probably right."

And so it proves. Not only has Aradhna befriended the farmer's daughter Maria, but she has received an invitation to come round after dinner to share a campfire and a few drinks with the Sonnleitners. Maria introduces herself, her English perfect, saying that they like having visitors but not many make it to the farm in its remoteness. Maria is back home for the summer from Linz where she has been working as a nurse.

We park Roxy where the road permits and make dinner, marvelling at how lovely the valley is, alpine grasslands dotted with apple trees and fringed by forest. Behind the green hills, snowy mountains loom, adding drama. Once more we have got lucky.

That night, after eating, we take some beers with us and head to the Sonnleitner's farm, where the flames of their campfire illuminate the deep country darkness. As well as Maria, we are greeted by her ruddy-cheeked and ever-smiling mother (also called Maria), along with her sister Elizabeth, father Joseph and little brother David, who quickly falls peacefully asleep[1]. Kind and inquisitive, the daughters show us how to spike homemade bread dough on sticks and toast it over the flames; the result is surprisingly delicious.

Patriarch and father of seven, Joseph senior smiles benevolently as we share our beer with him. He speaks no English at all but seems happy enough to watch his daughters practise theirs.

Later on, Maria senior gets her guitar out and plays a couple of songs, including hits by the Beatles and "Country Roads" by John Denver[2]. The elder Maria has lived on the farm for decades, but is remarkably worldly too, having travelled widely in her youth, including South America, Morocco and even Istanbul. Her English is almost as good as her daughter's. We walk happily back to Roxy a couple of hours later, having been invited to return for breakfast the next morning (a relief as our camping gas has just run out and a morning without tea is unthinkable).

---

1    There were seven siblings in total but we met "only" five of them.
2    Who I was once accused of resembling, during a "large glasses" phase of my unfashionable youth.

\*\*\*

An impressive spread almost entirely homemade awaits us at breakfast, including yoghurt and unpasteurised milk, bread and jam. The milk and yoghurt are sourced from the Sonnleitner's own herd which rather puts London's "organic" offerings into perspective. We donate Yorkshire teabags. More of the family are present, including Anton, newly returned from agricultural college. Anton is expected to inherit and run the farm after his parents retire; he seems to relish the prospect and is keen to get to work, tending the cows. Aradhna asks if she could interview the Marias, so I set up the camera for her and she sits mother and daughter outside, in front of the cows, and conducts a long interview which also features Maria senior singing an Austrian folk song.

As well as being extremely reliable and resourceful, David proves himself to be spectacularly clumsy, in highly unlikely scenarios. Having already managed to fall through the ceiling hatch in Roxy (nothing damaged but his pride), David manages two further calamities within twenty-four hours. First, he topples down a slope on the Sonnleitner's pasture whilst taking a nocturnal pee. To obtain the hat-trick, he excels himself, somehow managing to get his intimate places wedged between a barbed wire fence and a tractor, whilst attempting a shortcut through the farm. Extracting David proves a delicate operation and cements his newfound reputation as light relief.

We take many photos and bid a regretful goodbye. Maria junior says she might be travelling soon and will get in touch if she passes through London. We say we'd gladly host any of the family and have a spare room waiting. Austrian hospitality fully taken advantage of, we drive away, negotiating winding single-track forest road, heading towards Hollenstein once more.

**KILOMETRES TRAVELLED: 1325;**
**KILOMETRES REMAINING: 2073**

# Chapter 9: Tales from the Vienna Woods

*Day 42*

I'm only running 32km a day on average. That said, I am running through the Alps, where a country mile easily equals two on the roads, in terms of the challenge it presents. I also have the heat and the blazing sun to contend with.

The morning brings another cloudless blue sky. We are almost becoming nostalgic about rain but our memories of those frozen mornings in France serve to remind us that this enduring heat is preferable. The sunshine means I must begin the day with a full (two-litre) water bladder and remember to refill it at lunchtime (a task I sometimes neglect). This of course also means my backpack is at its full 5kg weight.

Still, I have an easy enough route to follow on 21st April: along a cycle path that accompanies the river Ybbs through alpine valleys eastward. Young Maria Sonnleitner told me about an alternative route across the hills but my creeping fatigue, which now feels like a leaden weight within me, and the knowledge that I am 42 days in and not yet halfway there, makes the choice a simple one. Roads will do for today.

I hope to make it to Lunz am See today, a distance of over 30km. The cycle path is extremely pretty but also rarely shaded beneath a cloudless sky. Soon I am gulping down water and feeling the cumulative effects of salt loss. I take to dissolving a double dose of electrolyte tablets in my water, although this makes it taste sickly sweet and sticky. The Ybbs water is crystal clear and I occasionally cup a handful of it over my face and neck to cool down.

Through wildflower meadows I run, soon reaching the village of Sankt Georgen am Reith, where the cycle path follows a disused railway line. I wonder if the titular hero is the "English" Saint George and indeed he is. A piece of folk art painted on a roadside plaque depicts George and his fearsome foe. I also pass a similarly crude illustration of two small girls falling from a collapsing bridge into the river, which comes with a cautionary script warning of the perils of drowning.

By the time I reach Kogelsbach, I am really suffering the effects of running in the constant heat. I find a roadside shelter designed for cyclists and stop to eat some dried fruit and nuts, Haribo sweets and glucose gels and drink some water. I find myself fantasising about ice lollies and swimming pools. I've managed about 20km but it feels like twice the distance. After ten minutes' rest, I know I have to be on my way once more. Due to our late start after interviewing the Sonnleitners, I've planned today's run to be non-stop. There will be no "lunch" break. I plod on.

The river and route 31 wind south as far as Göstling, then North East to Lunz. I soon hit the marathon wall[1] and hide behind a road sign to get a bit of shade. Consulting Google Maps, my heart sinks. It appears I still have 24km left to run. Fortunately, the road signs suggest it is nearer 14km to Lunz, so I choose to believe them.

The last part of the day entails a long, straight slog along a ruler-straight road with little to divert me from my shattering fatigue. Three kilometres later I reach the weir on the river at Lunz and follow the instructions Aradhna has sent me to reach the campsite where she and David have parked for the night. They are off exploring the local town and countryside. I don't mind; I need some time to vegetate in peace.

I dump my backpack in Roxy and head to the river, where I dip my aching feet in ice-cold water whilst drinking a Radler (lemon-flavoured beer popular in the region). The sense of utter relief at having endured and made it to my intended destination without compromise is a powerful analgesic.

As it is his last evening with us, David treats us to dinner at a lakeside restaurant. It remains warm enough to sit outside on the wooden verandah. Aradhna has her new favourite local dish, spätzle while David orders the pork and I tuck into roast beef with crispy onions and potatoes. Dessert is equally delicious – warm chocolate pudding with ice cream. We try some of the local dessert wine too, then walk back under pin-sharp starlight.

***

We have to be up and out by 11am the following morning so that Aradhna can drive David to get his train. As usual, it's a challenge to get me started but I wave Roxy off and then follow her out onto the

---

1    That stage in a marathon (around 16-18 miles in) when you have burnt all the calories in your glycogen reserves and the body switches, with much protest, into pure fat-burning mode.

road. I expect to have to run on tarmac again this morning and don't relish it. As anticipated, everything aches. However, a little way out of Lunz I see national trail-markers and locate an off-road route towards Lackenhof.

I am now entering an area noted for its skiing and I begin to spot the telltale signs – rows of brightly painted chalets with steeply sloped roofs, restaurants, biergartens and empty car parks. It is very much the off-season now, although some snow still clings to shaded gullies on the higher peaks.

The streets of winter homes are eerily quiet, like some silent catastrophe has decimated the population. I see just one man out tidying his back garden and wave a hello as I head up into the trees. The road grows ever-steeper and the air chillier, a relief after yesterday's temperatures. The gradient is gradual enough for me to not really feel the incline, yet quickly ascend several hundred metres. Dramatic vistas can be glimpsed through gaps in the natural-looking pine forest. The trees are probably heavily managed, but at least are not distributed in serried ranks like you sometimes find in Scotland's plantations. As always, my breathing seems to become easier and more regular in the oxygen-rich environment of the forest.

After several kilometres the path levels and begins its inevitable (and welcome) descent. I find myself flying down the slope, paying close attention to where my feet are landing as the acceleration takes over. I run so well and so fast that when I reach Erlaufboden, with its impressive hydroelectric pipes plunging steeply down the mountainside, Aradhna is nowhere to be seen. She has not yet made it back from dropping David off at Amstetten and, to be fair, I am half an hour ahead of my predicted time of 3pm.

I while away a few minutes studying a noticeboard showing a map of a local running event, the Josef Steiner mountain marathon[1], then dip my feet in the river as I call Aradhna for an update. She is still several miles away and suggests I run on a few kilometres and she'll meet me at the village of Reith. I'm not hugely keen to keep running as I expended most of my available energy on my downhill dash. Nevertheless, I set off once more, grumbling inwardly as the road inevitably begins to climb … and climb … and climb. It's a little over 4km up to the top of the hill, but they are among the steepest and most brutal kilometres I've yet faced. Still, I refuse to be defeated and reduced to walking pace. Half an hour later, I can only muster a

---

1    At 70km over two days, with a total ascent of over 4400m, a challenging ultra!

grimace as Roxy chugs past and vanishes round the corner.

At Reith, I stagger up to the van and clamber into the passenger seat with a grimace. Aradhna is part-amused, part-apologetic and makes up for the ordeal she'd put me through with an endless offering of food, juice and sugary treats. Unfortunately, I am finding it hard to digest anything remotely dry, the hot weather having eradicated my saliva. In addition, my appetite seems to be a little low, rather worrying, given all the calories I burnt off. Plus, Roxy's cooking gas has not yet been replaced, meaning the only hot thing I'll consume will be tea brewed from hot water we'd put in our thermos flask that morning (some English tourists thoughtfully offered to boil our kettle for us). Finally, the peace is frequently shattered by the sound of a woman loudly berating her endlessly screaming child in the otherwise peaceful hamlet.

Given these obstacles, I am relatively glad to resume the run, although a little dejected from not having had the recuperation and sustenance I need. This feeling soon passes, fortunately. After lunch I locate another trail and then find myself following something called the Via Sacra. Part of an international network of pilgrimage trails, the Via Sacra runs from Vienna to Mariazell and has been walked by the devout for hundreds of years. It is, in fact, Austria's oldest such route. I hope its auspicious origins will bring this atheist luck, if not a divine blessing.

At lunch, Aradhna and I decide I will not run for much longer today. It is enough to follow the winding trail through forest and along small local roads as far as Annaberg, with its distinctive black-spired church with a golden clockface shining like a beacon near the top. From Annaberg, the road dips steeply downhill, giving impressive views along a lush valley dotted with farms and well-maintained pastureland. The signposts deflect me along a leafy pathway and then down a flight of rickety wooden steps and, to my surprise, I pop back onto the road at a large lay-by where Roxy and Aradhna are waiting. The evening's camping spot couldn't be more perfect.

\*\*\*

We still have the problem of having no gas with which to cook and the prospect of a cold supper does not appeal. I notice a lot of discarded wood lying around, ranging from small twigs to ankle-thick logs, as well as a lot of large rocks. Could we build a fire to cook on? It doesn't seem a completely ridiculous idea. It could definitely be done safely

– the ground of the lay-by is stony and I could make a ring of rocks to contain the fire. In addition, there is a small river nearby where we can draw water to ensure the flames are properly extinguished. Whether it is entirely legal is another matter but, apart from the occasional car, the road is quiet and we reckon we'll probably get away with it.

Fifteen minutes later, I surprise myself by creating a successful blaze lit with a single match, on which we cook potatoes baked in silver foil, a tin of peas and some cherry tomatoes on the vine (also cooked in foil). We accompany our campfire meal with a local rosé wine and feel very pleased with ourselves (whilst expecting a telling off from a passing local at any moment; it never comes). Later, we eradicate every trace of our misdemeanour, pouring several buckets of water over the embers before going to bed. The experience reminds us that we can be considerably more resourceful than one might assume.

It also makes us feel closer to one another, part of a shared adventure, rather than two parallel ones. I can't take Aradhna with me for most of my daily slog, but I can carry the memory of sharing a meal cooked on a homemade fire, sipping wine from plastic cups and watching woodsmoke spiral up towards the stars.

***

We wake on 23rd April feeling mutually lethargic and decide to channel some of our energy into cleaning a few things that we've been putting off and completing some outstanding chores. I manage to persuade Aradhna to fit the replacement tap we've been carrying with us for weeks. It's a fiddly task but a successful one – once more we have running water and can end our arduous daily ritual of filling every available flask, bottle and kettle with water. Our main tank holds 20 litres and we are finding that it lasts 3-4 days with ease.

Then we remove and clean the sink and waste pipe, as well as the kettle, which has been blackened with soot from its spell on the campfire. With everything shiny and renewed, I have no more excuses with which to procrastinate. I set off along the road, still following Via Sacra signs, which reassure me that I am at least entitled to be there as much as the cars and trucks that race or rumble past. The route contains plenty of reminders of its sacred origins – statues, carved wooden panels depicting biblical scenes and even a pretty white-domed chapel with pilgrims' drinking fountain and lavatories (sadly out of order). A little further on a golden Madonna lies hidden and recumbent in a niche low down in the rocky mountainside. The Via seems to follow the road closely (or vice versa), sometimes vanishing then reappearing as a looping strip of green beneath the trees.

Eventually, at Türnitz, I deviate onto a more promising looking cycle path which turns out to be a disused railway line. I immediately feel at home, having run many such routes around Colinton in Edinburgh, where my parents live. Even the long, dark tunnels don't faze me as I take the opportunity to stretch out a little and run at a reasonable pace.

Then, back on tarmac and halfway up a challenging hill, I prepare to jump over a stick only to watch the grey-green branch slither away from me. I am too fatigued to jump at the sight of the snake and mentally add another piece of local fauna to the checklist of animal encounters so far.

\*\*\*

Moosbach is the next "station" on my route, followed by the blossom-lined valley and village of Lehenrotte. The river idles by, alongside the cycle path as if encouraging me on as I try to keep pace with its gurgling currents. Evening light displays the village architecture under a golden glow as I reach the outskirts of Lilienfeld. A huge aluminium works does not spoil the picture-postcard appeal of this sheltered and verdant valley. Traisen is a little more industrial and functional, its Main Street even offering the odd spectacle of a "Scotish (sic) Pub" – I don't dare venture inside, since I am now chasing the dying evening sunlight.

Aradhna texts me that she's found a great spot by a quiet park in the next small town and I am eager to rest. The cycle path follows the river which has been channelled and civilised so that it almost resembles a canal. Just as the last dying embers of sunset are fading, I reach Sankt Veit an der Gölsen and grind to a grateful halt.

A late dinner of soup and bread and telephone calls home await us that evening. Aradhna has to fly home in a few weeks' time to spend a fortnight caring for her elderly grandmother while her parents are holidaying in Japan. My father has gamely agreed to reprise his support role from my last adventure (albeit without the film-making requirements). This is big of him, especially as we have no way of knowing yet which country I'll be in then, let alone which city he will have to fly to.

\*\*\*

## Day 45

Aradhna has been feeling a little left out of my adventures, and perhaps just a little bored after 45 days on the road, so we decide that she will cycle with me the next day, along route 42 towards Altenmarkt. Her presence really encourages me – my legs feel solid and I manage a good pace. Running with a cyclist is, for me, one of the best ways to increase and maintain speed, as well as providing useful distraction from any overall fatigue I might be feeling. Like the shared campfire of the previous day, travelling together helps unify our experiences too, so that we share more than evening chores and exhausted early nights.

A family of ducks entertains us by taking turns to slide down a miniature weir on the river Gölsen. The cycle route is well-maintained and relatively quiet towards Rohrbach and the sky has the decency to host a few fluffy clouds today, offering occasional shade. Vienna lies only a day or two away. Mountains have given way to decorous hills and given how good I am feeling, today is an opportunity to rack up the kilometres.

Aradhna turns back just outside Hainfeld, having cycled 9km with me. A little further on, an impressive brewery in the town might have diverted her, unhelpfully; perhaps it's just as well she heads back to Roxy.

After Ramsau's pretty main street, I head north east towards Altenmarkt, finding myself climbing into the hills and cutting through an idyllic valley sprinkled with dandelions and scattered with blossoming fruit trees loud with the buzzing of thousands of bees. I stop for a moment or two on a bench positioned at the head of the valley, admiring a view almost too perfect; a Hollywood CGI version of an Austrian pasture. All that it needs is Heidi to come skipping out of a log cabin to tip over into schmaltz.

Another national trail takes me off the cycle path finally and onto the Via Sacra once more. At Kaumberg, I have an unlikely audience, two pouting llamas, no doubt speculating on this odd creature entering their domain. Finally, Altenmarkt appears and traffic makes itself known once more. A dramatic war memorial (for both wars) stands at the town's entrance. It is the first WWII memorial I've seen outside of France, although that might say more about my powers of observation than Austria and Germany's unwillingness to honour Axis dead. The town's streets are as colourful as I've come to expect from the region – Austria just doesn't do pastel shades.

After lunch, I leave the Triesting river and head to Hafnerberg, feeling suddenly very fatigued and slightly nauseous. I begin to suspect I've not eaten enough. A steeply sloping field, containing a plastic archway which denotes the start of a kids' nature trail, reduces me to a walk – a rare occurrence since the beginning of this trip. Finally, the trail levels and I can stretch out into a loping run again, heading down narrow roads towards the small town of Maria Raisenmarkt. I feel this will be an amusing place to stop for the night, given Aradhna's intense dislike of raisins (she mourns the wine that could have been). After thirty minutes of driving around looking for a covert camping spot, we find a niche behind some trees on the edge of a forest.

*** 

After a long overdue coolant and oil check (we've been neglecting Roxy's maintenance a little, never a good idea when your primary mode of transport – apart from my legs – is also your home), I begin running the following day at 11am.

Yet another blue sky morning ushers me quickly between the meadows and patchy woodland to the town of Mayerling. For the first time since Munich, I see rows of identical houses in a distinctly suburban style – we are now entering the Viennese commuter belt. The famously pretty Vienna woods, so beloved of Strauss and von Horváth[1], lie between me and the Austrian capital. I am looking forward to today's run very much.

What I don't expect is a frantic call from Aradhna as I head down curving B-roads towards HeiligenKreuz, with its impressive abbey and mausoleum. It seems I have failed to fasten the coolant cap back on properly after the morning's checks. Most of the liquid has splashed out of its reservoir on the hilly Austrian roads and a warning light is flashing, indicating that the engine is dangerously overheating. I apologise profusely and we locate a local petrol station at which to meet.

Aradhna drives a struggling Roxy into the car park, wearing an expression that can best be described as unimpressed. We quickly discover that engine coolants are available in bewildering variety and also that the kind specified for Mazda Bongos is particularly rare. We decide to use plain water from now on. Roxy will hopefully forgive me. Aradhna manages to forgive me as well – even giving me my old

---

1    Author of the 1931 play *Tales from the Vienna Woods* which was inspired by the famous Strauss waltz.

coolant, an ice cream – before I set off once more.

The countryside begins to look almost English – deciduous trees begin to dominate over pines. The woods are cool and shady and remind me a little of a small woodland near my parents' home in Edinburgh, Dreghorn Woods, where Dad and I used to engage in such archaic pursuits as making rope swings and bows and arrows. A familiar calm descends upon me as I cut through the Wienerwald and exit at the hamlet of Sittendorf.

Spring blossom is in full bloom amongst the gardens and one home, at Sparbach, particularly catches my eye. An oddly tall structure with a brick lower floor and dark wood upper storey, it resembles a gothic haunted house. Nothing stirs within, thankfully. I leave the town and skirt the perimeter of another wedge of forest, with a sloping meadow on my right at the end of which I can faintly hear the thrum of an autobahn. A tollbooth filters commuter cars while I run gently on towards the last significant town before the capital.

The outskirts of Mödling provide some lunchtime respite from the growing heat of the day. Once out from under the shade of the trees, the running is uncomfortably hot. I duck into the dim shelter of the van, which Aradhna has cunningly parked in the last available spot opposite a parade of shops and beside a tiny brook. As ever, I am reluctant to head back out into the baking heat of the afternoon with a full stomach, but with Aradhna's encouragement I stumble off towards the town proper.

Mödling is a lively, modern town with a pedestrianised shopping street where shoppers pause at the outdoor tables of cafés to enjoy their coffees and late lunches. I quash my envy as I run through a cobbled square whose baroque fountain takes opulence to new heights. An array of saints, some brandishing staffs, lean out from a central column of curling clouds and cherubim, culminating in a golden metal sun. No water gushes, alas.

From here it seems straightforward enough to follow the 12 route straight into the heart of Vienna. As is often the case with European cities, Vienna seems to have swallowed up neighbouring towns in its various waves of expansion. Is Perchtoldsdorf a suburb or an entity in itself? Perhaps only the locals would have a definitive answer to that. However you define it, Vienna's sprawl means that I can mostly take to a reliable pavement, always a relief at the end of a long running day.

I say "mostly" because, even here, Google Maps seems determined to throw me a googly. In a brief hinterland between suburbs, a zone of car showrooms and road intersections has seemingly shrugged off any duty to pedestrians and their safety. I zig-zag between the shiny new BMWs and end up detouring through what seems to be a private riding school.

Soon pristine white factories and industrial estates give way to shopping zones and the overhead wires of trams appear. I soon cross a bridge under which run several train lines, surely the main route into the central station. I turn along a road parallel to the tracks and after ten more minutes, a rather squat series of glass and steel canopies appears beneath a towering skyscraper. Vienna's *hauptbahnhof* with its bold sans serif sign and clock is a little more impressive than Munich's but still a bit of a let down. Nevertheless, I am happy to locate Aradhna (waiting at a different entrance) and we mark the moment with a photograph.

We are more than a little disappointed to return to Roxy, parked on an unmarked side street, to discover we've fallen foul of Vienna's secretive parking zone regulations. A ticket flaps under one of Roxy's windscreen wipers. This does not improve Aradhna's stress levels, already significantly raised by the challenges of driving into and parking in an unfamiliar capital city. We decide to retreat to an out-of-town park for the night and are relieved to find a small community of campervans and caravans arrayed in lines under the shade of trees in a park by the Danube's west bank. Despite the cupboards being almost bare, Aradhna puts together a tasty omelette and we drink some Austrian beer to relax. Tomorrow we'll catch up with a bit of work and then head into Vienna for some sightseeing.

***

The following day we are determined to get our work out of the way as quickly as possible so we can enjoy playing at being tourists for the day. Unfortunately, the technological limitations of being a cut-price "digital nomad" become quickly apparent. We both need internet access and tethering our laptops to our mobile phones just doesn't seem to work. Eventually we locate a free Wi-Fi signal coming from a nearby restaurant (the Lusthaus) and park up nearby. We have neither the money nor the inclination to become patrons and I'm sure they will be loathe to have us there for hours, so we shamelessly piggy-back on their internet from the street outside.

Still, the signal proves intermittent at best so we relocate to a proper campsite and are successfully online by early afternoon. We must look fairly ridiculous, with Aradhna cross-legged in the roof space while I work downstairs, using the cooker top as a desk. Aradhna finishes her work at a sensible hour, but I am up until 3am outputting and struggling to upload large video files. Eventually I have to give up and go to bed.

***

This means we have a late start for our Viennese tourism the following day. It begins with a slightly underwhelming view over the city from Kahlenberg, where the viewpoint feels hemmed in by a purpose-built restaurant and other buildings. Then again, Salzburg's spectacular vantage point from the castle has probably spoiled us for such vistas.

We tour the grand boulevards and buildings of Vienna (Karlsplatz, the Opera House, Karlskirche), stopping off for the obligatory cake and coffee and find it all very grand and impressive but, overall, a little alienating. When everything is designed to show off wealth and prestige, the effect is often one of diminishing returns, with the antlike spectator rapidly getting "monument fatigue". We're both certain that radical, intimate Vienna must exist, but we don't find it.

However, later that evening the city redeems itself when majesty meets music at the Schönbrunn Palace, where we finish our day with a concert of Mozart and the Strausses (in a venue where many of their works were premiered for the Hapsburg royals) and a glass of bubbly. As we catch the subway back to our campsite, we decide to extend our sightseeing by one more morning and send me off running after lunch.

***

On 28th April, we have a continental breakfast at the Naschmarkt, an extended food market with stall after stall of tempting provender and aromatic spices. Then we visit the Museum Quartier and settle on MUMOK (the modern art gallery) for our dose of culture. Highlights include a private collection of 1950s and 60s abstract and situationist works including *Hahns Abendmahl* by Daniel Spoerri, who invited his friends round for supper and then stuck everything down onto the table when they left (cigarette butts, hunks of bread, half-finished coffee cups), preserving his soirée for posterity. There is also a contemporary work by Cécile B. Evans called *Amos'World* combining immersive art, video and the plastic arts in a piece about architectural idealism and alienation (fitting, given our experiences in the city the day before).

When I eventually begin my run later that day, sated with art and fancy cakes, we devise a plan to meet up on the northern side of the Danube, where Aradhna will cycle with me through a nature reserve.

Alas, things don't quite turn out that way.

**KILOMETRES TRAVELLED: 1500;**
**KILOMETRES REMAINING: 1898**

# Chapter 10: Jamaica Beach

*Day 46*

The day begins well enough, as running days often do.

The first part of my run is a functional jog through Vienna's industrial outskirts, past the red and white striped chimneys of a power station then an (orange and green) bio gas plant, finally hitting a sluggish green tributary of the Danube at Kaiserebersdorf. I call Aradhna and tell her I'll probably be meeting her soon at the start of the nature reserve.

As the river splits into parallel waterways around various islets, the first of several bridges crosses the Danube. This is an impressively modernist structure with giant winches and curved steel arches. Next I trot innocently over a pontoon bridge made from floating plastic sections and framed by two yellow pipes thrust into the air like cannons, or something less subtly phallic. What on earth lies beyond?

The island has the curious name of Jamaica Beach. After running along a grassy path for a few minutes, I begin to spot scantily-clad sunbathers emerging from bushes or small huts. On closer inspection, they appear to be even less than scantily-clad: most are entirely nude. Groups of sociable middle-aged and elderly naked people, with a preponderance of far from athletic male bodies make me strangely glad I am wearing sunglasses, although this might also make me look like more of a voyeur. I feel myself speeding up to get out of the nudist colony and the triangular signs on the pavement showing two humps (speed bumps) take on a double meaning. It is the first time in my experience a turn of speed has been inspired by embarrassment. Eventually, I race up some steps then down onto a service road and see a small metal bridge appear to my left, leading off the island.

Although the bridge looks singularly underused, with almost no traffic, I don't hesitate. I quickly realise why the route is so quiet, as I find myself running into what appears to be a massive chemical plant. Earlier, I passed an industrial complex where some wag had painted a gasometer with a long outflow pipe to look like a friendly creature with a giant nose. In contrast, my new surroundings are much less whimsical. I run along a quiet strip of tarmac alongside and under massive pipes, occasionally decorated with CCTV cameras. I haven't seen any "Ausgang" or "Verboten" signs but this doesn't look like a public route. Nevertheless, since I am heading in broadly the right direction, I persevere.

A little later Aradhna calls me. She too is having trouble driving round to the place I'd indicated we'd meet. I tell her I'm on my way but that she'll have to find another way round. Aradhna sounds frustrated but there is nothing I can do. I say I'll call her when I am somewhere more publicly accessible.

Quite sensibly, the site is surrounded by tall chain-link fences and, given the number of cameras trained on me, it doesn't seem wise to climb one. After running halfway around the perimeter, I spot a tiny gate left a little ajar and seemingly leading out into a small copse. Looking around me to see if there are are non-electronic spectators (there are none) I slip through and wander into a small cluster of decorative trees, finding myself at the base of a large slope of grass and weeds. I have found the bottom of the Danube's flood dam.

I scramble to the top and am gratified to find a gravel footpath and, beyond the dam, a service road. A little later, a Lycra-clad cyclist flashes past on this road, reassuringly. I call Aradhna.

She is not best pleased, given that she has spent the last hour or more trying to locate me. My Garmin satellite device pings out an accurate location signal every couple of minutes, but these are only aggregated and uploaded to our website every ten minutes. My circuitous path through a seemingly mazelike network of tributaries, islands and footpaths has proven impossible to follow. Our plan to spend time together has failed.

Aradhna blames me in part for being unclear about my plans and seeming unconcerned by her problems in finding me. In truth, I am so preoccupied with navigation and worrying about potentially trespassing within an industrial plant, that I am not especially sympathetic. I have been thinking about myself and my own predicament, to the exclusion of all else. Such behaviour is all too often the downside of the extreme focus I require to improve my running and shape my writing. However, I ought always to remember that somewhere Aradhna is facing her own obstacles and frustrations. When we finish the call, relations between my girlfriend and I could best be described as "frosty". This irks and worries me but I have to press on with the task at hand.

From here, our maps have revealed a 30km-long curving route through the nature reserve, which is now revealed to be the line of the embankment. I'd hoped to be able to see the Danube from here, but it is some way off to my right (to the south) beyond a thick slice of forest which is mirrored on my left, beyond the roadway. The nature reserve is pretty enough, especially if you like trees (and I do) but it's not quite the beauty spot I'd been anticipating. Still, the sun is shining and the blue sky contains only a few wispy cirrus clouds, so I have a great opportunity to get some useful kilometres under my belt.

The trees are mostly deciduous and there are flowering shrubs, butterflies and birds aplenty to keep me company, but no other pedestrians and only a few cyclists. Occasionally a reedy pond appears on my left, glowing like burnished copper in the light of a rapidly fading sun. Times like these, when I have the sun itself to race, tend to improve my pace and I find myself enjoying the challenge, despite the disappointments and worries of the day. I hope Aradhna will forgive my bullish determination to press on and text her to apologise for my earlier brusqueness and confirm a plan to reach a road cutting down to the river's edge at Orth an der Donau. This will require at least another hour of strong running.

\*\*\*

I hit construction work after a couple of miles, the surface of the cycle path degenerating into gravel and then mud. Striped tape and temporary fences do not stop me from progressing, however. As it's a Saturday evening, no workers are in sight, so I edge round a barrier and keep going. Soon a side road cuts through the dam and I turn off onto tarmac once more, heading for the river. Half a mile later, as the street lamps are coming on, I make it down to the Danube's edge at a waterside restaurant with a car park and a slipway for boats. Roxy is stationed there but my girlfriend is nowhere to be seen.

A footpath extends along the water's edge to the east and a few minutes later Aradhna emerges on her bike. She's been on a recce to find me, to no avail. I apologise profusely and we make up, then sit with a beer on a nearby bench and watch passenger boats and goods barges slipping down the Danube, their lights gleaming in chaotic reflections in the dark water.

\*\*\*

Following a leisurely breakfast and a coffee at the waterside restaurant, we decide to reboot our original plan to journey together the next day. Aradhna climbs on her bike and I trail her along the water's edge, padding along a leafy footpath with "no cycling" signs we feel obliged to ignore (as other cyclists do too), due to the impossibility of taking to our original route along the dam. Wild garlic adds a piquant edge to the breeze. Spied through a gap in the trees, a huge barge struggles valiantly against the tide as the swollen river slides east. I wonder if its currents are moving faster than I am. It seems likely.

After an enjoyable and easy start by the river's edge, we are forced by a small river back up onto the dam's long curve after a couple of miles. Fortunately, as the day becomes bakingly hot and we emerge onto the shade-free embankment once more, our route along the dam seems unimpeded and open for business. We enjoy the simple act of being together and achieving forward motion as birds circle overhead and butterflies flit amongst the grasses.

Pausing briefly by a couple of large cut tree trunks, which serve as a makeshift picnic table, we meet a lone walker, accompanied by a small, curious dog sniffing amongst the bushes. He's photographing butterflies and appears to be an amateur naturalist. He tells us about the local freshwater turtles who emerge from ponds at night to lay their eggs in pits dug into the side of the dam. We are glad to see another pedestrian and encouraged to stop malingering in the rising heat and press on. We can't let a dog-walker beat us.

A little while later we come to another road which cuts through the dam. On the other side there are a few buildings and the familiar profusion of fences and diggers, denoting more construction work. A pair of male cyclists stand staring at their phones, considering their options. It simply isn't in the Austrian psyche to climb between fences and ignore warning signs, it seems, so we bravely show the way, reasoning correctly that, this being Sunday, there will be nobody to stop us. My principle has always been that if it harms nobody and causes neither environmental impact nor danger to oneself, a bit of judicious trespassing is preferable to an undesirable and pointless detour.

Aradhna and I soon reach the bridge we'd planned to cross to continue south of the river towards Bratislava. It looms overhead, accessible only by a taped-off staircase. I shoulder Aradhna's bike and duck under the tape. In for a penny…

We make it back onto legitimate pavement and head over the bridge, past fields of newly-planted crops in rows so pristine it looks like they have been combed into place amongst the dusty soil. We soon see the town of Hainburg on the southern bank, its round hill surmounted by the ruins of an 11th-century castle. Aradhna had planned to leave me there but, once we locate the cycle route continuing along the southern bank, decides to stay with me a little longer. We've travelled 21km together at this point and having the company is making it painless for us both.

A little further on we spy a riverside restaurant, with tables right by the water's edge and cyclists resting and sipping beers or soft drinks. We decide to be a little naughty and join them. I plan to have a Coke but somehow end up downing a beer and eating strudel while Aradhna refreshes herself with a glass of white wine.

We chat briefly to two local cyclists who are exploring the riverside path (at a pace that feels easy for the more athletic of the two, challenging for his less experienced friend). They are serious enough to be sticking to soft drinks; chastened and determined, we finish up and continue on our way. As we begin to see signs for Bratislava, I do a quick calculation of how far we've gone so far.

"We've done about 25km. You'll be cycling at least twice that, by the time you get back to Roxy. Can you manage?" I ask Aradhna nervously.

"I think so," is her uncertain reply.

I want to believe her but begin to worry that we might be making a terrible mistake. What if she makes it all the way to Bratislava and then can't face the journey back? That would leave me with the task of cycling 35km back, having already run the distance. I don't feel quite ready for an impromptu duathlon. For now, I trust Aradhna's judgement, and keep most of my doubts to myself.

Fortunately, as we hit open fields of yellow and green across a flat plain, Aradhna's common sense gets the better of her ambition and she turns back. I wave her off, asking her to text or call me as soon as she makes it back to Roxy. She will have cycled 60km by then, far further than she's ever gone before on a bike. I run on, telling her I'll call her from Bratislava if I've not heard anything – there is a good chance I'll get to Slovakia first.

***

European Cycle Route 6 continues, well-signposted and used by many cyclists but no other runners. I reach the town of Wolfsthal, with its commemorative cast-iron silhouette of a rampant wolf, seemingly attacking a castle. A ploughed field and level path leads me on towards the hillside Slovakian capital of Bratislava, which I can just make out in the distance beyond the trees. A little later, a major road joins the cycle path, running parallel, carrying traffic towards the border. I realise that the functional but semi-derelict buildings up ahead are an old checkpoint, now unnecessary as the two Shengen neighbours allow free transit across the invisible line separating them. A more unexpected indicator of my entering a new country, and Eastern Europe, is a brightly-painted casino called Monaco, which sits just over the border on the less-regulated Slovakian side. I can just make out a sign on the road beside me indicating that I have run into "Slovensko", although there is no similar indicator for cyclists or pedestrians.

***

Slovakia! It's my first truly foreign country on this trip, about which I know little or nothing. I feel a powerful sense of anticipation as I commemorate the moment with a photo and press on.

**KILOMETRES TRAVELLED: 1567;**
**KILOMETRES REMAINING: 1831**

*Above:* Beast from the East.  *Below:* Hidden campsite, rural France.

*Above:* Aradhna cooking, France.

*Middle:* Wash day, Châtillons sur Marne.

*Right:* Man's best friend, Marne.

Grand French house, Marne Canal.

Giant trash-ball sculpture by Maarten Vanden Eynde.

First Orient station, Strasbourg.

*Above:* Black Forest trails. *Below:* Babenhausen, Germany.

*Above:*
Glowering skies at Schemmerhofen, Germany.

*Left:*
Marienplatz, Munich.

*Above:* Chiemsee, Germany.

*Below:* Meet the Millers, Chiemsee, Germany.

*Above:* Morning mist, German Alps.

*Below:* View down to Mondsee, Austria.

*Above:* St Gilgen, Austria.

*Below:* Running alongside the Danube.

*Above:* Walking home on Sonnleitner's farm, Austria.

*Left:* With the Sonnleitners.

*Below:* Alpine trail, Austria.

*Above:* Alpine lodge, Austria.

*Below:* Roxy in the Alps.

*Above:* Austrian meadow.

*Below:* The tiresome splendour of Vienna.

*Above:* Welcome to Monaco, sorry, Slovakia!

*Right:* To drink or not to drink, approaching Bratislava.

*Below:* Cold War era bunker BS-4, outside Bratislava.

*Above:* Warhol-themed tram-style bar, Bratislava.

*Left:* Street sculpture, Bratislava.

The heat of the Great Plain, Hungary.

*Above:* Evening crops, rural Hungary.

*Below:* Great Market Hall, Budapest.

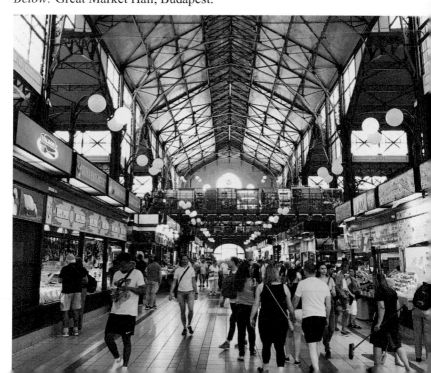

*Left:* Keleti Station (a proper railway station), Budapest.

*Below:* A Budapest street.

# PART TWO: NEW EUROPE

(Slovakia, Hungary, Romania)

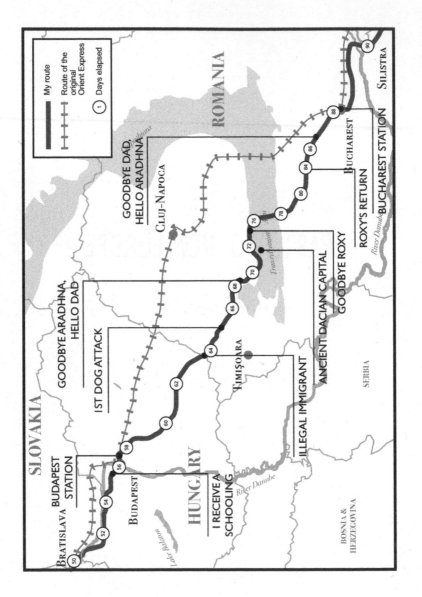

# Chapter 11: In Search of Andy Warhol

I know little or nothing about Eastern Europe. I'm dimly aware that much of it fell under the Soviet Bloc until the 1980s and that communist dictators held sway in many of the nations in the region – Ceauşescu in Romania, Tito in Yugoslavia, Hoxha in Albania. I know the Iron Curtain separated Soviet Europe from the capitalist West and post-revolutionary Turkey. Slovakia is a mystery to me and I confess I have done no research. In a way, this is exciting, since I literally have no idea what to expect.

It is also a little shameful – I can't just treat whole countries as conveyor belts for my feet. I vow to make up for my ignorance with judicious Googling wherever possible.

\*\*\*

### Day 50

I run on, as the low-angled, evening light illuminates everything with a brilliant bronze glow. Iron and concrete stars flank the pathway, reminders of the old Slovakian defences. There is even a decommissioned military bunker, now remodelled as a historical tourist attraction. Although it is closed this late on a Sunday, I run down an embankment towards the squat building following, to my surprise, a fellow runner! I find a footpath skirting the bunker and head off around the edge of a copse, still in the general direction of Bratislava. A metal barrel with a tap attached has been wedged between two trees and I notice a runner stop to drink there. I elect to take a risk and follow suit. The water is cool and refreshing.

The path takes me to the riverbank via a confusion of forest trails, then back onto a tarmac-covered path. I pass several evening walkers and then something like a UFO rises up out of the trees – a circular viewing gallery on top of the stanchion of a bridge. I've made it to my crossing point. Tired but happy, I weave through traffic on the road leading under the bridge, climb a staircase on wobbly legs and minutes later, am crossing the famous river once again, heading into another capital city.

***

My immediate impressions of Bratislava are that it is quite compact, very pretty and unexpectedly full of young people. Elegant women stride the cobbled squares while trendy young travellers join an impossibly long queue for an ice cream parlour. Decorative fountains form the centrepiece of a leafy pedestrian route ending in a square where the national theatre and art gallery reside. I sit down at a small café and order an exotic sounding pink lemonade, checking my phone and finding, with relief, a text from Aradhna – she has reached Roxy. I do some research to locate a likely pick-up spot and send her the directions.

Half an hour later, we meet up and locate a car park by the river which seems free on Sundays. We'll have to feed the meter the following morning but, for tonight, we'll sleep downstairs and "hide in plain sight". We decide to have dinner and drinks in town. Our first rule of travel is that you can't say you've visited a country unless you've gone for a wander and had a bite to eat. Airports don't count; the cities they serve do.

We cook a quick meal in the van. Aradhna hasn't eaten since morning so feeding her is priority number one[1]. Then, although our legs are aching from our exertions, we decide to walk the steep cobbled streets and explore. I've researched a fascinating bar I want to take Aradhna to – one filled with artworks, designed to look like the interior of a tram carriage and dedicated to Andy Warhol (or Andrew Warhola as he was born, to Slovakian parents[2]). We have an aperitif there, getting to the bar just as it is about to close. The minor disappointment of me shattering my glass on the cobbles halfway through my pint is eradicated by stunning views over the city. The vistas are even more impressive from the walkway by the castle – below us the bridge dominates a bend of the river decorated with the lights of many homes, threaded through with red and white veins of traffic winding along the valley.

In the city centre, groups of twenty-somethings roam from bar to bar and the public squares are bustling with diners and drinkers. Somehow, though, the stag-night sleaziness of other capital cities in

---

1   The consequences of doing so are dire indeed – Aradhna gets "hangry" when calorie deficient.
2   His parents hailed from the tiny village of Miková, near the border with Ukraine. It is about as far from Manhattan, culturally speaking, as you can get.

affordably foreign lands, has not spoilt Bratislava just yet. Its time will come, no doubt.

A series of strange bronze sculptures diverts us as we wander – a top-hatted gent saluting passers-by, a hard-hatted workman peeping out of a manhole, and Hans Christian Andersen accompanied, for some reason, by a giant snail[1]. We enjoy local wine and beer (Urpiner), people-watch from a wine bar on the main square, then stroll back to the van to surreptitiously sleep.

\*\*\*

The next day we have to beg a student café-worker for a refill for Roxy's water tank, before I set off over another bridge, with Aradhna cycling beside me once more (partly I think just to prove she can). I have another border in my sights now – the one separating Bratislava and Hungary just south of Čunovo. We consider continuing in Slovakia for a little longer before re-crossing the Danube, but our favoured route runs just south of the river for many kilometres and that seems likely to be both picturesque and free from navigational worries. To a certain extent, we are wrong on both counts.

On the south side of the river, the cycle path (route 6) continues, a die-straight track along another raised embankment, frequented by cyclists and rollerbladers. Aradhna doesn't stay with me very long; there isn't quite enough visual diversion from aching muscles. Plus, the parking we've paid for in Bratislava is due to expire and we have no idea how assiduous Slovakian traffic wardens are. I hug her goodbye and head off alone.

\*\*\*

The route takes me back to roads lined with impressively abstract graffiti, then back onto the self-same flood protection dam. By now, these structural defences are becoming monotonous, but at least they are easy to run, meaning I can maintain a steady pace. At one stage, I find myself pacing and leap-frogging a female rollerblader walking a small white dog on a lead as she zig-zags ahead of me in denim hotpants and a white t-shirt. I feel it is my duty to overtake her, but she leads me a merry race for around 10km before she finally turns off the path, leaving me alone with my aches and my fatigue.

A little further along the river, there's a community of houseboats on the opposite shore. I've never quite understood the appeal of

---

1    He once visited the city, apparently.

living in a box on stilts over water, neither a proper house, nor a boat you can unmoor and drift off in. That said, if you love the sight of a river sliding by, you can't get closer to your ideal. A little further on I begin to see another of the roadside "bufets" I've spotted a few times since leaving Bratislava. Basically, large shacks with outdoor seating serving beer and simple food, these eateries serve the cyclists, pedestrians and river travellers that frequent the route. I am sorely tempted to stop, given the searing heat of the day and my ever-present exhaustion, but I press on.

After a couple of hours, I take a ten-minute break amongst the trees along the side of the embankment, just to get out of the blazing sun, then continue on my way. The landscape opens out, the trees dwindling to reveal a wide curve of the Danube, swans bobbing upon the wind-blown waters. Wildflowers proliferate now, including daisies and vivid blue cornflowers.

When I reach the borderline, it is once again extremely downbeat. A tiny orange, white and green sign, a disused border control building and a circular plaque on the gravel, which at first I take to commemorate the writer Kafka, until I realise that the elaborate cursive capitals actually spelt Rafka, the name of a nearby town. What most dramatically marks my entrance into Hungary is a flight of soaring, wheeling, divebombing swifts, no doubt alarmed by the presence of this bipedal intruder. Like tiny fighter pilots they harry me as I run along a thinner, less surfaced trail into my fifth European nation.

\*\*\*

The Danube at this point arcs back on itself so frequently that a scattering of oxbow lakes has been created by its meanderings. I see no more cyclists or pedestrians for the next couple of hours and the solitude begins to feel almost sinister, given that I am running along a man-made structure and not through some remote wilderness.

With much relief, I finally leave the dam, following a shaded path between the trees to Dunakiliti, my first Hungarian town and lunch destination. The streets are quiet, lined with silver birches and neat, tiny bungalows with red-tiled roofs. Dogs bark at me as I run down the pavement, a different bark for almost every home I pass. Following Aradhna's texted instructions, I head for our traditional destination – the local church. I am so fatigued that I find it hard to express the right degree of appreciation for Aradhna's cheese on toast. Aradhna is not best pleased by my temperament and we argue. She is experiencing a perfect storm of period pains, hay fever, boredom and a tiredness of her own. To my shame, I do not pick up on her mood and probably exacerbate it. We part uneasily.

***

In contrast to the boxy houses, I run past the entrance to a German-styled *schloss*, a further reminder that I am back in a country that was once part of a mighty empire. The *schloss*, of course, is now a luxury spa and golf course. Further oxbow lakes add variety to my afternoon run, small wooden boats floating amongst the reeds at Dunasziget. I also begin to see bilingual signage. As well as Latinate letters, some place names are inscribed in a strange runic text, which a little Googling later reveals to be Old Hungarian, an ancient language which almost died out when Christianity and its Latinate script became prominent. Since the early twentieth century there has been a move to preserve the runic system, in tandem with a growing nationalist revivalism.

A traditional form of woodcraft is also in evidence – intricately carved portals, such as the one at the entrance to the park at Dunasziget, which also features a scaffold holding a single bell. Free-standing wooden belfries, often much more elaborate in design, are a common site in the Transdanubian and Carpathian regions. In the 17th century, the ruling Catholic Hapsburgs forbade the building of Protestant churches with prominent towers. To get around this, free-standing bell-towers were often built in the vicinity of the church. The Dunasziget scaffold is the ultimate reduction of this concept – a simple mechanism for a call to prayer and, in its quiet simplicity, the antithesis of Catholic excess.

***

Lilac blossoms decorate the hedgerows along the sides of the roads as I persevere, running now directly into a blazing ball of light (my sunglasses are a godsend). Approaching the town of Püski, across the fields, I seemingly manage to enrage every dog within a ten-mile radius – the cacophony is outrageous. I half expect a pack to chase me out of town but pass through unmolested. Some of the Hungarian place names have German equivalents, a reminder of the shifting borders in this region. Outside Kisbodak I pass a line of reconstructed ancient clay ovens, once used communally to bake bread. At the edge of a grassy field, a sign commemorates the tragic flood of July 1954, which displaced 20,000 Danubians from their homes, and whose effects extended as far as Vienna.

I meet up with Aradhna, who excitedly tells me about a lovely spot by a tributary she's found. Our lunchtime rancour is forgotten, fortunately. We drive to the rest spot, a quiet parking area by a small weir, but find it's a haven for mosquitos. We drive over the river at a shallow concrete ford and head for the Danube proper, but find swarms of midges there and yet more mosquitos. I can feel Aradhna's frustration rising and rack my brains for a solution. I feel we need to get away from standing water and the sort of dappled evening sunlight midges love. Further exploration of the forest takes us to the perfect spot, under tall trees, away from the river and at a wide stretch of path, allowing forestry vehicles and fishermen's cars to pass.

Fortunately, we are not disturbed at night by any other vehicles but, asleep in the roof-tent, we awake to the loudest concert of early-morning birdsong I've ever heard. It's almost comedic how raucous the forest has suddenly become. Aradhna manages to sleep through it, somehow. One bird sounds uncannily like a creaking door in a horror film.

\*\*\*

As is my custom, once sleep has become impossible, I let myself down through the trapdoor in the roof and begin preparing breakfast. For me, that means a species of granola with fresh fruit followed by various pastries or toast. Carbs and sugar are my staples, along with a generous helping of fat.

Then it's farewell to my other half and back to the insect-buzzing, thickly-vegetated path by the river. Nobody, bar the odd fisherman, seems to use this path and it has none of the infrastructure common to hiking routes or trails. I am in a weird no man's land between road and river. Still, it proves an easy enough run and, for today at least, so long as I keep the water to my left, I'll be heading the right way. Or so I assume.

At Dunaremete, I am surprised to encounter a small ferry terminal. The tiny vessel, currently unmanned and tied to the bank, reminds me of the small Caledonian MacBrayne ferries I'd been on as a child, usually crossing the fearsome Minch to a Hebridean island. This looks like it might hold one or two cars and a handful of passengers at best. I wonder how long it has been in operation and how they deal with passport control, since its eventual destination on the opposite bank is Slovakia.

The path becomes rarified once more, with standing ponds of mosquito-infested water and waterlogged forests attesting to previous floods. The air is hot and humid, the trees liveried in a reddish bark. Shortly, it becomes evident why gravel has become tramped-down mud and grass underfoot, as the track peters out by the side of a cascading weir, bringing water down from a parallel tributary into the Danube.

The river is a furious torrent and surely impassable. It looks like I've done it again.

**KILOMETRES TRAVELLED: 1649;**
**KILOMETRES REMAINING: 1749**

# Chapter 12: Lessons at the American School

Hopping over the rocks to the weir, I can see that there has once been a road or fording point here. Slabs of crumbling concrete lie amongst the boulders. Water rushes through a fifteen-feet-wide gap at great speed. I consider wading, then look up to see a picnicking family emerge from their car on the far bank. I don't want my foolhardiness to result in potential embarrassment or, worse, a rescue attempt by these holidaymakers, so this time I turn around and run back the way I've come.

I dash the next 5km back to the turning at 4.5min/km pace, highly unusual for me on this trip. I am irritated by my poor map-reading. I should have known that the pointy bit of land would denote a dead-end. If such adventures have taught me anything, it's never to anticipate a bridge where none is mapped. Wasting 45 minutes isn't a disaster but, given that I am still failing to live up to my intended 50km a day target, it constitutes a costly error. I maintain a faster pace for the rest of that morning, hoping to make up time.

*\*\**

When I finally locate it, the correct road leads me over the tributary and round to the town of Ásványráró. The homes here are a little more suburban looking, with back gardens filled with lines of washing, kids' bikes and what look like the modern equivalent of those clay ovens I saw at Kisbodak, but perhaps just some species of chimenea. I am back on the flood dam once more under the baking hot sun. A quick weather app check reveals it is 28 degrees Celsius and will remain so for at least a week. Not exactly Badwater[1] temperatures, but far from comfortable. As ever, the path is quiet, although I see a few fishermen's cars parked in the shade. A family on bicycles appears, stopping to ask in broken English how far it is back to Ásványráró. I surprise myself by being able to help them (about 8km), and it feels

---

1     The annual Badwater Ultramarathon is held in Death Valley in the height of summer. Runners have to endure temperatures of up to 54 degrees as they cover 135 miles on foot to the base of Mount Whitney. It is not for the faint-hearted!

good to have even limited local knowledge to pass on.

There are intermittent pumping houses and what look like grassed-over salt pans (unlikely) or water purification pools along the way. At Pátkanyos, one such station has a depth measure on its side and markings indicating significant past floods. From this I learn that on 7th June 2013, the water reached a depth of 840cm, just 60cm short of the top of the scale (and less than that from the top of the dam).

Finally, I am able to leave the dam for a bit and cross a major road at Vámosszabadi, then follow a cycle path round to quieter backroads near Nagybajcs, where farm roads carry me into the village. Texting Aradhna to tell her where I am, I slump down on a bench, exhausted after a "mere" 38km. The heat is really sapping my stamina, usually the one factor I can rely on to help build mileage. I enjoy a short rest before my pick-up and we locate a quiet camping spot by the river, by driving up and over the dam, probably illegally.

Fittingly, it is Labour Day in America and May Day elsewhere. The day has certainly felt laborious but I stopped short of having to issue a distress call. Somehow, I persevered. Of more personal significance is the fact that we've passed another milestone – I've topped 1000 miles on my original, estimated route[1].

*** 

Aradhna has had her own missions to accomplish today. Daftly, we didn't realise that Hungary does not use the Euro (and nor would Romania, Bulgaria or Turkey) so she drives into the biggest city nearby – Győr – to get some forints. Opportunities to pay for things in plastic are becoming few and far between. Locals trust hard cash and little else. Fortunately, Aradhna discovers she can withdraw local currency from a cash machine, a pleasant surprise. We have both accomplished our goals and earned our respite. As we rest for the evening, a few fishermen drive by, seeking their own solitude, leaving us alone to ours.

*** 

Day 53 starts well, although I feel a creeping exhaustion taking over my body, perpetually dropping me into second gear. I catch myself slowing to just above a walk and have to consciously add in the "bounce" that makes it a proper run. Still, the task at hand is simple enough – cross the Danube once more, avoid Győr and head out into

---

1    Actually, I've run 1024 miles, or 1649km.

the Great Hungarian Plain towards Budapest. I distract myself by admiring the roses decorating the village streets and the vivid crimson poppies sprinkled across the fields.

Things go wrong, as they are wont to do whenever I over-rely on my online maps. My planned route has directed me towards a major crossing but, as I draw nearer, it seems that significant construction work is underway. Mounds of bulldozed earth separate me from the slipway up to the crossing and I leap drainage ditches and wave at construction workers as I make my faltering way to a sign proclaiming that the bridge, although open to vehicles, is closed to pedestrians. I can see why – in the distance, a crew seem to be spraying down the walkways with something, clouds of mist blowing over the streaming vehicles. I consider ducking under the tape, then think better of it. Trespassing with no witnesses is one thing; doing so deliberately and provocatively in front of officials seems unwise to say the least.

I consult my maps. There is of course another bridge, around 10km downstream, at Győr, exactly the place I'm aiming to avoid. It means returning to the damned dam. I sigh and set off, after calling Aradhna to relay the news. This will add around 15km to today's intended route but it can't be avoided.

Halfway along the dam, I duck into a small shelter by some mysterious but sculptural rocks whose significance goes unsignposted, to get a bit of shade. I feel a little out of control and chaotic in my thinking – do I really have any idea where I am going today? I have little choice but to press on, however. Following a plan, however random or arbitrary it may seem, is generally better than having no plan at all.

In contrast with the tiny bungalows I've seen in the villages and the larger bungalows in the provincial towns, the fringes of Győr look well-to-do. Some of the houses even have more than one storey (I begin to wonder if there is a tax or building restrictions on multiple floors). The whitewashed, pantiled, blocky buildings arrayed in regular lines look comfortable, if a little clinical. A partly-shaded path down by the water's edge takes me along to a small bridge and then a road straight into the heart of the town.

As with all such encounters with population centres, I now feel oddly out of place, even though I surely stand out more in the villages. It doesn't help that Hungarian turns out to be an incredibly foreign language, with few of the linguistic clues of a Latinate or Germanic language[1]. English borrows very little from Hungarian, bar a few stolen meat dishes, the biro pen and, the word "coach", which Wikipedia convincingly argues was invented in the Hungarian village of Kocs.

I don't tarry long, locating arterial roads past shopping malls and industrial parks then, most curiously, a goods train laden with many new Audis, presumably from the huge nearby factory which, by October 2017, had constructed half a million cars. I stop at a roadside shack for a Coke and hide in a triangle of shade; it is becoming another oven of a day. Rest stop over, I head out along a footpath through a brownfield site which connects with cycle route 6 once more. There are very few users of the route, which proceeds in a fairly unpicturesque straight line along the side of a major road, but I can feel my legs rejoicing in the chance to stretch out and run.

Győrszentiván comes and goes, with its pretty church and well-tended kitchen gardens on the outskirts of town. Irises are in bloom along the verges, luminous fields of rapeseed shining under the relentless sun. I pass a sign for a place called Szentendre and realise that this means Saint Andrew, Scotland's patron saint. I am grateful for the tenuous link.

Although it remains hot, a cooler breeze springs up now and again and I don't slurp as much of my precious reserve of water. Fortunately, there are plentiful public fountains too, and occasionally even older hand pumps which still work, along the route. These largely replace the old wells I've seen in the villages, with their round wheels for pulling up full buckets, although some of these look like they might still be in use too.

At Nagyszentjános (Hungarians do like their saints) I spy further evidence that this bone dry weather is not a seasonal fluke. An immense irrigation system stands spread out across a huge field of crops. A line of wheels and metal frames several hundred metres long supports a pipe with many sprinklers. The whole structure can be pushed along metre by metre, covering the field like a wet comb. Brown horses eye me from behind rustic fences. I locate the church (where else?) that is our chosen lunch spot and gratefully slump into the fold-out chair Aradhna produces for me. Despite the fact that I've run 36km already, recently a full running day's distance, Aradhna coaxes me out of the shade after I've filled my belly and I head out once more.

---

1    It has more in common with Finnish and other Uralic languages, whose common ancient ancestors lived either in Central Russia or around the Liao River region in north-eastern China (depending on which theory you subscribe to). Continental migration is not a modern phenomenon – humans have always been peripatetic.

\*\*\*

The route is now very rural, as I cross endless huge flat fields of wheat or fallow plots of earth ploughed into decorative whorls and grooves. My shadow drifts before me, allowing me to monitor my gait as I run away from the setting sun. Soon I take to a quiet farm road alongside a railway, lined on both sides with headily fragrant trees with cascading yellow-white blossoms. I later discover these are the sinister-sounding black locust shrub. Every two minutes a local train comes thundering past, many no doubt heading for Budapest. Encouraged, I keep up a healthy pace. At Ács I finally run out of steam, a fitting metaphor as I come face to face with an ancient steam engine, in need of a good lick of paint but preserved as a local landmark.

As night falls, I find myself running along a rather dangerous main road (the 1, no less), past signs warning of tractors and horse-pulled carts, looking for the entrance to the campsite Aradhna has found for us.

\*\*\*

It is time for a bit of basic comfort – a shower, a washing machine and a peaceful night's sleep without the fear of being moved on. As I take off my socks, I discover I had a pronounced "dirt tan", everything below the ankles being vividly white, everything above coated in grime. The shower, and our reward beers are wholeheartedly appreciated.

When he heard what our crazy adventure entails, the campsite owner Laszlo invites us to join him and some of his guests for an evening drink. Aradhna, perhaps knowingly, leaves me to it. Laszlo's hospitality means strong beer and a compulsory shot of his homemade pálinka, a fiery spirit distilled from plums. I find it just sweet enough to gulp down without grimacing. Everyone laughs and I realise the various Dutch guests (everyone seems to be from the Netherlands) are sipping theirs.

Laszlo's friends, whom I learn visit the campsite most years, are in their 50s and 60s. I find myself explaining how important I feel European solidarity is and what a shame it is that Britain is leaving the European Union. Whiskers are tousled thoughtfully. I expect sympathy; none comes. My new friends are all fervent armchair Brexiteers, expressing admiration that Britain is showing the way and teaching those pesky Eurocrats a lesson. I quickly change the subject and guiltily slink back to Aradhna, who hasn't minded my absence at all and is quietly getting on with some of our endless chores, primarily washing my disgusting laundry.

I go to bed content that night. I've proven I can shake off even the most profound fatigue; when I tot up the distance covered I'd run an amazing 49km[1]. Would I pay for it tomorrow though?

***

### Day 54

We are both lethargic the following morning and the campsite is a relaxing place to rest so we declare an admin half-day and get some vital chores done. I also have some film editing work to complete (or attempt to do, since technical gremlins are still making it a near-impossibility) and this takes such a long time that I don't start running until 3:30pm.

Once more I follow the railway heading east, this time on a more forgiving dirt track around fields. At one stage, the trail seems to be heading me off in the wrong direction, until I spot a desire path leading over a mound of earth to another footpath. This leads me to the outskirts of Komárom, through busy suburbs then on into countryside again. The red dot of a trail-marker briefly excites me, although I've already realised that although trails in Hungary might be occasionally marked, they seldom appear on maps and there are very few official signs or facilities along the way. Basically, if you don't already know the trail, you'll have a hard time following it, which does appear to rather defeat the purpose of the markers.

Beyond Komárom, I spot a very grand mansion house nestling amongst the trees. Perhaps some of the relics of the kind of aristocracy Patrick Leigh Fermor encountered when he hiked a similar route between the wars still remain[2]. The ground, which has been almost distressingly level for several days now (it's not called the Great Plain for nothing), is beginning to shows signs of undulation. Is that an actual hill that lies ahead? I wonder, looking in the direction of Lake Tata, where we've decided to stop for the night.

***

I am so distracted by the improving scenery and by some huge warehouse-like structures behind the fields that I fail to notice the road under my feet becoming a steep downhill gradient covered with a thin

---

1    I would later discover it was my highest mileage day, joint winner with Saturday 12th May.
2    As recounted in his classic trilogy beginning with *A Time of Gifts* (John Murray, 1977).

gravel. A misplaced foot slips and I tumble, sprawling forward and putting my hands instinctively down onto the tiny sharp shards. My knees and elbows take a pounding too but, as I pick myself up and dust myself down, it is my right hand that has borne the brunt. A deep red gash glistens in the middle of my palm, the blood oddly oozing out, rather than dripping. It looks deep and livid. Lacking anything more sensible to wipe it on, I press the wound against my t-shirt, smearing blood on my side. I feel the kick of adrenalin coursing in my veins now and run on with my hand throbbing with an insistent but bearable pain.

After a little while, I spot Aradhna riding her bike towards me. She is pleased to see me and expresses sympathy when she sees my injury. I am grateful for her company as we run and cycle into the pretty town of Tata, with its towering twin-spired church, cobbled streets and a yellow-painted archway marking the route down to the water. Aradhna assures me that Roxy is only about a kilometre or two round the lakeside and I grimace in acceptance, the pain in my hand and arm now more insistent.

It's an idyllic scene – the blue lake reflecting a cloudless sky as families and couples walk the lakeside path past sculptures and statues, including the first female equestrian statue I've ever seen[1]. Yachts and rowing boats stud the mirror-smooth lake. A dragon-boat hoves by, its cox banging a giant drum while two dozen middle-aged rowers keep in sync.

After what seems an age, I spot Roxy nestling in a wooded car park area and collapse gratefully into a canvas chair. Aradhna tends to my wound, cleaning the gash with antiseptic cream before applying a cloth bandage. It's going to be hard to keep it covered, given my sweaty skin and the position of the gash. I hope it doesn't become infected. I've not had a tetanus jab for many years, something I should probably have remedied before we left.

That night we treat ourselves to dinner and drinks by one of the lakeside restaurants. I tuck into something called a "Castle Defender's Roast" while Aradhna has a grilled tofu salad. We then share a local dessert speciality called Somloi Galuska, a soft sponge with chocolate, nuts and cream. I can feel my body drinking in the calories and preparing to repair today's damage.

\*\*\*

---

1    *Tatai Diana* by Béla Thóth. The lady is also pictured holding a falcon.

Making up for yesterday, 4th May sees me leave the van at 11:15am, not especially early but early enough, given the heat and the lengthening days. Today is cooler than yesterday and a partly clouded blue sky greets me as I dash along the grass verge by the busy route 10 towards Komárom. I've not been able to find a decent alternative to the main road and keep having to leap off the tarmac to escape speeding trucks, not a terribly relaxing way to start my 54th day of running.

As I run through the village of Baj, I enrage many dogs and perplex the locals. I can sense curious looks as I head off into farmland again. The valley ahead is unusually lush and there are many insects to avoid swallowing, including red-winged flying beetles and iridescent butterflies. After the town of Agostyán, with its welcome sign in three languages, I spot the first of many roadside shrines – a white cross surmounting a tree stump containing miniature lanterns and candleholders.

There have been many examples of casual and/or reckless driving since I reached Hungary. While the Germans and Austrians drive as fast as humanly possible whilst, broadly speaking, obeying basic road safety, Hungarians throw all caution to the wind. I watch a motorcyclist, with pillion passenger, overtake a car around a tight curve, skimming past me on my side of the road. Last night, a car passed by with a broken front headlight. Today another battered vehicle rattles past with both headlights and front bumper missing. I give all of them a wide berth.

The road begins to climb, ascending the distant hill I saw yesterday. My hand is aching and the sweat has soaked away the adhesive on the plaster beneath the bandage. I take it off and stuff it into my backpack, then retie the grubby cloth. Its minimal protection is better than nothing. I rest briefly by two carved wooden totem poles at the entrance to an arboretum I'd love to explore[1]. There is simply no time – there are hillsides to cross.

Vértestolna features rows of smart whitewashed or yellow-plastered homes with bright blue painted hand pumps lining the street. An intricately carved sign displays the regional crest. Many bicycles are in evidence, often propped against the sides of fences and never chained up. They are cheap and functional – no 24-speed racers here – and evidently undesirable to thieves. Either that or there are no thieves – the very remoteness of such places means that miscreants stand out a mile and every neighbourhood is at watch.

---

1    http://verteserdo.hu/hu/arboretumok-parkerdok/agostyani-arboretum/

Another village boasts a series of twelve shrines strung along Main Street with painted scenes of the seven sacraments and other religious iconography. Many homes and plots of land are marked "Elade", which I come to realise means "for sale". It feels like these rural outposts are eroding away, as their young population flees for the cities.

At Tarján I pass a miniature lake, the only standing water for many kilometres, and discover a ring of holiday chalets surrounding it. A tree stands netted in woolly cobwebs. I manage to take a wrong turning somehow and then make the cardinal error of improvising without a map. Phone reception becomes erratic as I strike out along a vehicle track across fields, then through a grassy valley, over a hillside and down to dense forest. I quickly become entangled in impossible-to-follow paths made by animals, which lead me nowhere useful. My Garmin indicates a road or track about 500 metres ahead but I can't get anywhere near it. I can't even see that turning back would help and am genuinely stumped.

In frustration and cursing vividly, I eventually just blast through the dense thorny thickets, forcing vegetation aside, ignoring the stings and bites, the cobwebs and thorns until I burst out onto a dusty red dirt path leading downhill. My shins are livid with scratches and throbbing with discomfort, but I feel relieved to be able to run once more.

By the time I get to the peaceful town of Gyarmatpuszta, I am thoroughly exhausted and slump down at a picnic table in a small park which features an outdoor stage and lines of bench seating. I wonder what rousing speeches, school prize-givings and music nights have taken place here. At the moment the buzzing of insects is the only sound disturbing my rest until the familiar timbre of Roxy's engine announces that lunch has arrived. I have rarely felt so grateful.

\*\*\*

After lunch the trails begin to climb again, into lush hillsides where a series of small towns lies between me and Budapest. Outside Gyermely, I briefly think my fatigued brain is hallucinating; someone has erected a ten-foot-tall "Transformers"-styled scarecrow from old car parts. I run along the dusty edges of commuter towns, then past fields etched with ploughlines, the scent of black locust carrying on the evening breeze. At dusk, in the town of Máriahalom, I discover Aradhna and Roxy and we locate a quiet spot on the edge of a field of rapeseed to rest for the night.

\*\*\*

## Day 56

Today brings more pin-sharp sunlight and another cloudless blue sky.

Boy, it's hot! I've given up on cloth bandages for my damaged hand and have cleaned the wound once more and covered it with a large plaster and then layers of stretchy black KT Tape[1]. As I head up a dusty, rocky path into the hills once more, the heat is so intense that beads of sweat are rising through the black fabric and glinting in the light.

Once I leave the villages, a route across the driest field I've yet seen, so barren that it looks baked, leads me towards a forested hillside and the only proper inclines I've seen in Hungary so far. I pass a father and son mountain-biking towards me, which reassures me as ever that I'm not just wandering in the wilderness. The cool tunnel of woodland is refreshing, even as my calves and quads protest the climb. A little later, I notice a yellow and white trail-marker. Good – I am back on track. I pause briefly to look out over the valley – even from this small hill, the view is impressive, given how level the surroundings are. Heat haze enhances the sense of distance and everything looks greener than I had expected.

I belt down the other side of the hill, the track here feeling like many of those I've run during British ultra races – hard-packed mud, leaves and pebbles. Around one bend, I pass two men with a small table and what looks like a petition of some sort. I wave hello but have no time to stop. I'll never know what they were petitioning against, or for. The trail leads me out into the town of Nagykovácsi, which feels very much like a commuter town, the houses larger, with taller fences and bigger gardens. How odd these little allocations of land and barricaded properties are beginning to feel after two months on the road with the open countryside as our back garden.

I see a frankly terrifying poster for the Circul Americano Vargas (the number 1 circus in Romania, apparently), which doesn't help dispel my apprehensions about my next country destination. As if the insane laughing clown head isn't bad enough, the circus also features alligators, it appears. A little while later, in contrast, my run takes me past a pretty florist and an elegant avenue of chestnut trees. This is definitely a more moneyed place than many of the villages I've run through. I find a scrap of shade by a wall outside the American School,

---

1    Kinaesthetic tape, primarily used by runners to strap up muscular injuries.

and wait for Roxy.

When Aradhna arrives, I am still feeling the creeping exhaustion from recent days, combined with dehydration and a growing sense of repetition. Day after day of running in stiflingly hot conditions is taking its toll on my spirit. I am leaning against a wall, studying my phone and largely ignoring Aradhna as my girlfriend opens the back of the van to get out a folding chair for me. I hear a muffled ouch, but think little of it. After all, living in a space about 12 cubic metres in volume for so long means we are regularly bumping things.

Aradhna storms out from behind the van, evidently peeved.

"Did you not hear me hurt myself?"

I am taken aback. Where is this coming from?

"I heard ... but it didn't sound very serious."

Wrong answer. Aradhna is enraged that I haven't even asked if she is okay. As tempers rise, I make my usual mistake of trying to defend or explain my actions instead of just apologising and letting Aradhna vent.

"This isn't just about this one moment," she says, frustrated. "Your whole attitude stinks."

I try to mollify her but without really listening to the implications of what she is saying. I haven't been appreciative enough of the rigours of her role and the loneliness she is feeling being by herself for 8 to 10 hours a day in a country where she can't speak a word of the language. I feel my anger rising too.

"Don't you get it?" I plead. "I'm so exhausted, even raising a smile is an effort! Okay, I'm self-obsessed but to do this, I kind of have to be. If I'm going to get through this, well ... in a way, my needs just *are* more important than yours."

Aradhna has heard enough. Something snaps in her and she slams the back door shut, gets in the van and starts the engine. Surely she's bluffing – she wouldn't leave me stranded here without food or water, would she?

"My water ran out about an hour ago," I mutter.

A bottle of water bounces across the concrete by my feet as Aradhna spins Roxy in a tight U-turn and drives off down the road, and quickly out of sight.

\*\*\*

Damn. I feel more than a little guilty, hurt and confused as I pick up the water bottle and slurp the cold liquid down. I wait a few minutes but

Aradhna does not return. Clearly some sort of explanation – no, strike that, apology – is in order. But what am I apologising for? It takes a while for the subtext of Aradhna's rage to sink in. I can be a little slow to understand emotional subtleties and my ability to empathise seems to diminish when I'm tired. Whatever I've done or not done, or should have done but didn't, she feels neglected and abused and I have to do something about it. I send her a craven text message, then wait a bit and follow up with a call.

"I'm sorry," I begin. Grudgingly, she agrees to come back and provide the thousands of calories and pints of liquid I need. She hopes I've learned a valuable lesson. So do I.

**KILOMETRES TRAVELLED: 1792;**
**KILOMETRES REMAINING: 1606**

## Tips for Multi-Day Runners – 5. Support

More important than almost any other consideration when planning a multi-day running adventure, is thinking carefully about who you choose to support your run and how. There are broadly speaking three options:

1. *Fully Supported.* You will have a support vehicle and one or more crew following your progress. At the very least, they will see you off in the morning, meet you at lunchtime and collect you at the end of the day. In especially challenging circumstances, or if you are filming the experience, you may require more frequent encounters with your crew. The big benefit of having a support vehicle in which to sleep is that you can make spontaneous decisions to stop and make camp or keep going a little longer. The biggest drawback is the toll such intense support takes upon your crew members, unusually friends or family.

2. *Partly Supported.* One or more crew members will track your progress from a static location, perhaps a car or hotel / bed and breakfast, offering support as and when required. They will not follow you during your run and you may not have recourse to a vehicle in which to sleep or escape the rain. They will probably help with things like booking accommodation, social media, charging any devices you may have, possibly washing running kit and restocking your nutrition. You may have to be more disciplined with your own pacing and making sure you get to the agreed stopping points in good time.

3. *Unsupported.* You'll have total freedom as well as earn the bragging rights of having had an adventure solo and unsupported. In reality, you will probably have a lot of visitors and well-wishers offering varying degrees of helpful or irrelevant assistance, making "unsupported" something of a misnomer. You'll also have to bring everything with you or arrange to have care packages sent on ahead for you. This is not a great option for anyone who doesn't like too much of their own company or who balks at

putting up a tent in a thunderstorm in a pub car park in darkest Dorset.

The type and level of support you choose is dictated by the sort of adventure you want to have and the kinds of experiences you value. What are you trying to achieve with your running? Is it important to you to share those unforgettable moments?

Whatever you do, remember to be courteous, considerate and thankful. As I learnt the hard way, you may think there's such a thing as implicit gratitude but there isn't. Gratitude must be stated and demonstrated. Show your supporters how much you value them and they will go above and beyond. Neglect them and you may find yourself knee-deep in a Scottish bog at sunset, surrounded by midges, without anyone to call.

# Chapter 13: Buda / Pest to Fantasia

Running in cities requires a whole different skillset from trail-running. The obstacles you are negotiating are mobile and some of them – i.e. cars – can kill you. You have to factor in traffic lights, pedestrian crossings and heighten your proprioception to include tracking the likely trajectories of dozens of road users to keep up your pace and avoid calamity. It is seldom relaxing but can be extremely good exercise. I haven't done a lot of it on this trip but one of the biggest urban challenges looms today – Hungary's capital, a city of nearly 10 million people.

***

Finding a sensible route into Budapest has been a real challenge. We study the maps intensively to find a route that looks runnable. There is simply no way to avoid the major arteries into the city as we enter through District 2. I find a few parallel roads via commuter belt zones of blocky modernist houses and leafy gardens in full summer bloom. Although pretty, these routes inevitably end with a right turn back onto the main road, down which trucks and cars roar ceaselessly. Eventually, I just grit my teeth, turn onto the Nagykovácsi Út and head for "Centrum" (apparently I am already within the city boundaries, although I'd not noticed any signs to that effect).

The first definitive indicator that I have reached the capital is the towering drum-like shape of the Hotel Budapest. Then, joy of joys, a cycle path appears, most probably one that will take me all the way into the centre. There will be no more running head-on at oncoming vehicles whose drivers have evidently never seen anyone running in the road before.

Before long I begin to see shops and increasing numbers of pedestrians. I am reminded of the complexity and singularity of Hungarian when I stop to photograph a shop whose sign reads "Vegyeskereskedés" (general store). Then it's over the bridge and time to say hello to the Danube once again.

The mighty European river looks its bluest and best as cruise ships slide slowly by below. The opposite bank is dominated by a government building every bit as ornate as our own Houses of Parliament. A silken off-white stonework dominates the grand edifices ahead and I am impressed to note that the bridge I've chosen to cross (one of eight) has a kink in it, giving a view of the intricate wrought ironwork of its substructure.

Entering the centre, I watch lovely old trams negotiate the narrower streets and then pass a grand covered market, a triangular glass canopy suspended between two ornate, mirror-image halls. Some of the older tenement buildings have wooden trellises and awnings and their brick and plasterwork bear the grime of centuries (like some of Edinburgh's did[1] before the modern era sandblasted them clean). Old Budapest's streets are less daunting than Vienna's but no less beautiful.

Best of all is still to come. I see it shining gold and yellow in evening light as I approach. Keleti Pályaudvar – the east station. At last – a historic station that lives up to its status and position as junction and meeting place of nations. The front of the station boasts Doric columns supporting a complex glass arched window, in the centre of which is set a clock. It is 6:30pm, almost to the minute, when I come to a halt in front of the majestic station and begin looking for Aradhna. She duly appears, with a sports drink and a hug for me. She seems tired but resolute, if still a little bruised from my behaviour at lunchtime. I hold her tight and pose for selfies, wanting her to share the triumphant moment with me. We've hit our fourth major station stop on the journey and I've covered almost 1800km.

We can't park on the side street we spotted earlier on Park4Night, since that whole section of riverbank (on the Buda side of the river) has been turned into a giant street party with live music, beer and food stalls, massage tents and the corporate sponsorship paraphernalia that goes along with such public extravaganzas. We wander through it all in a kind of daze, considering joining in the fun, but lacking the energy to. We badly need to decompress. Tomorrow will bring a day off and a chance to do just that.

✳✳✳

A day that begins with homemade pancakes is a day begun well. We feel pleasantly sated as we emerge into pleasant sunlight and clouds of drifting seeds by the university buildings. Aradhna and I have made

---

1    Giving it the nickname "auld reekie".

a hazy sort of shortlist of what we want to see in Budapest. First we explore the hilly Buda area, climbing on aching legs up to the Citadel with its triumphal statuary. The view down to the arcing river and distant hills is breathtaking and whets our appetite for exploring the opposite bank – the sprawling Pest region.

As we wander through the bustling streets, past pavement cafés and colourful murals, there is a lot to see and a lot to distract. Aradhna is talking and I find myself having trouble listening. A lengthy anecdote is in progress and I've failed to follow the thread of what she is saying. Stupidly, I think the best thing to do is nod along and try to catch up. Aradhna cottons on to what I am doing and asks me if I'm listening. I assure her that I am, afraid that I'll raise her ire once more if I admit that I haven't been. Eventually, things come to a head with Aradhna, rightly, accusing me of counterfeiting interest in what she is saying. We find ourselves in a convoluted argument once more with me making poor judgement calls, as ever, about how to dampen down the flames. It's probably not a great idea to tell your enraged other half that you were pretending to listen because you thought you'd "get away with it".

We don't quite reach the heights of fury of the previous day, but Aradhna's anger continues to simmer while I walk behind her through a covered market, unable to think of a way to improve the situation. I feel desolate, knowing the secret mission I am on may be in real danger. By the time I ask Aradhna to marry me, will she be wholeheartedly sick of me and laugh in my face?

While I am busy catastrophising, time provides the healing we need, time and a city as fascinating and varied as we could hope for. Aradhna has researched a "ruin bar" for us to visit after lunch – Szimpla, a crumbling old tenement deliberately left in a distressed state and filled with a cornucopia of weird and wonderful decorations, its many rooms graffitied by thousands of visitors and bewilderingly maze-like in their arrangement. Everything centres on an open courtyard with multi-coloured vertical drapes slicing up the blue of the sky. We buy beers and take it all in. Aradhna laughs at something I say and I breathe a sigh of relief. Perhaps the day can be salvaged.

After Szimpla we cross back to the Buda side of the river to climb to the famous Fisherman's Bastion, a fairytale structure on the hillside of pristine white stone. Built in the late nineteenth century on the site of a medieval look-out post, it was once protected by the fishermen's guild. The neo-Gothic and neo-Romanesque flourishes are like something from a Disney backdrop, a fantasy structure drawing the cameras of the many tourists enjoying the views. Afternoon sunlight casts a perfect honeyed glow over everything as we take photos in front of the conical turrets and towering spire of the Matthias church. Then we stop for another drink at a small bar before crossing a different bridge back into Pest and walking the wide pedestrian boulevard towards St Stephen's Basilica.

After dinner it's back to Szimpla for a live jazz jam session, where sax players trade licks with one another and the rhythm section settles into a dance groove in front of a crowd relaxed (and alcoholically lubricated) enough to indulge the laid-back vibe. We walk back to the van, having covered at least eight miles on foot, without wondering why we've never once tried to use public transport. We decide that Budapest rivals Strasbourg as our favourite city destination so far.

\*\*\*

## Day 58

As is now our custom, we choose to extend our tourism for the following morning and get up early enough to explore the vast Grand Market with its panoply of food-stalls and snack kiosks. The upper level proves too crowded for us so we spend most of our time downstairs, marvelling at the range of baked goods on sale, a multiplicity of flavoured brandics and endless varieties of sausage. We snack on a cinnamon roll before walking back down to the riverside and treating ourselves to coffee and cake at a smart chain restaurant called Escobar. Inappropriately, our plates come dusted with the bar's name written in stencilled icing sugar. I suppose if you're going to celebrate a Colombian drug lord, you might as well pull out all the stops.

Reluctant to leave the fragile peace and warmth between us that the day had rekindled, I don't start running until 4pm. Attempting to make up for lost time, I hare out of town on the straightest road I can find, past construction sites and the imposing Dreher brewery. The suburbs seem endless, as befits a thriving and growing capital. I run past a showroom for kids' playhouses and a wall decorated in graffiti featuring the Starship Enterprise.

By 6:30, the city is finally releasing me from its grasp, as ranch-style homes appear in giant grassy meadows fringed with skinny trees. This is a new and even drier geography than any I've passed through to date. The "road" here is a dirt track through grasslands, sprinkled with daisies and punctuated by the occasional crimson poppy.

\*\*\*

Some of the off-road routes I am now taking are considerably less salubrious than the country roads of recent days. I pass lanes littered with the shameful leavings of fly-tippers. It seems to be a near-constant blight on the countryside just outside of major towns.

Aiming for Monor, I look for ways to avoid the busy E71 road and the motorways. This inevitably brings me to a confluence of roadways not designed for pedestrians to cross. After much confusion, I dash over a junction and run the gauntlet of trucks and commuters along a slip-road, before turning off onto what seems to be a retired A-road, barred with a striped pole but with nothing to dissuade runners.

As I approach the barricade I notice two suspiciously parked cars and wonder why on earth anyone would liaise in a remote and nondescript spot like this? Then I spot figures beyond the cars – a man and a woman, the latter hurriedly rising to her feet, the man handing her something. I pretend I'd seen nothing (in truth, I'm not sure I have) and race past the illicit couple. Ducking round the barrier, I next pass a teenager on a BMX bike, and skirt a small outpost of scattered homes before the fields reclaim me.

I run down a blossom-covered lane and out into wheat fields as a golden light, which the film-maker Terrence Malick would have envied, bathes the crops. A skinny brown horse chews hay impassively as I enter Péteri at sunset.

The sun is dying in a golden and crimson blaze and we have found a quiet spot by a miniature lake for the night. I've not quite made it to the intended target of Monor but I've managed 34km in 4 hours and that will have to do, particularly as we will shortly hit the halfway point in my journey (1850 of my intended 3700 kilometres)[1].

\*\*\*

The road to Monor is inevitably stressful with trucks careening past constantly. Still, I feel safer than the chap who rattles past me on a fully-reclining bicycle, effectively lying down and using his hands to propel

---

1   As ever with such estimates, I expected the final total to be around 10 – 15% more or less in the final summation, dependent on course alterations, errors in approximation and my remarkable ability to get lost. The Garmin also only pings out my location every two minutes and draws straight lines between then, losing me up to 20% of actual kilometres covered on particularly twisty paths.

himself along. Monor itself is smart and grander than I was expecting, although its wide-paved streets soon give way to pavement-free, bungalow-filled suburbs and gravel roadways. The traffic continues to keep me on my toes and after an hour of verge-jumping, I've had enough and plot a new route through small commuter towns, farms and smallholdings.

Poppies are blooming everywhere; I've never seen quite so many and they brighten my way. At Pilis I pause to drink a coke and admire another of the impressive wooden carvings carrying the village's emblems (a bunch of grapes remind me I am entering Hungary's wine-growing region). Two Jehovah's Witness ladies hand out leaflets to passers-by but leave me well alone. Perhaps I look beyond even Jesus's help.

I soon give up local roads for even more basic farm tracks – troughs of pale grey-brown dust, finer than sand, mark the passing of many off-road vehicles. Running through a forest of skinny trees, I catch the scent of aniseed. Distant dogs bark disconsolately, unable to see the intruder they sense at the fringes of their domain. The way forward is pancake-flat and frying-pan-hot, with many parcels of land sporting hand-written "Elado" signs. Making a farm work in this dustbowl is clearly a real challenge. One farmer I pass is painstakingly watering his entire field, the size of at least a dozen football pitches, by hand using an antique tractor pulling a tanker of water and pesticide.

Lunch takes place at another quiet village, Ceglédbercel, in the shade of a smart junior school. As I eat voraciously, we are serenaded by a class of kids around ten years old learning a song by rote, perhaps for a school play. Aradhna is highly amused that, by the time I am ready to leave, I can sing most of the Hungarian lyrics myself.

As I run out of town, I pause to photograph the imposing statue of a medieval ruler carrying a mighty broadsword, finished in black and burnished gold. This is the 11th-century founder of the kingdom of Hungary, Stephen I, later sanctified. As well as a distinguished warrior-king, Stephen was also instrumental in promulgating Christianity within the kingdom, founding bishoprics and monasteries in the region, independent of Rome. He has a feast day and public holiday designated in his honour (20th August)[1].

In a playing field on the outskirts of town, a fairground is assembling, colourful trucks parked in a circle like frontier wagons.

---

1    Not to be confused with St Stephen's Day (26th December) commemorated in the Christmas carol "Good King Wenceslas". That's a whole different Saint Stephen.

Then I head out across the vineyards, a sight that always makes me thirsty. Hand-painted barrels act as nameplates for "Kökény és Fia", a winery with accommodation and health spa.

I am now running towards Cegléd, the biggest town in the region, but the route still holds picturesque charms, including wooden street signs containing flower-boxes, a blue-painted drinking water fountain with carved wooden totems and, by the railroad tracks, a house painted mustard yellow on its gable end but fronted by a colourful mural of a train with a perky cartoon face. I am also passed by the first horse and cart I've seen so far, this one carrying fragrant manure and pulled by two light brown ponies. Once more, the meadows are dotted with poppies and soon, over the fields, I begin to see a line of lakehouses.

Further into town, a pavement appears, along with brightly-painted two- and three-storey buildings, then a modest but pretty square with flowerbeds, statuary and a towering church spire. Pavement cafés and restaurants are filled with locals enjoying a cooler afternoon than I'd experienced recently. The temperature drop presages a shower of rain, which quickly grows to a torrent as I hunt for Roxy. Although heavy, the shower is cooling, refreshing and brief.

Nevertheless, I am happy to see our home from home glinting in a shaft of sunlight at the edge of a small park. There is even a small (but smelly) portaloo by a kids' swingpark and a drinking water fountain. These basic amenities constitute luxury to us these days and we avail ourselves of them fully. I have stopped running rather earlier than usual (5:30pm), which allows Aradhna and I to spend some proper time together. We are still repairing the tears in our relationship that have appeared lately. Fortunately, other than the incessant barking of a dog, nothing disturbs a full night's sleep. It would stand me in good stead.

\*\*\*

The sixtieth day of our adventure sees me leaving Cegléd and running along a horribly busy road before ducking left onto a dusty farm track. A huge farm vehicle hoves into view and I stand aside to let it pass, before crossing rail tracks once more and heading into yet more sandy, dusty forest. A logging truck lies seemingly abandoned in the middle of a plain and many hares scurry from my path, their long ears perking up at my approach and their massive rear feet propelling them across the fields at a speed I can only envy. Bounding from the hedgerows, small deer give the hares an evenly-matched race; both leave this flat-footed jogger in the dust.

Even amongst the heat and arid soil, pink blossoming trees abound and the fragrance of black locust drifts into my nostrils. Familiar but unexpected purple thistles surprise me amongst the long grasses. Poppies and daisies begin to fill the fields to the extent I have to imagine they are farmed or at least encouraged to improve the local bee population. It is slightly cooler today, with a slight breeze that challenges the plentiful butterflies and dragonflies that hover before me like miniature helicopters. The forest takes on the regularity of a plantation, although of what I haven't the horticultural knowledge to identify.

Then – a surprise and a mystery. The trees fall away and a small mound of long grass contains a carved wooden marker and an information sign in inscrutable Hungarian. I imagine it to be a burial mound or barrow of some sort. Later research proves this supposition largely correct. Most probably a kurgan, or pit-grave, the site could even be of Celtic origin – the Celts had conquered the entire region of modern-day Hungary by 230BC.

Every so often I am reminded that these fields and plantations contain homesteads too – lines of skinny postboxes by the sides of the track allow the postal service to link these remote farms with the rest of civilisation. By 2pm the heat has risen once more and my calculations put the end of this long, winding rural trail at 20km away. I will be lucky to reach a town by nightfall and fatigue is building irrepressibly. Consulting with Aradhna, we decide to divert to a nearby campsite. The path ahead is long, straight and utterly exposed. The only footprints in the dust apart from mine are the V-shaped tracks of the giant black beetles I regularly side-step.

The dust gives way to distressed concrete after around eight kilometres and the strip of tarmac passes huge semi-cylindrical cowsheds and a sewage treatment works. I have run 10km in almost a straight line and am grateful to spot the roofed gate of a ranch, then bales of cut hay indicating another farm, one that I know borders the campsite. Amazingly, my phone still has signal, which proves hugely useful when locating the site, which is tiny and hidden by hedges and a copse of trees. A small handwritten "Camping" sign with an arrow directs me to the entrance in time to spot Roxy coming towards me from a different direction. I consider racing her but decide to let Aradhna pass with a friendly wave. She looks confused, having been lost for quite a while.

I've covered 39km and am happy with that. Although fatigued,

I'm not at death's door which allows me to chat to the Fantázia Tanya campsite owners, Vera and Fred. The couple are from, respectively, Holland and Curaçao[1] in the Caribbean, and own a dog-breeding business as well as their quiet oasis amongst the farms. All their neighbours are farmers and a few of their friends have come to visit. Vera and Fred are laid-back and contented, laughing frequently and enjoying their comparative solitude with like-minded neighbours and regular visitors. They give us beer and gift us a small bottle of their homemade red wine and we make friends with their bulldog, who seems friendly enough, yet no doubt could be a formidable guard animal too.

The following morning, Aradhna conducts an interview with the four friends for her film and I do some editing, complete the inevitable chores and help Aradhna operate the camera. Then I get dressed, proudly posing for a photograph in all my gear, too fatigued and forgetful to notice that I am still wearing Crocs instead of running shoes. I get going again at 1:30pm, determined to run as far as possible, despite the baking heat, which persists despite a sky decorated with thick grey-white clouds. The humidity is oppressive as I run through brown fields of livid young vegetables and endless rows of vines outside Szentkirály. A sign for the amusingly-named Fafarago prompts one of the strange comic ditties with which I amuse myself on long, challenging sections of the run. Nobody knows how Fafarago…

Most of the afternoon produces more of the same experiences as yesterday – blossoming trees, long dusty tracks, poppies, farmsteads, hares. In places, the dust beneath my feet is so thick that it sucks my feet backwards like dry sand, making speedy progress difficult. I pass lines of hives, confirming my suspicions about some of the wildflower meadows – we are in a region beloved of bees. Some of the homes are prettily decorated – a rusty bicycle parked outside one is laden with boxes of red roses.

Tiszaalpár provides a pleasant spot to stop for lunch – teenage girls squint at me, amused as a middle-aged, red-faced runner slumps down in their town square, gulping water from a nearby hand-pump. A statue of a local hero, the hurdy-gurdy-playing[2] folk musician Miháli Bársony keeps me company while I wait for Roxy.

---

1  I remembered there is a liqueur distilled there, made from the Laraha citrus fruit which, Wikipedia informs me, grows only on the island. I am somewhat sceptical.

2  In Hungarian, tekerözik, an instrument dating back to the medieval period, which creates sounds by means of a wheel rotating against strings which are pressed against it using a set of keys, producing continuous tones.

The afternoon takes me past yet more wineries and perfectly flat meadows, some of which feature tiny tumbledown shacks. Near another substantial town, plastic-covered crops nestle under a sky that is layered in grey and brilliant cream-coloured clouds, giving the light a dramatic cast.

I've reached tarmac once more, greeting its solidity with gratitude. This means I can lengthen my stride and noticeably speed up. My muscles can relax too, no longer having to actively drive each step forward through shifting sands. This brief respite doesn't last, however, since my route skirts the town proper. All I see are the edges of factories and rows of parked trucks at a logistics depot, then it's out into the fields again. By now the sky is glowering, promising rain, and lots of it. I can see the storm break ahead of me, a black column of misery coming my way. I am now racing against time – can I get to our final destination (Csongrád) before the weather assaults me?

**KILOMETRES TRAVELLED: 1944;**
**KILOMETRES REMAINING: 1454**

# Chapter 14: The Forever Road

Ultrarunning in unfamiliar places, you must always accept the premise that, no matter how tough things seem, they can always get tougher. Paradoxically, accepting that you have no control over geography and weather can set you free from frustration. You must take what is thrown at you and battle through it. No degree of fitness and preparedness will suffice if your mental attitude begins to slip.

As I watch the storm gathering ahead, almost beckoning me into its watery embrace, I lose my way. Not metaphorically, literally. The path I'd plotted, with Google Maps' help, appears to vanish into yet another impenetrable thicket of spiky bushes and knee-high grass. I curse aloud, with nobody to hear me and sympathise, although the swearing helps. The tyre treads lead on into jungle-like vegetation, giving me no option but to force a way through or turn back and improvise. I dig in, leaping over tiny trees and feeling the long grasses whipping against my naked legs. I hope there are no nasty ticks lurking in wait – a dose of Lyme's disease would really spoil our trip.

Then, inevitably, the skies open and huge, cold raindrops turn the footpaths into swollen streams in minutes. This is not the refreshing sprinkling of the previous day – this deluge is merciless. Soon I am wet through, to the point where I can no longer use my phone because I have nothing remotely dry to wipe it with. Once drenched, there is no point in hiding beneath the trees – I galumph on through puddles and icy rivulets, emerging eventually into a clearing where a series of shrines stand oddly illuminated in heavenly light. Were I religious, I might have taken the sun peeking out in this precise moment as some kind of sign.

From now on, the rain is drizzly at worst and the route ahead to Csongrád becomes damp roadway and empty cycle-path, well-marked with a yellow-dotted line receding into the distance.

A decorative wine press stands beneath the hand-painted wooden town sign at Csongrád and the rain-wetted streets reflect the low early-evening sun as I run to where Aradhna has parked Roxy, at a Penny

Markt store opposite an old brick-walled factory. I am soaked through and shivering, but I've somehow managed another 36km. Tonight's rest-spot is at the end of an abandoned B-road, at a lay-by used by fishermen, a fact we realise when I discover one of their makeshift loos (a spider-infested shed where a plank-bench with a hole in it suffices for a toilet seat). This "facility" is still preferable to crouching amongst the snakes and nettles.

***

## Day 62

Leaving Csongrád on May 11th, I am back in the land of sunshine, leafy pavements and decorative oxbow lakes where raised wooden platforms allow birdwatchers and fishermen to follow their enthusiasms. I run past our parking spot from the previous night and find a river, the Tisa, then take to the regular line of its flood-protection dam. I am pleased that my iPhone on shuffle chooses to play Led Zeppelin's "When the Levee Breaks", which seems strangely fitting. If the Tisa ever broke the dam's banks, a massive area would be devastated. A green horseshoe-shaped trail-marker and passing cyclists make me realise I am no longer in no man's land. This is an actual, sensible route by which to head east.

The most surreal encounter that morning is with an out-of-town Tesco! I hadn't realised Hungary had our familiar supermarket chain and the sight is both comforting and ever so slightly wrong. I haven't come 1990km to shop at Tesco; I run on.

Szentes is an attractive town, demonstrating civic pride with grand statuary and a park by a sculpted bend of the river. Strangely, a fountain springs from the middle of the river itself, as if the Tisa had sprung a vertical leak. School and college kids are in abundance, wandering in groups along the shady streets. As grand houses give way to tiny suburban homes, a towering communications tower dwarfs the houses like a menacing ice cream cone.

Then the brief respite of civilisation gives way once more to farm tracks through flat fields, this time a little easier to run, the dust dampened down by recent rains. Music helps me keep the pace going and stave off pangs of boredom. I feel almost guilty to admit that I am becoming bored, but it has been weeks now since I've seen mountains, and months since the sea and as a Brit, I tend to long for both.

In my John O'Groats to Land's End journey, I had my father or other support driver to encounter at regular intervals (since they were filming me) and occasionally another runner to join me. Here I have nobody, save brief encounters with Aradhna at lunchtime and our tired, time-pressured evenings. I am missing variety and mental stimulation. Music helps a little – The Doors, Zeppelin, Queen and others drive me on (nothing very cutting edge; this trip seems to require muscular rock music). I'd not expected ennui to become an enemy, but here it is, tempting me to stop early. I resist.

Then, nearing Nagymágocs, I take to the road again, which alternates intermittently with bits of cycle path in a fairly relentless, near-straight line heading for the town of Orosháza. I find myself grabbing moments of diversion where I can – a yellow-painted roadside hostelry, with bikes leaning in the shade outside, a sign warning of leaping deer, shrines to fallen drivers and cyclists (the implications of which keep me on my toes on blind corners). After 35km, I stop for late lunch by a graveyard, just outside Nagymágocs, but quickly move on, eager to get to our end point for the day. At Orosháza, a couple of men tootle by on electric bicycles, almost the only humans I've seen all afternoon. There are odd blue signs showing a head submerged in water – an invitation, rather than a warning. I believe there are bathing ponds nearby.

Aradhna directs me to a small lake, which is aflame with another beautiful sunset when I arrive. I, however, feel low and oddly dispirited, despite another high mileage day (46km). When Aradhna asks if I want to walk down to the lakeside, I prefer to sit with my aching feet steeping in a bucket of hot water and some of the soothing salts the Millers have given us. At first, I give no thought to Aradhna's feelings, although she just wants some company, having spent the whole day alone. Then it dawns on me how selfish I am being, so I make her a foot bath too and admire the photos she's taken of the lake. I hope my mood will brighten soon as we take early to bed, Aradhna suffering with her hay fever, which has been chronic for days. Two months on the road is taking its toll and, realistically, we have at least one more month before we hit Istanbul.

*\*\*\**

The suburbs are adorned with red roses but the road ahead is, once again, featureless, flat and straight as a die. I veer off as soon as I can – at least the dirt offers adventure, even though it often comes with a side order of frustration. The earth here is less dusty, more hard-packed and I run past a series of small derricks – perhaps they are drilling for oil in the region? Most of the derricks seem to be inactive, making me wonder if there had been small pockets of oil here that were now exhausted. Such speculations carry me eastwards, providing the mental stimulation I need.

More overgrown paths test my speed, making me go faster to avoid the bugs and beasties. Chickens roam the streets of Pusztaföldvár and purple wildflowers amongst the barley draw my lens. Lunch occurs at a place with the challenging name of Magyarbánhegyes, but to get there I have to run along the most dishearteningly straight route yet, which I quickly dub the Forever Road – a ten-kilometre strip of tarmac fringed with grass, straggly trees and not much else. At last, near the end of the ordeal by tedium, cobblestones take over from tarmac, marking this out as some sort of historic route, possibly a Roman road.

I pass a junction for Nagybánhegyes, which I hope Aradhna hasn't confused with Magyarbánhegyes (she hasn't) since I do not want to be doubling back on the Forever Road. I eventually reach the town with its city square and marble monument to local Marxist and political martyr István Anyyal, who died in 1958, aged just thirty.

A pleasant lunch gives way to another absolute scorcher of an afternoon as I run alongside wheatfields in the golden hour, a seemingly idyllic experience I still am not in the right frame of mind to appreciate. I don't know what's wrong with me – is it fatigue, boredom, a sense of dread that I am a little over halfway and the distance that lies ahead of me (over 1600km) seems insurmountable?

Whatever is the case, it doesn't help that my mapping apps lead me, once more, into trouble. The overgrown path becomes an impassable jungle of waist-high grasses, thorny bushes and overgrown trees, reducing me to more of a wade than a run. I have to divert from the plotted route and hope that I can circumvent the section that has evidently returned to nature.

This proves challenging. By the time I can see a clear route ahead through the fields, I am on the wrong side of a young crop of some sort of vegetable. Although I wouldn't normally do anything of the sort, I look all around me, see no signs of life and belt across the soil on tiptoes to the other side.

Back on course, a dirt road leads me on a race against the sun. I am now several miles from the road crossing where Aradhna is due to meet me and I remember that I have not packed my head torch. After dark, progress will be very slow indeed if I have to pick my way along by moon and starlight.

Fortunately, Aradhna has been impetuous too. Receiving angsty texts from my battery-drained phone, she decides to try to intercept me, driving along what looks like a reasonable farm road until it becomes a muddy, rutted track only suitable for 4x4s and tractors. Still she perseveres, hoping we'll intersect.

After what seems like an age, running with an already impressive turn of speed, given my fatigue, I spy a familiar figure step out onto the path ahead. Aradhna is lit in a golden glow by the fading sun and I accelerate to a sprint to hug her in a smelly embrace. She tells me the road proper is probably about half a mile ahead and she doesn't want to have to come back here tomorrow on the dubious farm tracks. I have no choice but to run on. Perhaps a little oxygen-deprived, I decide to run as fast as humanly possible to the roadway.

As Roxy trundles behind me, I belt at seven-minute-mile pace for about two kilometres to the road, as sunset gives way to dusk. I feel my spirits rise suddenly, knowing I have this reservoir of untapped energy in me. I've been in a bit of a slump for a couple of days but perhaps there is light ahead. The following day will bring another massive milestone – if our calculations are correct, I will cross another border, into Romania, which feels like both an exciting and a fearful prospect.

\*\*\*

That night, after a tiresome search for a sensible place to camp, we park outside an agricultural machinery factory near a watermelon farm. For the first time, our presence alerts the local police. They knock on our door as Aradhna is preparing dinner. We fear the worst – moving on now will be unpleasant, and cost us valuable downtime.

However, the two policemen only want to know if we are planning on staying long and where we were going. The answers to both questions – one night and Romania – seem to satisfy them and they nod their assent and leave us alone.

**KILOMETRES TRAVELLED: 2039;**
**KILOMETRES REMAINING: 1359**

# Chapter 15: An Illegal Scottish Immigrant

### Day 64

On 13th May 2018, and not in an attempt to make a political point or engage in an act of symbolic irony, I manage to become an illegal immigrant in Romania. This dubious achievement begins with a fairly arbitrary bit of route-planning.

Looking at our maps, we realise that the quickest way into Romania will be via the long, straight Aradi Utca, which as its name suggests, leads straight to Arad, one of Romania's wealthiest cities and a major financial centre. Whilst planning the trip, knowing very little about Romania and finding few official hiking trails, we randomly plotted a line through this region. It seemed fun to Aradhna to pass through a city whose name was similar to her own. We have no better reason to head through Arad, other than that it gives us a reasonably direct route east.

There isn't much traffic on Aradi Utca, which might have rung alarm bells, except that Aradhna drives ahead and reports back that a few miles further on, the road ends at a barrier to traffic, but not one that ought to trouble me. There are no obvious checkpoints or signs warning walkers not to cross. As naïve as it seems, this puts my mind at ease, explaining as it does the lack of traffic. Although Aradi Utca is far from fascinating or especially picturesque it's easy to run and peaceful and that's all I need this morning.

I pass a crucified Jesus, comparatively rare in Hungary, although omnipresent further west. Next, I am passed by a horse and cart carrying a chest of drawers, bales of hay and several brown-skinned family members – could this be my first sighting of true Romanies? I return their cheery waves and watch their ramshackle vehicle recede into the vanishing point of another straight-as-hell road.

I pass through Kisdombegyház, with its impressive graveyard, and stop at a shop in the neighbouring town for a Coke and a Mars bar. Everything bar the grocery store is closed, this being a Sunday. The road next takes me along rosebush-lined streets out of town and past a massive refinery and then I reach the barrier.

Doubt creeps in – there is a small white booth, but it's unmanned. Nobody is about, but a parked car stands about 200 yards away on the Romanian side. I get my passport out, just in case, duck under the bar and take a couple of photos by the Romanian flag and sign, then jog on, just in time to see two burly police officers emerge from the parked car. Uh-oh. I slow to a walk as they approach.

"There was nobody there. Here, I have my passport," I pre-empt, with a sinking feeling in my stomach. The Romanian police do not look best pleased. I have a sudden flood of panic, wondering if I'll end up in a featureless concrete cell, with only Aradhna to plead for my release.

A shake of the head. "No photos."

I proffer the passport again. The thinner, taller officer gives it a cursory look.

"No Schengen," he says, dourly. "Delete please."

Suddenly I understand. Although Romania is a full member of the EU, it has not joined the Schengen Agreement[1], meaning that passport controls are still compulsory. The border post I've blithely ducked under is not open for business.

While the shorter officer ensures I delete my photos (from my main album; I craftily leave them in my deleted items folder) the other waves his arm towards the checkpoint.

"You must go back. Proper crossing."

Of course. He wants me to cross at Battonya, where Aradhna is heading. There is no way to argue my case. I have to turn back.

Meanwhile, Aradhna has just cleared passport control and is about to leave the booth at the Romanian side when I call, explain my situation and ask her to drive back to collect me. For me to run around to the Battonya crossing is an impossibility – a journey of 12km that will add at least half a day to my schedule.

It is with some embarrassment that my girlfriend has to explain to the Romanian border control officers that, yes, she has only been in their country for five minutes but now she has to return to Hungary to pick up her errant partner. They shrug, mildly confused and let her do a U-turn. Aradhna then has to explain to the Hungarians that she's not been refused entry, but has seemingly changed her mind. Since there is no European law against cross-border dithering, they let her

---

1    The treaty, first signed in 1985, allowed free passage without border controls between 26 EU and EU-neighbouring countries (at time of writing).

through.

Once she picks me up from the conveniently-positioned picnic table under the trees on Aradi Utca, Aradhna and I return to Battonya to further bewilder the officials. In fact, they are simply amused and when Aradhna mimes "running" to explain my odd attire, one even nods with what appears a sympathetic expression, as if Aradhna is my carer or responsible adult, which in a sense, she is.

The Romanian border control police on Aradi Utca are likewise bemused to see me emerge from Roxy near their unmarked squad car. However, Aradhna charms them immediately. Somehow she explains, via mime and pidgin English, what I am up to.

"He is running ... from Paris. Long way."

The truth dawns.

"Ah ... sport," the officer nods, as if this word explains all my eccentricities.

Laughing and shaking their heads (in a good way) they allow me to start from the Romanian side of the barrier and jog past them in the Arad direction. It is probably the most unexpected thing to happen to these officers today and I am, as ever, happy to provide comic relief for all concerned.

***

The road continues to be comparatively quiet as it winds towards Arad. Wide fields, lined with irrigation ditches are straddled by lines of red and white striped pylons. Small boxy houses on the horizon are not too dissimilar to those in Hungarian villages. The churches are very different, however – here they wear shiny metallic "witches' hats" on top of square white towers, some burnished to a reflective silvery hue.

My legs are aching and I can feel the suggestion of a blister rising on my left heel. On my last epic run, I suffered from no blisters at all, largely because I kept my feet dry and wore two-ply socks (or two pairs of socks) every day. For some reason, this strategy isn't working this time around – perhaps dust or sand is getting into my socks from the perpetually hot, dry roads and trails. I do the only thing I can do and try not to think about it.

Soon I begin to see city signifiers – industrial plants on the edge of town, tramlines and Communist-era housing blocks that could most politely be termed "functional" but have, at least, been painted bright red and yellow in recent years. The high-density housing contrasts vividly with round-towered brick churches with a suggestion of the

Ottoman Empire about them – domes and cupolas, shady arches surmounting Corinthian columns.

The trams in Arad are quaintly narrow, sky blue and rattling by on narrow rails. I follow Google's suggestion for a final destination, and find it wanting, although it does take me past a fitting mural of a pair of fiery trainers. Google seems to think the city centre is a nondescript, quiet part of the suburbs. I call Aradhna and follow her instructions instead to a covert camping spot she's found by the river Mureș.

*** 

A high embankment provides ample parking spaces, while the other side of the street is lined with tenement housing and shops. On top of the embankment runs a public walkway, beyond it a small park and then the river, looping east. I wash quickly and then Aradhna and I walk down to the riverbank, find a pleasantly unpretentious bar and have our first Romanian beer – an Ursa. Nearby, some young men have ordered what appears to be a gigantic glass jar full of lager, complete with its own tap. Over our head, a colourfully-illuminated bridge arcs towards clubs and restaurants on the far bank.

We have a rudimentary meal (I enjoy some local lamb sausages and mash; Aradhna has to make do with fries and ketchup) before wandering over the bridge to another bar-restaurant where a grumpy maître d' tells us off for trying to sit in a reserved outdoor booth. Dismayed, our response to being made unwelcome is typically British – we say nothing and vote with our feet. A city centre ice cream parlour offers a warmer welcome, the waitress having spent three years living in Guildford, of all places.

We walk around town, finding the main square flanked by grand public buildings and a feeling of moneyed comfort. There are a lot of well-dressed young Romanians out and about and a young teen cycles circles around the mosaic-decorated square in front of City Hall, while a small child dances on the tiles. There are grand museums and theatres, and fancy cars roar past at untenable speeds. This, Romania's 12th largest city, was the second to rise up against Nicolae Ceaușescu in 1989's revolution (following Timișoara's lead) and has evidently prospered since the fall of communism. We would later discover that not everything is as it appears in Romania, however, as the contrast with what I'd experience in Arad County's more rural areas would attest.

As we head to bed rather later than usual, we realise we are now in a time zone two hours ahead of the UK. Back in Britain the *Ten O'Clock News* will just be ending. We are half a continent away but it is already beginning to feel like another world entirely.

\*\*\*

A somewhat disturbed night's sleep ensues, and it appears the road we've chosen to park on is a local cut-through for rush-hour traffic. We have some operational issues to solve this morning – we must repark Roxy due to local restrictions and locate a café so we can use their lavatories. I find myself lingering over my coffee and cake, the vestiges of my recent weakness of will remaining.

I shake it loose with an enjoyable run along the embankment by the Mureş, then off onto suburban roads and past some of the most immense gas pipes I've ever seen – they are at least three feet in diameter and suspended above ground, so much of an eyesore they almost transcend ugliness to achieve architectural drama. At one point, these immense conduits are raised ten metres into a U-shaped "gate", allowing citizens access to a leafy park.

I run in the direction of Deva, under a grey-blue cloudy sky, finding that the cycle path ends at a now-familiar hinterland of big-box stores and industrial estates. I run through the car park of a "Jumbo" toy superstore and locate another scrap of somewhat-concealed cycle path and pavement alongside a major road heading for Bucharest.

Vladimirescu is the first town I pass, with an excellent example of the brightly-painted churches typical of the region. Frescoes of saints decorate each panel around the church's perimeter, adding colour and vibrancy to a rather grey morning. At the town's limit, a sign proclaims "Drum Bun!", an amusing phrase in English but just the Romanian for "farewell". In this newly unfamiliar version of Europe, I take this scrap of encouragement to heart. I am running into an increasingly "in-between" landscape of roads, scrubby fields and billboards advertising inscrutable products and services. One baffling poster trumpets "Zoo Spa", and has an image of a giraffe and a pair of suntanned legs.

Romania quickly trumps all previous nations through which we pass in one shameful respect – roadside memorials. Rusting crosses sprout in great profusion by the congested road, looking rather neglected, their dilapidation giving the lie to their *in memoriam*s. Poppies sprout in their own form of commemoration and at Mândruloc I do a double-take before their World War I memorial. The dates throw me. 1914-1919. Later I discover that Romania fought a war with then-communist Hungary over disputed territories in 1918 and 1919, even going so far as to occupy Budapest. Romania did rather better than Hungary out of the complex negotiations that followed, but not without the loss or injury of around 13,000 fighters.

Pensiones and hotels line the road, as well as truck stops and rudimentary cafés. Lorries are in superabundance and, inevitably, the cycle route expires (I'd seen nobody using it but me) and leaves me to play chicken with the 18-wheelers. I decline the challenge and take to the fields, skirting a strawberry patch where two leathery men are hawking punnets to whatever passing trade they can muster. Roadside fruit-sellers will be a common sight in Romania, and I know it's only a matter of time before I succumb to the lure of all that natural sugar.

\*\*\*

Hills begin to undulate to the north; between them and the river, grander houses are in evidence, featuring round towers and balconies, decoratively tiled roofs and wrought iron gates. Some of these appear to have been abandoned mid-build. We later learn that it is common for Romanians to work abroad for several years, amass savings and pour them into property back home, often in the same poor villages from which these transient workers originated. This strategy doesn't always work out, however, and the financial collapse of 2008 can't have helped, hence the large number of projects "on hold".

On the outskirts of a satellite settlement, I run through a poorer neighbourhood and see a host of grubby-faced children playing in the street. They all stare and point like I am a spaceman fallen to earth. I wave and run on.

I continue to seek out alternatives to choking on carbon monoxide and staring down truckers. I find what seems to be a gravel farm road and head towards the Mureş. As I do so, a series of massive lorries overtakes me, throwing up clouds of yellow dust. So much for avoiding heavy traffic!

*Aruncarea Guiunoailor – Strict Interzisa Amenda. De la 500 La 1000 Lei.*

The sign is worrying. I translate it on my phone, revealing a warning against throwing guinea pigs. I imagine a scenario where unwanted pets are "set free", only to go feral and breed uncontrollably in the wild. Another attempt produces a more mundane translation – a stern prohibition on littering as I enter a nature reserve.

\*\*\*

Running alongside yet another flood dam, I scare a hedgehog back into the undergrowth and struggle to create a sensible route through the dried-out mud runnels and long grasses. The trucks have diverted towards a construction site on the south side of the river and have left me without a road. Nevertheless, I see a horse and cart ahead, so I know my chosen route leads somewhere vaguely sensible, hopefully not onto private land. I have no knowledge of Romanian trespassing laws or how accommodating the local farmers are.

As well as hedgehogs and plentiful insects, I witness a wheeling, flashing aerial ballet of bee-eaters. This colourful bird migrates to Africa in the winter months and gives the swift a run for its money in aerobatic skill. I spend a few minutes trying to creep up on them to get a photo, to no avail. They vanish as suddenly as they appear, nesting amongst concrete pilings by the side of the embankment. I later spot them under the eaves of village houses, preying on the bees that service the abundant roses and flowering shrubs.

Herds of sheep are soon visible as a path emerges on the river's flood-plain. As diggers and construction vehicles chop up the opposite bank, farmers can be seen driving shambolic cars around their land. Dogs, thankfully fenced off, bark in impotent rage as I pass. I make it back to the road with a sense of relief, only to return to running the gauntlet of reckless motorists. A weird vehicle with immense tyres and a body raised four feet from the ground passes, perhaps some sort of crop sprayer but looking like an escapee from a cyberpunk movie.

The truck superhighway carries me south-east, and I pass an unlikely souvenir stall selling rugs, clay pots, baskets and garden gnomes. I take a shortcut via Lipova's close neighbour Radna[1] and cross railway tracks via a crumbling concrete bridge into Lipova itself. The town has the look of a Ballardian dystopia, all rust and overgrown vegetation. A footbridge crosses the river and carries me over to smart Georgian-style buildings flanking a small park by the water's edge. There I find Roxy waiting and we decide I've run enough for the day, having managed 34km. We eschew the local ice cream stall but do use the frankly horrible portaloos in the park, which would instil traumatic memories in even the most seasoned vanlifer.

\*\*\*

---

[1]   That's right – the day saw me running from Arad to Radna – was my girlfriend trying to tell me something?

I ease my double layer of socks off and inspect the blisters. As expected, they are taut and angry and want attention. Soon will come a day when I'll have to lance them; today will not be that day.

**KILOMETRES TRAVELLED: 2119;**
**KILOMETRES REMAINING: 1279**

## Tips for Multi-Day Runners - 6. Injuries

If you're exceptionally lucky, eat properly, sleep sufficiently and pace yourself well, you may avoid significant injuries, even on a 3000km run across a continent. I was injured several times during my JOGLE, where I averaged 26 miles per day (42km). For running the Orient, I dropped this down to 20 miles (32km) and had no problematic injuries to contend with. I acknowledge that I may have just been exceptionally fortunate.

To give yourself the best chance to be as lucky as I was, follow these guidelines:

1.  *Eat plenty of protein*, whether in the form of meat, dairy, pulses or nuts. Protein helps muscles repair. It also helps in hormone production, helpful for pain limitation.

2.  *Build up slowly.* If you plan to average 30km a day over 100 days, consider starting at 15-20km for the first week, then increasing over the next 3-4 weeks. You may have to run some 35km+ days towards the end of your adventure to maintain your average, but you'll be stronger by then and your body will be used to the repeated mileage.

3.  *Stretch and warm-up,* if this is something you generally find useful. I don't, but many long-distance runners swear by it, so if you prefer to stretch on long training runs, do it during your journey too.

4.  *Make sure your shoes are suitably supportive.* Unless you're a seasoned barefoot runner, you'll probably need to ensure your shoes aren't rapidly running out of tread. Evenly flat shoes are better than well-cushioned ones in a state of distress. It's generally recommended you change them every 500 miles or so.

5.  *Notice the niggles.* Keep an eye out for little pains, strains and sprains that could become injuries. Ice, elevate and support swollen joints when you finish up each day. A bag of frozen peas

taped to your ankle can work wonders to ease the discomfort of shin splints.

6. *Recognise the really serious problems.* It's partly an instinctive thing, but you should get to know your body well enough to know when an injury isn't something you can just run through. Don't hesitate to seek professional help if an injury only worsens or causes you to unhelpfully alter your gait to the extent that other issues arise. An hour with a physiotherapist or getting an X-ray taken can reveal and clarify difficulties immediately. During my JOGLE, a persistent ankle swelling was revealed at X-ray to have been caused by a congenital spur of bone on my left shin rubbing against soft tissue. There wasn't really anything I could do, except ice and elevate it, but nor would it cause me any lasting harm. Knowing this gave me the confidence to keep on running, taking whatever steps I could to manage the pain.

# Chapter 16: Man's Best Friend

***Day 66***

I heard rumours that Romania has a feral dog problem. I made light of it. I like dogs and find it hard to imagine that domestic animals would form packs in the wild and threaten travellers. Yet, on 15th May, I find myself face to face with two vicious, snarling and very large dogs, whose hackles are up and whose every sinew screams latent violence. The rumours I've heard are inadequate and, as my heart pounds in my chest, I vow never to dismiss anything I've heard about the places I'll be running through. Reality frequently outguns mere rumour.

***

Several hours earlier, the day begins innocently enough. Yet another lazy start is mitigated by the fact that we manage to fill our water tank at a tap in the gardens and empty the waste water. At least I can leave Aradhna with fewer chores to complete during the day.

Lipova backstreets quickly dissolve into rutted gravel and puddles. It has rained heavily overnight. A steep lane merges seamlessly into farmland. I jog past a few young children coming downhill, who look at me as if I am something utterly alien. What on earth am I doing running into the countryside in shorts and a t-shirt? I often wonder this myself.

The gently rolling green hills begin to remind me of the Pentlands south west of Edinburgh, near my parents' home. I'd done some of my winter training there, panting red-faced up steep gravel tracks and sheep-paths, all the while blasted by an icy wind. The weather east of Lipova is far balmier than Scotland, but my legs and lungs feel the incline and the challenge of wet cobbles and oozing mud. I jog past a small farm, giving it as wide a berth as possible, following what my phone has assured me is a through-route towards Bata.

Just then, a volley of angry barking announces a pack of five medium-sized dogs, including one Alsatian, bounding over the grass towards me.

The animals seem to be running away from a farmer who has emerged from the homestead I passed. He bellows at them, as I wave my rolled-up laminated map at the pack like a baton. The dogs fan out, teeth bared and snarling. Every time I retreat, they advance, yet pause a few yards away, as if awaiting a cue from the alpha dog to tear me to shreds. The farmer lopes over and calls them away; reluctantly they obey. He is half-apologising, half-warning me (I think) in Romanian and all I can do is make the universal palms-up mime for "Sorry, I have no idea what's happening". I point the way I intend to run, and he nods as if giving permission, grabbing the collar of the largest of the dogs.

I walk away, gradually increase my pace, as the disgruntled barking diminishes. Eventually, I am able to run again. Except that half a mile further on I spot another farm and, almost inevitably, a pack of even wilder dogs. This time they are seven-strong, lolloping from the trees to my right, their curiosity piqued and infused with growing outrage. I slow to a walk once more, but they come at me nonetheless. This time I scan the ground and quickly grab a stick, swinging it before me like a sword. These dogs look too motley a crew to be farm dogs; I guess they are some of the feral animals I've been warned about.

In the early 1980s, Ceaușescu's regime was attempting to populate the cities and increase their number, his flavour of communism valuing urban expansion over collectivised farming and rural values. His ideal was to double the number of cities by 1990. As with most Western countries, there had already been a gradual depopulation of villages since the industrial revolution in favour of city-dwelling. Ceaușescu simply forced the pace of change. He declared villages with populations beneath 1000 to be "irrational" and enforced resettlement policies which required citizens to leave their livestock and pets behind. Many of the dogs were killed, others escaped into the wilds or were released by their owners. I am facing down some of the mongrel descendants of these ex-pets, now free to let their lupine instincts rise to the fore.

Although it might be true that few of these animals would attack me, I'm not going to take any chances. I bellow and wave my stick and the animals circle around me but do not pounce. I've heard others had not been so lucky, including a four-year-old boy mauled to death by street dogs in Bucharest in 2014.

Various Romanians I later speak to, and reports I read[1], point to

---

1    Including http://www.fes.ro/media/2015_news/FES_Report_Straydogs_en.pdf

an ongoing problem with dog owners failing to neuter their animals or abandoning puppies if they prove ineffective as guard dogs (or are the result of unplanned pregnancies). A vast literature exists online discussing possible solutions to the problem. Over the last 30 years, the government has variously experimented with culls, mass neutering and more recently, programmes of education in humane animal ownership.[1]

Charities are increasingly active in the country, rescuing and repatriating abandoned animals. My parents have a Romanian rescue dog, Maia, a floppy-eared and perky Kooikerhondje, who is one of the best-natured and, living near the Pentland Hills, best-exercised pet dogs you'd ever meet. It is hard for me to imagine her living rough on the streets of a Romanian village or city, even less running with a pack, yet that's the kind of life she must once have led.

Knowing this stirs up a conflict between sympathy and fear. I feel mean threatening these once-beloved pets, but I simply have to show aggression, to be "top dog", in order to fend them off. I will not hesitate to thump one if it runs at me with murderous intent.

Fortunately, this pack too lets me pass. I race through the farm's back-yard, past scatterings of voluble geese and out onto a proper track once more. I run on gravel and hard-packed dirt alongside fields of rippling grasses.

*\*\*\**

The village of Ususău appears, and with it, tarmac roads again. I exhale in relief. Ususău is a strange mix of impoverished bungalows, some literally falling down with trees growing through their roofs, and more grandiose builds, with pagoda-styled roofs and breezeblock walls not yet plastered (with little promise that they ever will be). A boy of about eight years old with unruly shoulder-length hair pedals his bike along the brick-lined pavement before me. Nobody else is in sight, apart from the sentinel storks perched in their nests atop the telegraph posts. These birds are a familiar sight in rural Romania, tending to their impressive nests, feeding their young or just standing guard, unfazed by the humans scurrying below.

The more cultivated gardens often extend beyond each house onto a grassy border between pavement and street; one house features a series of varnished flower-boxes constructed from wine barrels and carved-out logs filled with marigolds.

The only villagers in evidence are older people sitting on little benches in front of their gardens, with whom passers-by stop and chat. Skins textured with wrinkles and long hours of exposure to summer sunshine are shaded under headscarves or caps, heads turning to follow me as I run. I smile and wave, hoping to seem harmless in a place in which I can never hope to belong.

I run straight through the first village and out the other side without stopping. Like most hamlets I pass through, the homes are strung out along one main road. Outside the village a mile marker informs me that it is 7km to Zăbalţ and 45km to Făget. These stone markers prove very useful, allowing me to better structure my day and keep my pace up. I eagerly "collect" the markers and watch the miles roll by. The road I run on now is quiet, save the occasional truck, and the sky is clouding over, keeping the temperature down.

As I approach Zăbalţ, a line of thin haystacks resembles voodoo figurines under a sky that is now a doom-laden dark grey. A cool breeze springs up and the clouds promise rain, blackening ominously as I dodge a truck which roars out of nowhere and almost hits me. I curse under my breath and vow not to be so complacent. As far as I have seen, nobody runs for fun in Romania – I am a curio on the roadside.

Running through another village, an old man jokes amiably with me – he seems to be miming an umbrella over his head. I laugh politely and huff my way up an incline. Moments later, the skies open and hurl sheets of icy rain down. I tramp on, hatless, feeling the water running in rivulets down my back. Nearing Zăbalţ, the first flashes of lightning and cataclysmic crashes of thunder announce that we'll soon be getting a proper storm. If the streets have been quiet earlier in the day, they are desolate now, the small, boxy homes squatting in dank lawns, weathered and functional, with tiny shuttered windows. The road begins to climb through forestry land and there are piles of roughly cut logs and occasionally a hut or metal trailer, where the loggers can hide and eat their meals.

I carry on to Bata which, if anything, is even more derelict than the previous villages I've passed through. It's hard to believe that I am still in Arad County and that these neglected places fall under the same jurisdiction as that smart mercantile city on the banks of the Mureş.

\*\*\*

Aradhna and Roxy are waiting for me at the end of town opposite the police station. I am grateful to duck in out of the rain for a little while. I throw on a couple of dry layers but don't take anything off that I'll have to put on again. As we sit warming up, it is silent save the sound of perpetual drizzle. I reflect that we've developed quite an efficient and comforting routine by now, a little more than two months into the adventure. Aradhna says she's sorry she'll have to miss a couple of weeks very soon. She'll miss me but she'll also miss Roxy and our ongoing mission / voyage of discovery.

My girlfriend's elderly grandmother has been living with Aradhna's parents for a few months, but now the folks are due to holiday in Japan and Aradhna has to head home to Surrey to look after the octogenarian for a fortnight. Aradhna is very close to Veerbala, who once moved me to tears by saying in Hindi that she had known me for years but I had now become a friend[1]. Nobody else trustworthy is available to look after Aradhna's *nani* and we've both long known this day was coming but it opens up a void of uncertainty for us.

My father, himself nearly 75, will be filling in for Aradhna and we've only been able to give the vaguest notion of where we might be. I thought I'd reach Bucharest, but it seems a little unlikely. I'll probably still be north of the southern Romanian Alps, part of the L-shaped Carpathian range that divides the country. He has booked a flight to Cluj-Napoca, 100km north of the mountains and we'll be picking him up in two days' time. We have allowed for a single handover day, before Aradhna has to leave, also from Cluj. We value quiet moments of togetherness like this, sheltering in our home on wheels as the rain drums on Roxy's roof, because we know we'll miss them.

\*\*\*

Outside Bata, after lunch, I am surprised to pass a large spa hotel, so unexpected amidst the farms and impoverished villages. I realise we are getting closer to the mountains and thereby closer to popular tourist routes and destinations. The rest of the afternoon sees me passing village after village, fending off small yappy street dogs with the shovel we usually use for toiletary purposes.

Băcaul de Mijloc, Ostrov, Virişmort, Birchiş – after the rain has

---

1    Sadly, she passed away in August 2019, after a lasting illness. She spent her last hours at home, surrounded by her family as she had wanted, and was able to say her goodbyes.

stopped the villages are now full of life, but most of it scurries away from me on webbed feet or stares balefully at me with bovine eyes. A woman stands guarding her prize cow, goad at the ready, as it munches fresh grass at the side of the road.

A meadow at Virişmort contains two free-standing pillars, presumably once the main gate in a fence around a grand property, now a lookout perch for magpies. At Birchiş, three men laze around a fishing pond, the sun having finally broken out. A little later, two small dogs emerge from a house and run at me, barking. Behind them, their owner watches me wave his hounds away. I am swearing loudly, hoarse and worn down by all the dog attacks. He seems unfazed; this is just a part of life.

At Birchiş, I stop running, gratefully grabbing hold of Roxy's side. It has been a challenging day with a lot to absorb and I've covered 33km. We find a quiet field to park in, away from prying eyes, and I strip off for my bucket bath, too tired to bother putting the shower tent up. That night the thunder, rain and wild lightning assault Roxy's rooftop tent, but I snore through most of it. So far, Romania has been many things; what it certainly isn't, is boring.

**KILOMETRES TRAVELLED: 2207;**
**KILOMETRES REMAINING: 1191**

# Chapter 17: If You Go Down to the Woods Today

It rains all night and continues relentlessly into the morning of Day 67. I dither and don't get started until noon, meaning this will be one of those days when I'll drop the lunch break. Today is something of a milestone, since we calculate that I've run 1300 miles and therefore have less than 1000 miles to run[1]. Dipping to triple figures in mileage might not seem entirely encouraging when that still equals 38 marathons, but it comes as something of a relief to this exhausted runner. We reverse Roxy carefully out of what is quickly becoming a morass of liquid mud and drive back to Birchiş. I record a piece to camera about my expectations for the day (mostly entailing getting wet). It is hilariously grim weather, in an odd way making up for the seemingly endless parade of sunny days I have experienced of late.

Heading out once more to do battle with the rain and the dogs, I feel better prepared for what the day might fling at me. At Căpâlnaş, I pass a clay football pitch, netted and vacant, the first indicator that some Romanians, at least, are sporty rather than sedentary. Colourfully-painted houses hide amongst the trees in hillside villages guarded by tiny dogs with fierce attitudes. I quickly learn that if the stick doesn't work, bending to gather (or pretend to gather) a handful of stones sends these street dogs scampering away.

The road withers away to a gravel path as I take an unpopular turning towards Căprioara[2], chasing the Mureş once more, then heading into the hills. There is something beautiful about the landscape drenched in rain – the greens more vivid, veils of mist draped over the dark hillsides. Less lovely are the endless puddles on the gravel roads, whose trees encroach with fallen limbs and overgrown branches. The trees offer some cover, but the rain soon finds a way through and pelts me at every opportunity. I am so wet, there is no point in avoiding the puddles anymore. I splash through them, maniacally.

A little way into the forested region, a little car pulls up beside

---

1    Or 2092km and 1609km respectively. Measured subsequently, I'd actually run 1371 miles.
2    Rather poetically, the town is also the Romanian word for "deer", presumably common fauna in the region.

me. A jovial middle-aged couple beckon me in and look confused when I decline. Oddly, I find myself having to mime the thing I've actually been doing, namely running. Finally, they understand, shake their heads in amusement and drive away. I can't fault them for their confusion – surely only a madman would choose to run in this deluge.

\*\*\*

I encounter no more wild dogs until moments after I misjudge one puddle and fall sprawling to my knees. I pick myself up and find a black Labrador staring at me balefully. It barks a couple of times but I raise the stick I'd recently found and roar and my nemesis makes off into the underbrush. I christen the stick Gandalf II and slide it into the straps of my backpack for safe-keeping.

\*\*\*

I am now in the foothills of the Carpathians and the villages are becoming more concealed and derelict in appearance, although some homeowners have decided to shout from the wilderness by painting their houses in acid green or bright orange hues. The storms of yesterday have scattered broken branches across the gravel roads and I run alongside overhanging cliffs with an eye out for falling rocks or mudslides.

In the commune[1] of Zam comes a road so potholed I wonder how anything can drive along it. Minutes later, I have a demonstration of just how, as Roxy, following the same navigational suggestion from Google, appears behind me. For half an hour she trundles alongside, weaving in and out of the biggest puddles while I plunge through or leap over them. I enjoy Aradhna's company, for once not worried about feral dog attacks. The road opens out onto a high plain and we pass a huge herd of sheep being driven to pasture by a shepherd, complete with crook. We reach tarmac once more at Tisa, and Roxy and Aradhna leave me to my own devices.

Tisa is far smarter and prettier than the wild places I've passed and here the weather changes too, brightening and revealing glimpses of blue sky. I pass a tilted stone cross in a field, massive and lichen-covered; a no-nonsense nod to the almighty. Soon, my peace is shattered by the first of a volley of massive trucks, screaming along the narrow main road towards Dobra, the largest town in the province, and my next destination. I feel I have to find a different route. After an

---

1    Administrative region.

hour of facing down the horrible traffic, Dobra appears – an attractive village entirely spoilt by having an unending stream of massive lorries using it as a cut-through.

Aradhna and I stand aghast as an elderly couple hobble between 18-wheelers to get to some sort of local fête taking place near the town hall. There are women in brightly-coloured folk garb and leathery-skinned Romany men sporting trilbies at a jaunty angle as well as kids playing by the side of the road, blithely unconcerned by the potential vehicular mayhem just inches from their fragile bodies. We can't see anywhere to fill our water tank so we decide to flee the town and seek quietude.

We find too much of that on a farm road which leads us to an ominous gravel clearing ringed with derelict concrete structures, much graffitied and resembling exactly the kind of place you'd go to get murdered. We backtrack and find a scrap of farm road half a mile away where we can pull off onto a verge at the edge of silent fields. We spend much of the evening hand-washing my running clothes in a bucket and hanging them up to dry on Roxy's bike rack.

***

### Day 69

Aware that soon we won't have one another to fall back upon, Aradhna and I decide to share the adventure more fully on 18th May. She will cycle with me along side streets and back into the countryside, away from the hideous E673 and its unending smoggy roar.

The villages of the foothills are distinctly more well-to-do than those I've seen in Arad County; we are now in Hunedoara. Roşcani's dogs announce their dislike of me from behind stout fences and new, completed villas express confidence and style without excess, although some of them boast swimming pools, the first I've seen since Austria. Roses bloom in pink profusion and today's sky is an effortless blue as we happily meander towards the hills.

A sparkling river weaves its way through a cultivated valley, past haystacks and well-tended farmsteads. The only disconcerting moment comes when we pass a half-naked man talking to two cyclists as he stands by his ramshackle car, which seems to have a flat tyre. He gives us a very odd look in response to our greeting. It is the kind of look that yokels give naïve travellers at the start of Appalachian-set horror films. We laugh it off and run or cycle on.

Outside the forested trailhead where we part ways, a wooden shelter bears the inscription *Grija de Padure este eminamente grija zile de mihe, este simtul solidaritatii cu viit* (care of the forest is daily self-care, it is a kind of solidarity with all life), attributed to Marin Drăcea, a mid 20th-century silviculturist[1]. I feel happy to be entering the first established walking and hiking region I've encountered for weeks. Aradhna has to turn back when the trail surface becomes too challenging for her hybrid bike. A puncture here would mean a very long walk back to Roxy.

*\*\*\**

I enter a green tunnel of forest with a nagging sense of fear. I've been so preoccupied with feral dogs that I've entirely forgotten that the Carpathian Mountains are home to around 6000 brown bears. Bears have become public enemy number one in rural regions of Romania in recent years, with a 2017 ban on trophy hunting (generally the province of the elite) forever in danger of being repealed. A government-sanctioned cull was permitted in 2018 and conservationists now fear this will open the door to less regulated persecution of these fearsome but magnificent animals.

I deliberately read very little about bears before planning to run through their habitat. However, I do know that attempting to out-sprint an angry bear is futile (they can run up to 40mph; Usain Bolt has managed a comparatively measly 28mph in comparison). Bears are capable swimmers, so fording a stream would probably prove ineffectual. Finally, climbing a tree is no guarantee of escape – most bears can climb. All in all, if you get between an angry bear and her cubs, you'd better just submit and play dead.

That said, bears will seldom approach humans and will actively avoid us if we make our presence known and they are not protecting their young. You probably don't want to leave food out if you are sleeping under canvas (the usual advice is to suspend it from a tree a little way outside your camping spot). I'd also been advised to talk loudly to myself or sing, to announce my approach round blind bends.

I suspect that these foothills are still too populous and hope I am running at the wrong altitude to encounter our ursine friends, but I remember what my research has recommended and sing inane ditties to "Mr Bear" as I round each blind corner[2].

---

1     One who deals with the stewardship and environmental care of forests.
2     An example of one such piece of doggerel is given in Appendix IV.

I've almost persuaded myself that my fears are groundless when I come upon an odd relic – two small posters on a noticeboard wrapped in plastic to protect them from the rain. In front of the board is a partly-collapsed bench and table, as if someone has once sold something here. These posters, though faded and almost colourless, are reproductions of paintings in a naïve, rural style featuring, on the right, a buck-toothed rabbit bounding towards the viewer and, on the left, an adult bear fishing with massive claws over a placid river. This bucolic sight is no comfort at all and I sing even louder as I race through the now bear-laden domain.

Belying the summer's day beyond the forest, these paths are dank and damp, yesterday's rain having soaked deep into the leafy mulch. Mushrooms bloom from rotten logs over which fat black slugs crawl. A red triangular warning sign depicts falling boulders, adding to the air of potential threat. I come upon a rustic, treacherous-looking plank footbridge over the swollen river and decide not to go that way – it looks disreputable.

After a couple of hours of running, two signposts at a fork in the road offer Vadu Dobrii (20km) or Bătrâna (10km). Unfortunately, I am heading in neither of those directions. I want to see Feregi appear as a potential destination, but it is not to be. A little later I see a derelict brick house decorated with neo-Nazi slogans and swastikas. I now have no idea whether to keep progressing on the main path or find a turn-off.

Fortunately, my Garmin tracking device proves even more useful than usual. Aradhna has been parked up somewhere, nervously following my progress through the forest on the interactive map on our website. Every ten minutes my location is updated. Aradhna is able to call me and warn me that the turn-off I want is imminent but might be unmarked, since it appears on the Garmin map but not Google. She catches me just in time as I spot an unmarked forestry road entrance on my left and decide to try it.

The path carries me up through the trees and away from the valley floor. Closer to the bear's habitat I assume, until I begin to notice hoof prints, in plentiful supply, in the mud beneath my feet. This is no forest access route; it's a drovers' path.

The way broadens, climbing above the treeline to end at a rustic wooden gate. I have no idea if Romanian trespass laws allow egress into fenced-off pasture but I have little choice. I climb the fence and trot into some of the most beautiful alpine meadows I've ever seen.

The stepped fields, carpeted with buttercups and vivid purple flowers and flickering with red admirals, fall dramatically away down to the forested valley below. A kilometre of climbing later, I hit another fence, scale it and run around the corner to be faced with a danger I'd not yet considered, but which stops me in my tracks.

The path has narrowed, squeezing me between a walled terrace of thorny bushes on my right and a barbed wire fence and hedgerow to my left. In front of me stands a golden-brown cow with impressive horns, lazily chewing the cud and eyeing me with deep suspicion. Behind it, eight or nine sisters stand, also chewing the grass, berries and leaves. Their munching explains why everything looks so well-groomed and garden-like.

During my JOGLE I'd encountered many herds of cattle and all the reading I'd done in preparation for that trip had advised me to give cows with calves a wide berth. There is just one problem – these animals have me all but surrounded. I can either retreat or slink past them, risking a goring.

The animal immediately before me seems like the ringleader, occasionally turning to butt an unruly calf or wayward companion out of the way. If anything, the bovines are advancing, rather than retreating, but I refuse to be beaten. I have a few oblique choices. I could run at the animals, shouting (as advised by Richard E Grant in the film *Withnail and I*, when faced with an angry bull[1]). I don't really trust Bruce Robinson, that film's writer-director, as an expert in animal husbandry, so I quickly rule this strategy out. I could attempt to climb the barbed wire fence and squeeze through the hedgerow. Assessing this option, I judge that my chances of emerging into the field below without a twisted ankle or ruptured testicle are slim.

I could try to scale the small terraced wall to my right and weave between the more rarified herd up there. That seems a dangerous idea too, since there are several calves mooching amongst the mulberries; their mothers might not take kindly to me running at them. Of course, I could turn back and waste several kilometres finding another way to Feregi. If you know anything about me by now, you'll know that I dismiss this last plan out of hand.

The only rational thing left to do is wait. The cows are gradually advancing, literally eating their way towards me. I press myself into

---

1    Paul McGann's character's reply: "A coward you are, Withnail! An expert on bulls you are not!"

the hedgerow and keep as still as possible. All I have to do is remain as unthreatening and as quiet as possible.

My phone trills, obnoxiously loudly. I answer with a whisper.

"Can't really talk right now. I'm surrounded."

"What on earth do you mean?" asks Aradhna, quite reasonably perplexed.

"Cows. I'm waiting them out. I may be some time."

To her credit, Aradhna gives me the benefit of the doubt, apologises in hushed tones and hangs up. I put my phone away and wait as the chief cow turns its rear end to me, rarely a sign of respect in the animal kingdom, and begins to brush one hoof on the ground, as a warning to one of its more obstreperous companions. I don't want to be the object of that ultimatum – the animal looks ferocious.

I wait, and wait. Fifteen minutes pass and the cows have advanced by perhaps ten feet. Boss cow is now within petting distance. At this rate, I'll be lucky to get through the herd by nightfall. I have to take my chances before the animals draw alongside me, trapping me entirely. I bolt for the wall to my right, leap onto it and wriggle my way through the herd before any of the ruminants have a chance to react. It works! To the soundtrack of a few limp bellows, I round the last cow and sprint down a muddy track and through an open gate onto a small, quiet road. I feel immediately pathetic and triumphant at the same time, a unique cocktail of emotions.

\*\*\*

Feregi is a tiny hamlet perched on top of a ridge of hills, extremely insular in appearance, with my luminous yellow-clad figure the oddest anomaly to pass their way for some time. I am so strange to the few elderly villagers that watch me pass by twice, as I struggle to locate the right road towards Roxy, that they largely forget to react. Aradhna later tells me that one of the old women had been rather helpful in showing her how to work the village hand-pump about an hour previously. Aradhna, however, looks comparatively normal. I am evidently an escapee from an asylum or a townie who is very, very lost. I smile inanely and shout "Buna!" and leg it out of town.

Aradhna has parked Roxy by the side of one of those country roads beloved of the producers of *Top Gear*, a twisting, rollercoaster of tarmac through beautifully silent countryside. There is a rocky hummock to duck behind for a pee and glorious views in all directions. Sadly, we can't linger. There is a lot to do before my father's arrival the following evening and we have to make it to Cluj-Napoca, 190km away, by tomorrow afternoon. We decide to head for a Park4Night location in Hunedoara.

\*\*\*

Aradhna wants to drive on, not back, taking a leaf from my book in terms of a refusal to backtrack. A turn-off onto a muddy lane seems a risk, but our generally reliable online mapping resource informs us that this is a proper road which will connect with the main thoroughfare to Hunedoara. Minutes into the "short cut" we realise we've potentially made a terrible mistake. A day of constant rain has reduced the steep, curving track into a muddy morass. We feel Roxy slipping diagonally away to the left as her tyres struggle to find purchase. Fortunately, the vegetation on either side of the road is densely packed, giving us nowhere to go, but there remains the possibility of getting stuck. We will never be able to push Roxy back up the slope. There is little choice but to press on.

Eventually, the precipitous path weaves its way down to a forested valley which is eerily dark and quiet. A skein of mist swirls in the centre of a green meadow. I realise with some trepidation that I'll be running this way tomorrow. We make it out onto the main road and drive down to the city at dusk, pausing to photograph the first real Transylvanian castle we've encountered. It stands on one side of a gully overlooking Hunedoara, illuminated from below, linked to the road by a wooden bridge and exceptionally dramatic with its twin turreted towers surmounted by one round and one square spire. A row of staterooms featuring ornately arched windows faces us.

Amongst the other sightseers are a group of Romanians who are touring their homeland together, in part to help one of them plan the itinerary for his new travel company. We get talking and find them very intellectually curious and insightful. These are middle-class Romanians with white-collar jobs and a healthy dose of suspicion levelled at politicians and bureaucrats, whom they suspect spend much of their time employing family members and lining their own pockets. I tell them about my experiences in Arad County and they tell me that such disparities in income and public utilities are commonplace. Many of the more remote rural locations lack a reliable electricity supply and very few have piped gas. Although there are water mains in most parts of the country, some homes still rely on the village well or pump.

Romania is a rapidly developing economy, with many showy displays of wealth among the mercantile classes, but it is also, they believe, still steeped in governmental corruption entrenched since Ceauşescu's era. That said, they all seem to love the country they call home (although one couple now live in Munich) and are doing their bit for the economy. We talk for the best part of an hour and feel it's a shame we are all going in different directions the following day, or else they would have made excellent interview subjects for Aradhna's film.

*** 

Once we get on the road again, we realise we've entirely failed to source a tank of diesel and are running dangerously low. We can't hand Roxy over to Dad when it's running on fumes. There follows a tricky conversation with a petrol station attendant where he doesn't know the English word "diesel" and we can't identify which brand of fuel won't fatally damage Roxy's innards (this is our first fill-up in Romania). A fellow motorist with rudimentary English solves our dilemma and we refuel and drive to a small parking place near a major hospital to settle down for the night.

It also seems to be a meeting-place for kids to rev car engines, smoke joints and play loud hip-hop. Fortunately, the party ends at 12:45am and we slide gratefully into sleep

**KILOMETRES TRAVELLED: 2233;**
**KILOMETRES REMAINING: 1165**

# Chapter 18: Enter Boyter Senior

Now that the time has come to say goodbye to Aradhna, albeit temporarily, I can't help thinking how vital she has been to the whole endeavour, from coming up with the idea to thinking through the logistical and budgetary challenges we'd face.

But more than this, she has been a rock in a torrential river – something for me to cling onto to keep from drowning in pain and self-pity when things get tough. I am loathe to let her go, although I know my dad, in his own unique and sometimes frustrating way, is ready to face the challenge of filling her shoes for a fortnight. Aradhna is a tough act to follow, however, and we will miss one another deeply. We decide to linger over our leave-taking.

***

### Day 68

We set off early the next day towards Cluj and stop for lunch at Alba Iulia, grabbing an opportunity to do a bit of sightseeing in the historic city, a place that has sported many names (including Karlsburg, Gyulafehérvár, Erdel Belgradı and Apulum) in its illustrious history. Once a Dacian and then Roman settlement, Alba was later the capital of the Eastern Hungarian Kingdom and then an autonomous principality within Hungary's purview. It is the largest city in the historical region of Transylvania, the "land beyond the forest".

We enjoy a walk around the citadel, a walled hilltop fortress complete with (now dry) moat, drawbridge and period-clad "guards" to entertain the tourists, of which there are several hundred. At moat-level a public square is filled with food stalls offering local produce. There is nothing that quite whets our appetites, although I'm sure the sausages, artisan honey and pastries are perfectly tasty. We make instead for a nearby Italian restaurant, a sudden pizza craving having come upon us (one dish it is impossible to cook in a campervan).

While we are eating on the restaurant's pavement terrace, a thin but reasonably well-dressed man passes by with a small boy in tow. Both of them look hungry and the father holds out a shaking hand. Aradhna hands them the two remaining slices of her pizza and they thank us profusely and walk away, eating happily. We've heard that Romanies are considered something of an underclass in Romania (as they are in the UK too, although we make "amusing" ethnographic reality shows and period dramas about them[1]) and are sometimes mistreated; we wonder if the father and son are gypsies adrift in the city. We feel a little like that ourselves sometimes, although our resources are considerable, compared to the recipients of our casual kindness.

\*\*\*

We can't tarry. Next stop is Cluj-Napoca, to drop off laundry that we'll collect after picking up my father. We also manage an epic Lidl shop – the reliable low-cost supermarket chain has practically fuelled the entirety of my run so far and we like how easy the predictability of goods makes the process of stocking up. My stockpiles of Haribo, piles of pastries and mountain of yoghurts might turn a few shoppers' heads but it keeps us prepared and within budget.

The laundry owner, Vasila, is extremely friendly and talkative and has some rather strong views about Transylvania's superiority over the rest of Romania. He has the same sort of loathing for Bucharest that northerners or Scots often profess for London (until circumstances drive them there and they learn to make peace with the teeming millions, ludicrous house prices and general sense of entitlement). We want to know why he feels so ardently patriotic towards the long-disputed region. He relates a story about an encounter in the capital with a rude bus driver, where the casual disinterest he experienced made him feel unwelcome. It is a familiar lament – the casual alienation of the city – but evidently this moment affected Vasila deeply.

After retrieving our immaculately dried and folded laundry, we have a welcome / farewell dinner together – pasta and tiramisu – and give Dad the pep talk. We warn him about the dogs, the untrustworthiness of online maps, the scarcity of resources and lack of camping infrastructure. Aradhna talks him through my daily routine, having already sent him an outline of what she daily does for me so detailed that his immediate knee-jerk response is, "Well, he won't be getting that from me."

I don't expect he'll be quite so assiduously patient or as well-organised as Aradhna, who is exceptional in those respects. However,

---

1    *My Big Fat Gypsy Wedding* (Channel 4) and *Peaky Blinders* (BBC).

I do trust that, having looked after me before on an epic run, he'll know something of what to expect.

That said, on our length-of-Britain run, we stayed in comfortable bed and breakfast places or hotels, with all-you-can-eat breakfast buffets (or at least, that was how I interpreted them). This time round, Dad will have few of his expected creature comforts. No television, hot showers or en suite lavatory. Before I was born, Mum and Dad lived in a mobile home in Loanhead, near Edinburgh, and a static caravan in Bungay, Suffolk, while Dad worked for a local printer. They were in such basic accommodation for five years. That said, their little trailer in the late sixties still boasted three rooms and a toilet (albeit a chemical one that needed to be emptied by hand).

Our camping is an order of magnitude more basic. We had family holidays when I was little, in our VW campervan (of the kind that hipsters now revere and which regularly change hands for £15,000 online). We always stayed at campsites; there had been no true "wild" camping, despite the fact that it is legal in Scotland.

Aradhna and I have to allay Dad's fears whilst ensuring that he follows the daily plan and remembers the cycle of chores and mundane checks that will ensure the adventure progresses smoothly. Ideally, we would have had Dad there for a couple of days while he learnt the ropes from Aradhna, but the timings of the flights don't allow for an overlap. I can see Aradhna becoming emotional as she talks Dad through everything. Despite the stresses and strains this experience has put her through daily, she doesn't want to miss a substantial part of the adventure, especially in a country as foreign and fascinating as Romania. It can't be helped though; her family need her.

We sleep that night in a busy car park by the river Someşul, taking a bit of a risk as we have to raise the roof so that Aradhna and I can sleep there, while my dad snores downstairs. A group of kids decide to spend an hour or so driving "doughnuts" in their cars but they leave by midnight and we pass a fitful night's sleep.

*** 

At 4:45am, the sky is a vivid red wound as the sun blooms over the still river. I rise uncharacteristically early to drive Aradhna to the airport. In the car park outside the terminal, Aradhna throws her arms wide … around Roxy! Our home on wheels really has become a third character in our story and Aradhna feels she is saying goodbye to two close companions. Inside the terminal, the humans say their emotional goodbyes (I try and fail not to cry in front of my father) and I am left to the tender mercies of Boyter senior. We drive back to Feregi as fast as the traffic will reasonably allow.

*\*\**

The hillside is swathed in mist and very, very green and I am glad that the first Romanian vista Dad will experience is so beautiful. It is 4:15pm by the time I've downed a quick meal of cheese rolls and yoghurt, so I'll have only a half day's running ahead of me today.

I've been fretting a little about Dad's arrival for a while and not just because his appearance signals the loss of my girlfriend for a fortnight. He supported me well during my JOGLE but this trip is significantly more complex and he is three years older now and a little less agile. Plus, like me, he knew little or nothing about Romania before committing to coming here and ignorance often breeds prejudice and inchoate fears.

I skitter down the treacherous muddy descent into the valley, which now seems far longer, more sinister and even more steeped in solitude than it had the previous evening when we drove that way. A wooden forester's hut sits vacant, an empty picnic table in front of it. I even pass the entrance to a small, dark cave but don't dare investigate, although it piques the curious child inside me. It looks cosy, somehow. Were I a bear, I'd move in straight away.

Emerging in early evening light near Cerbăl, I take the 587J as far as Ciulpăz, then head over the hills once more, in the direction of Josani. I seem to be following a drovers' path and have to wait for an immense flock of sheep, driven by several shepherds and their dogs, to cross my path before I can progress. The sudden appearance behind me of a sporty 4x4 decorated in adventurous decals, helps hurry the animals up and I am finally able to tear downhill to Josani, where Google Maps informs me I'll find another hill road towards Hunedoara.

I run past a rustic wagon and its ever-patient carthorse and head up a gravel roadway that dissipates into a grassy smear. Nevertheless, a battered old hatchback trundles down this numbered "road" towards me and stops by my side. The driver rolls down the window. He is bearing an equally battered hat that somehow makes me assume he's Romani and he talks to me in an inscrutable language that doesn't sound quite like the Romanian I've heard so far. I smile and shake my head, hoping that he is just offering me a lift. I mime that I want to continue up the hillside and he mutters something and leaves me to it.

I later suspect he was trying to warn me off.

Further up the curving, saddle-shaped hillside I can see two encampments of crude shacks with corrugated iron roofs and small animal pens. Unfortunately, although the geese may be fenced in, the dogs are not. From the first shack tears a group of four mongrel dogs, belting towards me, utterly without fear.

I pull Gandalf II from my backback, and bellow at them. At the sound of my voice, a man emerges from the hut and, with some difficulty, calls them back. I walk and then run on, turning now and again, to check that I'm not being followed.

With tiresome predictability now, two more massive, shaggy monsters leap from the second shack, fangs bared, looking more like the direwolves from *Game of Thrones* than domestic dogs. These animals seem more than just pets or guard dogs – these are attack dogs. I turn to face them, stick at the ready. A stout woman, in a colourful dress and headscarf is running towards me too, frantically trying to call the hounds back, anger and fear in her voice, both seemingly directed as much at me as her dogs.

Am I trespassing? It seems so. And yet, this is a marked public roadway, with its own number (119) and not private land. Perhaps the locals have a sort of agreement with the Romanies, to leave one another alone. Ignorant as ever, here am I doing something patently bizarre – running in shorts and a luminous top – across their fields. To the dogs, I am at best impertinent, and at worst, dinner.

My stick looks like it is going to be utterly ineffectual, and the Romani woman is now clearly hurling a volume of abuse my way. I jog past, reluctant to just walk and extend the amount of time I spend near the animals. "Geddaway!" is the only English phrase that rings out amongst a flurry of Romani, this admonishment directed at the dogs, although I do my best to get away.

Unfortunately, whenever I begin to run towards the brow of the hill, the dogs bolt free from their owner to have another go at attacking me. Each time this happens I stop, shouting myself hoarse and waving my stick. Eventually, about 500 metres away from the camp, the dogs give up and turn tail, duty discharged – they have seen me off their land.

Shaken and flooded with adrenalin, I vow not to take any more of these unpaved hillside paths, if this is the kind of reception I am likely to receive. Fortunately, the path takes me quietly down to the village of Pestişu Mic, where I begin to see the lights of Hunedoara shining in the distance. At Pestişu Mare I encounter the spectacularly huge and ugly Arcelor Mittal steelworks, which almost raises hideousness to an artform, and turn south through suburban streets, whose comfortable familiarity erases much of the tension I've been carrying since the canine attacks. I've packed a decent number of kilometres into my four hours of running (34km) and am relieved to reach the relatively civilised environs of a city once more.

***

The rain comes on as I run along a cycle path under the cover of small trees and locate the square where Dad has parked. We decide to treat ourselves to some comfort food as it feels a little bit late to cook. I spot a restaurant called "New Orleans" and we decide to go there for no better reason than my dad being an avid jazz fan. There is, however, no jazz on offer, just piped pop music. I order sausage and bean stew and beer for me and a fried chicken salad for my dad. I recount my experiences at the Romany camp whilst I shovel away the calories. I'm sure Dad wonders what on earth he's gotten himself into. The meal comes to less than £10, which impresses him.

We retire to the same hospital car park we slept in two days ago. Once more, the local kids descend with their cars and bass-bins blaring, like mosquitos to a warm neck, but we are both too tired to move on and sleep comes in due course, erasing all tensions.

***

The following day brings more morning chores – stocking up with food, replacing my now hopelessly worn-out running shoes and solving Dad's communication issues. He had been assured that his phone would work throughout Europe, including the data allowance. Nevertheless, although he can make and receive phone calls, he can't access the internet, meaning that he has no way of tracking my progress on our website. After over an hour talking to Andrei, a very helpful young assistant in a Hunedoara phone shop, we buy a small Wi-Fi hotspot and sim card and are back in action once more.

I don my new, pristine red running shoes and a matching top and feel remarkably fit as I set off in glorious sunshine along leafy suburban streets. After yesterday's stresses, an easy-going day will be most welcome.

I am a little disappointed, given how welcoming and helpful everyone has been lately, to see the whitewashed side of a house sprayed with the slogan, "White revolution is the only solution!" and a little later, on the base of a tower block, "Refugees not welcome". I reflect that there are idiotic racists everywhere and that supportive, inclusive messages are seldom graffitied. More amusingly, the same tower-block boasts the "London Cafe". I am not able to stop and check if they sell bacon butties and tea in chipped mugs, but I hope so.

It seems that I'll be running a largely urban route today, so I leave Gandalf II behind. Sod's Law of course decrees that Google Maps will send me immediately back out into the countryside. I am hesitant to do so, but at least this "road" looks more heavily driven, though still basically a dirt track. A few half-constructed houses stand at the base of the hills and two men working in a yard offer me some water from a hosepipe. My backpack full, I decline, but it is nice of them to offer and at this stage, any encouragement helps alleviate my fears of running across open country.

I pass one farm, but the two dogs that run at me are quickly called back by an attentive farmer and by now, I am becoming a little inured to canine assault. The hill track descends to Batiz, where I rejoin the tarmac. Crossing a state border into the Băcia province, I run a road lined with many flags, then a 13km-stretch in which I pass six separate roadside memorials. Despite the vehicular manslaughter in evidence, I am encouraged to see that walking alongside major roads is not at all unusual in Romania. I later learn that it is relatively common for poorer people not to own a car. It feels good to have some perambulatory companionship, if only in passing.

After a short break in the highway for a bit of Kendal Mint Cake, I battle on along the small strip of gravel at the edge of the road, facing down oncoming traffic. Every so often, someone honks their horn, sharply and quickly, and not prompted by anything other than my presence. It doesn't seem like the drivers are angry as much as concerned and gently supportive. I begin to relax and even enjoy the monotony of feet pounding tarmac. I notice the hills rising into something more spectacular to the south – the Carpathians. If all goes well, I'll be there within a couple of days.

\*\*\*

As I climb gently towards the brow of a hill, a strange sculpture hoves into view on the horizon – an immense horn raised point-first to the heavens. A monster's tooth?

It marks the site of a reconstructed ancient village settlement, comprising several stone huts and religious buildings arranged in a grassy field by the main road. There are no interpretive boards in multiple languages to help me make sense of it, yet it is impressively constructed. Only two other people – a young couple – are perusing the unfinished attraction and I do a brief circuit, peering into primitive dwellings like a visitor from space; I then return to my road. I don't know it yet, but I have had my first encounter with the ancient Dacians, the Transylvanians who preceded the Romans in this region.

A services sign is incongruously labelled "Arsenal Park", although not I suspect in a tribute to the Gunners[1]. A little while later, my tarmac-bruised feet pass the immense Orăştie sign (this region's town signs put other Romanian communes to shame) and I long to stop for lunch.

I find Dad parked near a police station in a leafy public square. Following Aradhna's instructions, Dad has laid on an epic spread and I wolf down pastries, cheese rolls, yoghurts, biscuits and fruit until I feel sufficiently refuelled to battle on. I am impressed; Dad has done well. On the other hand, he tells me that earlier that morning he managed to leave the interior lights on for hours, flattening the battery. A local couple helped provide the necessary jump start and Dad took their photo as a keepsake. He has survived his first calamity well.

Having run 20km before lunch, we decide that 14km more would be adequate for the afternoon. I am finding that a roughly 60/40 percentage split for morning/afternoon sessions works best for me. Stopping for lunch and then having to run an equal distance on a full stomach and leaden legs, would not have worked.

In Orăştie, a cobbled pedestrian precinct leads to a fearsome public sculpture of a wolf's head, not a reference to the dangerous street dogs, but a symbol of ancient Dacia, found on much of the gold jewellery which has been unearthed in recent decades in the region.

Just 30km away, the pre-Roman capital city Sarmizegetusa once stood, which I'd written about in a horror spec-script called *Legion of Shadows*. In the supernatural action-driven tale, I'd pitted a lost scouting party of Roman legionnaires and Dacian barbarians against a host of seven-foot-tall vampires. It'd been great fun to write but my research had not, alas, included a trip to Dacia. Perhaps now we'll have a chance to rectify that. As I run past a signpost indicating the road to the archaeological site of the remaining city ruins, I formulate a plan.

The road towards the hills continues – straight, increasingly

---

1    It is in fact a leisure attraction featuring the incongruous juxtaposition of a waterpark and a battery of decommissioned tanks and field guns (a military museum).

humming with traffic, and more than a little dull. I take moments of diversion where I can. A rundown roadside bar which resembles a seedy brothel, a small red-painted steam engine with a fly-strewn dead dog lying on the grass in front of it, a grey-green AgroSem factory; these provide some fuel for my fervent imagination while my legs drive me mechanically on.

A road sign at one junction directs motorists towards Bucharest via two different directions, Sebeș and Sibiu. We've already decided on Sibiu via our first official Romanian campsite at a village just off the main road. Fortunately, the old 7 road twists around the newer A1 motorway, giving me a more manageable route to run.

Eventually, I come to the entrance to the village named after the famous airman, Aurel Vlaicu. A reconstruction of one of his early rubber-band powered test gliders perches atop the town sign. It reminds me of the little balsa wood planes I'd tossed around as a kid, powered by an elastic band attached to the propellor and tightly wound behind it. Vlaicu is famous enough to have a university named after him, in Arad, as well as being featured on the reverse of the 50 Lei note. I don't know any of this when I take a left into the little village and I certainly don't expect my own modest fame to precede me.

I have forgotten Dad's tendency to tell all and sundry about his son's excessive running exploits, a habit he formed on my JOGLE. It had been helpful then, since people would clap as I ran by and call me by name, encouraging me towards each day's finish line. Here it mildly perplexes me as I pass my father, and turn into the campsite, only to be greeted by an excited woman who wants me to pose for a photo with her.

She's the campsite owner and Dad has told her all about my 3400km challenge. I am happy to oblige and it's nice to have some brief company, having spoken to almost nobody all day. I then have a hugely welcome shower. That night, I realise that everything will be okay – Dad can handle this. So long as no calamities occur, we'll survive Romania and my eastward odyssey will continue unabated.

**KILOMETRES TRAVELLED: 2328;**
**KILOMETRES REMAINING: 1070**

# Tips for Multi-Day Runners – 7. Pacing

How seriously you pay attention to the pace at which you are running depends on several factors:

1. *Whether the journey is predicated upon reaching a specific place by the end of each day*
2. *Whether you are attempting to hit an overall time target or beat a record of some sort.*
3. *Whether, to be frank, it really matters at all.*

Ultimately, so long as you are running at a pace brisker than a fast walk, you are achieving something singular, something that very few (if any) will have attempted before you. That's your baseline achievement and you'll have a happier experience if you accept the almost certain truth that you will run slower than you expect to.

In training and planning stages, it's easier to make blue sky assumptions about pace ("I run 8-minute-mile marathons in training so I should certainly be able to hit 9-10-minute miles"). I know – I've made this mistake myself. Running all day, every day, takes its toll. I found that achieving a 10-12-minute-mile pace on average made me enjoy the experience significantly more than if I'd hammered out 8-minute miles and then collapsed midway into the second week.

However, if you do want to stick to a specific pace, remember to take into account cumulative fatigue, unfamiliar and unpredictable terrain and the little breaks you will have to take to navigate, refill water, take photographs, and so forth. I found it helpful to identify "gears" – set paces I could recognise and slip in and out of (i.e. a brisk walk is first gear, a slow jog is second gear, etc). When I found myself fatigued and slipping down into first, I'd make a conscious effort to add "bounce" to my step, taking me up to second gear and the minimum acceptable pace I'd set for myself.

A rule of thumb I adopted was to run at a pace where, were someone with me, I could have held a faltering conversation. This means your cardiovascular system isn't overstretched and can therefore keep going, potentially for hours. That said, if you experience an attack of "rocket legs" and your body urges you to pick up the pace and fly, then go for it. The body knows best what it wants and can handle.

# Chapter 19: Legion of Shadows

### Day 72

I've run many Roman roads, both in Britain and all across Europe, but I've never seen anything quite like this – a thirty-metre by ten-metre rectangle of moss-coated, square blocks, laid in a pristine pavement, with a higher kerb, perfectly flat but angled downhill towards the main Sarmizegetusa site.

A layer of turf and earth, laid down by the passing millennia, has been dug away to reveal exactly what a Roman thoroughfare really resembled, and it is even more impressive than I'd imagined, and incredibly well-preserved. The blocks themselves seem so perfectly cube-shaped that they could have been cut with a circular saw.

Dad and I stand under the tall, thin trees of the forested hillside that comprises the Sarmizegetusa Regia site, admiring ancient Roman construction. We rose unusually early, around 6:30am, in order to drive the 47km from Aurel Vlaicu to here. We took a long, winding road into the hills, then parked with only two other vehicles and began walking up a cobbled lane to the archaeological site. There are only four other people there this early in the morning, but a security guard shadows us as we walk through the impressive Dacian perimeter walls and into the stronghold.

At the foot of the Roman road, a clearing, more modest in size than we were expecting, contains all that remains of the capital of the Dacian peoples. Labelled barbarians by the Romans, because they followed other gods, the Dacian people had more in common with the Romans than most far-flung races incorporated into the empire. For one thing, Emperor Trajan believed his own people came from the same stock as the Dacians, and was thereby even keener to bring them under the aegis of Rome. When one military campaign and a round of dictatorial diplomacy failed, a second campaign resulted in the sack of Sarmizegetusa and an execution for the rebel King Decebalus. The people were deported and Trajan built his own Dacian capital 40km away at a site now known as Ulpia Traiana Sarmizegetusa.

There is much evidence that the Dacians, far from being a barbarian people, were just as sophisticated as their conquerors. The design and construction of the variously circular or rectangular structures appeared geometrical and orderly, although little remained but the bases of columns and piles of dressed stone. Nevertheless, archaeologists have unearthed many ceramic and metal objects that point to a developed society, including jewellery, sickles, pruning hooks, ploughshares and even medical tweezers.

The most mysterious aspect of the site is a round dais with a single catwalk of stone projecting from it, sometimes referred to as the "andesite sun"[1]. There is some speculation that this contained a sundial and that the Dacians were influenced by Hellenistic geometry and astronomy. Personally, I find the perfectly straight and still functional drainage channels to be just as fascinating, since they still serve to carry groundwater away from the sacred site almost two thousand years on, although their ceramic pipes have long been destroyed or purloined.

While Dad and I visit, a bespectacled young man is using an odd collection of white spheres on miniature tripods and a tablet, to create a virtual 3D laser reconstruction of the site. It will take him several weeks, he admits. Our curiosity gets the better of us and we corner him with questions.

"Believe it or not, only about 5% has been excavated so far," the archaeologist reveals. Just last week, they found a store of Dacian jewellery."

A cache of gold torcs and other precious artefacts, engraved with the archetypal Dacian wolf's head, were found. Apparently, the Dacians took to melting down Roman gold coins since they could trade more widely (presumably, beyond the Empire) with the resulting precious metal. Oh, to have a metal detector, and to be able to slip from the prying eyes of our ever-present guard.

The archaeologist tells us that the skulls of wolves have been discovered adapted into headpieces, with bone flutes attached to create a howling sound. This might have explained why Trajan had to fight more than one battle against the Dacians – the sight of mounted cavalry wielding large curved scimitars, wearing wolf-masks and howling whilst bearing down upon the legions must have proven terrifying, even to an army as disciplined as the Romans.

We spend an hour and a half exploring the site but I feel the old

---

1    Andesite is an igneous, volcanic rock similar to basalt.

restlessness building up; once again, this is beginning to resemble a holiday of sorts, when it is supposed to be a feat of endurance, isn't it? Still, as we head back down to Roxy to resume our adventure I feel vindicated in setting my horror/action movie here – it is an atmospheric and fascinating place.

*\*\**

The E86 road to Sebeş seems considerably more prosaic after our discoveries in the forests of Transylvania. Nevertheless, like a legion on the march, I have to press on. Behind me, black storm clouds are gathering, lending a sense of drama. I have 27km to run to Sebeş and that ought to be quite manageable. That said, the road is relentlessly straight and comparatively featureless and I have a two-foot-wide strip of tarmac and gravel between me and the white line indicating the edge of the main road. Like they did in Austria, the mountains ahead of me seem to be teasing me with their refusal to arrive.

*\*\**

An insalubrious-looking roadside establishment ahead of me seems to be a local pick-up spot for prostitutes and their clients. A young woman in an extremely short skirt stands talking to a driver through his window, then gets in and they roar off as I approach. Occasionally, I spot a tractor-path in a neighbouring field and manage to hop off the hot tarmac for a little while, to run alongside scatterings of poppies and leap over puddles. Some sections of the road, particularly on long, arcing bends, are hemmed in by crash barriers and I clamber over these and run on the top of the embankment, behind the protective metal. Anything to get me away from the ludicrously-speeding traffic.

A concrete underpass sports a spray-painted slogan and Romanian flag. I've seen it a couple of times already. *Basarabia e Romania!* I later learn that Basarabia (or Bessarabia as it is sometimes spelt), comprising Moldova and part of Ukraine, was ceded to Russia from Romania following the Russo-Turkish war, as part of reparations. Evidently, there is still a movement, among Romanians with long memories, to take it back.

I have a couple of near-misses with cars simply not moving an inch to allow for a pedestrian in the road. It seems like this is not even an established act of courtesy in these parts. I'm not, however, the only traveller without a car.

A pair of covered Romany carts rattle by on the opposite side of the road, each one pulled by a pair of horses. A family peers out at me from under the canvas covering of one wagon and wave, highly amused by my eccentricity. I watch vehicles swerve around the Romanies, almost as if they are invisible until moments before collision. I begin to wonder if some of the victims listed on the dozens of roadside memorials come from the gypsy community. As I near Sebeş, two more wagons pass by, each pulled by two horses, the rear one accompanied by a third horse walking alongside.

My only other encounter is with a skittish dog a few kilometres outside of Sebeş. It cowers away from me at the picnic area at which I stop for a brief rest. I leave it a handful of nuts and raisins and as soon as I leave, the starving animal creeps over to sniff suspiciously at my offerings.

My first impression of Sebeş is that it isn't an overly pretty place but things improve when I reach the town centre, where there are decorative flower-boxes hanging from railings and parades of shops. Dad and I locate a likely camping area by an out-of-town park and hotel, where we pass a relaxingly quiet and undisturbed evening, the first for several days.

***

*Day 73* brings a familiar quandary – whether to press on toward Bucharest via the main roads or take to the hills. We know that, whatever we do, we will have to cross the Carpathian chain of mountains to the south and there are only a few potential crossing points. We decide that to preserve my sanity, and so as not to waste an opportunity for some beautiful scenery, I'll find some sort of trail across the Carpathians. I can't run these horrific roads for much longer.

After a coffee (and loo stop) in a local café/bar overlooking an ornamental pond, I set off south from Sebeş, pausing to admire the unusual ornamentation on the high street – a pair of khaki green field guns. My route immediately sends me over rough ground and around the back of new-built suburban homes.

A young girl of around twelve is running in front of me for a couple of streets, probably not for exercise but either for the fun of it, or because she is late for something. I can't help but notice that she had a good, economical running gait. I hope her school encourages her. I am a firm believer that if a child enjoys running and is good at it, it is a thing to be cherished and nurtured. Unfortunately, my own school did little to support whatever athletic abilities I possessed and I was too shy and timid to push for it. I suspect they are far better at this now, but back in the 1980s you didn't attend Firrhill High School to develop sporting prowess.

My route to the hills takes me past the watchful eyes of a herd of mottled cows. At Petreşti I find a route around the side of a small reservoir before the road forks and presents me with a 50/50 chance of choosing the correct turning. For once, I get it right and run along another miniature flood protection dam by the side of a small river, its banks sprinkled with violets. An elderly man squeaks by on an even older bicycle, turning in the saddle to give me a gap-toothed and curious smile.

I reach Sebeşel and turn back onto the 67C road, the Transalpina, which should carry me through a series of small villages until I hit the Carpathians proper. I will probably not be able to cross the mountains today but hopefully soon I'll find a trailhead or entry point into the forest.

Săsciori proves pretty, a village nestling in the rising valley through which I am running, its homes extending precariously up the rocky hillsides. I begin to sense an alpine influence – larger houses have steeply sloped roofs and a few cars with German plates pass. A Săsciori grocery store displays a handwritten sign advertising German produce. Even the roadside shrines take on a more elaborate form – metal crosses are replaced by miniature chapels, like abandoned dolls' houses.

There are quite a few villagers in evidence, walking along the roadside or at play in their gardens. Perhaps it's the school holidays. Every so often a heavily-laden logging truck tears past, creating a rumbling like distant thunder. The road follows the course of a river, both of them slicing through crumbling walls of reddish mica schist. Iron pyrites (fool's gold) sparkles in folded seams amongst the exposed rock. A green meadow opens up below me south of Căpâlna; rows of brightly-coloured beehives explain the many signs offering *miere*, a common local product. I wonder if the different colour combinations on these boxes are meant to help the bees navigate back to the right hive[1]. Such musings help me resist fatigue – my mind carrying me away from my body into flights of fantasy and speculation.

---

1    Interestingly, bees see the world in terms of three primary colours – blue, green and ultraviolet. It is thought they see red as indistinguishable from green and therefore take longer to home in on red blooms, most of which are bird-pollinated. See: https://www.ncbi.nlm.nih.gov/pmc/articles/PMC521733/

My idyll is a little spoilt by four separate dog "attacks", including one where an elderly lady resting on a wall has to hurl her walking stick at her animal as it runs at me from the undergrowth. I try not to take it personally. A handful of gathered stones works wonders, and I rarely have to throw any. The local dogs have evidently had many stones hurled their way.

At Căpâlna, I also pass my first dam, a grey wall of concrete topped by a striped red and white fence. At Mărtinie, a carved wooden gateway, high enough to let logging trucks pass underneath, stands welcoming visitors to a well-to-do area of painted guest houses and piles of chopped timber ready for home hearths. The expensive cars parked outside make it clear that this is an area of second homes or holiday chalets as well as entrenched locals.

I pause to refuel with peach iced tea and a Mars bar. Still uncertain of the best route across the mountains, I decide to turn off the 67C and head up one of the hillsides towards Jina, where Dad says he will meet me.

The road climbs to Şugag. Its church features a tower whose clock-faces have painted-on hands. At least it will tell the correct time twice a day. Next, I run through a quiet village rather confusingly named Dobra (hadn't I passed through there several days prior?) Things are becoming a little bit strange, when the road to Jina begins to twist and turn its way up a ludicrously steep mountain slope. The switchbacks are tight and I keep to their outside edges to avoid calamity. I maintain a jogging pace as much as possible, reluctant to let the incline reduce me to a walk.

Ten minutes into the climb, I pass a nattily-hatted and weathered man, possibly a shepherd, who is standing at the side of the road. He laughs and says something in Romanian (or perhaps Romani?) and I mime an exaggerated picture of a man struggling to run uphill, probably unnecessarily, since that's exactly what I am doing. About half an hour later, an industrial digger passes, with this man standing on the rear bucket, holding on with one hand and waving with the other as he trundles merrily uphill.

My water unfortunately runs out halfway up the 8km slope; since this is a day when I've not stopped for lunch, I have not refilled it. Fortunately, I come to an ornate spring decorated with a religious frieze, where a chipped blue tin mug serves as my chalice. The water issuing from the pipe is cold and refreshing. Knowing the end of my day is near, I don't fill the bladder – a few restorative gulps should suffice.

I allow myself to half-walk, half-run the remaining few kilometres, pausing briefly at a large white crucifix above the treeline to admire a view of forested valleys and peaks. Ten minutes later I stagger into Jina and see Roxy parked in the sunlight by a house under construction. To the sound of banging hammers, I crash down onto the grass and pull my cap over my eyes while Dad procures a cold drink. I am exhausted but happy – I'll swap the creeping fatigue that mountains bring for the doldrums of A-road running any day. It is so breezy that it takes a pot of water 20 minutes to heat up sufficiently so I can enjoy boiled eggs. In fact, they end up soft-boiled, since the gas runs out midway.

Although it's still early afternoon, we decide to stop. We ought to replace the gas whilst we are in reasonable travelling distance of a major town. Unfortunately, the quest is far from simple. The large Camping Gaz canister is quite unknown here and we collect perplexed looks and indifferent shrugs from Sibiu's Decathlon, a DIY superstore, local garages and even a campsite. A quick call to Aradhna for advice leads her to recommend the two local suppliers listed on the Camping Gaz website. These are both in Sibiu but will now be closed. We park up and vow to do battle again the following day.

There seems to be a music concert winding down and a lot of Hunedoarans, young and old, are enjoying the summer warmth at a nearby complex of cafés and shops. We eat pizza, drink a couple of beers and people-watch. Fortunately, once most of the shops and restaurants close, the locals dissipate, with only the ubiquitous groups of kids loitering, reluctant to return to their families. Eventually, all falls silent in the car park, and nobody bothers us.

\*\*\*

We manage to get up at 7am the following day (my father is an early riser, a trait I have not quite inherited) so we can wander into picturesque Sibiu in search of the elusive camping gas. A medieval wall surrounds the old town, with red stone watchtowers, cobbled streets and pretty fountains.

The impressive town square seems to be gearing up for an outdoor concert, but the crew putting together the seating stalls are the only workers in evidence – none of the cafés open until 9 or 10am. We wander, wait and then eat two of the tiniest continental breakfasts I've ever seen. I have a croissant no bigger than my thumb. I'd need ten such breakfasts to fuel the running day ahead (but we don't have time for seconds). Fortunately the coffee is excellent.

Refreshed, we return to Roxy to fill her water tank and drive to our potential gas suppliers. At both of these, we draw a blank. The only gas for sale comes in miniature cans with a totally different fitting. We have one more lead – a camping supply shop that turns out to be just off the square where we breakfasted two hours ago. It will prove my salvation.

As well as two tiny fold-up gas burners and six small canisters of gas, I buy a hiking map for the section of the Carpathians I'm due to cross. When I describe my plan to hike the ridge heading east then cut south, the shopkeeper, a young but experienced mountaineer, shakes his head vehemently.

"Not a good idea. Peaks will still be deep in snow some places. Weather can turn dramatically. You don't want to be caught out in blizzard without proper gear."

We ask his advice and he unfolds his map and points to the middle of the three road crossings.

"Take this. The more easterly one could still be blocked by snow. This one should be open."

He is pointing at the 67C, which wiggles south from Alba Iulia and Sebeș, passes a couple of reservoirs and emerges out of the mountains at Novaci. It is of course the road I'd started on yesterday, before turning off towards Sugag and Jina. Despite the backtracking required, this route seems eminently sensible. I worry aloud that it might lack the drama of the mountain trails. The shopkeeper shakes his head.

"It is my favourite part of the mountains here. Very beautiful."

**KILOMETRES TRAVELLED: 2374;**
**KILOMETRES REMAINING: 1024**

# Chapter 20: Into the Carpathians

As did I, the Orient Express had to negotiate two major mountain ranges, in its journey east. The Alps were previously crossed by means of the Simplon Pass, a looping, hilly track through France, Switzerland and Italy, negotiated only by carriages pulled by teams of horses. A tunnel was first mooted in 1857 but was not commissioned until 1895, primarily due to the huge feat of engineering proposed – a twelve-mile tunnel through mountains up to 1300 metres in height. Work began in 1898 and the tunnel was finally completed in 1906, dug by teams of men working in temperatures of up to 131°F.

The second range to conquer was, of course, the Carpathians, which the Orient Express crossed by means of a valley through the more modest foothills to the west, skirting the border with Serbia at Orşova, before heading east, passing south of the range. Passengers who had chosen to sit on the left side of the carriages must have had the preferred view, with the mountains rising up in an unbroken wall for two hundred miles.

I missed the opportunity for a simpler route when we decided to head east from Arad instead of south, towards Timişoara. Now, there's nothing for it but to go over the mountains, in all their menacing glory.

\*\*\*

*Day 74*

With the shopkeeper's advice in mind, a radical rethink is required. I try plotting a route from Jina onwards but it makes no sense. To reach the Transalpina (67C) will involve backtracking 8km down the steep hill from Jina and taking the other fork in the road, towards Novaci. I've already run that bit so it will simply waste time. We drive back down to the turn-off instead and I begin my afternoon's running there, heading for the Oaşa reservoir. There are smaller hydroelectric dams en route, with mysterious concrete tunnels bored into the mountainside, presumably leading to control facilities and generators. Overhanging rocks on the roadside add to a sense of danger and I pass numerous signs saying *cazare*, evidently some sort of holiday rental property[1].

Smaller streams run from tributary valleys and there are meadows dotted with individual houses and caravans belonging to the alpine farmers. I wonder what life must be like here, surrounded by nature in all its various moods but comparatively cut off from shops and services (sometimes literally cut off, when the heavy snowfall comes). Locals must have to do a lot of pre-planning for inclement weather, stocking up on fuel, canned and dried goods or storing up spring water for the dry spells.

Occasionally, groups of bikers roar past, this evidently being a popular motorcycle touring route. This makes sense of all the "biker friendly" signs I've seen in the shops and cafés at lower altitude. Empty logging trucks trundle by, heading uphill as full ones speed down towards me at breakneck pace. I notice that the potholes and cracks in the road surface are largely on the left-hand side of the road as I climb, because this is the side the most heavily-laden vehicles use.

Craning my neck as I run, I see spindly pines projecting up cliffs a hundred feet high, with rocky bluffs protruding from them, the perfect spot for a timber wolf to howl at the moon. The ravine has deepened suddenly, closing in on me like a sinister smile. I feel safe from bears, mostly, because the traffic is frequent enough to scare them off, or so I assume. I encounter just one dog, a scavenger emerging from the bushes but running from my imaginary stones. Its barks echo from rockface to rockface.

Every so often, a spring gushes from a small spout at the side of the road, a concrete siding spray-painted with an arrow and the word "APA"; no *keine trinkwasser* here. The weather is comparatively cool so I don't drink much, but it is good to know that refills are on hand if I need them. Above one of these springs there stands a faded, framed print of the last supper, postcards of saints wedged in behind the weathered gilt frame.

At Tău Bistra I pass my first proper reservoir. I expect to see Dad there, but he's somehow managed to drive past the large body of standing water without noticing it and is 20km uphill at the next reservoir. Our communication is further complicated by having only limited and intermittent phone signal, unsurprising given the terrain. Since I am running well, I don't really mind missing the scheduled lunch stop. It will be good to rack up a few more kilometres.

I run past a few closed concession stands but not over the dam

---

1    It translates most simply as "accommodation".

itself – that road would lead me deep into the mountains and towards the east, via more artificial lakes. Instead I take a southerly route alongside the water, which I can only occasionally make out through dense vegetation to my left. Warning signs prepare me for bumps in the road (not a problem) and falling rocks (more of a worry) for a mere 30km.

However, the afternoon's running remains pleasantly picturesque as I rise higher into the pinewoods and eventually emerge from the shaded roadway by some smartly whitewashed buildings with rows of motorbikes and cars parked outside. There is a view down to a sparkling body of water, trapped in the ravine. This wasn't the Oaşa reservoir yet but just the most southerly extent of Tău Bistra.

I come to a grateful halt outside the Popasul Regelui restaurant and guest house, where a beer garden beckons invitingly. I call Dad, who has driven on to locate a likely camping spot. After some difficulty communicating with the staccato phone signal, I give him my location. He drives back down the 67C to find me tucking into beer and a plate of fries.

***

Dad is quite excitable as we bump up the road again and round what will no doubt be some challenging hairpins, to Oaşa. Several times larger than Tău Bistra, this reservoir has many more holiday chalets and concession stands around its roadside perimeter, although these are closed as the summer season is a month or more away. Dad tells me he has met some other eccentric long-distance pedestrians, two Belgian hikers called Joka and Björn and their "pack" of three dogs[1], which pulled a sled loaded with their possessions, including a tiny tent. They have been "walking the pack" for over eight months and logging their adventures across eight countries on a website. Dad is eager for me to meet them, although he can see I am tired and not especially keen to socialise.

We pull off the main road and head up a rough track to a clearing where it is evident many people have camped before. Aside from the litter, much of which we later clear, there is a frame lashed together from branches enclosing what would have been a small room, with scraps of tarpaulin clinging to it and shelving wedged between tree limbs. There are signs of cooking fires having been made and even a

---

1    Named Kamiel (a dobrador), Thor (Siberian husky) and Nazca (white shepherd). See https://walkthepackpackthewalk.wordpress.com/ for more on their exploits.

makeshift loo (a plank with a hole) which we decline to use in favour of the time-honoured freshly-dug pit. As we come to a rest, I could see the khaki tent of our fellow travellers and two of their dogs lazing in the dying heat of the day.

Joka, angular and bronzed, her blonde hair weather-tousled, is preparing to feed the animals while Björn rests (with the remaining dog for company). She tells us he has not been feeling well lately but might appear from the tent soon. Once I hear their story, I know it would be great to get an interview for Aradhna's film. Their version of "home" would surely prove unique. I decide to ask them tomorrow morning if we might capture their story on video.

Dad and I make camp a respectful distance away and the following day, we meet Björn, who seems much-improved, flashing a wry smile beneath a mop of unruly hair. He too has the rangy look of the eternal pedestrian, all limbs and energy efficiency. The couple are happy to talk on camera with great enthusiasm about their notion of what makes a place a home. For them, it boils down to just two ingredients, it seems – wide open spaces and their dogs. Both have given up challenging, mental health jobs, providing companionship animals for vulnerable adults. Now their own dogs are providing them with their own sort of therapy.

\*\*\*

The following day begins with a walk down to the lakeside, where the perfectly still water mirrors the forests on the other side with complete clarity. I am looking forward to crossing the mountains, over the next couple of days. It feels like once I am on the downhill section of the main Carpathian ridge, I will be entering the (albeit almost 1000-mile-long) final straight of my challenge. There won't be any mountains as significant as these between here and Istanbul. I must savour the coming days.

\*\*\*

After conducting our interview with Joka and Björn (with my father's main contribution being absent-mindedly wandering into shot several times), we prepare to leave. Before I head off, Björn suggests Dad and I walk with the pack for a video clip for their social media and we gladly agree. I am surprised by how easily the dogs pull the heavily-laden, wheeled sled. We continue for a few yards then wave them on their way and go back to the clearing to break camp. Dad drives me back down to the hotel to begin my ascent to Oaşa. I'll have a constant uphill section of 21km to run to get back to where we spent the night.

I enjoy a steady pace as the road climbs past more hydroelectric stations, steep cliff-faces and half-hidden chalets. The weather is so perfectly warm and the river to my right so inviting that I half-expect to see a whole family of bears playing there, tormenting the fish. I still can't decide whether I want this experience more than I fear it but for now at least, I am the only carnivore in sight. Purple thistles, of a variety I've not seen before, bristle by the roadside as I run under the dappled shade of overhanging trees.

No bears are to be seen but I do pass some extremely free-range cows clopping their way along the road and munching the verges. I wonder if they have escaped from a pasture somewhere or perhaps the road simply passes through their domain and cow perambulation is entirely normal here.

I run past the chalets and trinket stalls by the dam, slowing to bypass a dog that hops out of a sentry booth at its far end. Neither the man inside nor his dog are much bothered by my presence, fortunately. I pass our clearing and camping spot from the previous night, where Dad has re-parked, imagining that I might stop there for lunch. I want to press on because my legs feel good and the route around the reservoir will be reasonably flat. We decide that he'll wait 90 minutes and then drive to catch me up and we'll stop wherever I get to.

A signpost directs me to the next place of human habitation – Obarsia Lotrului – 23km away. I hope I might make it that far today after lunch but the great benefit of having Roxy with us is that it doesn't really matter. We can sleep wherever fate (and my protesting body) carry me. The road continues around one full side of the lake, climbing a little way above the water to give a spectacular view from a parking area where some local has daubed the word "ALICE", without further editorialising. What does it mean? Perhaps only Alice would know. Yellow and orange wildflowers sprout in vivid clumps on the lip of the cliff high above the water.

I have become quite relaxed about the rumoured bears until I pass a piece of folky art daubed as a warning on a rock face. A plaid-clad fisherman is depicted obliviously enjoying his day while a massive bear creeps up behind him with bared fangs and huge curved claws. Excellent, I think, before resuming my odd habit of singing doggerel whilst turning corners. I run alongside the most perfect fishing spot for bears, a tumbling river with many flat rocks to perch upon. A little later I spot a fisherman whose English is rudimentary at best. I try to mime an angry bear and ask if the fisherman knows of any in the area. I am not reassured by his cheery, "Oh, yes!" said with a smile that suggests he thinks I am actively seeking them.

The traffic, save the occasional logging truck, remains light. I reach a steeply curving road where several pine trees, listing into the road, seem on the verge of collapsing altogether. I know the feeling. Dad catches up with me conveniently close to a lay-by, opposite which is a shack of some sort. A minivan pulls up and a man steps out with two plastic buckets and vanishes into the trees behind the house, re-emerging a little later with water, then drives off. Dad goes to investigate, taking our water carrier, but returning to declare that the stream is of questionable hygiene. In such matters you have to, perhaps literally, follow your gut instinct.

We drive in search of a camping spot for the night and find it about 8km further up the mountain, where the road finally plateaus and there is another mysterious log cabin, locked and seemingly uninhabited. We pull in by the side of the house and set about making camp. There is just one snag – the electronically-operated roof sleeping compartment will not rise. It lifts about three-quarters of the way then grinds to a halt with a low whine. This is a significant problem. If we can't keep the roof up I'll be forced to top and tail with my father, not something a 47-year-old is especially keen to do.

We improvise. I find a stout branch and measure how long it needs to be to act as a prop for the roof. My dad suggests leaning it against the side of the cabin and hitting it with a sharp rock to break it. This proves highly ineffectual, catapulting the rock towards me instead, like a missile. My father has mixed experiences with DIY; he once managed to rupture his own ear drum with a sound wave projected back at him from a long plank he'd hit with a hammer[1].

I remember that I have a small Leatherman tool in our "useful things" box, which contains a small saw. My dad is sceptical but I manage to cut through the branch in about five minutes. Wedged in place, it provides sufficient reassurance that the roof won't collapse on me and I get a reasonable night's sleep.

---

[1]  This is the strangest injury story in our family since I once managed to cut myself with coffee. I was cleaning the inside of a glass coffee pot, in the café bar where I worked. I'd left the hotplate on overnight and the liquid had boiled away, leaving a hard layer of shellac-like dried coffee adhered to its base. As I scrubbed, frantically trying to atone for my error, a shard sheared off and sliced through my thumb.

\*\*\*

I say "reasonable" because I am awoken around 5am by what I am convinced is a bear snuffling around Roxy, possibly looking for a way to climb up into the flimsy canvas structure on the roof and investigate the intriguing smells of last night's dinner (vegetable and mushroom omelette). I hear snorting and what my imagination assures me are wet, throaty breaths. Something does seem to be moving outside the van, but unzipping just a section of the canvas and peeking out, I can see nothing moving in the pale blue dawn light. Suddenly, there is an especially loud snort and I decide I'd be better off in the hard metal interior of the van. I alarm my dad (whose snoring almost certainly constitutes the "bear" sounds I have been hearing), by dropping through the ceiling trapdoor in my pants.

"I'm coming down!" I shout. "I think there's bears outside."

"Don't be daft," my father counters, but tolerates my intrusion in good grace, possibly flashing back to those times in my childhood when a nightmare prompted a similar privacy invasion.

When we both emerge after breakfast, there are no signs of inquisitive bears, although we are far from experts in ursine spoor. My worries are almost certainly unfounded but we discover we have more concrete problems. There is a fairly obvious reason why the roof has not opened properly – our main battery is almost completely dead. What power remained we squandered on the LED lights last night; now only a pitiful clonking sound accompanies any attempt to start the van or lower the roof.

We are in the middle of the remote Carpathians, potentially surrounded by bears, without a functioning form of transport. Oh dear.

**KILOMETRES TRAVELLED: 2403;**
**KILOMETRES REMAINING: 995**

# Tips for Multi-Day Runners – 8. Nutrition

I'm far from a nutritional expert (see Appendix III for an example of my daily calorific intake) but I have come to a few basic conclusions about what works during multi-day running challenges.

1. *Eat what you want.* This isn't quite as dumb as it sounds. After burning thousands and thousands of calories per day for many days, your body will literally tell you what it is craving. If you're low on electrolytes, you may find yourself craving salty snacks, if you're sugar-deficient, you'll be fantasising about sweets and cakes and if your vitamin or fibre levels are down, you'll want some vegetables. Listen to what your body is telling you.

2. *Eat smart.* This may seem a direct contradiction to the above point, but ensure you have a balance of the 5 food groups in what you eat each day. At times, the constant agitation of your gut may make you nauseous. This might tempt you to skip food or be selective but try to be a little clever about it. If the thought of crunchy vegetables turns your stomach, try pulping them into a soup. If you feel you have no saliva with which to digest anything dry (as happened to me a lot in hot conditions) try starting a meal with cut-up pieces of soft fruit (watermelon and strawberries, for instance). There are usually clever ways to make almost anything palatable and this is a key area in which your support crew (if you have any) can help immeasurably.

3. *Eat little and often.* If you can't stomach a full meal at lunchtime, make sure you take a lot of snacks with you and top up your calorific reserves frequently. Eat small bites with plenty of water if you want to keep moving.

4. *Try energy gels.* Although a little grim, these sugary supplements slip down easily and deliver focused calories in large quantities when you need it most. For multi-day trips you'll want to use them as supplements for demanding days, rather than as substitutes for solid food.

5. *Don't eat too late.* Try to have your evening meal and snacks no later than an hour and a half before you go to bed. This will aid sleep and digestion.

6. *Don't skip breakfast!* In fact, have two breakfasts, one as soon as possible after you rise and one around an hour before you set off. Wholemeal granola with fresh fruit is my go-to morning meal – it works wonders.

7. *Never miss dessert* – this is one time in your life where, if you have a sweet tooth, you can indulge without fear of weight gain or ill health. Your body will burn through those calories with no difficulty at all. I swear by Scottish fudge or tablet – it's basically condensed milk and sugar.

These tips come with the usual caveat that you should consult your GP or a professional nutritionist if you want to make significant changes to your diet. Also bear in mind that, when you do finally reach the end of your journey, weaning yourself off such feats of gluttony will be challenging in its own right.

# Chapter 21: Farewell Roxy

*Day 76*

My life is measured out in vehicular calamity. In my early teens I remember my father's chagrin when he realised he had filled our car up with diesel instead of petrol, just outside of Saint Etienne in France. It was Easter Sunday, pouring with rain, and we were extremely lucky to find a garage whose owner left his family brunch to open just for us and flush out the engine in the downpour, saving our holiday.

Aged 18, I had a blow-out on the motorway, and wrote off my first car (not to mention terrifying three passengers) by colliding with and destroying the crash barrier, and most of the embankment we finally came to rest upon. It was my first brush with potential fatality.

My JOGLE was interspersed with support vehicles stranded on ramps, in ditches or untenable wet driveways, or rattling along with warning lights flashing and spark plugs failing.

Today's tribulation is nothing new, therefore, and my father and I quickly move from lamentation to the practical problem of how to get us quickly back on the road. We need another jump start, the third of this trip. I have a sudden brainwave, wondering if we can draw power from the leisure battery to the starter motor. I use our jump cables to connect the two, wait a few minutes and turn the key.

Success! We get the engine running, quickly put the roof down and head back to the Popasul Regelui hotel. We can't risk Dad driving around in a vehicle with a battery that keeps discharging, seemingly at random, particularly in the middle of the Carpathian Mountains. The drive down to Tău Bistra gives Roxy a 45-minute chance to recharge her battery, but on arrival, when we turn her off and try to restart her, the same problem ensues – the starter motor can't draw enough power. We realise it might be the starter, perhaps the alternator, rather than the battery. I call Aradhna, who tells me where to locate the number of our European breakdown service, affiliated with the RAC. Our cover is comprehensive and will allow for a tow, full service and replacement vehicle, although this is unlikely to be a campervan.

The saga begins. We wait four hours and the French office admits they have not yet ordered the tow truck, despite me having given detailed directions and a description of the model, measurements and likely weight of our vehicle. I am assured it will arrive soon ("within 45 minutes"). It does not. An astonishing 20 phone calls later, with Aradhna joining in from England and my dad helping out when I become too infuriated to speak, we are assured that a tow truck will be with us "within the next three hours". Part of the problem is the chain of phone calls flying back and forth between the UK RAC, their European partners' head office in France and the local recovery services in Romania. Lots of promises are being made but it appears nobody but us is checking those promises are being kept. I have to ask several times if a courtesy car is on order and where we might pick it up. Even when the tow truck finally appears, twelve hours after it was first promised, as we are having dinner in the hotel and trying to block out the sounds of hilariously bad 80s Europop coming over the sound system, we still have no idea where we are sleeping. The breakdown service did not realise we need a hotel.

***

Watching Roxy being pulled up onto the flatbed trailer is an emotional moment. It feels almost like a member of our family is sick, the diagnosis and prognosis unknown. We are driven at alarming speed in the tow truck around the twisting road to Alba Iulia, where the nearest garage that could handle our vehicle is based. The journey takes around two hours and we are nodding off by the time we pick up our replacement vehicle – a white Skoda – and drive to the hotel we finally persuaded the RAC to book for us.

I've lost a day's running and the future of the trip is in question. We have no idea if Roxy can be saved and our budget will not support 30-plus nights in hotels. Our cover will only compensate us for seven nights and we'll have to return the courtesy car within that time too.

***

The drive back to the mountains the following day gives me a rare insight into how far I've come and the dramatic nature of what I am doing, as we retrace my running route from Sebeș to the lay-by where I stopped running two days prior. It feels like an even more epic distance driven in the Skoda, oddly enough, than it did running.

We had an odd breakfast experience. Not all Romanian hotels do buffet-styled morning spreads so we have to choose from a menu instead. Neither my dad nor myself are that into cooked breakfasts or cold meat in the morning so I order cereal (chocolate flakes swimming in at least a pint of milk) then pancakes and a fruit cocktail to finish. Dad embarrasses me a little by ordering exactly the same thing (although I have absolutely no idea why this is an issue). The waiter's expression makes it clear that we are both lunatics. Nevertheless, I get the calories I need and Dad enjoys his unusually filling breakfast. He'll probably need it – supporting an ultrarunner in the mountains can be a taxing challenge.

I start my run up the rest of the curving road to the camping spot where it all went wrong. Every so often, I spy my dad from the roadside, taking pictures, or videoing me on his phone. It is good to have him there, since I am still a little worried about bears. I stop for a sneaky squat in a ditch by a sort of tunnel under the road and it is only when I am filling in the hole I've scraped out amongst the rubble that I realise the tunnel is probably to help bears and other animals pass surreptitiously under the 67C. I jump out of there with much haste.

The uphill stretch lasts for 3.5km and then, as the sky begins to turn a stormy tobacco hue, the road levels and leads me on a steep, bone-jolting descent as the massing clouds pour buckets of icy rain over me. A thick mist makes the hillsides recede in stepped diagonals as I shorten and quicken my pace to prevent calamity. A slip on wet tarmac here, or twisted ankle, will ruin my day. A few cars drive past, foglights on, their drivers no doubt wondering who this madman is belting down the road. It has turned remarkably cold and I tuck my thumbs into my palms and run faster, to maintain my core temperature.

The weather breaks as I reach the bottom of a wide forested valley and a junction with the 7A heading west to east. When I'd plotted out the route back in London I'd planned to run this road, past the largest artificial lake in Romania, the Lacul Vidra. Although no doubt a picturesque road in its own right, I decide to stick to the plan, even though Dad chooses the moment to call me with a warning.

"The road ahead goes up and up and up. It's really steep and really long," he offers, helpfully. What kind of weird pep talk is this? I am not to be dissuaded, although Dad offers to drive back down to meet me.

"I feel fine. I'll keep going," I say.

I don't want to wait in the rain and, although there is one souvenir shop and a café open nearby, they don't look massively inviting and

I have mountains to run. I turn west along the 7A, then south on the next portion of the Transalpina. Enlarging the map on my phone, I can see the line of the road ahead double back on itself dozens of times, as if it had been obsessively folded. My quads had better get used to climbing.

I traverse a wide, flat valley, through which a river meanders, cutting off miniature oxbows and stranding tiny islets. It's surrounded by young conifer forest and looks like a perfect playground for bears looking for lunch. For once I am unequivocally keen to see some, ideally romping on the far side of the river. There are none to be seen, however, and I feel disappointed. As if bears aren't worrying enough, a notice pinned to a tree warns of "vipers" and contains a useful illustration of the scaly menace. I'll have to watch my step even more carefully than usual.

A few kilometres further on, I begin to hit the section where the hairpin bends begin and rapidly climb above the treeline. Blue-grey peaks surface from the pines, dotted with snowdrifts, their ridges lost in layered veils of cloud so that each successive peak pales further into nothingness than the one before it. As the road begins to snake upwards, I defer the moment when I will have to walk, arbitrarily deciding that I'll continue at a run all the way to the top. Admittedly, this will be a very slow run – probably no faster than eight minutes per kilometre – but it feels important to prove to myself that my legs still have what it takes to make this a running challenge, rather than an extended hike.

My heart pounds and my breathing quickens as the various muscle groups go into overdrive to push me up the dramatically concertinaed roadway. The traffic here is a little heavier than I've experienced so far, but motorists are crawling along, scarcely faster than I am, as they negotiate the fearful bends, most of which are accompanied by steep drops with little more than the occasional boulder to mark the edge of the safe strip of wet tarmac. Occasionally a horn sounds, a driver alerting me to their presence, or just expressing how impressed they are to see me running towards the top of the mountains.

The air grows cooler, the climate at this altitude more wintry than springlike. I pass cows munching their unending breakfast. The bovines turn a lazy eye in my direction as I shuffle past. The views across the peaks and down the dark blue ribbons of road, tied in bows around the conifers beneath me, are breathtaking. My determination grows, even as fatigue begins to fill me. I remember the training runs in

Edinburgh through the Pentland Hills, where I tried to run impossible slopes and came to a lactic-acid induced halt amongst the sheep. Here the incline is gentler, apart from at the furthest extent of each hairpin, where it takes on a rollercoaster quality.

Around two thirds of my way up the mountainside, I reach a rocky plateau where there is a food stall selling inscrutable meat stews, polenta and coffee, as well as craft stalls and a half-full car park. Families are in abundance; I remember that today is the first day in a three-day weekend, 28th April being orthodox Whit Monday in Romania.

The Skoda and my father are there, with lunch in preparation and a kettle of tea on the boil, al fresco, amongst a backdrop of huge mountains. Kids are having their photographs taken in traditional shaggy wooden robes once worn by shepherds.

Dad is in an excitable mood.

"Look what I found," he says, proffering a knobbly stone towards his exhausted son.

"What is it?" I gasp, wondering why he isn't handing me a Lucozade or something I can eat.

"It's a Stone Age tool," he explains, having somehow turned into a prehistoric archaeologist. "This is where he would have gripped it. There's the sharp edge. He could have used this to skin animals."

In my fatigued confusion, I wonder who this putative tool owner had been but it seems my dad is still lost in his flight of fancy.

"He's even put his initials here. And it says 'Ian'. Well, almost."

Here my polite nodding turns into laughter as I examine a series of crude lines that could be anything, or nothing. For all I know, this pebble had been dumped here off the back of a lorry carrying aggregate to surface this car park. Still, I do have to acknowledge that the rest of his theory wasn't entirely without merit. Perhaps, on this wind-blasted hillside, a prehistoric hunter had once skinned a carcass with this piece of flinty rock. I feign as much enthusiasm as I can then beg for sustenance.

When the kettle eventually boils, some twenty minutes later[1], I gulp the tea down with gratitude. Its warmth is just what I need, as I begin to shiver in the chilly interior of the van, munching down cheese rolls, cherry tomatoes and pastries. We take some photos and watch as

---

[1] At higher altitude it should actually take less heat to boil water, due to the decreased air pressure, meaning kettles should boil quicker. This theory is fine if you have a well-sheltered flame and the wind isn't constantly stealing it away from the kettle's base.

a huge, lumbering, bear-like wild dog tries to make friends (and find scraps to eat) amongst the day-tripping Romanians. Most people are kind to this gentle giant, who nuzzles me impetuously as I head off once more, before lolloping in front of me.

A small car tears past, moving at speed as the dog waddles in front of it. The driver, who can clearly see the animal in the middle of the road, simply bashes the poor hound out of the way. The dog yelps and limps away as my father and I, and one or two others, shout abuse at the driver.

Saddened by this display of deliberate animal cruelty, I keep up my jogging pace, past families taking photographs amongst the snowdrifts; past cars parked in tiny lay-bys so their inhabitants can take in the view; past two amateur geologists – a father and son – tapping at the rocks with small hammers. Near the summit, I stand upon a mound of rocks to take a windblown selfie, watching thick swathes of cumulus clouds blowing across the dappled green valleys. The road ahead arcs up to the pinnacle of the ridge where, unbelievably, there is a row of wooden stalls selling trinkets and local produce. Imagine finding concession stalls on the top of Ben Nevis! I suppose if there was a road taking you up there, commercial interests might win the day. Here it's disappointing, but carries a feeling of inevitability. Eastern Europe is a place that has embraced capitalism with a vigour that "old" Europe has almost abandoned. Having lived under the yolk of communism for so long, perhaps it's no wonder that unfettered trade is so assiduously celebrated. I ignore the imploring voices of traders, calling like drowning sailors from drifting oceans of cloud pouring over the ridge, take some photos and run on.

\*\*\*

Visitors have carved initials and declarations of love within crude heart-shapes into the side of some of the snowdrifts I pass. The road now throws its loops downhill, slightly less dramatically than on my ascent, except that now I am looking down across endless vistas of mountains and hills. If there are towns and villages out there, I can't see them. I know that somewhere below lies the village of Rânca, the first I'll pass and a likely stopping point for the day. My calves ache as I cut corners, checking that no traffic is likely to sneak up on me first. Words painted onto the tarmac announce a new administrative region – I am leaving Jud Vâlcea for Jud Gorj.

\*\*\*

My descent is necessarily slow, but I keep a wary eye on lightning flashing from glowering skies to my right. I really don't want to become caught in another storm. After an hour, I finally spot the village riding a saddle of hillside down below. The houses and hotels look like they are clinging to the brow of the hill like limpets. The road takes its time meandering down to Rânca, but when I get there, the place is atmospheric and melancholy – lots of unfinished hotels and apartments attesting to the financial collapse of 2008, which must have hit ephemeral tourist stop-offs like this especially hard.

Banks of grey and white clouds are obliquely illuminated by early evening sun, creating a polarised sharpness that adds to Rânca's frontier-like vibe. The Skoda draws up alongside me as I stand shivering in the sharp wind. I gladly jump in and we make for the Novaci hotel that Aradhna has kindly booked for us, my dad having enlisted her assistance due to his lack of internet connectability.

We have a little trouble locating the hotel, our satnav seemingly sending us to a rather rough-looking neighbourhood where an overweight bald man is practising football manoeuvres topless in the rain. We get some of the least friendly looks we've received so far, do a three-point turn at the end of a dead-end dirt lane, and get the hell out of there.

When we finally find the hotel, its second building still awaiting completion, the staff seems oddly offhand and distracted. We soon understood why. We are the only two residents not attending a wedding whose guests have filled the main building and who are already in the early stages of a fancy dinner. The hotelier assures us we will be looked after, but we are a little sceptical, as we edge our way up a set of marble stairs without a handrail and with exposed electrical wiring in places. Still, the rooms are comparatively quiet and the revelry from the main house doesn't carry quite as loudly as I imagined it would.

Violently heavy rain begins to pelt down as Dad and I dash across the car park a little later to the wedding venue, where we've been told we can dine. Several long trestle tables are set with around fifty guests in attendance. We are shown to a table for two at the edge of the party, by the reception desk, very much the last seats in the house. Some of the guests nod in greeting, amused to see us seemingly crashing their party. We are given no menus but the maître d', who also appears to be the hotel owner, tells us we can have what the wedding party are having. Confused and just going with the flow, we assent. We are then treated to a three-course meal including a sharing platter of mixed starters, then a second course of traditional meat and potatoes wrapped in cabbage and served with polenta and a seriously hot chilli.

Finally, just when we think it's over, a main course is offered – either beef or chicken. We both order the chicken, which comes in the form of a breaded escalope with plenty of fries. I decide I need to shovel everything down, balking only at the red cabbage coleslaw (I hate coleslaw), washing it down with two and a half beers (the half belongs to my dad, who mistakenly orders a second Ursa.

Entertainment comes in the form of a singer and small band (keyboard, accordion, saxophone). The singer's repertoire alternates between Sinatra-sequence crooning, with a folk lilt and frenetically-paced songs which prompt the younger guests to get to their feet and form odd hopping circles. The folk dancing resembles an energetic blend of Russian Cossack leaping and Irish hands-free jigging.

Dad is more impressed by the sax player than by the dancers. As a jazz saxophonist himself, he is dumbfounded by how fast the young man with the horn is able to play, breakneck runs of notes cascading from his instrument and impelling the guests to ever-faster gyrations. Predictably, Dad accosts the sax-player between sets and the two musicians start a faltering but mutually-fascinated discussion of circular breathing and "slap-tonguing" technique. I just sit back, rubbing my distended belly and wondering how the celebrating Romanians can consider leaping about with a stomach full of such dense food.

We stagger back to our rooms just after eleven, but are later told the party went on until 4am, as evidenced by how exhausted the proprietor and her staff look at breakfast the following morning. Clearly they have hardly slept. We go easy on them and dine on coffee and leftovers, then begin the drive back up to Rânca.

*** 

## Day 78

Huge white clouds are blowing over the hillsides around Rânca blurring the distinction between land and sky. A pale, eggshell blue emerges and vanishes from one moment to the next. We stop briefly to take photos by a viewpoint where a giant wooden cross stands, a crack running down its length as if it has been split by lightning (or a jealous God). There is something momentous about the scenery phasing in and out of view as we rise into a "pea-souper" of dense, wet fog. Despite the weather, lots of families are out and about in Rânca, making the most of the holiday weekend. The cafés are full and guest houses look livelier than they had the previous evening. Wrapped-up toddlers totter around like tiny Michelin men in the unseasonably wintry weather.

I run down the foggy high street and out into a sea of mist where the road's vanishing point ... vanishes. I have to look out for car headlights and prepare to leap onto the concrete sidings or grassy verges. Visibility is fifty feet, at best; then it abruptly diminishes to twenty feet and I have to use my hearing as much as my eyes to spot approaching vehicles. I pass a further line of food and craft stalls, their owners shivering under anoraks as a cold rain begins to add to the fun.

A little later, I emerge from the clouds and the rain lessens. A herd of pigs by the roadside grunt at me and I pass another unimpressed cow. I see a desperately mournful bit of graffiti, carefully daubed on the concrete siding:

*"Am intire din viata care a trecut ieu aici am flins mai mult lacrimile au curs parau dupa copile sul meude: cand a flecat din lume hu mai zuht zile semime zilelehele din viata sau prins au hoursiciata. De ghe baloi 13 sect 1982 tatal ghe baloi."*

"Memory from my past: I come to this place to pour a bucket of tears over my child. Since he passed from this life I haven't had a clear day – my world is cloudy and foggy. From Ghe (George) Baloi, Father, 13th September 1982." (liberal translation)

\*\*\*

The foothills continue in grassy undulating slopes, until a wide, flat valley opens up. The town of Novaci lies down below, briefly revealed by a gap in the seething banks of cloud. I pass a sign boldly pronouncing that we are in the homeland of Constantin Brâncuşi. I am pleasantly surprised, since the minimalist 20th-century sculptor is one of my favourite artists, especially his distillation of a soaring bird into a shiny bronze spear pointing at the sky[1]. I also love his "Endless Column"[2], a series of 17 and a half rhomboid shapes stacked on top of one another, 29 metres into the sky and symbolising Romania's World War I sacrifice.

---

1    Pasărea în Văzduh (Bird in Space), 1923.
2    1938, at *Târgu Jiu.*

The artist lived and worked in the Gorj province. Unfortunately, I'll not be passing his home village of Hobita, which lies to the west. Nevertheless, I do seemingly pass a sculptor's home on the outskirts of Novaci – a series of carved, smiling stone heads lies gathering moss beside a wooden fence, like benevolent guardians of the road. An elaborate gate, its white-painted arch carved and patterned, suggests a creative presence within.

***

My route will now take me south-east to Bucharest, over the plains and between the farms of the fertile south. Novaci has more of the same red-tiled bungalows, some colourfully painted in yellow or green. A profusion of orange day lilies decorates the roadside as I seek the turning for Baia de Fier, to avoid the busy 67 road. The sky has an oddly orange glow on the horizon, although it is only 3pm. I begin to notice that the soil underfoot is a little sandier that in the Carpathians, perhaps affecting the kinds of crops I might see as I wind my way east. It begins to rain and, once more, lightning flashes and thunder rumbles in the angry skies ahead.

I meet Dad at Baia, by the town hall, and grab a quick lunch. I am running well so I head off within the hour, crossing a tumbling river, swollen by rains. The road rises a little into low hills and I spot a metal cross with a small square of wrought-iron fence around it – a memorial with a glorious view over deciduous woodland and green hills.

***

Polovragi after the rains seems abandoned by all humans, leaving just a horse tethered to an unoccupied cart and a cat eyeing me warily from a roadside bench. A house in the next village – Racoviţa – comes with its own hen house and fenced-off enclosure where a dozen pullets perambulate.

A sign announces the third village – Cerna – but I reach a crossroads where Dad has parked the Skoda, without finding any signs of habitation. We drive around, trying to locate a guest house. Aradhna's first suggestion looks decidedly insalubrious so we drive further east, to Horezu, where the main hotel is full. The receptionist makes a call for us to a friend who runs a nearby guest house and minutes later we are checking in to Alex and Tedi's comfortable residence a few hundred yards up the street, having been led there by a very helpful waitress.

***

Alex greets us and immediately offers me a shot of pálinka. I say I'd prefer a coffee but he insists, and I remember I've read somewhere that pálinka is a traditional drink of welcome. I swig down the fiery liquid and Alex laughs, in appreciation. I suggest Dad does the same, but he isn't to be swayed. Before checking us in, Alex shows us a large tourist map of various local places of interest. As well as numerous ceramics workshops (intricately patterned plates are a speciality of the region), salt mines and the ubiquitous museums, an illustration of several perfectly round boulders catches my eye.

These, Alex explains, are a geological oddity of the region, often used as decorative garden ornaments by locals, seemingly carved into perfect spheres but actually created by entirely natural processes. Called trovants[1], these are rounded rocks which "grow" when accreted sandstone layers are deposited by a chemical reaction between their intrinsic minerals and rainwater (effectively layering them in cement). They have been known to roll into new positions, as they expand and become unstable. An open-air museum dedicated to these remarkable rocks was even created in Costeşti in 2004.

Unfortunately, being an entirely different kind of rolling stone, I'll have to give that peculiar attraction a miss. Instead, my route will take me directly south-east towards Piştesti and, eventually, Bucharest.

**KILOMETRES TRAVELLED: 2458;
KILOMETRES REMAINING: 940**

---

1  Literally "living stone".

# Chapter 22: Troubled Bridge over Water

*Day 79*

The following day, Dad and I struggle with another meat-heavy breakfast, which I manage to finish, following my "food is fuel" principle, whereby I remind myself of the consequences of being calorie-deficient whilst running dozens of kilometres. We say goodbye to Alex and Tedi and I set off from the Cerna crossroads in a set of almost-dry running clothes (Alex has kindly washed them for us but they've not had time to dry properly).

It is to prove a day of rolling but significant hills, with 10 to 12% inclines. A series of pretty towns comes and goes, with streets lined with vividly coloured rose bushes (I have never seen so many roses as in Romania). Nut-brown mares stare inquisitively from a field outside Vaideeni and I fend off a couple of semi-wild village dogs, including two whose indifferent owners watch from their garden as their dogs bound some way down the road after me, barking furiously. As ever, crouching to gather a handful of stones makes the smaller dogs flee and the large hounds keep out of range of my ever-present stick.

At Vaideeni, the rain begins, a brutal downpour that soon turns drainpipes into miniature waterfalls and the streets into a slick mirror reflecting multitudes of grey clouds. Here, south of the Carpathians, it feels a significantly damper place than the northern reaches of the country and perhaps the climate explains why there are so many roses. Local people dash from their cars to their homes, sheltering under newspapers or traumatised umbrellas. Rivers of water run down the main street, quickly overflowing the drains, and veils of mist begin to rise from the damp fields.

The dog attacks continue, to the point where it seems word of my canine-baiting presence must have somehow got out, prompting four-legged challengers. Over the course of the day I fend off a dozen dogs in nine separate incidents. I find myself becoming braver, almost blasé in my approach; I gather stones and bark back, sometimes even throwing a few missiles, aiming always to miss.

Horezu boasted a three-towered church and one of the most beautifully floral main roads I've yet encountered, vivid blooms seemingly obsessively tended by every citizen on the square of green beyond their individual gardens. I *buna* as many locals as I can and most are either welcoming or just bemused. I never meet any active hostility, save the canine variety.

Beyond Horezu, I reach a famous street of craft shops and ceramics workshops, passing stalls where traditional white shirts with patterned fringes and short sleeves hang in the breeze. Then, remarkably, a two-storey shop shaped like a terracotta vase appears, surmounted by a square roof like a mortar board hat. Lots of tourists are perusing the wares of at least two dozen separate ceramicists in a market that stretches for a quarter mile. The plates are decorated with whirling geometric designs – intricate chevrons and earthy colours. I take some photos and pause briefly, but there can be no stopping. How would I run with a hand-painted earthenware plate, no matter how exquisite? I hope Dad passes this way and explores too, and text him accordingly.

I am now running the 87, a main road. Many poorer Romanians don't have cars and can often be seen walking along the side of roads such as this, which makes me feel a kinship whilst worrying me at the same time. Some of the more lunatic drivers have a rather grudging attitude to giving room for pedestrians and Romanians drive just as fast as Austrians, but in significantly less roadworthy vehicles. I grab my chance to get off the 87 as soon as my mapping systems permit, heading over a scrap of rough ground and alongside the river Bistricioara, a tributary of the Olt. The footpath narrows through some denser undergrowth and stubby trees, then emerges close to the riverbank in front of the most rickety footbridge I've ever seen.

Around 300 metres of marshy land separates me from the river, itself a further twenty metres wide. A series of rustic planks, each about 18 inches wide, are held loosely together by rusting metal bars and weathered nails. The minimalist bridge projects out over the river on skinny wooden props, with an untrustworthy handrail on one side and on the other, a four-metre-drop to the rain-swollen river below. I have no way of knowing if this bridge is a long-abandoned route in semi-ruin, and therefore possibly lethal, or whether the locals just like it this way. I think it's fair to say that Eastern Europe does not adhere to the rigid, perhaps overly bureaucratic, approach to health and safety we follow in the West.

I take a tentative first step and find it sound, then begin to lightly jog over the marshy section, trying to be fleet of foot, yet alert for impending calamity. When I reach the water's edge I hesitate. Am I really going to trust, if not my life, then my health and comfort, to this deathtrap? I focus my attention on what my feet are telling me about the planks, their solidity and trustworthiness and trot across, taking photos from the opposite bank so I can remember the crazy experience.

The mud track on the opposite side takes me past a little village then into a forested region where I quickly become lost. Google has me following a vague impression of a path through a grassy meadow, although in hindsight, I remember there were a few branches laid across the entrance to the field, as if to dissuade travellers. I am seldom dissuaded. Minutes later I am thoroughly baffled as I try to negotiate a network of half-formed paths and trails in a hilly forest without signposts or markings of any kind.

As I clamber up a hillside strewn with crisp leaves and broken branches, I remember the viper warning in the Carpathians and hope the serpents are a northern phenomenon. Occasionally a bluebell peeps out from the mulch and papery remnants of last autumn. These bright blue blooms cheer me disproportionately as the run becomes a struggle – something familiar amongst the frustrating unknown. I take out my Garmin and use it to navigate in the general direction of a proper road, winding up and down overgrown forest paths, until I find something muddy but built upon a rocky base, which leads me down past an elaborate covered well, which contains benches and a place for country workers to gather and refresh themselves – farmers and shepherds perhaps?

\*\*\*

I arrive down into Baia de Fier, exhausted and happy to slump down lifeless in the small ornate garden in front of the town hall, while Dad serves me whatever I still have the saliva to digest. It has been a challenging morning and early afternoon, although Dad has been pleasantly surprised by a local offering to fill his water tank. The latter part of the day takes me along leafy suburban roads, though I still have to watch for groups of small dogs exploding from the undergrowth (I carry a reassuring pocket full of pebbles to hurl). In one place, the road has partially subsided, presumably under horrible weather conditions, a diagonal crack splitting it in two. Fortunately, the Skoda will not have to come this way.

A truck parked in a nearby field seems to sport a psychedelic chessboard pattern on its side. Running closer, I notice that the colourful squares are the doors of pigment-delineated hives. It's a clever solution to the scarcity of wildflowers: drive the bees to the blooms. I wonder how long it takes the bees to remember where their hives are, given that they move from time to time. Or perhaps this is a meaningless question with bees and they have spatial awareness which is infinitely superior to bumbling humans. However they do it, the system works – I pass numerous signs advertising "Vand Miere" (Honey for Sale) along my route.

As I approach Băile Govora, leaden-legged and longing for the guilty pleasure of white cotton sheets, the city outskirts appear and I run through a pleasant park full of afternoon walkers and kids playing with the water from ornate fountains. A footpath carries me past some immensely grand hotels – five-star edifices like slabs of vanilla ice cream that wouldn't be out of place on the Croisette at Cannes. We won't be aiming for quite that level of luxury, but we have booked ourselves into a four-star place in Râmnicu Vâlcea, a bustling town on the banks of the Olt. I spur myself on at this thought, emerging from the outskirts of Govora to a major road junction where one of the now-familiar roadside bars is stationed.

Running the gauntlet of gimlet-eyed and aged locals (all men), I order a Pepsi and sit at a table outside, having called Dad for a pick up. His highly fallible navigational skills mean I have to wait another 30 minutes for him to locate the crossroads, but I don't much mind. I am happy with my running and getting used to the level of muscular and all-over fatigue with which I end each day. After 79 days on the road, exhaustion is now normalised.

***

The Grand Hotel Sofianu is a shock to the system – my room has twin beds (doubles are rare in Romania), so I use one for my clothing and the other to sleep in. An en suite shower seems, after Roxy's limited facilities, the height of luxury. Sunlight flows behind airy net curtains, over which I am able to throw thick velvet drapes to block out the sunlight entirely. I call Aradhna and describe the environment we now find ourselves in, joking that the endurance aspect of my trip has been compromised. In truth, I feel no real embarrassment in treating myself to a proper bed. It might not last long, but anything that can recharge my batteries is strategically and emotionally welcome. Aradhna expresses envy and warns me not to get too used to it. I'll be back to bucket baths and digging holes in the bushes before long, assuming Roxy can be repaired. I concur but still sleep like a particularly well-behaved baby, my consciousness annihilated by deep-in-the-bones fatigue.

The following morning we enjoy a full breakfast buffet, the perfect solution to an ultrarunner's need for an absurd number of calories. I fill my stomach and struggle not to doze off as we drive back to the junction outside Băile Govora. The morning begins uneventfully, with no dog attacks and long, dull roads through level fields of pasture, separated by very English-looking hedgerows. I could be in Somerset or Devon or Kent, were it not for the hayricks built alongside cottages in the villages, latticework sides open to the air so that the grass can dry, beneath steeply angled roofs. These are like nothing I've seen in the UK.

Mihăeşti, Căzăneşti … the villages begin to merge into one another. The latter place even has a nearby twin with exactly the same name. I call Dad to clarify that it will be the second Căzăneşti where we'll meet for lunch. First I have to negotiate the industrial outskirts of Râmnicu Vâlcea. I run down access roads, stepping out of the way of passing trucks, dodging huge puddles and passing under immense pipes between power plants and factories. The architecture is unapologetically functional, and yet it has a strange beauty, sculptural concrete forms and snaking metal pipes, spherical gas tanks and metallic gantries. It makes for dynamic photographs and is a distinct improvement from the endless agricultural plains and empty villages.

Leaving the factories, I run alongside a major road, dodging in and out of parked cars as lorries roar past, raising knee-high dust clouds. Even here, painted churches are plentiful, the spiritual coexisting with the prosaic and earthbound. Hot and thirsty, I stop at a roadside bar for a drink but find I have insufficient change. A local man steps in and buys it for me. I thank him profusely and down it before trotting on.

\*\*\*

At Budeşti, there's an architectural monstrosity, a many-roomed mansion circled by ornate balconies and staircases and topped by intersecting pyramidal roofs like stacked witches' hats. Is this an abandoned folly or a Grey Gardens-like remnant of faded grandeur?[1] It is hard to tell but there are no signs of life behind the uncurtained

---

1    A 1975 documentary film by the Maysles brothers, telling the story of a couple of eccentric, fading socialites in their decaying and overgrown mansion, reflecting sadly on their glorious and fading youth.

windows. Romania wears its recessions on its sleeve.

\*\*\*

Soon the busy 81 road, bordered by gravel desire paths in the absence of a pavement and occasionally walked or cycled along by the very brave (or foolhardy), takes a treacherous turn, swooping up a steep hillside and winding back on itself in a succession of blind corners. This would be bad enough on a quiet country lane; here, on the truck superhighway to Budapest (as it sometimes feels) it would be very dangerous to run. I spy what looks like a forest path and duck into the underbrush.

I quickly realise I am following a dried-up stream bed, which becomes entangled in briars, leaving me to haul myself up muddy banks using tree roots and young saplings. When I get to the top of the rise, a thicket of thorny bushes bars my way. Unwilling to backtrack (*quelle surprise*), I pull myself through the spiky fence, bursting out, scratched and red-faced, onto the 81 at the end of its windings.

I'm not willing to keep going on the nightmarish road, so I consult my phone and find an alternative route past hillside homes via rocky tracks. Flustered cockerels scatter before me and families out for an afternoon stroll gawp as I race down a steeply curving backroad to the hamlet of Milcoiu, where Dad has parked the Skoda in the shade of an old barn. The afternoon sun is relentless, so I am grateful for his foresight, as I devour lunch then get on the road again.

The other Căzăneşti appears, with prettier, grander houses, many more roses and yet more hayricks. I find myself inevitably back on the E81 and running cheek to cheek with trucks again. More alarmingly, a man in front of me is swaying drunkenly along the verge, a hedge-trimmer draped rakishly across one shoulder, walking a bicycle with his free hand. As an 18-wheeler rumbles past, I am certain a wing-mirror will catch the trimmer and send it and gardener spinning under the wheels. Quickly I catch up to the inebriate and overtake him, not keen to witness the causal process behind all those roadside memorials. Hopefully the itinerant and soused gardener lives to cut hedges another day.

Eventually, I find another diversion from what I begin to term the "hell road", a series of pathways through villages and fields where immense stacks of seasoning tree branches are piled into huge pyramids. Having forgotten to fill my water at lunch, I am suffering under a cloudless blue sky. A village fountain satisfies my thirst, really little more than a rusty pipe protruding from the hillside and filling a mossy stone trough. Heat exhaustion begins to take its toll, nevertheless, reducing me to a walk through a shaded forest section before I tackle the last challenge, a ruler-straight dash along an exposed gravel path to my pick-up point at Morăreşti.

*\*\*\**

My inner reserves are running low by this point in the adventure and I have many kilometres and two countries yet to run – will I make it before my body rebels completely?

**KILOMETRES TRAVELLED: 2531;**
**KILOMETRES REMAINING: 867**

# Chapter 23: Which One's Mr White?

*Day 81* begins with me malingering somewhat, feeling overwhelming fatigue and a wearing-down of my enthusiasm. I have now been running (with a day off here and there) for two and a half months and a primitive part of my brain seems to be worried that this state of affairs will never end. Consciously I know that we are about two thirds of the way through the adventure and beyond the last mountain range. It should be relatively straightforward to run to Bucharest then Varna, then down the coast (mostly) to Istanbul.

That said, I also know I still have around 750km to run, a not inconsiderable distance. Too many busy roads and the repetition of flat farms and tiny villages are taking their toll. A multi-day runner craves variety. Romania has offered plenty of that so far but my enthusiasm is wearing a little thin.

Fortunately, we start the day with a diversion – six large gypsy wagons, with arched coverings and entire families ensconced within, trundle past me as I run (and wave). Several curious urchins salute back as the odd Lycra figure shuffles past. Each wagon has eight large plastic barrels tied to the sides of the roof and I guess that they might be transporting something to trade, although what exactly, I couldn't tell. Home-distilled pálinka, perhaps?

My father, packing the car up behind me, misses several opportunities to take photos of the Romanies he spots while driving; I text him to let him know who is coming his way. He gets out his camera and is about to take a photo when one spindly child jumps down from the back of the first vehicle, hands outstretched for an offering. The kid sports a worn leather jacket and strikes a pose like a seasoned catwalk model. Several other kids and several other photos ensue and Dad hands out a few crumpled lei.

Meanwhile, I continue over fields and onto rough ground, only to reach a tall chain-link fence. I tentatively try the gate, seeing no signs prohibiting walkers. It squeals open and I close it behind me and run on. I seem to be in a giant, well-kept pasture, almost alpine in character, dotted with yellow wildflowers and occasionally a small, smartly-maintained hut, probably shelters for shepherds. A herd of around a hundred cows graze in a hollow, but leave me well alone. I run along a gravel path and then into a small forest, where, of course, I immediately lose my way.

I am wary of meeting packs of wild dogs, but nothing menaces me from the undergrowth as I struggle up a thickly-wooded and leaf-strewn bank, over a rise and down towards a rural backroad. Wild roses border the red-ochre path and I am able to look down over a gently undulating valley dotted with small homesteads, some of which sport their own barns and hayricks. The region reminds me a little of the part of Hungary where smallholdings cluster, little parcels of land run by a single family, or the Sonnleitner's farm in Austria. Small wooden shrines and shelters hold icons of the Virgin Mary, or local saint, awaiting veneration.

Next, I enter a region where logging is taking place, rows of young conifers all exactly the same height testifying to comparatively recent planting. A couple of dogs chase me for a while, but showing them my stick and gathering up a few stones soon sends them on their way. I make it to Tutana, where the local shrine is surrounded with carved wooden crosses, evidently a local variant on a traditional graveyard, but where are the bodies buried? Tutana feels pretty in an almost Teutonic way, with dogs firmly tied up or fenced off, a pristine, whitewashed church whose metal roof is undergoing a polish, and a local well decorated with plastic flowers. There is evidence of wealth here with large, Austrian-styled houses, albeit constructed from brick, stone and metal rather than wood. Even the local pony and cart, waiting patiently for its owner by the roadside, looks immaculate.

Finally, I reach the Vâlcele reservoir, one of a series of 17 on the Argeș river. I make it round the western side on the 704H road and grind to a halt in the hot afternoon sun, by the service road that crosses the dam. There is a place for Dad to pull in. The sun and dehydration have been draining my resources and, given how I've been feeling at the start of the day, I decide to stop. I manage to run 27km but the tank is empty. I call my dad, who seems to have no idea where I am. I give instructions as clearly as I can, then hang up and wait.

One hour later, the Skoda pulls up. Dad has been driving up and down the road adjacent to an entirely different reservoir. I am less than amused, especially as I've been baking slowly in the afternoon sun, without a scrap of shade. Nevertheless, I have learnt not to expect Dad to be as efficient or prepared as Aradhna; practically nobody is. In fact, faced with a problem or dilemma, Dad and I have already started using, "What would Aradhna do?" as a guiding principle.

Quite apart from her superior organisational capabilities, I am missing Aradhna's company. It is great to see Dad; we've not spent so much time together since our last adventure, in 2015. However, nothing can replace Aradhna's support, companionship and love. I'm sure Dad won't be offended if I reveal that now, on day 82, I am literally counting the hours.

After a second night in the Grand Hotel, I decide to take advantage of their swimming pool, managing around 25 lengths before breakfast. I feel that using different muscle groups in the gentle environment of the water will help loosen me up. Wear a 5kg backpack for 81 days straight and there will be consequences, often for the lower back.

\*\*\*

### Day 82

A canine welcoming committee awaits us back at the dam that morning. A motley pack comes sniffing around us as I quickly eat a second breakfast. Fortunately, these real-life reservoir dogs express their hunger through inquisitive friendliness. Dad throws them a few dried-out rolls, which they wolf down as if they were lamb chops. Later that day, he posts a small video of them on Facebook, revealing the location of the dam and copying in the rescue charity who provided Maia. Someone from the charity thanks him, but suggests he not reveal the exact location of these animals in case state-sponsored animal exterminators seek them out.

I jog downhill past the dam and find the 7C, making for Pitești and points south-east. Although better than the dreaded 81, the narrow 7C has its share of trucks roaring by. Fortunately, it also boasts a foot or more of gravel beyond the white line at the edge of the road and occasional picnic stops, where I can escape for a minute or two. More white elephant mansions grace the side of the road, awaiting a layer of plaster that might never come, their balconies a roost for pigeons. Bascov boasts a war memorial flanked by field guns, adding a layer of irony to the pathos.

I reach Pitești by noon, the suburbs characterised by towering housing blocks, recently painted in welcoming shades, to offset the concrete brutalism. I buy an iced tea, since I am losing a lot of fluid under the relentless sunshine. Piteşti's picuresque but comparatively modest churches remind my father of an incredible story he'd read about the communist era in Bucharest.

At the outlandish suggestion of civil engineer Eugeniu Iordăchescu, numerous orthodox churches were relocated to make way for Ceauşescu's grandiose redesign of public spaces. Disinclined to care about the feelings of the faithful, the communist dictator was persuaded by Iordăchescu to try this audacious alternative to wholesale destruction. The historical buildings, some of them dating from the 16th century, would be mounted on platforms and literally wheeled on rails to their new locations, sometimes as far as 250 metres away. Amazingly, this unusually literal strategy worked and in total, thirteen churches were moved. I am looking forward to checking out some of these relocated buildings in Bucharest, including a monastery weighing over 9000 tonnes, shunted 24 metres away from its original location. There will be much to marvel at in the capital and I am beginning to feel that it is becoming imperative to get there soon.

***

I leave Piteşti's leafy suburbs and pass more monolithic housing blocks, cross the river Argeş and am making good progress towards Ştefăneştii Noi on the 7 when a call comes in from Aradhna with long-awaited good news. The mechanics in Sebeş have managed to fix Roxy and are wondering if we might be able to pick her up. I call Dad and arrange to wait for him outside the Nidec[1] factory.

We decide to drive back to Sebeş but realise we will not reach the garage before it closes for the day. Instead, we book into a hotel and retrieve Roxy first thing the following morning. We have to drop off the hire car in Alba Iulia first (I already called a few days before to extend out six-day hire to ten).

We manage to make it back and over the Carpathians, this time via the picturesque 7 route via Sibiu. The next day, after a quick valeting, we hand back the hire car and take a taxi to the garage in Sebeş for the emotional reunion.

## KILOMETRES TRAVELLED: 2599; KILOMETRES REMAINING: 799

---

1    International manufacturers of motors for the white goods industry.

# Tips for Multi-Day Runners – 9. Hydration

It's no great revelation to say that you'll need to drink an awful lot of water if you're planning to run all day, every day. What may surprise you is the sheer extent of consumption you'll require. On my pan-European run I found I would easily empty a two-litre reservoir in the morning and again in the afternoon session. In addition, I'd probably consume another litre at lunchtime and one more at the end of each day. That's six litres in a day, three times what I would normally drink.

Plan your route around where you might obtain water. If you're tempted to refill at mountain streams (and this is really a last resort) make sure the stream is fast flowing, running through rocks and near no farmland where manure or pesticides might seep into the water. If you are camping at night, do boil any stream or meltwater you consume.

Also remember that it is not just water your body is losing when you sweat or urinate. You'll need to regularly top up your electrolytes with salty snacks or (ideally) electrolyte tablets you can dissolve in your water reservoir (as a rule I'd use one per day or two on exceptionally hot days).

Finally, when you stop running, do not be tempted to glug down litres of water to replace lost fluid. Drinking too much too quickly can lead to hyponatremia, where the blood's sodium content has become excessively diluted, which in extreme cases, can be fatal.[1]

*Signs of dehydration to watch out for:*
Dark urine, not urinating, dry skin, dizziness, rapid heartbeat, confusion, feeling faint

*Signs of electrolyte deficiency:*
Nausea and vomiting, headaches, confusion, muscle spasms or cramps, dizziness

*Signs of hyponatremia:*
Nausea and vomiting, headaches, drowsiness, restlessness or irritability, muscle cramps

---

[1] Such as in the case of a 28-year-old runner who collapsed and died during the 2002 Boston Marathon: https://newrepublic.com/article/86985/the-boston-marathon-and-drinking-too-much-water As recently as 2018, during the hottest London Marathon for decades, Johanna Pakenham, a 53-year-old female marathon runner collapsed and was diagnosed with hyponatremia.

# Chapter 24: Two Reunions

## Day 83

The following morning, we get up at 6:30am and recover Roxy who, it appears, has been suffering diode difficulties in her alternator. Part of the delay in repairing her has been the wait for spare parts. Frustratingly, with the correct diodes, she could probably have been repaired in an hour by the side of the road where we broke down. Dad and I are gratified when she starts first time and, after refuelling, we head out along the Transalpina again. It is fascinating driving in full the route I'd run. Dad enjoyed the manoeuvrability of the Skoda and its familiar manual transmission[1]. Despite our four-star luxury, I nevertheless missed what feels more like a home from home than any luxury hotel could. How quickly we become institutionalised. In addition, Dad and I no longer face much of a drive at the end or start of a new day to locate a mystery hotel – we can take our shell with us, once more.

We pause at the clearing where we met Joka, Björn and the pack. Deep cleaning will be needed as greasy, dusty mechanics have climbed all over Roxy's interior and, in truth, a few days' luxury have revealed how grubby Roxy's interior has become. We set about performing a much-needed spring clean, both inside and outside. Following a tip from Mum, we fill the "isolation box" with soapy water and my foul dirty clothing and put the lid back on. The rest of our drive over the mountains should provide all the sloshing and cleaning my gear requires.

The spring clean, enabled by carrying many buckets of water up from the lake, takes three hours. At its conclusion, Roxy has a spotless exterior, immaculate interior and, we assume, all will be shipshape for Aradhna's return. I see it as a kind of devotional act but, in truth, it is little more than me finally pulling my weight.

I then begin to drive Roxy towards the Transalpina's steepest section, trying to give Dad some respite. Sadly, I start to nod off, a

---

1   Roxy is an automatic.

highly dangerous habit on a road with so many hairpins, blind corners and sudden drops. Although I enjoy the novelty of driving Roxy, Dad has to take over for the final stretch back to Piteşti. Evidently it has recently rained, but the sun is now baking the tarmac and lifting a fine veil of mist over the foothills. We stop in Rânca for dinner on a sunlit terrace restaurant then press on to Piteşti. We don't reach the city until 11pm and although I suggest sleeping in Roxy, Dad isn't keen, so we treat ourselves to one final night of comparative luxury.

*** 

It is business as usual on day 84. In all, Roxy's collapse has probably cost us three days. The only advantage of this delay is that we'll probably only just hit Bucharest in time for Aradhna's return; she is keen to explore the city with me and I don't want to be in the position of deliberately not seeing it with my dad, to save the experience for my girlfriend. That doesn't seem fair. Nevertheless, this is no excuse to slacken off. We begin the 2nd June at 10:30am, which I feel is reasonable after yesterday's early start. I vow to make up for lost time and pile a few more dozen kilometres under the belt.

From Piteşti to Bucharest, the 7 route seems the straightest and sanest choice. The E81, which runs largely parallel, is unthinkable. The day is searingly hot and I really feel I am running into summer in Southern Europe, after a comparatively balmy spring. I tuck my head down, the brim of my cap and sunglasses protecting me from the worst of the heat. I keep hydrated with regular sips of tepid water and run. Running is now quite literally a way of life and I no longer have to think about the process very much, especially on predictable and easy terrain such as this.

I pass pretty churches and a shrine devoted to that ubiquitous of saints, George, a gold-armoured knight attacking a cowering serpent beneath a rearing white stallion. Then I hit the Bucharest commuter belt proper, with decidedly chic homes at Viioşoara complete with substantial gardens and multiple storeys. Topoloveni proves a more substantial place still, where estates are protected behind ornate wooden gates, similar to those I saw in Hungary. In the sweltering heat, swarms of flies are in plentiful supply, making the task of breathing more challenging than usual.

All along the roadside, fruit-sellers have set out their rudimentary stalls, loaded with plums, watermelons and, most frequently, cherries. Pyramids of freshly-plucked red and black fruit lie shining in the sunlight while their sellers relax in the shade of roadside trees, occasionally stepping out to entice passers-by into a purchase. Nobody expects me, a passing runner, to buy anything and yet I do, outside Glambocata, from a man exclusively selling red cherries from a stack of crates. He gladly takes my 5 lei note (about £0.90) and hands me a kilo of fruit. I assume I am near to where Dad has parked Roxy, but soon find the task of balancing this extra kilo in my outstretched right hand something of a challenge as I run the next 5km to Leordeni, passing at least a dozen other cherry-sellers stationed much closer to the van.

Dad has parked in the only spot he could find, a dusty farm track just off the main road with a scrap of shade provided by a giant golf umbrella balanced between the open passenger door and the side of the van. I crouch in this triangle of respite and wolf down my calories, including a handful of the deliciously ripe and sweet cherries which I presented to my father as a surprise gift. It later transpires that I could have pretty much plucked them for free from the trees further along my route. The boughs I duck under in the smaller villages are often burgeoning with fruit.

***

Heat fatigue means I can only manage an additional 13km after lunch, reaching Găeşti by means of an unforgivingly hot, straight section of the 7, stumbling up to the van parked just beyond the town's name marker and begging for liquids. Dad has booked his last hotel, happily abandoning all pretence at vanlife in favour of a comfortable night's sleep. This is made a little less convenient by having to drive back to Găeşti to obtain cash, since the trucker motel he chose doesn't do plastic. This is not quite the Grand Hotel Sofianu but the rooms, although small, are clean and cool.

Aradhna is arriving the next day, so once I've washed off the day's grime, I log onto the motel's Wi-Fi and do a bit of research into Bucharest. We'll be picking her up there and we've decided to start the second phase of our time together with a day off in the capital, even though I haven't quite reached it on foot yet.

Aradhna is flying in on an afternoon plane, so we know we'll have another short running day on 4th June. Găeşti provides a pleasant start, however, with impressively marked cycle lanes, pretty gardens heavy with roses, and public parks. I even see a dog being walked on a lead along the high street, a first in my experience of Romania. We are very much in a middle-class enclave. Gone are the wild-roaming farm animals and there is a distinct increase in the number of warehouses and factories, business parks and shopping precincts.

Continuing along the 7 to the Dâmbovița region, I pass one factory whose exterior wall boasts a mural at least sixty-feet long, showing industrialists and scientists at work. Less positively, the car park next door contains a very recent shrine, surrounded by fresh flowers, dedicated to a woman called Juliana who evidently died here in March, just shy of her 40th birthday.

\*\*\*

There follows a tough few kilometres, after Mătăsaru, where the road stretches straight out ahead, vanishing at the horizon, entirely featureless, with not so much as a tree to provide scale amidst the daunting perspective. The thermometer is topping out at thirty degrees, lower than the forty-degree furnace I once ran in back home, but that hadn't been an all-day, every-day run. The endless perspiration and need to ration my sips of water soon take their toll. I manage to misplace my iPod so not even music can help me endure the tedious heat. The mysterious reservoir of determination within will be drawn deeply upon instead, although I know we'll have to stop by 1pm to head to the airport, so I have only four, rather than eight, hours of this.

In the pastureland between towns, lazy horses swish away the flies with their tails under a sky where swirls of cirrus clouds are thankfully forming, offering moments of shade. I stop running at Titu, deliriously pleased by the town's name which, laid out vertically on the welcome sign, possesses a satisfying symmetry. Many are the peculiar observations of the exhausted ultrarunner.

\*\*\*

Dad and I give Roxy a quick second spring clean by the roadside, to ensure she's sparkling clean for Aradhna's return. I am looking forward to the reunion with huge anticipation and feel strangely glad I've not reached the capital before we can experience it as a couple. Dad is relieved to be heading home too. He has enjoyed his time in Romania, discovering a country far more surprising and varied than he'd ever imagined, but misses Edinburgh, Kathleen (my mum) and his lazily bohemian routine of painting and playing jazz. I think he's done a wonderful job in trying circumstances. He'll never ascend to

Aradhna's heights of tolerance and adaptability and makes a point of telling her, "I don't know how you've done this for so long." However, in his own way, he has proven doggedly determined and resourceful. In short, he's earned his rest.

\*\*\*

Aradhna bounds through the arrivals lounge to hug us both, but I suspect she saves her biggest embrace for Roxy, whom she admits she missed to an extent that shocks her. Our pocket-sized life in a van has become the norm, with its endlessly different vistas and casual impermanence. Adjusting to being transported back to a home that never moves, and a set of concrete responsibilities that have nothing to do with adventure, has been hard. Once more, I shed a tear or two, as we say hello and wave Dad off. Aradhna started this trip with me and now we will finish it together, in our reinstated home on wheels.

**KILOMETRES TRAVELLED: 2631;**
**KILOMETRES REMAINING: 767**

# Chapter 25: Palace of the Parliament

*Day 86*

This far into the adventure, introspection has become a way of life for me, given how much time I have to think. So the question arises – what exactly is home for Aradha and me?

It's a tricky question, since we've both travelled enough and lived in sufficiently varied environments to know that it's not about bricks and mortar anymore.

Nor are we the radically free spirits that Björn and Joka seem to be, pursuing their dogs over endlessly changing horizons. For us, home is an uneasy balance of comfort and change – a movable locus of well-being and familiarity. It's being in a place where we can relax, be our most honest selves, and plan our adventures together.

Of course, the more entrenched is one's sense of home, the more house-proud one becomes.

Before she left the UK, Aradnha's friends gave her the farewell gift of a hangover and, although she is happy that we tidied Roxy, she can't help but spot details we missed. Particularly egregious are our tea mugs, each lined with a heavy brown tannin stain (Dad and I rinsed but never scrubbed them). I accept an earful for that and other transgressions, quietly glad her eye for detail is back, even as I endure the tongue-lashings. Home is where the heart is.

\*\*\*

I drive us into Bucharest, and we locate a quiet street beside a public park, where we feel safe to leave Roxy. Then we head out to explore, first walking through the Parcul Carol, past a towering modernist war memorial, silhouetted against the sky like a giant orange squeezer. Soldiers stand sentry, guarding the eternal flame at its base. We walk down the steps to a fountain I have imagined, but never seen.

Several months previously, I wrote my first novel, a crime story centring on Elena, an illegal Romanian immigrant who investigates the murder of a friend and neighbour when the police close the case as an evident suicide. Although set largely in London, I referenced key memories from Elena's past in Bucharest. Having never been there, I was at the mercy of internet searches and Google's street view to find locations to set various scenes. One fictional encounter, with an Englishman who subsequently disappears, takes place at this very fountain (the Fantana Zodiac). I am delighted to discover that the real fountain is ornate and picturesque and perfect for my book. Mimicking the scene I wrote, Aradhna and I take selfies in front of the cascading water, before moving on in search of an evening meal.

\*\*\*

The following day doesn't have an ideal start – Aradhna still feels poorly, yesterday's "hangover" possibly a red herring and she wants to reassert some order in the van. I warn her that everything won't be quite as she left it when my dad took over, but the period of readjustment is proving challenging. Eventually, I coax her away from the cleaning products and out to brunch in a small local café. Suitably refreshed, it's time to put my research to good use.

Hiding under our giant golf umbrella as the rain begins, we walk through the streets to the Palace of the Parliament, the monstrous government building that is Ceauşescu's most absurd legacy. Covering an area of 365,000 square metres with 1,100 rooms, the "palace" is the second biggest public sector building in the world, after the Pentagon. As ornately decorated as Britain's Parliament building, yet at least ten times bigger and styled more like a city-sized hotel, this Xanadu is so vast, that its interior space is 70% empty, despite housing almost all of the current Romanian government. Its enormous underground car parks were even featured in an edition of the BBC's *Top Gear* (in pre-Clarkson disgrace era), where the three man-boys raced fast cars around to their hearts' content. Looking at my map, I suddenly realise the immense, totalitarian wall we are gawping at is only the *side* elevation of the famous folly. Its front facade is even more ridiculously ginormous.

In search of a spectacle more modest, we hunt down one of the monasteries that Iordescu relocated on his mission to save the potentially desecrated holy buildings of Romania's major cities. The monastery features a beautifully painted arched entrance-way, but we are too timid to investigate further, given that it is still in active use.

En route to our next stop, we stop to watch a tram-driver hop out of his carriage at a junction and insert a metal pole into a hole in the ground. With a little effort, he levers a set of points to one side, then hops back in to take his vehicle in a different direction from the way the previous tram had gone. A straightforward approach to a technological problem, but not one suited to the absent-minded.

Bucharest is as modern and bustling as Budapest, with colourful street cafés (rather desolate under the ceaseless rain) and a peculiar statue of a bear suckling two infant humans[1]. We decide to duck out of the weather to a shabby-chic cocktail bar, the Dianei 4, where we down delicious gin and tonics among the faded grandeur of a once imposing private house. Round the corner, I spy a beautiful example of art deco, the ArCuB, a cultural centre as decorous as a 1920s ocean liner.

Bucharest's boulevards are as wide and leafy as those of Paris or Vienna and there is plenty of bold modern architecture on display, including a small glass and steel skyscraper built over and around the facade of a 19th-century townhouse. We can't decide if this is twisted genius or a catastrophic lapse in taste.

In one of several grand squares, an immense stone pinnacle pierces a nest-like metal doughnut with expressionistic figures at its base. This was erected in honour of the "heroes of the Romanian revolution". The extent to which it has been defaced and spray-painted suggests this memorial isn't universally applauded. Giant equestrian statues, neoclassical theatres and grand gardens begin to induce what we might call "Vienna Syndrome", a fatigue engendered by epic public buildings and monuments. We begin to long for something more intimate.

I think we've found it at the Green Hours jazz bar, with its quiet courtyard and tasty local food and Pilsners, but there is no live music tonight, unfortunately. Still, Aradhna is enjoying our day off together and expresses gratitude that, for once, it's me who has done the necessary research. We polish off sausages, fries and roasted vegetables (me) and bean curd with pickles and bread (Aradhna), then go for a less regimented wander around the city streets, past busy restaurants and bars, over the sluggish river, gliding un-prettily in its concrete channel, and back towards Roxy, via a quick stop for a nightcap and cheesecake at a "steampunk" themed bar called District 42.

Not being quite ready to call it a night, we then pop into one fashionable-looking courtyard of bars and design workshops, called

---

1    Romulus and Remus, presented to the city by the Italian state in 1906, to commemorate Romania's Roman origins.

Fabrica, where we have nightcap number two. The wave of trendy craft beer has well and truly hit Romania, so we have plenty of choice. Tomorrow will bring a much-needed full running day, however, so we don't stay up late.

**KILOMETRES TRAVELLED: 2631;**
**KILOMETRES REMAINING: 767**

# Tips for Multi-Day Runners – 10. Clothing

Multi-day runs require you to be prepared for every eventuality and even in the balmiest climes weather can be unpredictable and treacherous. You should have the following on your person, in your pack or close to hand:

> *Leggings as well as shorts*
> *Compact Waterproof jacket*
> *Waterproof trousers*
> *Two-ply socks*
> *Cap with visor (and possibly neck-covering)*
> *Woolly hat*
> *Running gloves*
> *Trail shoes to substitute for road shoes*
> *Sunglasses*
> *Fleece for recovery (your temperature dips significantly after a long run so you'll need to quickly throw on a layer or two when you stop).*

For more detail on why you'll want leggings and shorts and two-ply socks in particular, see Tip 11.

You can now buy running gloves that have rubberised fingerips, allowing you to use your smartphone without having to take them off all the time.

Make sure you visit a large sports clothing store before you stock up for your challenge, so that you have maximum choice. Clothing is not something you'll want to skimp on, particularly in sub-zero conditions. Do ensure enough of your clothing is high-vis too, particularly if you are going to be running on roads after dark.

Once again, make sure you have enough of everything, or else you'll be doing an awful lot of washing (or running with your own special atmosphere, à la Pig-Pen from *Peanuts*).

# Chapter 26: Bye Bye Bucharest

Bucharest feels like a watershed destination, somehow. Once I make it to the station in Romania's capital, there will be just one station left to encounter on the Orient Line – Constantinople itself. However, on Day 87, there is still 55km of major road lying between me and the city centre at Bucharest, with heavy traffic, heat and fumes to contend with. The surreal vision of a small truck apparently laden with pink cherry-blossom passes us by as we drive back to Titu. I kiss a still-queasy Aradhna goodbye and resume the eternal slog. I hope to cover at least half the distance that remains to the capital. Were I less fatigued, I'd be capable of running all of it, but the journey is taking its toll, a creeping exhaustion colouring everything. And with Aradhna under the weather, it doesn't feel fair to subject her to a whole day of coping alone.

I miss mountains, although I know that in my present state, they would finish me. Tiny clouds drift pointlessly across the blue expanse of sky, as if taunting me with their ineffectual cover. There is little but huge flat fields of crops on either side of the road, some of them in the process of being irrigated with immense sprinklers. Were there not so many farm workers supervising the drenching, I'd be tempted to run through the fields myself, bathing in a cool shower as I leap cabbages.

To pass the time and steal brief respite stops as much as anything else, I find myself photographing agricultural equipment and strange domed farm buildings. Commuter belt villages and communes pass by quite anonymously – Lunguleţu, Slobozia Moară, Tărtăşeşti – dusty tractors parked alongside the trucks at roadside stops. A parched tree outside Slobozia throws its charcoal limbs up to the merciless sky, looking every bit as dried-out as I feel.

After 14 miles I stop at a petrol station for a Mars bar and iced tea, enjoying both more than is surely reasonable. Tărtăşeşti offers another minor comfort – a pavement – but little else to divert me from the growing ache. Three kilometres further on, Aradhna and Roxy wait. I grind to a halt, hugely relieved.

We drive to a nearby small town – Ciocăneşti – where we find a bit of rough ground by a pond where local boys are splashing around and stray dogs are prowling feebly in the evening heat. Taking pity, I find half a cured sausage which I don't fancy consuming and hurl it towards the hungry animals. They scarper, thinking it a missile. Later, I prop it up on its end in the middle of the lay-by and leave it there; by morning it is gone.

I manage a few outstanding DIY chores. Aradhna cooks us a delicious meal to which my only contribution is regular stirring. We settle quickly back into our regular, comfortable routine and it is a blessed relief.

***

6th June begins with a mundane but deeply vital mission – finding me a quiet niche to dig a hole and relieve myself, no easy task in this flat, sparsely forested region. We drive around while I probe various disappointingly public paths until I finally creep into a farmer's field and sneak through a gap in a dense hedgerow to do as nature intended. We joke that just as Aradhna occasionally experiences "hanger" (hunger disguised as anger) I experience "full bowel sorrow", my melancholy lifting miraculously the moment I lighten my load. I don't want to harp on at unnecessary length about such things but in vanlife, and particularly in multi-day running whilst living in a van, the gut is king and must be obeyed. Duly liberated, I run.

Tărtăşeşti's pavements soon end, depositing me back on the 7 with only a scrap of runnable gravel and tarmac between the edge of the road and the bushes. Immense electrical pylons spread their arms like Space Invaders across the billiard-table-flat landscape. Passing cars occasionally beep at me and I have no idea whether these noises are friendly in intent or translate as, "You have no right being here." In more urbanised villages, I pass far fewer pedestrians and none on the tougher stretches where trucks roar incessantly by.

At Ciocăneşti, a large sprawling reservoir appears. A lone fisherman sits on the concrete dam by the water's edge, a shaggy mongrel dozing in the sunshine a little way off. I join the 1A, another major road artery into Bucharest, since it is impossible to avoid one or other of the bigger roads leading into the city. Fortunately, this road features pavements and I soon pass through Mogoşoaia, a commuter town developed enough to have a large garden centre, lurid with roses.

Replenished with a can of "Hell", the local energy drink, which tastes exactly like Red Bull, I redouble my efforts to reach the capital. A leering sign for a *Spalatore Auto* depicts a busty, bikini-clad lovely on the bonnet of a sports car, ostensibly washing it. Carwashes denote major towns, don't they? I ask my exhausted brain. Minutes later I realise that I am in Sector 1 Bucharest, one of the outlying regions of the city.

The only city sign I pass is a large billboard advertising a construction business but I soon notice blocks of tenement housing rising up on one side of the road and then, surprisingly, a film lab (Cinelab Romania) and a little later a large gilded vertical mosaic depicting saints venerating the Virgin Mary.

Reaching the city proper, ducking and weaving between pedestrians, I pass a building midway between a grand hotel and Alexandra Palace transmitter in London. This is the Casa Presei Libere (House of the Free Press), a somewhat ironic title for a building that once housed all of Bucharest's heavily censored printing presses, newsrooms and their staff. Some national newspapers are still based there but, post-revolution, freedom of the press is a little less ambiguous.

I run past the huge "RomeExpo" exhibition centre and cut through a financial district, following the commands of my phone's mapping apps. Once I begin to pass glass-fronted modern hotels and a branch of our lifesaving Lidl, I know I am nearing the centre. The region around the central station is not one we explored two days previously, so my urban orienteering remains a challenge.

When the Gara de Nord appears, it is surprisingly elegant and understated, part Soviet neoclassicism, part art deco, its shoulders decorated with what look like ascending angels. Aradhna is there waiting for me, with her bike, planning to cycle me back to our waiting conveyance. We take the requisite triumphant photographs and I muster enough energy to follow Aradhna a further three miles through the city, across the Izvor park and garden, around the Palace of the Parliament and back to the same quiet spot we found two nights prior.

***

Our shared mood is ebullient – we've reached the penultimate station stop. That said, two countries remain, one I know almost nothing about and one we are a little fearful of. We discuss the road ahead over celebratory pizza and beers[1] in Fabrica that evening. It is our third

---

1    A Silva pale ale for Aradhna and a Gambrinus Pilsner styled lager for me, craft beer aficionados.

night in Bucharest and we are beginning to feel we know the place, at least better than most towns we skim through. After 88 days on the road, you hold tight to whatever scraps of geographical familiarity you can. In four to five days we should be crossing another border and all our local knowledge will reset to zero, like an odometer cheated back to factory settings.

After a mildly traumatic trip to the portaloos in the park, day 89 begins with a lovely run along a footpath past sloping gardens, with intermittent glimpses through the trees of the city laid out below me. Then I weave through a children's playground of impressive scale and variety, complete with fountains, a miniature monorail where the carriages are tiny, brightly coloured aeroplanes, benches constructed from giant pencils and bike racks made from immense padlocks, before exiting through a Disneyesque palatial gateway.

The suburbs change quickly from massive, communist-era housing blocks to leafy lanes and rows of local shops. On the outskirts of town, things get a little poorer, rougher and more random with the paving stones crumbling away to gravel beneath my feet. I have to keep up a nimble pace and use my peripheral vision to dodge speeding scooters and unpredictable pedestrians. Like every major city, the sprawl continues for many kilometres.

An industrial zone puts paid to the pavements and I am back to running along a thick strip of sandy soil at the edge of the tarmac. There are still some grand modern-built houses set back from the road, but the countryside is beginning to assert itself once more as I take the decision to turn off the 4. I am now in Călăraşi County and will wind my way through a succession of small hamlets before being forced back onto the highway once more.

A handful of goats busy cropping the grass tell me I have finally escaped the last vestiges of the city. Orăşti provides a cool oasis in the form of a picturesque lake and fields of rippling corn, as perfect as a cereal box illustration. In contrast, one of the off-road shortcuts I take leads to a hotspot for fly-tippers, including a dozen or more smashed car windscreens glinting up at the sun from the side of the trail.

\*\*\*

Frumuşani features more lakeside homes, although there is evidence of abandoned self-builds amongst the flourishing properties; dreams have foundered here. A couple of shepherds nod happily at me from the shade of a row of trees, their flock grazing nearby, as I navigate my way back up to the main road. The succession of small lakes continues and I spy what I think is a supermarket and decide it might make a good place to stop for a bit in the shade and call Aradhna. We are running low on provisions and this might be an opportunity to stock up.

Unfortunately, after I call her I notice the warehouse-sized store has shut down and a much smaller shop has opened in an adjacent lot. There I buy some iced tea and a chocolate bar called "Roxy" (can't resist) and sit on some garden furniture in the shade of a giant parasol. When Aradhna arrives, our chance of a pleasant rest looks likely to be spoilt by some locals burning odiferous trash nearby. We drive Roxy away from the smoke and down to the lakeside.

After eating and feeding the ubiquitous stray dog, I run along the water's edge then follow a trail back up to the road. A little way off is a very stylish modern home, fenced off from the road and nosey neighbours. It has a swimming pool, angled solar panels and five small barking dogs that run to see me as I pause to take a surreptitious photo.

Unfortunately, although the owners have surrounded their tennis court with chicken wire, they have made no such provision at their front gate, where the bars are just wide enough for two smallest dogs to squeeze through and come barrelling down the road after me. Evidently they have never faced such barefaced provocation as this dayglo runner. The anguished owner appears and calls them back to safety.

The traffic remains mercifully light for the afternoon and the verge by the side of the road, although small, protects me from what little traffic there is. Speed limits in Romania are, at best, a wistful aspiration, as for a life-ambition forever beyond one's grasp. Budeşti's grand church shines brightly through the distant trees and I make for the town with renewed energy, the end of today's comparatively brief afternoon session in sight.

***

Aradhna and I drive Roxy down to a farm track near a small river. It leads across rutted dirt sprinkled with occasional puddles. One of them is deep enough to warrant sending Aradhna out in wellies to test its depth before Roxy can be driven across (she is less than amused but also the only one with waterproof boots). We find a very quiet spot between the fields and cook an al fresco meal on our camping stoves and fold-up table.

## Day 90

The next day I set off from the outskirts of Budeşti, aiming to leave the 4 for the quieter 403 route via Mânăstirea. At Şoldanu I am amused to see that the concrete pavement bears an impression of a set of small dog footprints, evidence, if any were needed, that dogs are literally everywhere in Romania, including spoiling road workers' cement pours. The roadside after the turn off is dappled with crimson poppies, in a profusion I've not seen since Hungary. Were I to choose an emblematic flower for the run, the humble poppy might well bear that honour.

I use music today, tired of the eternally flat landscapes of fields, tiny villages, whitewashed churches and trucks. That said, Luica boasts one of the most pristine and colourfully painted places of worship I've yet seen, as well as a picturesque lake. Such pleasures are a brief respite from the unending highway, tall pylons only serving to enhance the sense of an epic distance left to run. Music helps provide a rhythm for my feet and breathing and a distraction from the most featureless stretches. The weather remains boiling hot, though a strong headwind serves to both challenge and cool me.

Eventually a stretch of forest appears, throwing some shade over me as I belt through its seemingly unending length, knowing Aradhna and Roxy are waiting at the other side. Butterflies flit from the verges in front of my sweat-stung eyes as I feel fatigue setting in. After 10km I finally break out of the trees and see the van parked in the shade at the edge of a field. I feel so weak that I have to lie down for thirty minutes in the cool of the raised roof tent before I feel capable of moving again. Heatstroke, or something approaching it, is making me feel nauseous and limiting my ability to wolf down calories. I have no saliva with which to masticate dry carbs and instead focus on chopped vegetables, yoghurt and boiled eggs.

\*\*\*

After lunch, the farms on either side of the road are immense, agriculture on an industrial scale I've not seen in Romania. Huge irrigation trenches divide vast tracts of wheat and green crops, an occasional derelict concrete blockhouse or tumbledown bridge adding to an air of Ballardian dystopia[1].

---

1    I'm thinking of something like *The Drought* (J.G. Ballard, 1965, Jonathan Cape).

I find a path parallel to the main road by which to head for the reservoir at Mânăstirea, shaded by trees and leading around the back of some houses adjacent to the water's edge, as well as a builders' yard. Roxy is parked at the dam, just in front of an immense concrete embankment holding back millions of gallons of water. We drive along the track behind the houses and find a spot beside a builders' yard where we won't be bothered.

Romania, in keeping with most of Eastern Europe, has a very laid-back attitude to parking and camping. There don't seem to be the kind of busybodies you might find in Western Europe, eager to enforce their small-minded notions of what is appropriate or allowed. I suppose this might in part be due to the common sight of Romanies wandering far and wide and making the roadside their temporary home.

As the sun sinks low over the reservoir, we eat our evening meal in the company of several dozen geese, who are let loose on the overgrown verges at the water's edge. A woman armed with a stick for redirecting errant birds watches over them as they systematically denude the greenery. That night the gaggle of geese is replaced by the most astonishing cacophony of frogs imaginable, so loud it becomes a constant white noise of burping, rippling, throaty cries. Despite this, we both manage to slip off to sleep remarkably quickly. Exhaustion will do that to the weary traveller.

**KILOMETRES TRAVELLED: 2772;**
**KILOMETRES REMAINING: 626**

*Above:* An illegal border crossing.

*Below:* With Bjorn & Joka, on the Transalpina.

*Above:* Making tea on the Transalpina.

*Left:* Dad's washing day, Romania.

*Above:* Misty road near Rânca.

*Below:* My dog-deterring face (and Gandalf II).

*Above:* Romanies and their wagons.

*Below:* Romanian village scene.

*Above:* Carpathian foothills and rain.

*Right:* Running the Transalpina.

*Above:* Me on top of the Carpathians.
*Below:* A Transylvanian cow.

*Above:* Recovery in Romanian heat.
*Below:* Horezu – the street of ceramics.

*Above:* Bucharest street. *Below:* Cocktail bar, Bucharest-style.

*Right:* Crossing into Bulgaria.

*Below:* Lavender field, Bulgaria.

*Above, left:* A typical Bulgarian toll road. *Right:* Green river, Bulgaria.

*Below:* Resting with Sarah Bond at Kolartsi, Bulgaria.

*Right:* Bulgarian statuary.

*Below:* Sea near Varna, Bulgaria.

*Above:* Black Sea sunset.

*Left:* David and Aradhna on the beach.

*Below:* Boats on the Shattered Shore.

*Above:* Into the wet hills, Turkey.

*Below:* Running with company, Turkey.

*Above:* Hakki and family (round dinner table).

*Below:* Bay of Büyükçekmece, nearing Istanbul.

*Above:* Flytipping corridor, outside Istanbul.

*Below:* Istanbul city centre.

*Above:* Column of Constantine, Istanbul.

*Left:* Arriving at the station, Istanbul.

*Below:* Sirkeci Station, Istanbul.

# PART THREE: THE EDGE OF EUROPE

(Bulgaria, Turkey)

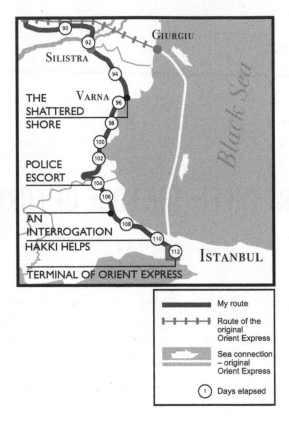

# Chapter 27: A Beach by the Danube

## *Day 92*

A family is picnicking on the concrete slope of the embankment, sitting on a large colourful blanket, as I head off the following morning. The dam's length is hard to estimate and I experience the same confusion of perspective and distance as I've previously encountered on Cornish beaches – it seems to extend limitlessly before me as I run the awkward camber.

Looking at the map that morning we realised it might just be possible to reach the border with Bulgaria today, if all goes well. Of the various options available, a river crossing at Călărași-Silistra seems the best idea – it's the closest border crossing, around 30km to the east, and will be my final encounter with the mighty Danube, before it slides off north to grudgingly meet the sea in the Ukraine, some 250km from here. It looks straightforward enough – a ferry from south of Călărași will transport Roxy, Aradhna and I over to Bulgaria.

We will have company once more. Aradhna's university friend, Sarah, will be accompanying us. A seasoned traveller who once lured Aradhna away for an impromptu month-long trip to Kerala, India, on a week's notice, Sarah is unfazed by the thought of flying into Romania and crossing into Bulgaria a few hours later. She's the kind of open-minded adventurer who will gladly drop everything for a chance to explore a new country and Aradhna is looking forward to her company hugely, it having been a while since we've had a visitor. Sarah flies into Bucharest; she happily agrees to journey cross-country by national and then local trains to meet us at Călărași. A runner herself, she's even promised to jog with me during her stay. After so long running alone, it will be a pleasing diversion to have some company.

As Sarah is closing in, I am enjoying my last experience with Romanian A-roads. As I run between the quiet villages, it seems that Romania is throwing a selection of "greatest hits" at me. I pass tiny, pristine churches, burgeoning beds of roses, storks nesting on telegraph poles, elaborate roadside memorials and a rundown dance hall with colourful glass windows in zig-zag patterns which goes by the unlikely name of Disco Esentza. Nothing has ever looked less like the essence of disco. A feeling of slight melancholy comes over me – I feel like I might be saying farewell to a newfound friend. Romania has taxed me, frightened me, surprised me and baffled me, but it has almost never bored me and for that I feel hugely grateful.

***

Confusingly, I pass through another town called Ciocăneşti, stopping to check my map to make sure I've not just run in an enormous circle. The village is stretched as thinly as a strand of toffee along the main road, a full 5km in length and lined with flowerbeds. Inevitably, it's a hot and humid day and I feel sluggish and weak, struggling to find sufficient distraction from the pain in my legs. I focus my attention on the little birds hopping in and out of tiny holes in the underside of storks' nests, like tiny feathered squatters benefiting from the host's largess.

At Bogata I find another reservoir and then a pavement and thoroughly signposted cycle lane, a rarity in Romania. The villages are now rubbing shoulders as I near the border, but the traffic heading for the crossing seems suspiciously light. It will be deeply irritating to reach Călăraşi and be forced to backtrack. These thoughts are shared in hindsight though; on 10th June I simply run, with the growing realisation that I might not quite manage to end the day in another country. I stop at a small shop, startling some leathery local men drinking beer at the shaded tables outside. I am so intent on downing my Coke and chocolate bar that I completely forgot that I laid my cap down on the counter to scour the shelves for sustenance. One kilometre down the road, I realise my error as the sun begins to scorch my forehead, but I haven't the energy to face turning back for it. I've brought spares in any case.

At Grădiştea, I stagger past a number of men and women tending to their roadside shrubs and roses as if competing for a "village in bloom" prize. Perhaps they are. I smile feebly and run on, back into the final stretch of open countryside before Călăraşi, where I've decided I'd stop for the day. Aradhna has to collect Sarah in around forty minutes' time and my legs have lost every shred of resilience. I can see a strip of water across the fields to my right – a Danube tributary – as I swap pavement for the shade of a long grove of trees for a while, my sights set on the final five kilometres to the town.

***

A mid 2000s BMW draws up alongside me and a well-dressed man with chunky gold rings and a skullcap, whose son sits awkwardly in the passenger seat looking away, addresses me:

"Kind sir. I wonder if I could trouble you. My wife is pregnant and I must drive her to the hospital but we need a tank of petroleum."

My interlocutor's English is more impressive than his logic, since he is clearly short of one pregnant passenger.

"I am a good Muslim and will repay you for this kindness."

I immediately feel an irrational guilt, knowing I'm not going to help him as he is almost certainly playing a short con. I begin to demur and he prises off the large signet ring on his forefinger and proffers it. I shake my head. He looks sad, thanks me with a cursory wave and drives off. Throughout the exchange, the teenage passenger I took to be his son steadfastly refuses to look at me, the biggest clue that his father is engaged in something shameful. Still, I feel a pang of remorse; have I just refused to help a sincere and desperate man? On balance, I feel probably not, but it leaves me ill at ease as I head for Călăraşi.

My mood is not improved by a guard dog – a snarling Alsatian – making for my legs as I run past a large industrial plant on the outskirts of town. The accompanying human guard scolds the dog, rather excessively I feel, given that it's evidently just doing its job.

I soon reach the suburbs and shopping streets of the town, a large sculptural signpost in the middle of a roundabout carrying the town's name. Evidently this isn't entirely the sleepy village I'd imagined. I find Roxy and collapse breathless into the passenger seat. Reading my mood well, Aradhna plies me with liquids and nibbles before we drive off to check out potential places to park for the night. On the way out of town we pass several runners trotting along the roadside verge. I feel a surge of kinship and a slight urge to join them, accompanied by that strange guilt that watching others run while I recline can inspire. This guilt feels particularly unnecessary given my six-plus hours of running today. More positively, I am encouraged to see that tomorrow I'll be running a route that others run. I wonder if it is customary to run from Călăraşi to the border and back.

We find a hotel/club with the unlikely name of Complex Albatros POD4, situated just west of a tributary of the Danube before it joins the main flow to the south. Hopefully we can sneak into the hotel bar to use the loos (and possibly have a drink, although we have stocked up on local beers at the nearby Lidl). There are a few other vehicles parked in the car park and people traipsing back from the riverside in skimpy summer clothes. We have no time to explore though as Sarah's arrival is imminent.

***

Aradhna and I have considerable difficulties locating the station at Călăraşi, which seems to be tucked away up a side street out of the reach of satnavs. When we find it, there's Sarah, beaming jovially, not at all perturbed by her journey and our tardiness. We drive back to the Hotel Albatros to investigate the rumoured beach, discovering as we cut through a gap in the trees that there is indeed an expansive sandy stretch by the side of the river, extending for about a kilometre opposite the hotel. The sand must surely have been trucked in but we take our lemon beers down to the grassy "dune" and sit watching a group of kids attempting and largely failing to light some Chinese lanterns. After setting the last one entirely alight and watching it flop pointlessly across the sand, the teenagers trudge off to seek other entertainment. We watch the sun sink below the horizon over the river's quiet waters.

***

We return the following morning, after a lazy breakfast, to have our coffee on the beach. The sun is out once more and there's already a throng of locals sunbathing or splashing in the water. A speedboat appears, a flying man attached to it by means of a snaking tube of high-powered water sucked up from the river and then blasted through two adjustable nozzles attached to his jetpack. We can't quite decide whether he looks impressive or ridiculous as he bobs his way down the river, wearing what looks like a white straw hat. Evidently there are modes of transport more ridiculous than my own.

Tempted to linger for longer, I have to remind myself that this is no holiday. After a quick stop off at the rather grim "squat over a hole" toilets in the hotel, we drive back to Călăraşi and the unglamorous Lidl car park where I stopped running the day before. I tell the ladies I'll see them at the ferry terminal and head off.

I quickly reach a bridge over the Danube tributary and run around an immense aggregate manufacturer which I know lies just north and across the river from the Albatros. Sure enough, I soon locate the turn-off and head through a forested region where shepherds drive herds of placid sheep through the shady trees. The traffic is light and the route easy to run and navigate. There are signs for the ferry and even one offering Varna and Istanbul as eventual destinations, some 140km and 580km away respectively, as well as Athens (1260km). I take a photo, realising with a shock that I am fast approaching my 2000th mile on this journey[1].

A few minutes later another sign directs me down to the water's edge and a local policeman stops me taking photos of the border checkpoint. It seems I'll be passing customs on this side of the Danube, although, strictly speaking, the border lies along the middle of the river. I find a questionable loo and then wait nearby for Aradhna and Sarah. We pass through the checkpoint together, with me jogging alongside the van. Even here, there will be no compromise. As much as possible, I'll take every metre of this journey on foot.

The ferry arrives within twenty minutes, chugging across from the other side to offload a few lorries and a scattering of cars and pedestrians. Only three trucks roll onto the ferry after Roxy, but we still feel a little hemmed in as we begin to cross the famous river for the last time. By now, it feels like an old friend. On the other side, I hop off the ramp and pace a truck up onto the road, waving goodbye and plunging straight into Bulgaria.

\*\*\*

What on earth do I know about Bulgaria? I know that it boasts a particularly potent folk singing scene[2], that Bulgar wheat might originate here and that *The Wombles*[3] had a character called Great Uncle Bulgaria, although I have no idea why. Nothing of consequence, in other words. I think I know that it had once been part of the communist bloc, but I have forgotten that its alphabet and most of its signage will be in Cyrillic. Indeed, I later discover, the Cyrillic alphabet was developed there in the 9th century, then spread throughout the region during the period of the first Bulgarian empire. I pass through the checkpoint at Silistra and encounter a commemorative plaque in a small park on the outskirts of town, not a word of which I can understand, except the date at the bottom – 1916. Okay, I think, I am now somewhere *else*.

Concrete tenements line the fringes of the town through which I run. The first car I see comes skidding sideways around a roundabout,

---

1    Although it will be two full weeks before we cross that particular milestone.
2    Such as the Trio Bulgarka, who worked memorably with Kate Bush on her 1989 *Sensual World* album.
3    British children's book series by Elizabeth Beresford and animated TV show in the mid 1970s.

as if being pursued. I've been warned that Bulgarian drivers are even crazier than Romanians; this feels like an almost hyperbolic demonstration of that assertion. It is an audaciously lunatic example of bad driving. Fortunately, as I progress through the country, I find that the bulk of Bulgarians are neither better nor worse than anyone else on European roads.

\*\*\*

My route out of town takes me past more vineyards, grapes full and green under the cloudless sky, and then a huge concrete sculpture by the side of the road. Two stern and whiskered knights stand shoulder to shoulder under a square pediment, immense swords pointing down. It's like something from *Lord of the Rings*, twin guardians protecting the road to Dobrich.

I soon see my first lavender field, which surprises me as I know nothing about the country's growing industry of lavender oil production[1]. Lilac fields provide a vivid burst of contrast to the green fields all around and their fragrance wafts gently over me as I run. It is by one of these fields that I encounter Roxy for our mid-afternoon rest-stop. Aradhna and Sarah prepare a picnic and we sit outside on our fold-out chairs, savouring the sunshine, and fragrant breeze.

Nearby stands an odd totem, one in a line of strange creations stretching a mile or so down the road. Looking more closely, we notice it's a dragonfly, constructed from empty plastic bottles and coloured cellophane draped around a wire frame. Other sculptures include a sailing ship, an immense tulip in the colours of the Bulgarian flag and a giant cone of green plastic bottles. The mystery artist has left no clues to his or her identity but we guess that they may live in the nearby farm. The roadside talismans cheer me up as I wake my aching limbs back into action.

\*\*\*

Finally, I reach the first town on the road south-east: Bogorovo. I trot down an overgrown pavement as the sun begins to set in a golden haze, then reach a crossroads of B-roads, where a drinking fountain stands by a small grove of trees. There is a dusty lay-by nearby, where Aradhna and Sarah have stopped to pick me up. Occasionally a local drives by and hops out of a car to fill plastic bottles from the fountain. Under the spout, a series of wide troughs serve as washing basins

---

1   In 2011, Bulgaria became the largest producer of lavender oil in the world (https://en.wikipedia.org/wiki/Lavender_oil)

and there's even a large flat concrete drying area and a metal rail for hanging things from.

Still, we don't feel confident that we can get away with camping with the roof up so close to the town's water supply. I spot a likely-looking road leading down to the side of a small lake and imagine it might be a fisherman's path. Ten minutes later we are bouncing down a rutted path towards the water. It feels a lot more remote than we expected, not at all like the path down to a popular picnic spot. There are some shacks by the water's edge and a few carcasses of cannibalised vehicles. Nobody is in sight but this feels very much like the kind of backwater where bad things happen.

I squint at a familiar-looking plant growing in profusion in a small plot near the shack and recognise it from t-shirts and movies – the splayed hand of the five-pointed cannabis leaf. Oops. We do a sharp three-point turn and hightail it out of there before any locals appear to ask questions.

Suddenly the fountain at Bogorovo looks very inviting indeed as we park up in the lay-by opposite. The traffic is extremely quiet, with a vehicle purring by only every 10-15 minutes. The main part of the village is up a small incline about 500m away, but we keep to ourselves by the fountain and I make the most of it by washing the contents of the "isolation box", and our general laundry, in buckets of soapy water. Aradhna and Sarah cook while I hang the wet washing on the bike rack (and Aradhna's bike).

***

The following day, as I run on, Sarah and Aradhna decide to wash their hair by the fountain. Hair-washing is a bit of an epic procedure for Aradhna, who has a lot of it, and it is all but impossible unless there is a constant source of running water. Some local women come by to wash a pile of rugs and Aradhna helps lay them out on the drying slab. My companions enjoy their morning by the fountain, which seems like a nexus for villagers from all walks of life, from local police officers filling drinking water bottles to housewives going about their daily chores.

Meanwhile I trot down the 71 towards Kolartsi in the baking heat. I pass a small airfield, with half a dozen tiny planes parked up beside the small landing strip. A sign depicts a sultry female pilot in purple leather jacket and goggles, offering passers-by the chance to "Fly 4 Fun. A ride with an airplane." It also suggests that any takers can "choose romance or adrenalin". I wonder why you can't have both.

*** 

The next few days see me heading for the coast, for Varna, a major town and tourist destination on the Black Sea shore. I am looking forward to seeing the sea. In the same way that hitting the Cornish coastal path at Newquay had marked the last leg of my JOGLE, reaching the Black Sea will mark the "home straight" of my 3000km run. The distance from Varna to Istanbul is 430km on foot. A significant distance but certainly achievable in two to three weeks. For now, I have to keep my spirits up and my energy levels in the black, since this stretch of Bulgaria offers little but a vast network of fields and challenging temperatures.

The villages in Bulgaria tend to be set off the main road, rather than built along it (as they often are in Romania), giving me even less to look at as I pass by.

Eventually I reach Središte, which is rather rundown and empty, save for a pristine complex behind a tall fence that I hope is a school. Kolartsi proves a little prettier, with a shady spot beneath the trees where Aradhna is able to park Roxy so we can all sit outside with our lunch. While I wait, I feel a nipping sensation around my ankles and notice some small houseflies buzzing around there. Could there be stinging flies in Bulgaria? Apparently so.

There's an amusing photograph taken in Kolartsi by Aradhna, with me looking exhausted and hot while Sarah is irrepressibly perky. It is a fairly accurate depiction of how I feel, although somehow Aradhna still persuades me to aim for a few more kilometres before calling it a day. As we eat delicious slices of melon, we are pestered by a peculiar insect with black and white polka-dotted wings and the body of a bee. For the lack of any entomological knowledge, I dub it the Muhammad Ali[1].

*** 

After lunch, I notice the terrain becoming a little hillier; oddly, this helps, as does the gentler early evening light. Beginning my running days in later morning might not be such a bad idea, since the challenging bit of each day is then run in the cool of the evening. Tiring of the 71, I decide to detour via a much smaller road towards Dobrich, the 7105. There is much less traffic as the road to Balik ramps up a hillside and then leads around the side of a hill overlooking a verdant valley with

---

1    Who famously boasted of his ability to "float like a butterfly, sting like a bee".

houses scattered between the meadows. A distant spire draws my eye and for a moment, I almost feel like I am running into some English village. Almost.

I turn a corner and there is Roxy, with Aradhna lifting her bicycle down off the rack. Aradhna and Sarah have been tracking my progress and have decided to help me along by respectively cycling and running with me. The companionship couldn't come at a better time, since they have caught me up as I am about to negotiate a significant hill (although all hills are significant after running 35km in the summer heat). I suspect this is no coincidence. The girls keep me moving at an acceptable pace and we decide to call my parents on speakerphone as we go, since we've not spoken to them for a couple of weeks.

While catching up with my dad's news, I spot a tortoise ambling from the grass on one side of the road and straight into the path of oncoming cars. A few locals whizz by, heading home at the end of their working day and I don't rate the tortoise's chances at a pace even slower than mine. I walk over, pick him (or her) up and carry him to the other side, releasing him into the long grass. While this happens, Aradhna narrates everything to my disbelieving dad. A few days later, we drive past some tortoise roadkill and I'm glad I am able to repeat the animal rescue episode from my last adventure (that time it had been a baby rabbit stuck half-out of its burrow[1]).

Aradhna has to turn back to get Roxy, leaving me and Sarah to tackle a monster of a hill and a gentler final 3km together. I'm glad to say I have enough energy left to finish with a tiny sprint, as we reach a wild camping spot my companions identified earlier. It's high on a hillside on a bit of rough ground at the edge of the road. We spend a very peaceful evening there watching the sun go down and shooing dozens of insects out of the roof so that Sarah can sleep unmolested.

The following morning, we find Sarah has not slept alone – a giant green grasshopper, fully two inches long, shared her quarters. She shrugs it off, saying she'd known it was there during the night but didn't want to make a fuss and wake us. What a trooper.

**KILOMETRES TRAVELLED: 2874;**
**KILOMETRES REMAINING: 524**

---

1    For the sceptical, there's a video of this (the rabbit rescue) online: https://youtu.be/bQo5bB0IDng

# Tips for Multi-Day Runners – 11. Blisters and Chafing

You're probably wondering if this topic really deserves its own dedicated section. Believe me, it does! If you are running 5 to 8 hours a day in often wet conditions, perspiring heavily, you're going to experience this perennial torment at some stage and it can be a truly miserable experience. Here are some tips to avoid the worst of it:

*FEET* – the abuse these extraordinary appendages will silently endure is phenomenal, but they need special care and attention, given the load they bear. Do wear two-ply socks (or even add another pair on cold days, times when you'll be running in wet grass or mud and on exceptionally hot days when your feet will sweat the most). More than anything else, this will prevent blisters from forming by stopping cloth rubbing directly against your skin. Do also dry and air your feet as much as possible and drain / disinfect and bandage any fluid-filled blisters that form as soon as you can. KT Tape is fantastic for covering plasters or bandages so that they do not rub off. Applying talcum powder after washing can help the skin dry and remain supple.

*INNER THIGH* – use plenty of Vaseline here and try wearing thin cycling shorts or leggings under your running shorts to add an extra layer and prevent abrasion. If you're feeling brave, you might also consider shaving this region.

*NIPPLES* – this is mainly a concern for men as women should be wearing sports bras. Vaseline is good here too but for long-term protection, sticking plasters on them daily works wonders.

*BACK, NECK and SHOULDERS* – your running backpack should be tight against you to prevent it bouncing and rubbing. I found that it rubbed my lower back raw and made my t-shirt ride up. Tying a thin jacket above my waist solved this problem, as might adding extra foam padding to places where the pack rubs.

# Chapter 28: To the Black Sea

### *Day 96*

The heat that persistently boils down upon me, and the sense of going frequently "off-map" on this adventure reminds me of my one and only solo adventure in my early 20s. It was 1993 and I wanted to take a European walking holiday, but had neither partner to go with, nor friend who I could trust as a three-week travelling companion. Two previous holidays with one particular buddy had proven a strange mixture of fun and frustration. Whenever we got lost in France, Italy or Egypt, which was frequently, my friend would become anxious and stressed. I've always had an absurdly optimistic outlook in such situations and generally take being lost in my stride. Our varying attitudes to calamity created a tension between my travelling companion and I. This time, I decided, I'd try going it alone.

I booked a return flight to Madrid, with the intention of taking the train down to Seville, Granada and Cordoba. I also planned to see Toledo and hunt out all the magnificent El Greco paintings hidden away in churches in that medieval city. What I didn't plan for was the loneliness of being by myself in a part of the country (Andalusia) where few people spoke more than rudimentary English. Furthermore, my Spanish consisted of being able to say please, thank you and order a cheese sandwich and a beer. I wrote a rather self-pitying and angsty journal during my three weeks, in which I got repeatedly lost, sunburnt and frustrated, whilst also having some unforgettable experiences, including walking 45km one day across the Sierra Morena hills with a 20kg backpack, about 250ml of water, some chocolate, a dry roll, a fruit yoghurt and a pear.

This formative memory of extended wandering on foot instilled the realisation that, whatever trouble I got myself in, I'd generally find both the inner resources and external help, to get out of it again. It also taught me the importance of maps, planning and having a navigational "plan B".

\*\*\*

Now, nearing the Eastern edge of Europe and the Black Sea, I feel myself relax. Surely I've conquered the difficult sections of my journey – the towering Alps and Carpathians; the dustbowl of the Great Hungarian Plain; the depths of a rural French winter; the dogs of Romania. As I near the sea, I find myself becoming less of an ultrarunner and more of a trusting tourist. The illusion of security and distraction of sightseeing serve me well, keeping me moving steadily east.

\*\*\*

Pchelnik proves a much prettier Bulgarian town than any passed through so far, with an ornate village well, modest yet tidy homes and gardens garlanded in fruit vines. On one front gate hangs a horseshoe, inverted from the traditional British "U" of good fortune, above it a red, white and green flag flying proudly. Beside the well stands a pristine white chapel, scarcely larger than a phone box (and in a sense fulfilling a similar function). A little way out of town the houses grow grander, set back from the road in a couple of private acres and heavily gated. The rolling hillsides and hedgerows continue to remind me of some of the places I ran through in England, perhaps in Somerset or Devon.

A line of tall fir trees surprises me along the next straight between villages. I'd not expected to see evergreens this far south. A little later they are replaced by a more familiar, but no less graceful grove of cypresses. A wall of red earth rises up, little birds hopping in and out of small holes bored into its crumbling face. The gentle inclines provide good variety for my aching limbs, alternating the muscle groups taking the strain.

The town of Jinitsa brings more lavender fields and on the main street, I see my first funeral noticeboard, covered with public epitaphs and notifications of upcoming ceremonies. These can be found in most Bulgarian villages, perhaps a testament to the aging rural population, although occasionally there's the photograph of a young person too, a tragic anomaly amongst the grandfathers and grandmothers.

\*\*\*

I begin today at 10am, unusually early for me, with the intention of running straight through until 2:30pm, so we can have a late lunch with Sarah before depositing her at the station. Her presence has been a fleeting but welcome diversion. We are anticipating another visitor in two days. Our friend David enjoyed his last visit so much that he decided to rejoin us, hopefully in time for us reaching the coast. David is self-avowedly semi-aquatic and relishes the opportunity to swim in the Black Sea. Having previously told Aradhna he can tread water without using his hands, he demonstrates this skill to her one afternoon, waving his hands in the air like a vogueing robot.

"I'm doing it; I'm doing it!" he cries, and a meme is born.

For the rest of our trip, whenever we need a laugh, Aradhna and I repeat this phrase to David, along with the accompanying hand gestures and it amuses us hugely. To his credit, David takes the ribbing in good spirits.

\*\*\*

The sun-baked road takes me out across marshy fields dotted with livid purple thistles, some of them taller than me. I thought Scotland was the home of the thistle; evidently not. Butterflies flicker between the blooms, many of a dusty orange variety I've never seen before[1]. I take their photo for later identification. Dark blue wildflowers join the lavender and thistles and the earth grows redder and rockier. Bulgaria is becoming a riot of colour, with giant yellow weeds clashing violently with it all.

I drink all my water by lunchtime, but the spring at Kozloduytsi has run dry and I have many kilometres to run to reach Dobrich under cloudless skies. I lick my dry lips and soldier on, past fields full of cylindrical hay bales that again remind me of home. Perhaps everything reminds you of home when you've been away too long.

Eventually the outskirts of town make themselves known – concrete water towers, telegraph poles; utilities preceding the people.

I received instructions from Aradhna about where in Dobrich they have parked – it seems a significant city. My route takes me up into hillside suburbs, then down into the centre, the rollercoaster roads reminding me oddly of Sheffield. Perhaps all the oblique similarities I am seeing are really the beginnings of a serious bout of homesickness. I've been on the road (quite literally) for over three months now and my brain is searching for the familiar amongst the unknown and unknowable.

---

1    Probably the Meadow Brown (*Maniola Jurtina*).

\*\*\*

My legs are aching viciously as I try in vain to negotiate a tangle of city streets, out of practice with urban orienteering. The blue dot that shows me my location is swimming around with equal uncertainty, heading me down the wrong turning or across the square in the wrong direction. A plethora of pedestrians taxes my abilities to dodge and weave on ruined legs. Finally, I spy Roxy parked in a shady side street and collapse in relief.

After showering, Aradhna leads me to a small restaurant she discovered with Sarah earlier that day. It's still bakingly hot, so we sit in the covered outdoor area, while a few locals sip tiny coffees or ice cold beers nearby. The menu has a surprisingly high vegetarian quotient and we discover some unexpected local delicacies, including a herby, yoghurt-based soup (tarator) and a dish of baked cheese, honey and nuts (sirene), which is fabulously tasty.

We then bid a fond farewell to Sarah at Varna airport. During the drive I literally sit with my eyes screwed shut to avoid glimpsing the Black Sea as we approach the coast. I don't want to spoil the reveal.

Aradhna and I drive back to Dobrich but stop a little way outside town, turning off onto a tiny forest road behind some houses, thinking the litter-strewn lay-by we end up in (after an hour's search for a suitable spot) will just have to do. We try to ignore all the bottle caps and used condoms and make the most of it.

My hair has become messily long and is irritating me, as is the almost-beard I've sprouted over the last week. Both have to go. Before I stop to question the wisdom of my choices, I agree to let Aradhna go at me with the kitchen scissors. Half an hour and much mutual anxiety later, I sit, shorn to a rough military crop, shaving with a selection of mostly blunt disposable razors. It's worth the struggle – soon I feel fresh-faced and considerably cleaner.

Our night is rudely interrupted by the arrival of some local youths around 1:30am who adhere to the international behavioural mode of loud music, marijuana and conversations held at the maximum volume. We peer out from our partially unzipped roof-tent to see if they are here to bother us but they're keeping (noisily) to themselves. Nevertheless, after 90 minutes of tossing and turning and screwing in earplugs, I decide I'd better go and reason with them.

Aradhna is a little worried – I have no idea what to expect, fearing gangsters. Fortunately, as I squint without my contact lenses at the silhouetted figures in the moonlight, a girl and a boy canoodling against the rear bumper, the body language is languid rather than threatening. There's another car parked behind the first and probably two or three other teenagers lurking within.

"Hi," I begin, trying to affect the posture and tone of voice of a cool (rather than uptight) middle-aged person. "We're trying to sleep. I've been running all day."

"Running?" says the boy.

"Yes. I'm running from Paris to Istanbul."

"Really?"

There then follows an exchange in Bulgarian with the unseen friends, in which I can only understand the words Paris and Istanbul. There is laughter.

"Yes. We're really tired. Are you planning on staying long?"

Something like a shrug follows, accompanied by a smile (I think).

"Right then. Well, goodnight."

I wave limply and they nod back. As I climb back into the roof, the music is still playing and I feel convinced I've achieved nothing but, surprisingly, within ten minutes, the music drops to an acceptable volume and a little later, engines rev and they're gone. Aradhna thanks me, turns over, and is unconscious in seconds. I follow her into oblivion just as quickly.

*** 

### Day 95

Our disturbed sleep makes for a slow start the following day. I feel drained of energy and Aradhna is under the weather. Neither of us feels inclined to rush back into action. We make it to Dobrich and park in the same shady spot as before. At my suggestion, Aradhna takes a short nap in the roof while I eat a second breakfast and plot my route. We head out a little later to rehydrate with juice coolers in a trendy bar in a bustling pedestrian precinct. The drinks are cool and delicious and we sit on a swing seat in the shade. At 2:15pm, I prise myself up and begin loping off through the afternoon crowds of shoppers.

I cross a pigeon-strewn square with leaping fountains, then cut down a leafy avenue and through a pretty park livid with roses. Then, putting all western equestrian statuary to shame, I encounter a blackly bronze 7th-century warrior-king, the Aspurah, sword held aloft in armour on a mighty steed. The statue stands out against the painfully blue sky, a full twenty feet high, and is accompanied by a similarly gigantic honour guard of warriors with staffs and shields.

Leaving such grandiosity behind, I locate a defunct farm road running parallel to the 71 route, a bit of quiet respite from the busy traffic.

We are due to collect David, our last visitor, at 7pm, from Varna airport. I'm not running towards Varna, however. Instead I'm taking a quieter route to the coast, aiming to hit the sea at Albena then run along the coastal road to Varna and beyond. I have roughly five hours to run 35km, which would normally be child's play for me, but after 95 days of accumulated fatigue, running under a scalding sun, my arrival at the seaside is not a foregone conclusion today.

After the attractive village of Branishte, I relinquish the pavement for the verge once more and take to quieter roads with plentiful teeth-rattling potholes to surprise the unwary. In Bulgaria you have to buy what's called a "vignette" to travel on certain toll roads (there are many). You might think this means those exclusive routes are better-maintained, but it is evident that very little of this revenue is spent on road repairs. These are the worst roads we've encountered in Europe by far. On foot it isn't a problem, but Roxy's suspension suffers a fair few brutal jolts, which probably doesn't help Aradhna's state of body or spirit.

*** 

An advertising billboard along one hot, straight route seems to tease me, featuring a horde of happy drinkers at a posh party. I long for beer and sup my warm water. Despite my lack of sleep, the 30-degree heat and my overall exhaustion, I feel my pace improving as I head towards the coast. The countryside remains pretty, like a sort of dried-out England, the Cotswolds during a hosepipe ban, and I am enjoying the challenge of running with a significant target (the sea) and a deadline (7pm).

Since crossing the border, I've seen so many lavender fields I begin to wonder if Bulgarians are as blasé about them as we are about acres of rapeseed. I get my answer shortly – a car sits parked on the roadside opposite one quadrangle of purple and a family are crouching amongst the flowers, taking photos. After they leave, I sneak in between the rows and take a shot or two myself, getting the colour fascination out of my system.

At Slaveevo I see another of the common kitchen gardens I've encountered across Eastern Europe. Devoting your whole back garden to rows of vegetables seems quite common here. Quite how they are maintained in such a healthy state in this boiling heat escapes me. Perhaps they don't have hosepipe bans in Bulgaria.

I run on, soon getting tantalisingly close to Albena, which tries to shake me off on its approach road, a snaking, climbing route with high cliffs of crumbling red and white stone and lots of vegetation. Coming around the corners, I feel I have to speed up to minimise my chances of an encounter with a hurtling truck, although the traffic is still comparatively light. A few steep loops later, I reach the top of the rise and descend towards the village of Obrochishte, where Roxy overtakes me and I wave her down.

Earlier, Aradhna went on ahead, searching for a petrol station and finding instead a seemingly quiet road to investigate for a sleeping spot. Now I hop in the van and we drive down another dusty track between fields where a farmer with a minimal grasp of English assumes we are seeking a hotel and shakes his head. We drive on, more in the hope of finding somewhere to turn around than anything else, then emerge at a circular clearing partly-shaded by trees beside a minimal fountain, just a copper pipe protruding from a concrete block. A local man is filling about a dozen five-litre plastic bottles with water. We've used up most of our own water in the couple of days since Bogorovo, a testament to both the heat and the added burden of another body in the van. We need to fill up but the spring is a mere trickle coming down from the gentle but distant hills and our neighbour will clearly be some time. He mimes jovially that he'd be happy to let us cut in, but we demur and head off to collect David instead. Once we pick up our returning visitor, we are able to spring the pleasant surprise of the idyllic spot on David, especially fun as it lies at the end of fifteen minutes of unpromising and rough track.

We have a pleasant evening together telling stories of our travels, sharing vegetarian spaghetti bolognese and a tasty bottle of local red and then make up for the sleep we lost the night before. At night the only sound is the distant howling of what we later find out are jackals, a far preferable lullaby to what we are now calling "boom-boom music", the bass-bin shaking sound of boy racers everywhere. Tomorrow we'll lull ourselves to sleep with the sounds of the sea.

*\*\**

The following day we wake to find a stream of people coming to visit the spring, which helps us get up and out a little earlier than we might have been inclined to. I am really looking forward to reaching the Black Sea and am especially pleased to find another forgotten road running parallel to the main one down into Albena, which announces itself with a massive sign in the centre of a roundabout and the motto "Oasis for Holidays". An LED readout informs me that it is just 26 degrees today, the few degrees cooler making all the difference as I negotiate a wide pedestrian avenue leading down to the beach and struggle to adjust to the sudden appearance of a fully-fledged holiday resort after days in rural remoteness.

This early in the season, the town is relatively quiet, but I can imagine a small forest of beach umbrellas appearing between the trees before me, shading thousands of sun-seekers in the weeks to come. The hot, fine sand sinks under my shoes as I tramp between the recliners and down to the bluest sea I've ever seen, a deep dark sapphire strip, lightening to yellow and capped with fine froth amongst the knee-high breakers. I strip off my shoes and socks and dip my feet in the water, delighted by how warm it feels. Perhaps it might be possible to swim here, I think, forgetting that, to many cultures, swimming in the sea is far more natural than running. Of course we can swim. It suddenly seems essential. The Black Sea appears anything other than black and very, very inviting.

**KILOMETRES TRAVELLED: 2934;**
**KILOMETRES REMAINING: 464**

# Chapter 29: The Shattered Shore

The beach at Albena is relatively quiet as I start running along the cambered strip of damp sand at the surf's edge, heading for a development of hotels and apartments half a kilometre away. Only a scattering of strollers, scampering kids and a couple of dogs share the sand with me. I decide I'll stick like a limpet to the shore, avoiding tarmac as much as possible, to give my traumatised feet a rest. I've been collecting blisters for weeks and lancing them with a hot needle, something I never had to do on my JOGLE, probably due to the increased perspiration, salt and dust in my sweaty socks.

As I wallow my way through the dunes at the far end of the beach, looking for a sensible route back onto tarmac, I come upon a middle-aged couple desperately trying to reverse their car out of a deep trough of sand. They have driven right down onto the beach and evidently haven't realised how soft and treacherous the dunes can be. The man, red-faced in summer flannels, is gunning the engine, frantically spinning the wheels while his wife, strong-looking and determined but clearly no weightlifter, is pushing from the front, trying to rock the vehicle out of its rut. I might have run right by and they look too embarrassed to ask for help but kindness gets the better of me.

"Do you need a hand?" I ask. The driver's shrug could be taken as, "I don't know what you're saying," or a sarcastic, "What do you think?" I choose to assume the former and join his wife at the front of the vehicle. We heave hard, our feet sliding back into the sand and the vehicle rocks a little but can get no traction. I look around for a solution, something to put under the wheels, but there's nothing useful in sight. Meanwhile, the driver has climbed out of the car and has gone to elicit additional assistance. Soon two other holidaymakers join us and he gets back behind the wheel (why not give your wife a go, I think, but don't suggest) and floors the accelerator again. After some five minutes of grunting effort, we manage to get the car out of its hole and send the harried couple off on their way. Thanks were cursory, disappointingly, but hopefully some sort of karma will chalk this act up in my favour.

Now a little more tired than necessary and thirty minutes behind in schedule, I reach the end of the sand and see a rocky coastline stretching ahead. Common sense would send me back onto roads but I am enjoying running with the waves at my side, so I get my phone out to use a visual translation app to decode the Cyrillic on a warning sign. It produces nothing but gobbledygook until I realise the sign is translucent and I am attempting to translate its reverse side. The sign warns the public about the beach and dunes being a wild conservation area. Considering myself not much of an environmental hazard, I press on past it and begin clambering over broken concrete slabs shattered by the waves and giant piled-up boulders.

There are remains of some sort of coastal road here, but it has long fallen into the sea, the fragments that remain looking like the aftermath of an earthquake. After half an hour of rock-hopping, I spy a homemade beachcomber's shack among the trees off to my right. I daren't investigate and hope I'm not being watched. Surely anyone who makes their home in a place as wild and trackless as this has something to hide.

Not long later, I finally get to the end of the region of boulders and hit sand again, then a slipway up to a concrete walkway where small fishing skiffs are stationed and makeshift wooden jetties enclose miniature harbours. Then comes a region of rocky wilderness and a section where tall cliffs have broken into striated slabs scattered over one another on the sand, like Weetabix. Bleached driftwood thrusts skeletal fingers towards me as I duck and dodge and try to keep my footing. It's fun but challenging, a reminder of the rock-running I did as a child on Fife beaches with my dad. I firmly believe this ingrained in me a sense of balance and daring, which makes progress steady, though scarcely speedy.

A tall, angular man with a small leather bag passes me, nodding a hello. I am relieved to see another human here, though wondering too what he is doing and where he came from exactly.

Next up is a once-inhabited zone evidently destroyed either by coastal erosion or an earthquake. Piles of broken furniture, masonry, carpets and abandoned possessions are heaped up amongst overgrown vegetation and fiery red shrubs. A path seems to have been made by many feet here, possibly scavengers, and it leads me around its various loops and twists past the edge of a collapsed building to a sight that makes my heart sink – a large wire fence and padlocked gate. There is a wooden shed and security signs indicating that I've just inadvertently trespassed into private property, or at the very least an area denoted too dangerous for the public.

I can't face backtracking, given what I know of the terrain I've come though. Looking around to check I'm not being watched and that there are no CCTV cameras in evidence, I grab the crossbar of the gate and begin to climb. Its rusty hinges immediately give way under my weight and I grab for something as I fall, bringing the gate partially with me. My hand scrapes an exposed piece of rusty wire and I feel the end dig into my palm, drawing blood. I land on my feet and leap back.

The gate is hanging by its padlocked chain and I can now just step over it. I feel guilty, but there is nobody around to confess to so I leg it, achieving my fastest pace of the day until I exit the service road to the waste ground. I emerge onto a dusty backroad, where I slow down and hide my bloody hand from a couple of vehicles coming my way. I hope none of them are plain clothes police or security personnel and run on.

The backroad leads up through the trees, giving a high vantage point over the little harbours and beach below. It brings me up onto the coastal road once more, where mega-hotels gleam like modern-day ziggurats. Amongst them stand the occasional remnants of an older age of tourism, such as the crumbling Hotel Villa Aqva, a quirky place with round towers, painted roof tiles and a domed greenhouse.

Google throws me a curveball next, sending me behind the houses and up some dirt tracks into the hills, where I am able to look down upon Varna's suburban sprawl. In one front garden, someone has painted an old Trabant Brit yellow and filled it with rose bushes and I am particularly taken by a 50s-styled ice cream parlour, which looks like the kind of place a young Natalie Woods might pop perkily out of. Today, despite the heat, its outside tables are empty.

*** 

While I am running, Aradhna and David are sunning themselves on the beach with ice creams and beers and sending me WhatsApp messages containing idyllic photos of sand and surf. I stop at a local shop, buy and devour a watermelon-flavoured ice lolly and a bottle of iced tea. I've crested the hill now and rouse myself to a final blaze down through the houses to the hotels and shopping streets by the Varna seafront.

I pass through a public park, leafy and popular with strolling locals and tourists alike. There are ornamental ponds with couples driving pedalos across the limpid water. As well as the usual park accoutrements such as fountains and benches with dedications to fallen loved ones, this park features massive field guns and the statue of a behatted general, turning his disapproving back on the water park antics behind him.

I make it through to the beach and find David and Aradhna still relaxing on the sand, having spent much of the day sunbathing and swimming. I am glad Aradhna is feeling better than she has lately and has had a chance to catch up with David and simply relax. I am also keen to join them so I dash back to the van, parked in a large municipal car park on the shore, change quickly into my swimming trunks and return for my first dip in the Black Sea.

The water isn't exactly warm but nor is it significantly cold. It becomes bearable in a minute or two and pleasant within five minutes. Aradhna and David join me and we all splash about and lie on the sand for another hour or so before going to get changed for dinner in Varna. I feel happy and my achievement is really beginning to sink in; I've just run from Paris to the Black Sea! Only a little crescent of coast lies between me and the end of this adventure. Surely nothing can stop me now.

\*\*\*

I should have known that Bulgaria and Turkey would reserve a few late surprises to spring on me. After all, an adventure is not an adventure without surprises.

**KILOMETRES TRAVELLED: 2966;**
**KILOMETRES REMAINING: 432**

# Tips for Multi-Day Runners – 12.
# Hills and How to Get Over Them

If you're like me, running uphill isn't your favourite thing in the world by any stretch of the imagination and yet I learned to love the uphill stretches for several reasons:

*Hills Build Stamina:* Hills are great for improving your cardiovascular health, strengthening your muscles and regulating your pace. Run enough of these early on and you'll see fast improvement.

*Enjoy the View:* Often (though not always) hills offer a chance to admire the scenery and check out the lay of the land. Make a pact with yourself to not look back until you reach the summit, saving the vista as a reward for your effort.

*Every Uphill Earns a Downhill:* Assuming you don't hate running downhill too, every hill will eventually reward you with a blissful downhill section where you can either relax and jog with ease or build pace and bang out some metres.

*Challenge Within a Challenge:* A couple of times on my pan-European run, I decided I would run every metre of a lengthy uphill stretch. Both times, I achieved my goal and felt a surge of confidence having done so. This helped me overcome a general feeling of sluggish fatigue.

*Walk it Out:* There will come a time when a hill will just be too ridiculously steep, or you'll simply have no energy left at all. In these situations, it's completely fine to walk it. Make sure you give yourself permission consciously when you do this and enjoy the respite your lungs and circulation will receive. Then run the next one.

# Chapter 30: Glittering Sky, Sparkling Sea

*Day 97*

We are all reluctant to leave Varna the following morning, so we have a late and lazy brunch at one of the seaside restaurants, then another swim and a bit of sunbathing. This time I feel the guilty tug of my mission and enjoy it a little less than yesterday as I mooch off at 3pm to begin my only session of the day. At the end of the beach, I turn left at an old schooner which has been turned into a theme restaurant and climb the steps to the harbour wall. A poignant sculpture of a seated boy pointing out to sea, while another shades his eyes, distracts me for a moment, then I shake off my lassitude and head past the car park and into town to locate the coastal road once more.

I have a theory that I can stick to the coastal road, and take the most direct route to the border, if I can run across the Asparuhov Bridge. The problem is, Google isn't sending me that way, as if it knows that pedestrians are not allowed. If I can't cross on foot, it will mean an embarrassed call to Aradhna to get a lift, which might spoil the break I am hoping she can continue to enjoy. Photos of the bridge seem to show a narrow path between railings but no walkers. I can only cross my fingers and hope.

I run the city streets and out through the suburbs and south to where the bridge's approach roads sprout, cutting though a desire path across a forgotten bit of waste ground, then up a flight of steps to the top of an off-ramp. I can see the long span of the curving bridge ahead of me, its towers and support cables looping away for kilometres, separating Lake Varna and its canals from the Black Sea and joining the Asparuhovo district to the southern regions of the city. It is a full two kilometres long and I can see that the narrow corridor on the left-hand side of the busy crossing is definitively not open to the public, being nothing more than a service route. I weigh my options. As usual, backtracking is off the table. Without enlisting Aradhna's help, and a 2km cheat, I'll have to run 23km to the western extent of Lake Varna to cut south. I'll then have to run an inland route to the border, which seems highly unappetising, compared to keeping the sparkling sea to my left.

Taking a deep breath, I dash across the off-ramp and clamber over the gated entrance to the walkway. I'm not sure it's possible to convey innocence whilst jogging but I try, affecting an air of, "I'm running over the bridge, so what?" If I am stopped by the police, I'll affect the idiot tourist and hope they take pity on me. The running is relatively easy, except that I have to turn my torso sideways to edge past the lamp posts, another clue that this is a forbidden route. Oddly, my limited research about the bridge has revealed that, until recently, it was possible to bungee jump off it, the terrifying experience provided at the midpoint of the bridge, over the waters of Lake Varna. Have thrill seekers really come this way? Around a kilometre into my run I spot an arched frame and a bench seat that might mark where the extreme sport had once taken place. I imagine leaping off this structure attached to a piece of elastic and feel glad I am simply trespassing. The views across to the berthed yachts and curve of blue water on my left-hand side are suitably spectacular and I realise that I am looking down from a vantage point that not even the drivers ten feet away can ever experience.

A few cars beep at me as I cross the bridge, but most ignore me, their drivers having more important things to worry about, perhaps. After all, I am doing no harm to anyone and endangering nobody but myself (and even then, not at all, really). I hope to find a set of service steps on the far end of the bridge and there they are. Eagerly, I hop over another fence and duck down the stairwell. I emerge on the side of another access ramp and duck into the bushes, in case I've been seen crossing the bridge and reported by someone. I allow myself a ten-minute rest in the shade, cooling and calming down, eating an energy bar and drinking some water. The preceding ten minutes crossing the water have proven far more adrenalin-inducing than anything since my first dog attacks in Romania.

\*\*\*

I take a hilly road towards Zvezditsa and follow a dirt road past farms to avoid a stretch of the E87, the main "motorway" south along the coast. I can't avoid it forever, unfortunately, and play chicken once more with speeding motorists through a succession of small towns such as Priseltsi and Bliznatsi, forced inland by the lack of a true coastal road, although yellow slices of beach on the map to the east taunt me with their inaccessibility. The road will hit the coast again at Byala, if I can endure the traffic long enough. Cars honk and slice past me at reckless speeds and I can feel my pulse rising disproportionately.

I take a brief respite stop at a petrol station, desperately looking for another way to run, but nothing presents itself. Then minutes after I leave the service station, I panic, thinking I've left my sunglasses behind. I am in the middle of texting Aradhna at the next town to ask her to drop by and pick them up for me when I find the glasses – firmly attached to my forehead. Clearly fatigue is taking its toll.

At Bliznatsi, I do finally find a quieter route – another dirt track behind a small hamlet where I finally collapse down onto the pavement near the junction with the E87, where Aradhna can easily spot me and turn in. A local man is climbing a ladder to cut cherries from a burgeoning tree that is spilling over into the street.

Seeing me dusty and dirty, sitting on the kerb, he perhaps mistakes me for a homeless man and presents me with a generous handful, beaming broadly as I thank him. When Aradhna and David turn up, he presses further handfuls into their hands too. They are the sweetest cherries I've ever tasted, a treat for once entirely earned.

***

We then go in search of a beach, determined to spend the night with the sound of the surf lulling us to sleep, if possible. The first place we find, at the end of a steep, winding road, ends at a beach restaurant and small adjacent car park. The proprietor rushes out towards us, gesturing wildly.

"No park here! No camper!"

Clearly this is not the first time he's had to warn off campervans. Then, more helpfully, he gestures along the beach, pointing at a spot about a mile away.

"There! There you camp. Is very nice."

With some difficulty we find our way there and drive along a single-track road past a half-dozen campervans and caravans. One caravan has a GB sticker, so Aradhna and David walk back to fact-find with our British near-neighbours.

Meanwhile I make camp, and in my exhausted impatience, manage to crack the side of Aradhna's clothes box by slapping it too hard with the flat of my hand. When she returns, with the good news that we are perfectly free to camp here, she is not best pleased by the damage that I've caused. We finish our preparations, parked just fifty yards from the surf, but also opposite a small beachfront bar that is playing loud Bulgarian pop music. Both tired and worn down by 97 days on the road, we snap at one another and things escalate.

Eventually, Aradhna and David leave for a walk along the beach while I quietly fume and finally, grudgingly, accept my part in the fight. I know exactly what do do, putting on the kettle and washing some cherries. Five minutes later I am jogging down the beach holding a flask of tea, three cups, a bag of pastries and a plastic plate loaded with cherries. Unfortunately, Aradhna and David have managed to make it almost a mile down the beach, so I add an additional couple of kilometres to my daily total catching up with them. Seeing what I've prepared, Aradhna forgives me and the three of us sit drinking tea and trying to tie cherry stalks with our mouths, as the sun lies upon the horizon, casting a golden-orange light all over us.

***

That night, after dancing and drinking a couple of beers in the beach bar, David has a daring idea. It's now entirely dark and empty on the beach, save a gibbous moon and an impressive flecking of stars against the inky blackness. We strip off our clothes and, wondering how wise this really is, run naked into the water. Although chilly, we quickly grow used to the temperature, marvelling at the skies and the reflections in the water.

I feel a tiny stinging sensation on my arms as I move them through the water.

"There's something in the water," Aradhna says, wide-eyed.

"It's probably just seaweed," I say, thinking she's just nervous of unknown fronds in the dark water.

"No, look! It glitters too," she insists. "And I can feel it."

"Gosh, yes," says David, half-afraid, half-delighted. "It stings a bit."

Then I feel and see it too, brushing my hand through the water and releasing clouds of pale green speckles and a slight prickling sensation. Tiny bioluminescent jellyfish, each no bigger than a peppercorn, are stinging us as we swim. The sensation is mildly irritating rather than painful and the dim green trails of sparkles are quite magical, like a mirroring in miniature of the stars above us. We marvel at the sight for a few minutes more, and then get out of the water to quickly dry ourselves and dress.

Still bruised by the argument we had earlier, I've been a reluctant participant in this experience to begin with, but I am glad I've allowed peer pressure to prevail. It remains an indelible memory: arcs of glittering light in midnight water.

**KILOMETRES TRAVELLED: 2989;**
**KILOMETRES REMAINING: 409**

# Chapter 31: A Channel Crossing

### Day 98

The plan on 16th June is to run from Bliznatsi to the coast once more, via the road we found the previous night, past the beachside restaurant and bar and then continue along the beach for as long as possible. On our maps, the sand stretches for 8km but it all looks passable, except for one small obstacle. There's a twenty-foot-wide channel running down onto the sand just a little way east of where we've camped.

Before setting off, David and I decide to attempt a test crossing. I take a long stick to use to probe ahead of us, looking for sudden dips, as we wade out into the water, while Aradhna films us from dry land. "Be careful!" she admonishes, very much uncertain whether this is a sensible course of action. I promise I will stay safe, discovering with relief that there is a hidden, snaking sandbar leading across to the other side, where someone has sunk a branch into the sand, perhaps as a marker. We make it across the waist-deep stream, turn and walk back, without mishap. I now feel confident that, so long as I don't mind running wet for the rest of the morning, I can ford this river safely.

Imagining ourselves fearless macho men, David and I are later shocked by Aradhna's photos of our exploits – with our t-shirts tied up under our armpits, we appear to be wearing camp crop-tops as we gingerly tiptoe through what looks like a placid streamlet.

*** 

From Bliznatsi, I quickly locate the turn-off with its array of signs promising holiday chalets and a campsite (we passed it the previous day and decided it more resembled a Soviet gulag than anywhere you'd want to spend a night). I make it down to the sand and head for the hard-packed strip by the water's edge. Anything drier will be impossible to run. The strip of fine yellow sand and the line of broken, frothing surf stretches out to the horizon, dotted with sunbathers, families with kids and the occasional fisherman. I duck around toddlers cavorting in the waves, sandcastles, and couples walking hand in hand. I feel a small ache, wishing that Aradhna could be here with me and feeling oddly lonely amongst more people than I've seen since Varna.

David and Aradhna drive further round the coast so I pass our camping spot alone and reach the fording point in the river, stepping gingerly over a tidemark of broken seashells. Halfway through the water, two local fishermen in waders come along the sandbar towards me, proving that my supposition is correct – this is an established crossing for locals in the know. The fishermen gesticulate that my backpack is trailing in the water but I motion that I know, whilst thanking them. They must consider me a peculiar sight as I galumph out of the water and slosh along a much quieter stretch of beach. Only one lone sunbather lounges nearby, reading her book under an umbrella. I wave hello and run on, to a land inhabited only by driftwood limbs, beached rowboats and resting flocks of gulls, which take to the wing as soon as I approach, slapping wet sand under my flat feet. I feel a little sorry for disturbing them, but I am a man with a mission, now feeling almost as if the finish line is in sight, even though it will take at least ten days to reach Istanbul.

I pass a man in a wetsuit standing up to his shoulders in the sea, poking some sort of instrument or probe into the sand at regular intervals. Perhaps he's a marine biologist. A few odd driftwood corrals amongst the dunes and the occasional beached dinghy are the only signs of a human presence for a kilometre or so before I spot a semi-derelict pier and another scattering of sunseekers. The day is warm but nowhere near as fearfully hot as it has been. I dry out quickly, following a patterning of bird footprints along the sand, which are soon joined by the tyre treadmarks of a beach-buggy or jeep.

As I reach the pier, a young man is clambering over a fence near its shore-end, his friend reaching over from the shore side to help. They jump down and pass two middle-aged fishermen who, remarkably, begin to climb the fence themselves, no doubt seeking a perfect fishing spot at its far end. Some teenagers are shouting and splashing in the water, taking turns to jump off the accessible bit of pier into the deep water. I sit and rest a while, putting my shoes and socks on with some reluctance – my feet have enjoyed the gentle massage of sand and seashells.

\*\*\*

I run up a green strip of astroturf past stacks of holiday apartments, then find a trail into woodland where I am quickly mobbed by hordes of mosquitos. These swarming menaces don't usually bite me, but they do fly into my eyes, ears, mouth and nose with great frequency and delight. I cover my head with my waterproof jacket and run with one hand waving in front of my face, spitting out the occasional damp mosquito. I've chosen to run in my glasses today, in order to rest my eyes and the layer of glass offers a little more protection. However, running while being pursued by swarms of biting insects is no fun at all. I have to curl my top lip down over my bottom lip and breathe in vertically to avoid sucking in the tiny pests. I haven't brought any repellent with me, which I vow to rectify as soon as possible.

As the day started rather lazily, this will be a single-session run again. The forest path twists over and down a hillside for a few kilometres before depositing me into open vineyards under a spectacular sky like something from a Dutch master painter – a skein of clouds lit in golden early evening light with the sun glaring, eye-like, behind them. I call Aradhna for guidance, knowing she is close but wondering how on earth she got here, given that the tracks I am running consist of furrowed clay and sand, ramped-up steep slopes that I suspect Roxy won't cope with. I needn't worry. Following a legitimate Park4Night recommendation, Aradhna drives up a farm track and, with David's encouragement, takes all the correct unmarked forks to bring the van out onto the lip of a grassy clifftop overlooking a small beach.

It's a truly idyllic spot and one we will share with a group of backpackers camping below us on the sand and one other well-equipped traveller, a lone middle-aged man, who is jovial, helpful and somewhat lacking in personal boundaries. Then again, a clear lesson we've learnt from our travels in Europe so far is that "staring" or standing and watching others is really only deemed impolite in the UK, where privacy is primary. Most of Europe doesn't seem to recognise the concept of being a "nosey parker".

I run down to Roxy and the others, who have already had their daily swim, a new and welcome addition to our day's routine. I admire our neighbour's giant awning, satellite dish, solar panel and moped, nod to him and go about my ablutions.

The sun sets gloriously as we dine al fresco (another treat we are fast becoming used to) and leaves us admiring the clear sight of Venus and Mars in the ascendant against a backdrop of a million stars. The night is so clear, as all our nights have been recently, that we can make out the smoky line of the Milky Way cutting a diagonal across the night sky. It is an incredible thing to realise that you are looking along the plane of a galaxy, of which the place you stand is an infinitesimally minute part.

*\*\*\**

17th June 2018: after a pancake breakfast and a quick dip in the cool ocean, where larger waves buffet us in a watery massage, we pack up, just as rain is spotting down upon Roxy's roof. I set off through the vineyards, starting the day with dramatic sea views and just-as-dramatic inclines under leaden legs. I have said my farewells to David, who will be leaving us today, Aradhna making yet another airport run while I make for the border with Turkey, some 150km away. It ought to take around four days to cross into our final nation, a momentous milestone.

The vineyards soon give way to the outskirts of the small town of Byala, which sports a selection of tall, thin wooden sculptures in a variety of styles, some biomorphic, some geometrical, some figurative. Less aesthetically pleasing is the sight of the dreaded E87 road, the major coastal route I'll have to take towards the border at Burgas, if I don't want to undertake a major diversion inland. I endure the traffic and tedium of the near-motorway as far as Obzor, where I feel I've had enough, first cutting down towards the seaside, past wooden holiday chalets and grand hotels, then heading west along the rutted, puddle-strewn 906. As I hop over the pools of standing water left by the sudden rains, a car draws up alongside me. A woman with a young son rolls down her window to warn me in pristine but accented English of feral dogs, suggesting I carry a stick.

"Don't worry," I say, "I've already run across Romania."

"Ah," she nods, getting my inference immediately. "Then you know."

A little later on (once I've actually picked up a stick) I pass the family once more. This time they have stopped the car to examine two kittens that appear to have been abandoned by the roadside. I hope they'll take pity and provide them with a loving home.

The day grows very humid and somewhat overcast as I climb into gentle hills along tarmac and red dirt roads. It feels like I am running through South America with the dripping green forest and fields and russet-red earth underfoot. The fields are spotted with wildflowers and the sky is glowing with a peachy hue which dims to a tobacco brown on the horizon. The towns I pass through are functional rather than pretty and there is very little traffic, possibly due to the immense rectangles of tarmac seemingly missing from the road and the giant potholes liberally strewn in my path.

Mosquitos crowd me whenever I slow, so I keep going, my head once more swathed in a waterproof jacket. Aradhna, returning from the airport at Varna, texts me to say she'll be there around 7:15pm, an hour later than planned. There is nothing I can do but forge on into the early evening. The sun begins to break through low-lying clouds as it approaches the horizon, creating a beautiful "golden hour" before sunset. I am also grateful to note that when we climb above the treeline and into cooler, open air, the mosquitos fall away. Approaching the town of Panitsovo at 7pm I decide to do my bit for the team and find a spot to stop for the night. A high meadow with a view down to a mist-blanketed valley seems the best of three possible options. When Aradhna arrives, I take her there and she pulls Roxy off the road, glad that I've found such a beautiful spot.

Hordes of grasshoppers spring away from our legs as we walk through the long grass and prep for nightfall. My mother's mobile laundry tip has again delivered a box of clean clothing to wring out (Aradhna) and hang up (my task). After a late supper, we retire to the sounds of a gathering storm, epic flashes of lightning and fearfully loud rumbles of thunder surrounding us. The display is both terrifying and exhilarating and is followed by torrential rain for most of the night. A few moments after my head hits the pillow I remember that the washing is still out. It is too late to prevent it getting a second rinsing and neither of us are keen to venture out into the storm.

\*\*\*

### Day 100

Since I stopped running at a suitable camping spot (a more common strategy these last few weeks), we don't have to pack up entirely before I set off the next morning. Today we have another milestone to celebrate – day 100 of our adventure. Five years ago, if you had told me that I'd run around 35km a day for almost 100 consecutive days, I'd not have believed you. I wouldn't have believed it was possible.

I have also run almost 1900 miles[1], which seems as ridiculous as it is impressive. That said, these achievements are coming at a cost. I have now lost about ten percent of my body weight, by my estimation,

---

1   3037km to be precise.

and am perpetually fatigued, with a deep in-the-bones exhaustion I can't shake with food, sleep or by slowing my pace. Thankfully, the end is fast approaching. We now have around 330-350km[1] to go to reach Sirkeci station in Istanbul.

\*\*\*

Day 100 provides a fittingly atmospheric start with thick clumps of mist clinging to the lower slopes of the valley spread out beneath us. If I can make it over this range of hills, I might even reach the lakes at Burgas by the end of today. I experience a moment of indignity to balance the grandeur – having to duck down mid-poo amongst the bushes as a team of Lycra-clad cyclists swoosh by. I wish I'd been able to wave encouragingly, but I am too busy avoiding the thistles and grasshoppers threatening my posterior.

After saying goodbye to Aradhna, I slog sluggishly uphill for around four kilometres, distracting myself with pleasant views and abundant butterflies and wildflowers, which I stop to photograph, as much to have regular moments of respite as to indulge in nature study. Finally, the rise levels off and I begin a descent, noting that I am high enough now for fir trees and the occasional logging truck. An almost dry riverbed, perhaps only irrigated by last night's rains, tells of a dry summer. I pass a strange shack near Gyulyovtsa, part tree-house and part hermit's hut, which appears to have a sign made from broken branches attached to its facade. I can't read the Cyrillic but take photos for later reference[2].

Gyulyovtsa offers a long, tree-lined main street with a domed, ornate chapel set in its own garden. Just outside the town is a peculiar architectural monstrosity – two giant trapeziums of concrete squat on either side of the road, announcing a county border. The villages now feel a little different. Do I imagine Ottoman influences in the geometric tiling and ornate gates I pass?[3] At Orizare, the decorative door-frame of a bar features a cartwheel inset into its lower half.

The azure sky is filling with tiny candyfloss clouds, crowding one another for space. I reach a vineyard bordering a small reservoir and am grateful for intermittent shade as the afternoon heat begins to rise. Aradhna passes by in Roxy and I beg her to stop nearby so that I can

---

1    By now any route estimation came with its own margin of uncertainty.
2    I entirely fail in this task, and then realise that it might read "The Kingdom of Pot" in English. Presumably a reference to marijuana, rather than a certain Cambodian demagogue.
3    My supposition later proves correct, as I am entering the mysterious Strandja region, which was once encompassed by the Ottoman Empire.

pause for a late lunch. A strong westerly wind springs up, cooling me but hindering forward motion. When running on dead legs, you feel the added burden of climatic conditions more keenly.

After crossing the dam-head, I see that Aradhna has pulled Roxy over into a small lane and I gratefully take my rest and refreshment, hindered only by the appearance of a giant black, white and green locust-like insect, which seems mostly interested in making its home in my running shoes. I have trouble eating, my stomach feeling unsettled, a mild nausea coming on. I decide to take an uncharacteristic nap in the roof-tent and although I don't drop off entirely, the ability to lie out in a comparatively cool, dark space, helps my mood considerably.

Feeling utterly fatigued but determined after my snooze, I start climbing a hill towards Burgas, the traffic increasing as I approach the city. Tour buses are especially frightening since their drivers seem loath to swerve out of my way when they fail to notice me until the last minute. I have to leap onto the grassy verge to keep moving. The sky continues to display a picturesque whorl of cumulus clouds as I run past fields of sunflowers and dry grasslands. There are a few more villages between me and the coast but I gladly take to a small strip of bridleway for a while, enjoying the feel of something other than tarmac under my feet.

\*\*\*

It's not long before I am funnelled back onto the E87 again, passing through another monumental concrete county line marker, this one softened by the presence nearby of a small cottage whose garden boasts a vivid array of flowers, attended by many yellow and black butterflies.

As my day draws to a close around 7:15pm, I find a lay-by alongside a field of horses and call Aradhna to come and get me. We find a Park4Night recommended spot on a spit of land to the north of Burgas, where we wait patiently for kids to stop driving in smoky, noisy circles in a nearby car park so we can sleep. Fortunately, they aren't there for an all-nighter and leave before twelve, leaving us to slip off into a dreamless sleep to the sound of crashing waves.

\*\*\*

### Day 101

Aradhna isn't feeling very well on 19th June and my legs are ruined so we call a much-needed admin and rest day. Some dog walkers and sunbathers can be seen on the small strip of sand below us and we decide to join them for a while. We swim and soak in the sun's benevolence for an hour or two, then set off to hunt down camping gas canisters and restock our food supplies. Both missions accomplished, we decide that we want to find a campsite, to avail ourselves of civilised washing facilities for ourselves and our clothes, as well as the all-important electrical hook-up.

Various chores later, we find the tiny private beach appended to the campsite and sit in our folding chairs contemplating the waves and all we've achieved to date. In just over a week from now, it will all be over (we hope). We've planned a leisurely journey back to London via several countries we've never visited before and might never again, including Albania, Montenegro and Croatia. First though, I have my secret mission, one linked inextricably to the small item I've hidden in my wash bag. That mission will reach fruition in a couple of weeks' time and preparations are already underway.

We finish our day off with some of my homemade chilli (sin carne), since I've not cooked for a while and am feeling guilty about my growing lassitude. I hope I can shake it off for Turkey and the grand finale – Istanbul.

**KILOMETRES TRAVELLED: 3070;**
**KILOMETRES REMAINING: 328**

# Tips for Multi-Day Runners - 13. To Film or Not to Film

Both my epic journeys to date have been filmed, in one sense or another. For this project, I used a cheap action camera on a steadying gimbal as a kind of visual Dictaphone, to record my thoughts whilst running and record the environments I passed through. On the JOGLE, the shooting was intended for a forthcoming documentary, so I also had my support crew film me with a DSLR camera as well as occasionally using a drone for spectacular landscape shots. There are distinct pros and cons to choosing to film your run:

*PROS* – you'll have a permanent record of the experience, to supplement your fading memories. Social media laps up video more than any other kind of content, which is invaluable if you are fundraising for charity or creating content for a sponsor.

*CONS* – you may have to carry bulky equipment with you, together with the onerous task of offloading the media and recharging batteries. This is particularly challenging if you're running without frequent access to mains power. I found a GoPro camera on a Fciyu gimbal was the best overall system for grabbing footage on the go, literally filming as I ran. I constructed a zippable shoulder-holster for the gimbal and camera, which worked extremely well.

Whatever you choose, remember to record times of adversity and your down moments as well as the epiphanies and triumphs – it's all part of the wonderful world of ultrarunning.

# Chapter 32: The Long-Forgotten Road

Uncharacteristically, I begin day 102 with a blood-red grapefruit, deciding that I need a vitamin C boost. It would not do to fall ill at this late stage in the adventure, particularly with some of the most arduous and dangerous stretches of road ahead, as the E87 becomes motorway-like towards Burgas. I find myself clinging to the white line beside a merciless crash-barrier, cars hooting as they blast past me. Google Maps on "walk" setting adds a strange loop to the route I'll have to take into Burgas, ignoring the direct road. I decide to ignore Google's idiosyncratic plan and stick to the road I am on.

I almost immediately regret it.

*\*\**

A mile outside of Burgas, I grind to a halt, facing a four-lane highway with no pavement or hard shoulder and buses and trucks roaring past every few seconds. Worse still, the next bit curves around a tight bend, with tall, overgrown bushes pushing their way into the roadway. I take a deep breath and begin to dash short sections between clumps of foliage, ducking in to let vehicles pass, then sprinting to the next scrap of verge between bushes.

After a few minutes of this, my nerves are shot, so I gratefully duck into a small lane leading down to what looks like hundreds of acres of flat fenland. Through this strangely peaceful scenery a small stream snakes, finding its way to the sea on my left, somewhere on the far side of the E87. I stand watching water birds feeding and feel my heart rate slow and my breathing quieten. I drink some water and eat some dried fruit and nuts. I can't lurk here for long, however, and so set off again after ten minutes, bolting past Burgas's immense sculptural sign and then a copse of small shrines and floral tributes to dead motorists (or pedestrians), hardly an encouraging sight.

Planes temporarily obscure the sun in a cloudless sky, coming in to land at the nearby airport. I grit my teeth and run as fast as my legs will take me down to a large roundabout, service station and the heavenly embrace of pavements. Another short break and snack stop later, I am passing imaginative street art and pastel-shaded high-rises, negotiating complex road junctions on raised walkways and crossing the railway tracks to access the Burgasian outskirts.

A cycle path surprises me (Bulgaria so far has featured very few cyclists) but I follow it assiduously over the following two hours, stopping once more for an ice lolly at yet another service station where a parked van branded "Runners" seems like a good omen. I am downing liquids at an alarming rate and immediately sweating them out under an unforgiving and relentless sun. Once more I find myself practising the diversionary tactic of scanning the environs for interesting distractions from my physical distress. A small police station, presumably decommissioned, is scrawled with graffitied genitalia. It's either defunct or local vandals are uncommonly brave and/or foolish. A hazard sign carries an illustration of a mother goose and three trailing goslings, a reminder of the protected wetlands adjacent to this bit of road.

Eventually, predictably, the cycle path ends abruptly and without warning. I've seen a single cyclist in the last two hours and this ending feels like a town planner's shrug of disillusionment. I imagine how busy this route would be in Germany or Hungary, both bicycle-loving nations in their very different ways. I wonder why Bulgarians have not embraced the bicycle. I am determined to seek out alternatives to the highway and find them in forgotten parallel roads and dirt tracks, leading me past a gap in the bushes which affords an impressive view out over the bite-shaped bay, whose far shore wears a necklace of barrel-shaped refineries.

A peaceful and shady interlude follows, in a small scrap of forest where I pass a grand garden with a volleyball net awaiting unseen players. However, I begin to feel the fatigue becoming all-consuming and it is with great relief that I hear Roxy's familiar engine noise behind me and wave her down into a lay-by for lunch. I try to persuade Aradhna that it is in both our best interests if I stop running for the day but she is having none of it. So close to the prize, she isn't going to allow me to slack off now.

*** 

On the south side of the bay I exchange the 99 for the much smaller 992, heading due south towards the town of Rosen, the first stop in a series of zig-zagging roads leading to the border at Malko Tarnovo. Rosen is prosaic, the bungalows red-roofed like British post-war homes, functional and affordable. I drag myself on, past ever-watchful storks and out into the countryside once more, finding myself running alongside a small lake. An adjacent field contains a sign saying the land is for sale; it looks like the advertisement has been there for some time. A youth is walking briskly along the road in front of me. I assume I'll catch him but don't. It is evidently a sign that the end of my running day has come.

Fortunately, Roxy stands parked in the long grass by the lake. I have no idea how Aradhna has got her there but if Aradhna feels confident enough to off-road Roxy in dry conditions like these, I will not challenge her – she's now by far the more experienced van driver. I pick my way over to her, through the thick vegetation, with much relief.

I stumble over to hug my girlfriend, having run 38km in total today, a very good result. We sleep accompanied by a gentler frog chorus than the one we heard at Manastirea in Romania. We awake to an insect-laden summer's day.

## Day 103

We leave our lake-view home and I head back up to the road while Aradhna does her final checks and packs up. The route I am taking is now a landscape of heavily wooded gentle hillsides, with fewer farms in sight than I've seen since the Carpathians. A large sign warns casual wanderers to look out for (but not pick) some of the rare flowers, including the red stars of sun-opened tulips. There is also an indication that tortoises roam wild here. Thistles up to six feet high line the roads, besieged by black and white butterflies with lacelike wing patterns.

Everything quickly becomes drier and rockier and it feels like I am approaching a geological boundary, if not yet a geographical one. The ground is tinder-dry and I wonder if wildfires are common here. Then, as if the visual comparisons to the African veldt are not prevalent enough, I come upon a herd of water buffalo, hard at work munching the crisp grass. No doubt another lake is nearby for the beasts to immerse themselves in. I am half-tempted to do the same.

I come to Veselie, whose streets are tiled in geometric mosaics of red, green, gold and white and lined with flowering bushes. I receive many enquiring looks from the villagers who are braving the noonday heat. Outside the town I find more public wilderness and a sign forbidding litter, open fires, camping and, apparently, the firing of semi-automatic weapons. A sluggish river, half empty, meanders at a pace even slower than my own and the local spring has evidently dried up, tin mugs nearby rendered redundant. I wonder when it last rained here.

\*\*\*

A denser forest crowds the road, bringing the promise of shade and the curse of mosquitos. Once more I don my makeshift hood and begin waving my hand in front of my face, clamping my mouth shut and breathing through my nose. The insects plague me as I climb slowly and then descend to the town of Yasna Polyana. Outside of town a series of wooden sculptures stands like totems by the side of the road – the first is a cubist collision of blocky letters and eyeholes, possibly spelling out the town's name in Cyrillic. The second is a twisted frame through which to survey a landscape of dry plains and distant, misty peaks. The third is a diver poised to leap from an immense pole but pierced by spears – sadly the artist's name is given in Cyrillic only.

Yasna itself, nestling in the knuckle at the base of a valley, is an exceptionally pretty place with neatly manicured flowerbeds and many more wooden sculptures, remnants of a woodcarving symposium held here in 2012. A carved and dopey stork poses amongst the marigolds, eyeing me with long woodshaving lashes. There is a grand public square with a substantial drinking fountain, where a driver is filling his water bottles.

\*\*\*

I've begun to see border patrol cars prowling the roads along which I now run, looking for intrepid and illegal immigrants from Turkey coming through the nearby fields[1]. It won't be long now. If not today, then tomorrow will see me enter Europe's sole Muslim-majority nation. Too conspicuous to be of real concern to the police, or so I think, I run past warehouses, then find a footpath out into forested countryside, leaving the tarmac for the relief of a trail.

During a brief pee stop I hear the voices of a man and woman calling to their horses (or so I imagine) but I never see the riders. A little later I run past a group of loggers, their truck parked in a clearing, having a cigarette break. As I run past, I nod hello but nobody seems especially concerned by or interested in my presence.

Clouds of midges now join the party swarming around my jacket-shrouded head. I find myself following a gurgling river, an experience I've not had since the Carpathians. Everything seems to be going well

---

1    At time of writing, these are mostly Syrians but by the time you read this, who knows what oppressive regime, war or famine may have displaced the world's most vulnerable peoples.

until the path abruptly turns down to the river and stops, leaving me floundering amongst the rocks, scratching my head for a way forward.

Wondering if I can hop over the rocks to the other side of the river without falling in, I begin to doubt the sense of the route Google Maps has found for me. This path through the woods has evidently not been travelled by anyone for years. Still, some shreds of it must remain, I hope, as I teeter over the river, plunging the habitual single foot accidentally into the flow.

Optimism always wins over common sense. My trail-finding takes on an archaeological dimension, sending me back in time, past the overgrown remains of a long-crumbled ancient bridge and roadway. I force myself through bushes and over fallen tree-trunks, eventually finding the preserved remains of a road which clearly hasn't been in use for at least sixty years. It once took locals through the forest but now the forest has taken it back.

The not-a-road sidles around rocky cliffs and cuts through densely packed trees until, abruptly, I hit a ten-metre-wide gap, two metres deep, where a hunk of the road surface has seemingly been bitten away. I clamber down and up the other side of the mini-ravine and press on, very sure now that I am on a path taken by nobody at all in recent memory. It is both exciting and frightening at the same time. If this way becomes impassable, what on earth will I do?

My pace slows to a crawl, with short stretches of running where ancient tarmac wins out briefly over the underbrush. I have no phone signal, so can't send a text and my situation isn't quite problematic enough to warrant an email from the Garmin (I have an allowance of only a handful of these per month). In a strange way, the sounds of distant logging (chainsaws and yelling) are almost comforting. I'm not the only human out here. I follow the mendacious blue line on Google Maps up a perilously steep forest path only to discover it's veering me off in entirely the wrong direction. I backtrack to where I missed the "junction" – this route is so long gone that all navigational definitions no longer make sense – and try again.

Finally, the road becomes a recently maintained gravel path and as I feel my feet lift once more into a trot, I hear a strange snort from somewhere to my left and squint through a gap in the hedgerow to see something that chills my blood and excites me in equal measure.

Wild boar! At least eight of them, as large as calves and a lot more dangerous, the creatures rumble on heavy hooves towards and past me on a thankfully parallel path.

Jet black with long tusks, shoulder muscles piled over one another like boulders, the herd is magnificent and terrifying in equal measure. In a moment, it's gone, leaving only the echo of hooves and the memory of something almost primeval. My thoughts wander to what I'd have done if they had charged towards me on my own path and I find myself unable to formulate a sensible answer.

Soon I'm running along a surface of hardpacked dirt – an actual road, of sorts. As soon as I get reception again, I begin texting Aradhna updates on my challenging progress. I am suddenly glad, though not entirely surprised, to see Roxy parked up at the side of the path. Aradhna has come to intercept me. She doesn't want me to stop running and quickly disabuses me of the notion that I might rest here. She has found a good spot to camp for the night and it's only 1.5km further on.

Only 1.5km. The charming naïveté of the non-runner. Aradhna is so used to me running 35-plus kilometres a day that this last 1500m seems inconsequential. And so it would have been – at the start of the day. I sigh and jog on as Roxy trundles behind me, then overtakes and drives slowly in front, like a faithful hound that's eager to speed off ahead but knows it must hold back. Actually, the enforced discipline helps. I maintain a good pace and am relieved to reach a junction where this half-road/half-trail meets the potholed 99.

A bit of scouting leads us to a turn off into a patch of grassy rough ground. It's peaceful and we're invisible from the road, but we also appear to be invisible to the hordes of huge but clumsy bees that smack noisily into Roxy's sides and windows, as if drunk on their own nectar. They are the least aerodynamic insects I've ever seen, hindered it seems by gigantic green eyes which bulge from their tiny heads. No amount of Googling can clarify exactly what these beasties are but they are an epic nuisance.

Finally, we can't take it any more and jump back in Roxy to see if we can drive back to the coast. After 10km on a road so rutted and potholed we can hardly believe it's a pay route, we decide to give up and head back to the bee-besieged meadow. We de-insect the interior and shut ourselves inside, and the peace and quiet is palpable, although I can't help but wonder if this is the proverbial calm before the storm.

**KILOMETRES TRAVELLED: 3136;**
**KILOMETRES REMAINING: 262**

# Chapter 33: A Police Escort

*Day 104*

When we return to the road junction where I stopped the previous day, a logging truck has broken down opposite, one of its front tyres evidently exploded, possibly as a consequence of the many gigantic potholes on the main road. The driver, wearing an expression midway between exasperation and resignation, speaks no English but seems to be calling for assistance, which, we gather, is on its way. He gratefully accepts Aradhna's gift of an iced tea and swigs the bottle down in one. We wonder how long he's been here.

Unencumbered by such fragile supports as pneumatic tyres, I jog off up the road while the driver looks on, amused. The day is hot, humid and very quiet, which is how I want it. The road continues to climb, offering views of hills veiled in mist and heat-haze. Young ponies in a neighbouring field snort and flick the many flies away with their blonde manes. I feel the familiar cloud of mosquitos gathering and don the hood once more. Running with my hand waving in front of my face is now second nature.

The town of Vizitsa appears, the first place of habitation I've passed for some time. Gardens are vivid with roses and trellised vines. I pause to slurp cool water from a spouting spring.

I turn onto the 99, the road that defeated Roxy yesterday, and make it to Gramatikovo, a town scattered amongst green hillsides. Like so many Bulgarian places, it is set away from the main road, so I bypass it on a road now so pockmarked that it resembles the surface of a much-abused moon. I keep climbing and soon pine trees are visible at the roadside, making it seem like I've looped back in time to my adventures in the Black Forest. Aradhna has decided to follow me closely to the border today and stops every so often to refill my water and check I am okay. Having her close by really helps, especially as the sky begins to darken ominously.

\*\*\*

I leap into Roxy's interior as a violent hailstorm begins, tossing down bean-sized balls of ice. The storm passes as abruptly as it began and I run on after lunch, planning on another eight to ten kilometres before calling it a day. Trees with an unusual red bark offer some variety in a landscape of myriad greens. Then, on one of the trunks, I spy a white triangle with a green stripe; an unmistakable trail-marker! The wet roadway ahead steams like a jungle floor as the sun forces its way through low cloud and heats up the crumbling tarmac. The rest of the afternoon brings sticky humidity and partly-shaded roads almost devoid of traffic, save the occasional border patrol car. As I crest one hill, I wonder whether the mist-swathed slopes in the distance are Turkish. If so, it looks like my final frontier will bring a few more challenges than I might have anticipated.

Towards the end of the day I stop on a high hillside, with open pastureland on the left and a distant wailing call I think might be the sound of the muezzin, drifting over the border at the start of evening prayers. Perhaps this is a fanciful notion but it fills me with a sense of excitement.

Aradhna and Roxy are waiting, parked just off the road in a convenient lay-by. The spot has a bench built into the limbs of a small tree and information boards advertising two bicycle trails in the vicinity. We are clearly in a country park of some sort and fortunately, the higher altitude and cool breeze keep the insects at bay. The view across the rolling valleys, farms alternating with patches of deciduous woodland, is soothing and pleasantly domestic in scale – the Chilterns rather than the Cairngorms. The sky has clouded over with shifting thin layers of grey through which a peachy sunset blooms.

Aradhna still feels a little poorly and takes a nap in the roof while I do the admin work and cook us both an omelette. A blessed peace descends, although something tells me it can't last.

Heavy, unrelenting rain batters Roxy overnight, complementing the distant howling of jackals. My mid-morning delaying tactics do not impress Aradhna and eventually I have to face the downpour and the ruined roadway as I run downhill towards Malko Tarnovo, the last town in Bulgaria (or this part of it, at least). At least the rain keeps the mosquitos away.

\*\*\*

Malko Tarnovo is a smallish town which displays its civic pride and its history in an unusual way – a display of cut-out and life-size figurines, with holes for faces through which passing tourists can peep for photographs. I resist and run on, scouting for a money exchange and water fountain for Aradhna, who is still packing up somewhere behind me. Aradhna successfully locates the former while I spy a drinking water fountain, ironically surrounded by a veritable river of rain cascading down the nearby streets.

After I lead Aradhna to the water and help her fill up, I squelch off, trying to make the best of it. I've been exceptionally fortunate with the weather throughout the trip, so I can't really begrudge a day of rain. I splash past a couple of dogs disconsolately mating in a nearby churchyard, while other dogs look on, unimpressed. None of them seems to be able to muster the energy to bark at me.

The misty mountains I spied the previous day come ever-closer as I make for the border. I pass a sign telling me that Turkey is a mere 3km away. Another sign confirms that I am in the Strandja Nature Park, evidently shared between the neighbouring countries[1]. I see a parked border patrol as I join the E87 route once more and am approached by a young officer. He asks where I am going and when I explain that I am running to the border and that Aradhna has driven on ahead with my passport, he simply nods.

"Your girlfriend? It's okay."

And he waves me on. Evidently Aradhna has already met this young man and explained why she is hovering at the roadside by the border in a van that might look ideal for people smuggling. I silently applaud her ability to convey innocence and trustworthiness, and run on, unstopped and feeling, for once, unstoppable.

Aradhna has mostly been waiting near the border for my benefit, but also so that I can accompany her across into Turkey. She has been nervous about entering the country as a lone woman driving a van, a fact I don't entirely appreciate. I've been downplaying her fears, partly because I don't share them and partly because if I really thought she was in danger I'd never be able to leave her at the mercy of her anxieties. It is, I now realise, more than a little dismissive of me. The subtle negotiations of personality required by any lasting relationship remain a challenge and our partnership permanently a work-in-progress.

---

1    Fantastic insights into this melancholy and spooky region can be found in Kapka Kassabova's book *Border* (Granta, 2018) which I read upon my return from our adventure, immediately recognising the landscape and the people I'd unfortunately had very little time to talk to as I ran through their world.

***

As I approach the border, I pass an abandoned and derelict sentry box only to discover that it is neither abandoned nor derelict, merely rather shabby and occupied by two bored thirty-something border policemen, with their large and boisterous Alsatian. They stop me and ask for my passport.

"Er, I don't have it. It's with my girlfriend. She's waiting at the border," I explain.

The officers look dubious and go to telephone a superior. I hover, annoyed by the delay, but determined to look accommodating and harmless. After around ten minutes, the officers reappear with their dog.

"We will come with you."

As I walk with them, I try to lighten the mood by suggesting that they might run with me. Unamused, they decline, sticking to a strolling pace. I try again.

"I suppose if I were to run now, he would chase me?" I ask, indicating the Alsatian.

"Oh, yes," the younger of the two officers replies, in a tone that suggests that this would be an unpleasant outcome for only one of us. The policemen exchange a laugh and are perfectly pleasant company for the kilometre or two it takes to stroll to the border checkpoint, where Aradhna is indeed waiting. Seeing me appear with my police escort, Aradhna blanches but is relieved when they simply examine our passports and nod us on with a smile. It's a world away from the summary border shootings and imprisonments of the former Soviet bloc country I am now intent on leaving.

***

After a short delay to obtain compulsory road insurance, we pass all the necessary checks and I jog into Turkey, noticing at once a vivid improvement in road quality. Gone are the collapsing Bulgarian roads with potholes like the craters of the moon. In their stead, a wide curve of almost empty highway stretches before me, newly-surfaced, with a hard shoulder as wide as many of the farm roads I've taken. Around this immaculate road, a much older and now abandoned single track road loops, leaving stranded sections behind like oxbow lakes on a river's floodplain.

A low mist floats on the road surface in places and plentiful springs are graffitied with the date 1914. Later research reminds me that this date marked the beginnings of the Armenian Genocide, when the Ottoman Empire forcibly murdered or expelled millions of its Armenian citizens, making them march into the Syrian Desert. In total, around 1.5 million Armenians died. Sadly, Turkey to this day does not accept the term genocide for these atrocities, despite international lobbying for its recognition.

We find a lay-by to stop for lunch just outside Dereköy and I wolf down plate after plate of food, including, randomly, slices of avocado, cheese and oatcakes and German spiced biscuits. Aradhna warns me that she has driven through Dereköy and, although picturesque, it wasn't a comfortable place for her and she received many stares. Although I try to allay her fears once more, I have to admit that the place has the feel of a pretty but remote hamlet through which strangers never pass, let alone athletic tourists from overseas and lone women driving campervans.

I keep up a good pace, nodding to a few locals (all dark-skinned men, all shabbily suited and most of them bewhiskered) as I make my way towards the gently rolling Thracian hills. I didn't know Turkey could be like this – humid and cool – imagining instead sunbaked plains and twisted olive trees.

A spaniel follows me a little way out of town and I feel a little ashamed that I have to turn and shout at my canine companion to get him to leave me behind. I head out through dirt tracks behind the houses and factories and finish my run against a blazing sunset and an impromptu rainbow, the combination of the two almost absurdly beautiful. Although I've only run an additional 8km since lunch, I decide to call it a day. Still uncertain about this new country, we elect to sleep downstairs, parked by the side of the road overlooking a small reservoir. The spot is quiet and pretty and we pass a thankfully uneventful first night in our eighth and final country.

*** 

## Day 106

Today begins with a wander down to the side of the reservoir. A few fishermen have driven 4x4s down to the water's edge and have cast their lines into the placid blue. They leave us quite alone and we enjoy a contemplative moment which includes watching a line of ants manoeuvring large bits of leaf and other edible remnants into the tiny entrance to their underground nest. There is something about the nature of their painstaking progress and collaborative determination that strikes a chord. Aradhna and I have got this far by being equally steadfast in both our goals and in our support of one another. In just a few days' time it will hopefully all pay off.

Meanwhile, my body has changed considerably. Although fatigued and jogging steadily with stiff legs, I feel lean and strong in my muscles and sinews. I am sleeping better, eating more, sweating less and urinating more frequently, as if my cooling system has learned to cope with my body temperature being raised for a significant part of each day. Once more I am reminded what remarkable machines our bodies are, capable of subtle adaption and great endurance.

I will have one more thing to endure today – heavy and constant rain as I head out along roads lined with red earth embankments and soon streaming with running water. I am wet through in minutes and then have to accept that I'll be covered in moisture all day.

Behind the small town of Karadere I find a country lane leading up into the hills, then forestry roads and gravel access paths carry me alongside a parade of giant wind turbines. I am so close to these monsters that I could touch their immense boles, yet do not. Something about their monumental and throbbing power keeps me at a safe distance. I don't fear stray dogs as I run; surely the weather is so inclement that even they will be sensibly tucked up under the protection of the trees.

Some of the hollows in the narrower forest trails have filled with mist, which makes running both spooky and atmospheric. Despite the season, latitude and country in which I am running, I also manage to feel a little cold whenever I pause to take a photo. After the zone of windmills, I run into hills less industrial, dotted with villages and even a questionable-looking campsite, which seems to consist of little more than a hand-written sign and a wooden gazebo in which a man is mysteriously lying on his back, hands propped behind his head. Drunk, meditating or deceased, I couldn't say. The rain drives me on.

A sign promised "Balaban" in 19km and that seems a likely place to stop for the day. I like that this is also the surname of a noted American character actor (Bob Balaban) and wonder if his family hailed from the area[1]. The paths I am following take me past a plantation of skinny trees and over a river swollen by the rains. A backdrop of misty hills

---

1  Apparently not – they are of Russian / Romanian Jewish origin.

adds mystery to the destination ahead and when I Google the name of one town through which I pass (Karanlik) its name translates as "darkness". I see precisely nobody on the roads but hardly expect to, given the rain.

A small rest stop soon beckons, with a spring, benches and tables and a Turkish flag which has wound itself around a tree branch in the wind. I unfurl it and let it fly. The road spirals and climbs through woodland (boughs heavy with crab apples) and I break out of a green tunnel abruptly onto a road open on one side, giving fantastic views across a leafy and sodden land, far from the bakingly hot and arid Turkey I'd imagined. Once more I come to realise how paltry my geographical general knowledge really is. So far the Turkish Strandja region has been as lush as anywhere in England, the steaming forest almost jungle-like.

Sarpdere's pretty houses and mosque remind me that this forest has people in it. I will now see as many minarets as I had seen church steeples in France and Germany, often hearing the amplified clerics calling the faithful to prayer before I am close enough to see the neighbourhood mosque rise up above its village. I pass a rest stop even larger than the previous one, with several parked cars and families gathering to refill their water tanks, picnic together, or sit upon the swings. I wave and move on, glad to have seen someone else out on the roads.

The road arcs down into a valley where open meadows are dotted with white and occasionally black sheep, munching away contentedly. A sign proclaiming Balaban appears and Roxy is parked by a large well, Aradhna sensibly ensconced within.

**KILOMETRES TRAVELLED: 3218;**
**KILOMETRES REMAINING: 180**

# Tips for Multi-Day Runners – 14. Fatigue

On multi-day running adventures, you'll certainly experience waves of exhaustion that will sap your energy reserves and threaten your will to continue. It is important to both recognise what these slumps are and find creative ways to combat them. Here are some of the tricks I used when the kilometres began to seem like a treadmill you can never get off.

*BREAK IT DOWN* – If you're facing 40km on dead legs, don't focus on that extreme number. Think instead about getting as far as the village that's 12km away, or getting out of the forest or over the next hill. Rest stops are great motivators, but they should be tied to a specified landmark or place.

*REWARD YOURSELF* – Make an internal bargain, "If I get to the next town, I'll be able to eat that chocolate bar" (you'll find food a great motivator). Rewards should be proportional to the size of the achievement and do remember to share end-of-the-day rewards with your long-suffering support crew.

*MUSIC* – I only run with music in long, boring stretches of featureless road or when my willpower is in serious decline. I find the pulse of rhythmic music energises me and provides a useful distraction from the endless slog. You might also find that podcasts or audiobooks work as mental deflection too.

*WALK IT OUT* – It is okay to take walking breaks when your muscles ache and energy levels are waning. Pick something in visual range and walk until you get there. Especially save your dwindling energy levels by walking steep hills. Make sure you do start running again when you reach the landmark you had in mind.

*EAT AND DRINK* – It may sound blindingly obvious but make sure you're not mistaking hunger or dehydration for deep-in-the-bones fatigue. This is when you'll draw upon those rather unappetising glucose gels. Put some electrolyte tablets in your water and drink a little more frequently than usual. Your body is a kind of energy-processing machine and you'll only get out what you put in.

*CAT NAPS* – If you have a safe place (ideally a vehicle) in which to grab 40 winks in the middle of a long day, then do so. Sleep encourages the production of HGH (human growth hormone), which is key to repairing and rebuilding muscles. Fatigue and cognitive performance should improve post-nap too.

*FOCUS ON THE ACHIEVEMENT* – Lastly, remind yourself how incredible what you're doing really is. Hardly anyone ever runs for days on end through some of the places you'll be exploring. Think ahead to how good you'll feel when you're resting and looking back on these difficult kilometres.

# Chapter 34: Tea and Rifles

I round the rocky hillside, still confused by the sight of what seemed to be a military lookout tower and wondering if it was sensible to step over the fallen gate I passed a mile or so back. As the evening light dims towards sunset, a white booth appears below me, two young men in military uniform standing nearby.

They are facing away from me, smoking and apparently blithely unaware of my approach. Given their shoulder-slung rifles, I realise I'd better announce myself. I clear my throat.

They turn, immediately alarmed and grabbing at their weapons. It is only then that I realise I am trespassing on a military base on the day of Turkey's presidential elections. This might not end well.

*** 

To understand my fears, we have to rewind to the beginning of that remarkable day when, leaving Balaban, I am reminded of the political situation in Turkey by the visage of current president, Recep Tayyip Erdoğan, printed on a sheet and proudly displayed from a well-to-do home on the outskirts of town. Today the country is due to hold its presidential and parliamentary elections and the incumbent president is the favourite to become head of both state and government, a situation some fear will bring about a communist-style rule by dictat (something the country's northern neighbours know too well). This democratic election could paradoxically engender a situation where one man holds total sway over his electorate. Erdoğan brought the election date forward from summer 2019 in order (critics feel) to prevent his opposition from mounting an effective campaign.

It is fair to say that Europe is closely observing its only majority-Muslim candidate member to see whether a Western-styled democracy can be maintained, amidst rumours of vote-stuffing and other manipulation[1].

---

[1] Turkey has been a candidate member since 1999 and negotiations for full membership began in 2005, but its legal and human rights record in recent decades has so far stymied its accession to the Union.

Ignorant as I am of the true situation as I run through the villages on 26th June, I know only that an election is happening soon. I think little of it and run on, the road out of town constructed of reddish gravel and so quiet that Aradhna is able to drive alongside me as I run. It makes a nice change to have her company and only once does she have to pull in behind me to allow a logging truck to sidle by. The weather is warm and humid, the road undulating up into the hills. Aradhna even films a shot of me ambling along, moving at a decent, if unheroic pace. We part company as the gravel road meets a broad, curving highway leading up a major slope.

I'd worry if the road had not such wide hard shoulders, allowing me to run separated from the trucks and cars by at least six feet. That is to say, except when I run a left-curving corner, often cut by drivers hurtling towards me, forcing me to press myself against the crash barrier. Happily, most motorists are generous, giving me a wide berth. The road provides amazing views over the lush, green fields and forests below and reaches its apex at a summit 810 metres high. I should add that it peaks only after almost 8km of constant ascent, leaving my quads and calves aching.

\*\*\*

I fancy I can almost see Istanbul in the far distance, or at least some housing blocks on its northern periphery, but the horizon is surely 50km away from my high vantage point. A quarry slices open the top of a nearby hill, reminding me that this is worked countryside, very much in service to the city. With gratitude, I swap my uphill slog for a downhill trot, letting other muscle groups take the strain. I am able to leave the truck-laden D-road outside Yenice, a pretty town of red pantiled roofs surrounded by small fields. The terrain has levelled out to a gently rolling patchwork of small roads and equally small plots of land lined with olive trees and dotted with wildflowers. Suddenly this feels like the Turkey I'd expected – a rich, sunbaked landscape with small villages centring on the local mosque, its minaret providing a visual pointer, a push-pin pressed into the world-map beneath.

There are fewer trees and the view over the lowlands allows me to see what lies before me, seemingly an easy ride down into Istanbul. But little in ultrarunning is as it first appears. The roads are generally good, the traffic intermittent and well-behaved. The farms I pass seem pocket-sized when compared with those on an industrial scale I saw in Hungary and Bulgaria. At Sergen, two dogs come running and yapping at me but are quickly cowed by the stick I hold, which now feels like as much a piece of my running kit as sunglasses, cap or backpack.

My strangest encounter is with, of all creatures, a small red-brown crab that scuttles quickly out of my way, either a freshwater dweller or someone's lunch, having executed a cunning escape. We lunch near Evrencik, having painstakingly levelled Roxy with my patented technique of digging trenches for her wheels to settle into. After eating, I am keen to be off, a whiff of the finishing line having hit me now. I locate a forest path suggested by Google Maps, forgetting once more how variable that resource can be.

***

The trail takes me along dusty lanes lit by evening light and a sentinel moon, three-quarters full. It glows pale blue in a bluer sky overhead. I see nobody but a few forestry workers having a cigarette break amongst the young plantation all around. Surprisingly, I spot oak and maple trees among the young saplings – destined for furniture I suppose. It looks like we'll find plenty of good wild camping spots, since there are many side paths and the tracks of vehicles amongst the reddish dust. I text Aradhna to ask her to find me somewhere on my current route, imagining Roxy hoving into sight over one of the small rises. I am beginning to feel extremely fatigued and the sun is skimming the horizon. I really don't want to get stuck running through this place under moonlight alone and, of course, I haven't packed my head torch.

Aradhna texts to warn me that she's encountered a large military base covering much of the land north of our intended stopping point, the town of Vize. I reason that signposts or fences would suffice to repel intruders – as long as I steer clear of anything obviously military I'll be fine. Inevitably, this is a naïve assumption.

The rocky hilltop and surrounding moorland is frequented by small skittish deer, which bound away at my approach. These animals distract me from further clues to where I am heading, including spent bullet cartridges and curls of barbed wire. There are a couple of warning signs on the plantation side of the hill in Turkish, which I guess have something to do with trespassing in the forest. I even hop over a fallen fence, the gate lying useless amongst the dust, assuming that if there were anything worth protecting beyond it, the fence would be properly maintained.

It is only when I encounter the two young armed sentries that I realise I have made a full set of false assumptions. As the frankly teenage soldiers grab at their guns, I begin to garble an explanation.

"I just ran over the hill. There were no signs. I'm running to Istanbul."

The young men pause to process my words, clearly unsure how to handle me.

"Running?"

"Yes. To Istanbul. I'm sorry, I must have taken a wrong turning."

Their expressions reveal that this is something of an understatement. One sentry begins to gabble into a walkie-talkie as they lead me down the hillside, guns in hand. On the way down, a large all-terrain truck rumbles up to meet us and I am instructed to climb in. I sit beside a young officer (let's call him a sergeant), who speaks better English than the younger privates (possibly doing national service) who accosted me. Once I explain what I am doing, he tells me with pride that he runs 10km per day. I congratulate him, thinking that any opportunity for bonding might stand me in good stead, when it comes to negotiating my release from a Turkish prison.

As we approach a group of blocky buildings and an imposing, well-guarded fence and gateway, it beccomes clear that I'm within the same military base Aradhna warned me about earlier. I jump down from the truck and am led into one of the buildings, into a small office and ordered to sit in front of a desk behind which sits a smiling forty-something officer, probably a grade higher than my fellow runner (let's call him the captain). He wears a non-committal and serious expression, with a hint of a smile.

"ID?" asks the captain. I shake my head ruefully, indicating my running apparel. Then I remember that I have the Turkish e-Visa on my phone. I ask permission to look through my iPhone and the captain nods. I find the visa and pass the phone over. The captain studies it and then calls his superior (I'm imagining a colonel seated somewhere comfortable). The conversation takes place over a mobile phone plugged into some mysterious white box, presumably to scramble the signal. I then hear a word from the sergeant that I think I recognise, but can't be sure.

"Chai?"

They can't really be offering me tea, can they? I decide to assume that they were.

"Sure," I nod vociferously. "Thanks."

A few moments later, while the captain is still considering what to do with me, a glass of hot, black tea appears, tasty and refreshing. I immediately relax, as any British person would. If they are offering me tea, surely they can't have any evil intentions.

Then my fellow runner passes me his phone. He's used Google Translate to render a phrase into English.

"It will be okay."

Once more, I relax. I type my own phrase, asking permission to tell Aradhna where I am. The officers nod agreement and I had the following exchange with my girlfriend:

*I'm with some soldiers. They're being nice to me, but I may be a while. X*

I turn my attention back to the captain and don't see Aradhna's reply:

*Ah. Are you being escorted? Are you okay?*

Meanwhile, I decline a second cup of tea, after the captain finishes his and requests more. The Sergeant shows me another message generated on his phone:

Erdoğan *won!!!*

He laughs heartily.

In that moment, I remember that the election is being held today and that there might be some controversy over the fairness of the result. Is this officer pro-Erdoğan? Is he being ironic, suggesting that the result is far from a surprise? I try to hedge my bets with my response, offering a small laugh and a half-shrug, as if to say, "Of course he did." Who knows what political allegiances these men have? I have seen the film *Midnight Express* many years ago and want more than anything to avoid ending up in a Turkish prison.

The captain hangs up from his lengthy chat with the putative colonel. He nods and says something to his sergeant, who turns to me.

"You can go."

Immense relief floods me. I ask if I can phone Aradhna for a pick-up and they agree, highly amused, as they lead me out of the fortified entrance, as Roxy draws up and Aradhna jumps out, wide-eyed. I bid a fond farewell to the running sergeant and his sentries. I climb into Roxy and feel just a little on edge as Aradhna backs the van out of the narrow concrete channel in which she'd been directed to park. We drive swiftly away from the scene of my trespass, past glimpses of street-parties and other festivities. Erdoğan's supporters are highly visible in Vize at least and are celebrating democracy dealing them a winning hand. I am just glad not to be squatting in a dark hole somewhere, begging for my freedom.

Freedom is something seldom appreciated until it is threatened.

**KILOMETRES TRAVELLED: 3292;**
**KILOMETRES REMAINING: 106**

# Chapter 35: A Rescued Sunflower

***Day 108***

We awake to a sea of sunflowers, having parked in darkness the previous night as an act of desperation, at the edge of a quiet farm road. We drove around the outskirts of Vize as the sun set, looking for a quiet spot and found one by a small spring. This morning we are rudely awakened by a gigantic combine harvester mounting the verge to ease by us; we make apologetic faces and wave it through. Then, after filling our tanks and my backpack with cool water, we head back to the gate by the military base, trying to be a little less conspicuous this time. A group of teenagers playing on their bikes wave me off, hopefully non-sarcastically.

Vize is the busiest town I've so far seen in Turkey and feels almost like a dry run for Istanbul. Triangular warning signs contain graphics of tanks, a vivid reminder of the town's military presence. I run past a garish statue of Atatürk and his family, gold-painted and apparently recently vandalised. The founder of modern Turkey is not without his detractors. A staunch nationalist and reformer, his secular ideals did not sit well with more Islamist factions within the country and seemingly still don't.

A high street not dissimilar to one in any provincial UK town leads to a small, smart mosque with a garden at its furthest extent. There are lots of shoppers out and about and I am even heckled (encouraged?) by some construction workers as I run. I expect that even here, so close to the capital, I am a peculiar and unusual sight.

Soon though I leave the shops and apartments behind and head out on the edge of the D20 route towards Istanbul. I am not looking forward to returning to the highways but I can't discern a more sensible way into the capital. A road sign informs me that today's target – Saray – lies 20km away with Istanbul itself 121km further still. Three to four days of good running, in other words. When we were planning this adventure, Aradhna calculated that we might finish at the end of June. At the time, I'd been a little scathing of what I felt to be a conservative estimate of my daily mileage. In this respect, as in most things, it looks like my better half is going to be spot on.

Combines and tractors crawl through fields of wheat under glowering grey skies which provide some of the first decent cloud cover I've experienced for weeks. There are many more sunflowers in evidence, with small stalls in some of the fields that might serve either as sales kiosks or places for itinerant farm-workers to pick up their wages. Today they are unmanned.

\*\*\*

Perhaps in part because of the cooler temperatures and also how close my goal is getting, I experience a phase of "rocket legs" for the first time in many weeks, picking up the pace as I run alongside the cars, managing almost 12kph. Trucks rumble by as I stick to a strip of gravel between 30cm and a metre wide. Sometimes a passing car sounds its horn and few drivers make much of an effort to pull out and give me space. Trucks certainly never do. I feel the hurtling vehicles' air streams ruffling my t-shirt as they pass.

A stepped and ornate wall with arched portals stretches ahead for around 1500 metres. It looks like the mock-up of a walled city exterior but proves to be merely the perimeter of a now-defunct factory complex. It must once have been rather prestigious, I surmise.

At Çakilli, a roadside café hides in a grove of trees and I am tempted to stop but decide to press on to lunch at Saray. The town is bustling and thick with traffic so I take to side streets, dirt-packed and lined with apartment blocks but still in use as a cut-through by huge lorries. I persevere along lively high streets, dodging broken paving stones, sleeping dogs and zig-zagging shoppers. One shop has a table outside upon which two pristine silver samovars stand, each four-spouted to dispense tea. We have lunch on a side street on the edge of town and after just 45 minutes I press on once more.

\*\*\*

Beyond Saray the D20 stretches out, straight, featureless and rather monotonous. I pass what looks like a large ranch, a sign outside featuring a man kneeling to his bride, suggesting a facility for weddings. It is the last building I'll pass for several hours. Thunder rumbles ominously in a sky the colour of the water an artist washes his brushes in (and just as murky). Inevitably, it begins to rain: a driving rain that soaks and chills me, making the afternoon's run a feat of endurance. Occasionally, I duck into the trees by the side of the road to attempt to wipe my phone dry and check where I am on the map. There are no visible landmarks, just forest and road.

Eventually, although sunset is at least two hours away, it becomes so dark and the rain so thick that the cars can no longer see me and there is no discernible verge. I stop at a forest access road and manage to call Aradhna. Ten minutes later, she drives back to pick me up. I take a selfie in the rain because I am almost certainly the wettest I've been so far on this trip. Then we drive further down the gravel road and find a quiet place to park and sleep.

A mangy dog with cut-off ears and hanging teats, indicating that she is either pregnant or has recently given birth, wanders up to the van and we feed her on biscuits and leftover bread.

As we prepare to sleep, a couple of large trucks rumble by; construction rather than logging vehicles. We guess there might be a development in progress somewhere down the road. Nobody bothers us, although a car screeches to a stop so that its driver can get out and hurl abuse and stones at the poor bitch we'd fed earlier. His behaviour towards the animal is so furious we can only imagine he's either an owner who tried to abandon the forlorn mutt, or he somehow sees her as a dangerous pest.

After the lightning, the air clears and the stars come out, accompanied, I discover, by the green Morse code flashes of fireflies. I call Aradhna out to see them, glad that it's me showing her something magical for a change (she sometimes asks me to look at the stars with her on the trip and, I confess, I am often too exhausted to work up the right degree of enthusiasm).

***

### Day 109

The following morning another spell of rain turns to violent hail. Rather than the usual pea-shaped pieces, this hailstorm throws down ice chips the size of cornflakes. I am doubly glad not to be running in it. Our canine friend has sensibly hidden under a tree and later, when I follow her to find a toilet spot, I find a still-frozen ice chip the size of my thumb, a full hour after the storm has passed. Before we leave, we make sure the desolate dog has a full breakfast, then bid her farewell. We don't want to dwell on what had happened to her puppies or how she lost her ears.

\*\*\*

The D20 begins to wind around low hills, much to my relief, quickly bringing me to the village of Safaalan. I stop to photograph a pretty town with several mosques, hearing the muezzin's call ringing across the valley and waving at an old woman who is walking, swathed in black, her head covered in a shawl. She smiles back, seemingly unperturbed by this Lycra-clad apparition.

Signs on the road forbid the firing of rifles (presumably illicit hunting) for which I am immensely grateful. Another sign informs me that I am in the administrative region of Istanbul and a third reassures me that I now have just 100km left to the city centre.

My first ultra race had been the 100km London to Brighton challenge, back in 2014, which I completed in a little over 13 hours. I suspect this 100km will take a little longer.

I begin to pass roadside "piknik" cafés and wood-built designer homes nestling amongst the trees. I sense I am running into a well-to-do commuter region. Many homes and businesses proudly display Turkish flags, something I'd seen a little less of in the villages. There are fewer EU flags than in most of the other European Union countries through which we passed. The inclement weather has broken and I am soon baking in the heat, passing pretty towns edged with cabbage fields, each with its pristine mosque. I pass Aydinlar and aim to have lunch at Gümüşpınar. My legs still feel surprisingly sprightly, if not quite as fast as yesterday.

A breeze helps make the heat manageable, as does a brief stop at a roadside fountain to splash water on my face and neck and refill my CamelBak. I stomp downhill, pounding round blind bends, dodging trucks, to make it to Gümüşpınar, where I find Roxy parked in the shade by a small walled cemetery. I lie down on a raised flat stone which I think might have been a flower stall, enjoying the cool granite on my back. Aradhna is feeling a little down and I am probably not as appreciative as I ought to be; we don't argue as such, but the mood at lunch is a little chilly. I set off wishing there is something I could do to show her how hugely grateful I am, despite my veneer of indifference.

I pass an innovative answer to traffic control a little way down the D20 – a life-size cardboard cut-out of a police car, complete with silhouettes of officers lurking in wait. Whether it works for locals, I don't know, but it fools me until I am a few metres away. I then have a kilometre or two running along a very challenging tarmac embankment with no crash barrier and a steep drop down to a bramble-strewn ditch. As trucks roar past, I have to step a foot or two down the perilous camber several times, then hop back up onto the road surface to dash a few hundred metres more. Nobody gives me much room, clearly neither expecting nor wanting me to be there. There are absolutely no cyclists, anywhere.

It is on one of these evasions that I spot my peace offering. A stray baby sunflower has somehow seeded itself into the edge of the road, its face turned to the traffic and just half a meter from being side-swiped into oblivion by an oblivious motorist. I feel it would be an act of kindness to rescue this wayward flower, as well as a cute present for Aradhna. We'd talked about having a plant or two in the van but had never got around to it. Here is our chance. I uproot the small sunflower and insert it gently into my backpack, after first wetting the roots. I just hope the stem won't break as I run.

Fortunately, for both me and my floral companion, I shortly locate a forest road forking off from the D20 and decide to take a bit of respite from the highway. That said, it turns out to be rather spooky, with parked cars amongst the small copses and a group of men having some sort of clandestine meeting; as ever I feign ignorance and run on. I end up crossing through a zone comprising large gravel pits, with no clear purpose. Fortunately, before too long it leads me out onto a proper road, albeit an exceptionally quiet one culminating in a seriously steep slope and an utterly monstrous climb. It is so vertiginous that it makes me burst out in incredulous laughter. Nothing but a Jeep or Range Rover should attempt this road. I decide to run all of it, just to prove to myself that I can. When I get to the top, lungs bursting and heart pounding, I am on the top of an attractive hillside overlooking a small town. I make it down another slope to a small spring and then locate Aradhna and Roxy nearby.

*****

I present Aradhna with the sunflower and she is equal parts pleased and bemused. We joke about names for the plant and somehow settle upon Bob. Bob takes up residency in one of the dashboard cup holders, for lack of anywhere more sensible, and we fill our water at the spring then drive back up the hill to seek a camping spot. After some off-roading along muddy farm tracks, we find a quiet fallow field, whose dry grass seems uncultivated enough to park on without incurring the wrath of angry farmers. We are a little troubled by some truly enormous bees and I find a rock which I am momentarily convinced is a coprolite (fossilised dinosaur faeces). Otherwise the evening passes uneventfully but relaxingly with a golden sunset and a delicious al fresco meal.

We play cards and draughts and go to bed unusually late (1am). We were enjoying ourselves and hadn't noticed the time. Bob is a bit of a daft romantic gesture but it helps break some of the ice that has formed between my partner and I.

***

## Day 110

A predictably late morning start sees me jogging south from İhsaniye towards the next town, Kabakca, via small local roads. I pass a succession of rather grand homes with fancy gates (one peculiarly decorated with the image of a giant web and spiders). Beyond wheat fields I spy rows of red-brick terraces. The scene could almost be somewhere in Northern England; Turkey is still surprising me at every turn.

The mansions grow truly palatial at İnceğiz, with acres of land behind the ornate metal fences, in which whitewashed ranch-style homes stand out against the deep blue sky. In contrast, when I turn off up a side street, I see a vintage car the colour of an old leather suitcase, crowned with horns and decorated with an intricate rug. A Turkish flag hangs from the aerial. Eccentrics are everywhere.

***

The next big town, Çatalca, is a place of contrasts. Smartly-painted multi-storey housing blocks with balconies are juxtaposed against a shack literally made from old pallets and forgotten detritus, which crouches directly opposite. The route through town takes me past a smart formal garden and busy marketplace where locals are checking out stalls of ripe melons and cheap but cheerful children's clothes. It is a scene of joyful chaos and my London run-commute stands me in good stead here, as I duck and weave between the shoppers[1].

I thought it would continue like this – larger and larger commuter towns and busy streets – but Google Maps has another surprise in store for me. I jog up a dusty road, alongside a vast quarry, with filthy

---

1 Two or three times a week I run either to or from work. It is a six-and-a-half-mile route from Archway to Vauxhall and not without its hills and pedestrian-shaped obstacles.

trucks grinding past me as I search for a surreptitious spot to pee. An entire mountainside seems to have been truncated and turned into aggregate and I can hear the sound of immense factories somewhere processing rock into gravel. I hoped I'd skirt this industrial zone but end up running up a service road directly towards a car park and security booth at the quarry's entrance. I should have backtracked but, as usual, I don't. I am listening to my iPod and allow the music to battle with the sounds of the quarry as I blithely run on into a concrete-floored yard where immense hoppers and conveyor belts are tipping aggregate into the back of trucks before they head out, presumably towards the main road.

I decide to pretend I belong there, perhaps an off-duty worker keeping fit by running home, and follow the route the full vehicles have taken. I pass hard-hatted workers in high-vis jackets, all of whom seem to either ignore me or not even notice my presence. At every moment I expect to be shouted at and sent packing but the call never comes. Perhaps because I myself am wearing a luminous outfit, I don't trouble the periphery of anyone's vision and like a trained operative in a cheesy spy movie, I evade capture and make it out the other end of the working quarry unchallenged.

A small road leads past some more unmanned security booths and out to a road junction. I breathe deeply in relief as I run another half-kilometre to where Roxy is parked.

After lunch I run through Muratbey, whose streets are festooned with red and white bunting. The decorations cheer me though I have nothing to do with the festivities that have occurred here. It is beginning to seem like everything is celebratory as I enjoy the final few days leading up to the grand finish. For a long time, I have been able to push the end goal to the back of my mind and concentrate on taking each day as it comes. Now I am on the fast track to completing a 3400km adventure and every experience seems ever more vivid.

*\*\*\**

The memories are peculiar and bright – a vibrant flower stall, a shop selling a porcelain swan with three miniature elephant "babies", a woman with bright red hair walking down the middle of the road between colourful bungalows. I pass one more quarry, cross the railway tracks and catch a glimpse of the bay of Büyükçekmece from a motorway overpass.

This bite from the southern shore of the narrow isthmus that joins

Turkey to the rest of Europe is really part of the Sea of Marmara, an almost landlocked body of water open to the Aegean at the narrow channel known as the Dardanelles and joined to the Black Sea via the even narrower Bosporus. Everything to the east of here is the capital. Without fanfare, I am suddenly on the outer western suburbs of Istanbul.

**KILOMETRES TRAVELLED: 3327;**
**KILOMETRES REMAINING: 71**

## Tips for Multi-Day Runners - 15. Social Media

Whether you are fundraising, satisfying a sponsor or just keeping in touch with friends or family, you'll probably want to engage with social media. Here are a few tips gleaned from my own limited use of such media.

There is a natural hierarchy of content, resulting in different degrees of engagement:

*Live video > video > photos > text.*

Of course, live streams only work if you've forewarned enough people that you are going live at a given time. Video content that is short and dramatic (under 90 seconds) beats long-form every time. Show people something they haven't seen; communicate your enthusiasm and the extent of the challenge ahead. Stay positive and look straight down the lens as much as possible. Talk as if you are addressing a close friend. If you film whilst running, please use stabilisation technology – shakicam will just make your viewers feel sick.

Everyone loves a sunset – don't stint on uploading photographs of the extraordinary places you are running through as well as the people you meet. Stills that capture a trail extending away into infinity always look good too. If you can enlist your support people in taking great photos of you running, that will certainly help.

Tweets and interactive maps are another great way to make your followers feel they are there with you in the moment. Be careful though – stopping to Tweet every half-hour will seriously impact upon your running pace. It would be better to do daily photo galleries or blog entries at the end of each day than try to upload your thoughts and experiences as they happen. Save live updating for the truly extraordinary moments you experience.

Social media can be a burden as well as an opportunity. Consider having a supportive friend or partner in charge of this aspect of your journey. Make sure you thank and reward them for their unstinting support, and extend the same gratitude to your followers. You may be building a following that will see you through many adventures and their enthusiasm will carry you through the hard times (as well as proving to potential sponsors that you are a viable influencer).

# Chapter 36: Full Steam Ahead

*Day 111*

The capital, once known as Constantinople, and in ancient times as Byzantium, covers an area of over 5,400 square kilometres and is home to over fifteen million people, making it the world's fourth most populous city. As well as humans, Istanbul is home to over 30,000 stray cats, by one estimate. As holy an animal within Islam as the cow is to Hindus, these street cats are cared for by everyone and nobody. In a strange way, seeing these domestic animals roaming the streets makes me feel more at home – a culture that cares for its feral cats surely nurtures caring for its own sake.

Given the immensity of the capital, I know that locating Sirkeci Station will be a task requiring at least one more day. On 28th June my task is simply to run as far east as possible. The simplest route seems to be following a flood dam (they have frequently been my friends on this trip) parallel to the E80, then cutting across the top of the bay of Büyükçekmece.

The route proves peaceful, flat and pretty, just what my aching limbs need. Reed-beds ripple at the edge of the bay, the occasional wading bird strutting in search of supper. At Bahşayiş I meet an immense black dog, who barks lazily at me, but turns tail and flees as I stoop for imaginary stones. The smart houses have gardens filled with scented Orange Jubilee bushes, their vivid bell-shaped flowers still bright in the dimming light.

The sky is scattered with dramatic clouds, through which the early evening sun throws shafts of light like search-beams behind me. I find myself running along a narrow causeway, with fairly light traffic, in contrast to the rushing river of cars on the E80 to my left. Hordes of fishermen have parked their vehicles on the sides of the road, slowing down the through-traffic in a way that would incite traffic wardens into apoplexy in the UK, but seems par for the course here. I appreciate the more relaxed pace as I climb a gradual incline back up to and across the main road. Apart from a momentarily frightening encounter with a pack of five dogs that are called away by a public-spirited local,

I make steady progress past a field of goats and through attractive suburbs to the pick-up point at Karaağaç.

\*\*\*

We backtrack to where the fishermen are and find a bit of rough ground upon which to perch for the night. Before the sun goes down we manage to do a final bit of washing of my running gear, which we hang up for the morning sun to dry. We look at potential routes to Sirkeci station for the next day and realise I have around 45km left to run through the complex city streets to reach the station. At my fittest, this distance, slightly more than a marathon, would be reasonable for a day's running. After 110 days on the road, including 100 days spent running, it feels like a big ask. Do I really want to finish after dark and exhausted when I could simply divide the last section into two days and enjoy both?

Given that this isn't a race and that it's a route that nobody else has run (as far as I know) it scarcely seems to matter. I will feel just as triumphant having run through eight countries and covered 3000km on foot in 112 days as I would in 111 days (pleasing numerology notwithstanding).

The decision is made – two more days and the adventure will be over.

**KILOMETRES TRAVELLED: 3359;**
**KILOMETRES REMAINING: 39**

# Chapter 37: The Indefatigable Hakki

***Day 111***

"Gavin?" Aradhna calls from inside the van.

"What?" I ask, probably with a slightly tetchy tone in my voice, given that I am shaving with a used blade and a tiny compact mirror balanced on my knee, a delicate operation.

"There's a car parked in the road and a man looking at us. He's been there for quite a while."

"Oh shit."

I stand up and look back at the road, face half sudsed. We are clearly in some sort of trouble. A pristine white Mercedes has stopped on the side of the road and a man in his early thirties is scrutinising our vehicle. The driver's door opens and he comes bounding out, an adult human with the energy level of a Labrador puppy. Dressed in what Alan Partridge would refer to as "sports casual", our visitor rushes up to within a foot and a half of my face and asks eagerly:

"Are you from Great Britain?"

I realise later that he might have been a little confused by the fact that Roxy sports both an Ecosse and a GB sticker.

"Yes, we are," I reply warily, as Aradhna sticks her head out of the door.

"I love Britain! I was there for study! Two years!"

The Turkish man, who is named Hakki, speaks with such open-hearted enthusiasm that we warm to him immediately, despite our ingrained sense of British reserve. Hakki has a rounded, boyish face and conveys a sense of excited urgency in everything he says. It is practically impossible to report his speech without liberal use of exclamation marks.

When he hears what we are doing in Turkey, Hakki's excitement level hits a new high.

"Amazing! You must let me help you! I own gas station. Is near here. You come!"

Aradhna and I share a look. This stranger is either incredibly friendly or a little touched. At this point, it is impossible to say which. Normally, we'd have a private chat about it but it doesn't look like Hakki is going to leave us alone to talk it through.

"Let me wash your car! We can have tea. You are exhausted."

He wasn't entirely wrong there. I feel drained, the adrenalin-fuelled dramatic finish not having quite kicked in yet. Aradhna has been feeling the strain of late and Roxy could certainly do with a wash – her exterior is filthy. Aradhna and I continue to communicate in surreptitious looks before we both shrug and nod, our body language expressing a shared decision to throw ourselves into one more mini-adventure. Hakki doesn't seem like the serial killer type and he has only offered to lead us to his petrol station. Roxy could also do with a fill-up.

Hakki is delighted when we assent to his plan and agrees to give us time to pack up (and for me to shave the other side of my face). He sits in his car waiting patiently for fifteen minutes while we fold away the dry laundry and break camp.

Hakki's petrol station, a smart blue-liveried franchise, turns out to be a good half an hour away but we are committed to following him and relieved when he pulls in and takes us to the office for tea and to meet his father, who it transpires, works there. More bizarrely, Hakki's two sisters turn up a little later to meet us and we realise that he is treating us as celebrities. We've become so accustomed to our daily routine that we've forgotten that running / driving 3000km across Europe with a self-built van is an activity that others frequently find impressive.

Hakki's father, a well-tanned gentleman in a well-ironed, short-sleeved shirt, speaks no English so his son translates our story. The effort to which he goes to entertain and inform his father is quite touching as we sit in the sweltering office sipping our tea. Aradhna and I are by now fully in "go with the flow" mode, although I am beginning to get slightly itchy feet. Hakki wants us to join the family for lunch but I really have to get running and he understands. We promise to return to the petrol station at the end of the day. Hakki is also keen to show us the football ground of "Istanbulspor", of which he is a vice-president. That too will have to wait for later.

We bade Hakki and father a fond farewell, having already decided amongst ourselves that we have to get them on camera for Aradhna's documentary. As we leave, Hakki's staff rush out of the station shop with armfuls of mineral water and sports drinks, with which we fill up Roxy. Once more we are impressed by his generosity and hospitality. Had we met Hakki at the start of our Turkish leg, any residual fears about the unknown country might have faded into insignificance. We now feel like we had a whole gang of local supporters egging us on and it is a great confidence booster.

\*\*\*

It is early afternoon by the time we get back to the suburban street where I stopped the night before. I'm dressed in a red t-shirt today and I have another one for tomorrow – it feels fitting to wear the colour of the Turkish flag. I guess that I am now running through a string of satellite towns that were absorbed into the Istanbul suburbs. Each has its own mosque, the most impressive of which is at Yeşilbayır, though the town itself is tiny. Religion holds a powerful place in these communities.

Scraps of pavement are a blessed relief from the busy streets, where I form a peculiar diversion for at least ten thousand Istanbul-dwellers as they drive past me, frequently beeping in what I decide is support. The lands surrounding the city are hilly and I spend the day testing my ankles and quads on steep descents and ascents. Eventually Google Maps has enough of commuter towns and sends me out into a hinterland of new-built housing blocks striped in colourful pastels and half-completed highways.

As with many of the places I've passed through in Eastern Europe, there is much evidence of development and of the abandonment of ambitious projects. I pass immaculate housing blocks which stand out against the horizon like modern-day ziggurats and find myself on a half-finished road which culminates with a rough path into what seems like a limitless rubbish tip. A narrow, rutted channel is flanked on both sides by piles of builders' rubble and domestic waste, extending for what seems kilometres. A few scavenger dogs roam here and there, or doze in the sunshine. A strong breeze blows, helping cool me as I negotiate puddles and duck out of the way of the small trucks and cars that prowl the fly-tipping corridor. There's so much waste material on this hilltop that it surely must be a sanctioned activity. The view from the high hilltop is of a sprawling city upon the horizon, surely central Istanbul. At the far end of wheat fields to my right, even more epic housing blocks are arranged in stepped formations, like wings.

I speed up in order to progress a little faster, grabbing a piece of rubber tubing to wave at the dogs. None of them bother me until I get to within a few hundred metres of the end of the wasteland, whereupon a group of five medium-sized dogs stand snarling at me from a pile of old tyres. Will this be my day? Will my adventure end here, with a vicious mauling?

Fortunately, as I yell at the pack, I am joined by a man who was sitting in a parked car nearby and together we fend the dogs off. I thank him and run downhill, past a legitimate recycling centre, where two tiny ponds seem to host at least four dozen geese. I suppose that, like Aradhna and I, these winged travellers stop where they can at the end of a long day's flying. We can't always chance upon paradise, sometimes a rubbish tip will have to do.

The gravel soon gives way to tarmac and takes me to the edge of yet another suburb, then up and down pavements until I reach a rise with shops and houses to my left and a view down to Istanbul's second coastal bight at Küçükçekmece. At last I feel like I might be making progress into the city – on the map of our trip I am now at the fingertip of the outstretched arm reaching from Gare de l'Est to Sirkeci. All that lies between me and success now is a maze of streets and my own flagging energy levels.

I begin to pass office blocks, a football ground (not Istanbulspor) and university buildings. I see teenagers and twenty-somethings in shorts and feel an inward sigh of relief – now I am not the only one dressed so casually. At the start of the day's running, Aradhna and I had agreed that I'll run 25km and then stop, leaving just 20km to the finish line the following day. It is now my challenge to find Roxy in a city swarming with people and parked grey vans. Aradhna has sent me her position with a mapping app and now I'm in the heart of the city, my phone signal is good, so finding her is easier than I imagined. I do manage, however, to run straight past the van at first, before backtracking (for once).

\*\*\*

As good as our word, although a little later than planned, we set off back to Hakki's petrol station, arriving around 5pm. There he arranges for Roxy to be power-washed, after receiving a good shampooing. She emerges sparkly and renewed (albeit still pretty stinky on the inside).

We then follow Hakki to Istanbulspor's ground and meet a couple of star players plus their manager, an ex-footballer of some renown I am embarrassed not to have heard of (I know nothing about the sport). We decide that with the fading light, it might be best to come back and do the interview here another day. Before we leave though, I have a professional weigh-in, the electronic scale revealing that I now weigh

71.6kg, a weight I've not been since a teenager.

Next we head off to Hakki's summer home, on the south coast, where we are honoured to share his family dinner table and meet his wife Semra, and daughters Serra and Berra. His mum (Sukran) and dad (Sebahattin) are already there. Their delicious home-cooked food, including stuffed vine leaves, fresh watermelon and *mihlama* (a dish of melted cheese and cornmeal, to be eaten with hunks of fresh bread, fondu-style) is exactly what I need. The family takes us for a short stroll around their well-to-do neighbourhood, saying hello to some of Serra's friends in passing (she exhibits none of the embarrassment such a social scenario might cause in the UK).

Finally, late and rather tired, Hakki insists that we can't spend our last running night in the van and that he must put us up in his city apartment. It takes the best part of an hour to get there, but when we do we find it comfortable and relaxing. We both sleep soundly, still amazed by this family's open-hearted generosity. So far, Istanbul has been exceptionally kind to us.

The following morning, as we all eat breakfast together, I take the opportunity to send a couple of emails, in preparation for the surprise I am planning for Aradhna a few days hence. I had to tell her I had something nice planned, in order to legitimately spend an hour staring at my phone, but I know she will not suspect its true nature. We also wash everything remaining in the "isolation box" in Hakki's washing machine, so that it won't stink up the van while we recover for three days in a luxury hotel that our wonderful friend David has kindly booked for us. We are grateful to be the recipients of such generosity, from so many supporters.

*** 

Bidding a final adieu to Hakki with a roadside brunch, I set off in the early afternoon. I have a "mere" 20km to run, but only about four hours of daylight in which to run it. This last stretch will be run as one final straight and I send Aradhna off to locate the station and find somewhere to park Roxy and wait. She plans to use Facebook's "Live" function to broadcast the grand finale on social media. I hope I can live up to the weight of expectation. A host of friends and family have been following our adventures for months now and I hope I will not disappoint them.

**KILOMETRES TRAVELLED: 3381;**
**KILOMETRES REMAINING: 17**

## Tips for Multi-Day Runners – 16. Safety

You're going to be spending a lot of time alone, sometimes in very remote locations, perhaps in treacherous weather conditions and maybe even with wild animals prowling the undergrowth. You'll need to follow some simple rules and carry some essential kit with you.

If you get lost, consider backtracking. I am terrible at following this rule; I always want to press on. However, the one thing you do know (generally) when you get lost, is how you got there. It's a good idea to have an emergency rendezvous point in mind so that your support crew and you can assemble there in case you become split up.

*Carry a satellite phone or communicator* (see Tip 4). It may become a vital lifeline, either for alerting emergency services or just letting your other half know you're alive. Carry a second phone, in case the first one runs out of batteries. Get one with a long-life battery and remember to charge any rechargeable devices whenever you get a chance.

*Take a survival blanket/bag with you, plus warm clothes.* The blanket is a fold-away sheet of thin metallic foil that, just like baking foil, keeps heat in. You may have seen marathon runners wearing them at the end of a race to combat the inevitable body temperature drop that follows. If you get stuck out after darkness, with little or no shelter, climbing into one of these just might save your life.

*Keep messaging your presence to your support crew*, at regular intervals, so that if you become lost or out of communication range rescuers will know when and (through GPS tracking) where you vanished off the beaten track. If your support driver is vulnerable and alone, make sure they have keys to a lockable vehicle.

*Run with a head torch and a change of clothes.* Neither need be especially heavy and they could be vital to your happiness or even survival.

*Don't take any risks greater than the situation requires.* If you have to walk five miles to cross a bridge, rather than fording a river, then do it. Know your own physical limits and always err on the side of overestimating how long it will take to run from A to B. I've probably broken most of these behavioural rules, but I now travel prepared, with GPS communicator, survival bag, head torch and two mobile phones.

# Chapter 38: Byzantium Beckons

### Day 112

The city once called Byzantium has been occupied since at least the second millennia BC. It was named in honour of the Greek king Byzas who settled colonists there in 667 BC. After the Greeks came the Romans, of course, and the city gained its second name, Constantinople, named after the emperor Constantine the Great, an early Christian convert. Thus the city exchanged pantheism for monotheism and gained many magnificent churches and cathedrals, including the famous Hagia Sophia, later converted to a mosque and finally a museum. Rarely has a city had such a vivid and complex history (perhaps only Jerusalem can compete), partly due to its geographical position as the apex of the land bridge between Asia and Europe, with the Bosporus acting as a vital trade conduit.

All in all, I couldn't have hoped for a more magical place to end our adventure. As I begin the last section, I can no longer remember a day when I haven't felt drained of energy, but this is no time for being pathetic. I trust that my muscles and cardiovascular system will kick into gear as ever and do their jobs.

\*\*\*

I find myself running through a large shopping area not far from the vast Mall of Istanbul, no doubt an air-conditioned haven in the high heat of summer. I've never much liked malls myself, finding them soulless and blatantly manipulative, but right now I could certainly do with some of that cool air.

The mosques grow grander and more impressive, with double minarets and golden domes. I run with my phone open at Google Maps, zig-zagging along side streets, including some spectacularly steep ones. Most of the hills are descents – fortunately, since the ache in my legs is a vivid reminder of how many miles I've put them through. I duck around pedestrians and shopkeepers, leaning against their storefronts in the sunshine. Political banners supporting Erdoğan are still in evidence, tied across the shopping precincts.

Running down a major road linking one part of the city to another, I spy three dogs, a motley pack of hobos, trotting uphill on the other side of the road. We let one another be. I descend to a pristine road junction with geometrical flower beds and wrought-iron-railed overpasses carrying pedestrians high above the traffic. It is civilised yet confusing; I take a wrong turning immediately and end up climbing a handrail to dreep[1] down onto a lower walkway.

At Merkez Efendi I reach the Roman-era city walls, built in the 5th century and subsequently restored and strengthened following numerous earthquakes and floods. I pass through the massive fortifications, which are intact enough to imagine the indomitable presence they must have had for any approaching visitors.

I am now within the Old Town, whose buildings are anything up to 1,500 years old[2]. The streets are hugely busy and I am a little surprised to see how few people are dressed in conservative Muslim attire. Bare arms and shoulders are on common display – perhaps largely tourists but also, I feel, an indicator of the inclusiveness and tolerance that makes the city one of the jewels of the Islamic world. I hope it will remain this way and feel absolutely at home as I run.

An age-darkened column, listing like the famous tower in Pisa, and seemingly held together with iron bands, draws my attention. Tourists are taking selfies in front of it. I later discover this is the Column of Constantine, built in 330AD by the Roman Emperor to commemorate Byzantium (renamed Constantinople) becoming the capital of the Roman Empire.

I am close now – the blue line on my phone indicates a mere 3km lies between me and achieving a goal we've dreamed about for over a year. Aradhna posts as much on Facebook and our social media accounts begin to go crazy. I get out my action camera and gimbal to record the final approach. Unbeknownst to me, Aradhna sets Facebook Live going and begins to record:

"I have actually no idea which direction Gavin is going to come from but I have his drink, as requested, and a little treat in my bag," she announces, looking around for me. Meanwhile, I am only a few streets away.

*** 

---

1   A fantastic Scots word meaning to dangle by one's fingertips from a wall or other high perch.
2   The Hagia Sophia dates back to 537AD and there are many Ottoman-era buildings from the 14th to 16th centuries.

I cross a fairly quiet stair, run down a cobbled street and spot a sign indicating "Marmaray" with a graphic depicting a train. Marmaray is the local station adjacent to Sirkeci. I turn a corner and remarkably, there it is – the end of the Orient line!

The arched portals and rounded windows are as beautiful as I'd seen in the illustrations, although the station is now partly under scaffolding (and, I am pleased to note, renovation). More importantly, Aradhna is there, filming on her phone. I run to her and we embrace, excited and happy but also a little baffled. What now? What's the protocol?

We take photos in front of the station's restaurant, fittingly called the "Orient Express" and wander into the lobby, imagining exhausted and excited Victorians disembarking here and walking out into the heat of the day with their parasols. A craft fair is taking place within, but Aradhna and I elect to sit quietly outside at one of the café tables, to drink a glass of Turkish tea and contemplate what has just happened. Aradhna feeds me some Turkish delight and takes a photo of this, a celebratory Indian tradition called *muh meetha karo* (literally "sweeten your mouth").

We sit back and watch some railway employees in orange dungarees taking a break as tourists wander by, looking for the modern, concrete and steel station adjacent to Sirkeci. What exactly have we just done?

We have run and driven across eight countries, through countless towns and villages, through vast forests, over epic mountain ranges, alongside rivers and lakes, reservoirs and seas. We have done this together, with a little help from friends old and new. We've met wonderful people and seen incredible things, with a new vista behind Roxy's windows every morning. The experience will be unforgettable – yes, some of the details will fade in time. The impermanence of memory is inescapable. But vitally, we have survived and shared a proper modern-day adventure.

***

Like those early Europeans, setting out on the Orient Express back in 1883, we are celebrating a continent and our ability to move freely within it. Back then, such mobility was the prerogative of the wealthy and adventurous. Now it is an experience open to all who want it. Our unity and commonality is under threat by the forces of small-minded insularity and xenophobia.

We contemporary Europeans need to fight for our place in a great continent, and within a vision of humanity that celebrates variety and open-mindedness.

If every adventure should end with a revelation, ours is that we really have far more in common with our French, Romanian and Turkish friends than we do with anyone who would deny our place in the cultural powerhouse that is Europe.

**KILOMETRES TRAVELLED: 3398;**
**KILOMETRES REMAINING: 0**

# Chapter 39: One More Adventure

One more discovery Aradhna and I make on our journey is more personal. We always said, semi-jokingly, that if we managed to make it 3000km across Europe in a tiny self-built campervan without killing one another, then we were meant to be together, forever. Now that we've made it to Istanbul, homicide-free, I want to show Aradhna how much I appreciate her sharing this journey with me. The big moment has arrived.

The covert emails I'd sent over the last week have borne fruit. One of the restaurants I contacted hasn't responded at all. Another said yes to most of my requests, but not all of them. The third was thoroughly accommodating and plans are in place to dine, three evenings hence, on the N-Terrace rooftop restaurant of the Sura Design Hotel. Over the next three days I will have to contend with one more physical obstacle as a direct result of all this running – my errant gut.

\*\*\*

Almost as soon as I stop running, I develop an upset stomach and bowel as well as flu-like symptoms of fever and nausea, topped off with muscular aches and pains. Nevertheless, I try to stay upbeat. We move into the lovely hotel room David has arranged for us and drink the champagne my sister Fiona gave us when we left (tagged "Do not open until Istanbul"), and which we transported intact across a continent, concealed in the recesses of the "cupboard of doom".

When we hand over Roxy's keys to the hotel concierge, we realise just how smelly and cramped her interior is compared with the opulence of our suite at the Palazzo Donizetti. We must seem eccentric at best, turning up in our jeans and t-shirts, with multiple carrier bags of clothes for our three-day stay.

To their credit, the hotel staff take it in their stride. As for us, it will take a while to become accustomed to luxury once more. I am, however, immediately grateful for the en-suite bathroom, which I make copious use of over the next few days. That said, on our first day, the toilet springs a leak and we miss sunset at our hotel's rooftop while waiting in for a plumber, surely something one ought not to have to do in a four-star hotel. It is quickly fixed, however, and we dine at dusk, eventually.

Despite my feebleness, we do manage to foray out now and again to visit a local art gallery, some nearby restaurants, the Grand Bazaar and the famed Blue Mosque, which slightly disappointingly is being renovated inside, its ceiling largely hidden by scaffolding. We find Istanbul varied, bustling and convivial, with Aradhna sparking up a lively debate with a local shopkeeper on the merits of Frida Kahlo as a female role model. We buy some delicious-looking sweets to take home for friends and work colleagues and souvenirs for family members.

I then take Aradhna out to buy a dress for our special dinner, which raises an eyebrow, since it's not something I do very often, not being much of a fashion aficionado. I pick up a new jacket and trousers, not quite a suit, but giving a similarly smart effect. Aradhna chooses a sweeping red, gold and black dress with a deep neckline.

\*\*\*

And so it is that, on 3rd July 2018, we step forth from our hotel into the warm evening air, hail a taxi and speed off to N-Terrace, a little late, which causes me palpitations as I am timing the evening to hit sunset on the terrace. We just make it in time and a very friendly maître d' shows us to our table, which has a spectacular view over the city, including the Bosporus and the fabled Blue Mosque. Our waiter is momentarily confused by my request for a bottle of champagne *before* the meal (especially as he knows my plans for after dinner). We eat our first two tasty vegetarian courses and then I excuse myself to double-check the proceedings with the maître d', who reassures me that all is in order.

As I take my seat again, one of our favourite songs begins to play over the restaurant's PA[1]. This probably confuses many of the diners since, up to then, we've been listening to vaguely ethnic ambient music. Aradhna now knows that something is up and is further clued-in by the waiter delivering our dessert – two chocolate and pistachio pancakes with words written in Turkish around the rim:

*benimle evlenir misin*

Geek that I am, I make my partner Google-translate these words,

---

1    "Whatever's Written in Your Heart" by Gerry Rafferty, from the 1978 *City to City* album.

which first requires me to decipher the cursive chocolate sauce text for her. I spell the letters out with the help of the waiter, who proffers a piece of paper with them written out in block capitals). This isn't happening quite as smoothly as I'd anticipated and my heart is pounding in my chest as Aradhna consults her phone's browser.

Meanwhile, I produce the secret item I've been hiding in my wash bag since March and Aradhna begins to giggle nervously as I hold out the sapphire ring. Immediately the waiters, who have mysteriously gathered, plus the dozen or so other customers on the terrace, begin to clap energetically and I laugh and remind them that Aradhna hasn't answered yet (and she reminds me later that I never actually spoke the words, "Will you marry me?"). Aradhna holds it together for long enough to nod her assent, then lets me put the ring on her finger and we have our Hollywood moment.

## Tips for Multi-Day Runners - 17. What's Next?

If you've just run 3400km in a few weeks, you'll probably want to rest and not think about things running-related for a while, but this complacency could be a mistake.

Now is the time to reflect on and record lessons learnt as well as completing any notes you might have taken to help you remember the detail. Upload your photos, celebrate the achievement, but also start thinking about what you might try next.

The starting point for me is always, "What sort of experience do I want to have?" But there are other key questions you might want to ask yourself, including:

*How will the experience build on what I've just done?*
*What have I learnt from the run I just completed?*
*How long do I need to recover?*
*Which countries do I long to visit?*
*How runnable are the places I'm considering?*
*What sort of support do I want?*
*What support is available?*
*How far is it?*
*How long will it take?*
*How do I want to record my experiences?*
*How will I use social media?*
*Will I be able to get sponsors involved?*
*Should I raise money for a worthy charity?*
*Who is coming with me?*
*How much will it cost?*
*When do I start?*

And believe it or not, this is not an exhaustive list! I believe you need a good 6-9 months minimum to plan an adventure run of one month or more. Certainly if you want to avoid stress headaches and the possibility of making calamitous mistakes, this should be your lead in.

# Backwards

Following the inevitable social media storm that accompanies any engagement (and given our recent adventure we begin to worry that we are Bogarting the limelight somewhat) we settle into the role of two holidaymakers whose only commitment is to a Calais-Dover ferry in six weeks' time. My body struggles to understand its new lassitude at first, with my energy levels fluctuating wildly and my gut taking its time to readjust. I like what the run has done to me, overall, being able to see muscle definition in my torso that hasn't been visible since my teens. I know that it won't and can't last. How do you replace six to eight hours of cardiovascular activity plus 6000-8000 calories per day with any sort of ad hoc, on-the-road exercise regime? Simple answer – you can't.

We spend two more blissful days in Istanbul, then check out of our hotel and get back into Roxy. With sadness we discover that we'd entirely forgotten about Bob, our adopted sunflower. After three days in a presumably subterranean car park, he is a withered husk. There might have been some life left in Bob, but I set him down temporarily on the kerb and then accidentally shut the passenger door on him. Bob is beheaded. It is an ignominious end to an all too brief life for our mascot. Aradhna and I hope this will not be an omen for our future parenting skills.

***

There is everything and nothing to say about our meandering journey home through countries including Greece, Albania, Montenegro, Croatia, Bosnia, Slovakia, Italy, Germany, Belgium and Luxembourg. The weather seems to universally bless us with warmth and sunlight. We pass through fascinating towns and cities such as Mostar in Bosnia, Dubrovnik, Verona and Trieste, near the Italian-Slovakian border. We white-water raft in Bosnia and admire ludicrously expensive yachts in Croatia, are moved to tears by a war museum in Bosnia and explore a huge communist-era bunker turned art exhibit in Albania. We swim in icy karst springs and placid warm Grecian lakes. We entirely fall in love with breathtaking Montenegro. We eat fabulously and drink to gleeful excess. We feel at home everywhere we go and are moved on exactly once (by a nightclub owner, politely, and as much for our own good, as his customers').

When I write that there is nothing to say, I mean merely that by the time we reached Istanbul we already knew our place in Europe and what it meant to us. The journey back is just idyllic reinforcement of a single, simple idea.

We are too small to be insular, too influential to turn our backs on a continent in whose culture we revel and whose history we are immutably a part of. The Orient Express first embodied this spirit of travel and adventure, linking rather than dividing nations. We are glad to have followed its well-worn route across eight countries. We know ourselves a little better, as well as discovering what Europe really means to us.

We are Europeans, and we always will be.

# Appendix I – Worn/Carried Kit

*On my person:*
Running / Trail shoes
2-ply socks (with optional second pair)
Cycling shorts / leggings
Over shorts
Technical t-shirt
Technical jacket
Cap (optional)
Sunglasses (optional)
iPhone 7 armband holster
iPhone 7
Homemade shoulder sling for action camera & gimbal

*In my backpack:*
Reservoir with 1.5 litres water and drinking tube
Energy gels
Electrolyte tablets
Fruit and nut snacks
Survival Blanket
Maps
Compass
Whistle
Head torch
Garmin inReach satellite device
Battery pack and charger cable
Compact waterproof jacket
Spare t-shirt
Dry face flannel in zip-lock bag
Factor 50 sunscreen
DEET insect-repellent
Paracetamol and ibuprofen
Local currency
Credit card
Spare batteries and SD card for action camera

# Appendix II – Roxy Kit

It's hard for this to be exhaustive as we discarded items along the way and picked up useful things too, but here's what we would certainly pack if we were doing another such trip.

*One 64L box each of clothes, including running gear*
*Isolation box for soiled kit*
*Empty recycling box*
*Bedding including duvet*
*Sleeping bag for guests*
*Towels and rags*
*Slippers*
*Flip-flops*
*Wellies*
*Large backpack*
*Sturdy shopping bags*

*Cooker with 2 gas rings plus grill*
*Gas canisters*
*2 x miniature fold-up gas burners*
*Miniature gas canisters*
*Kitchen implements*
*Melamine crockery*
*China mugs*
*Metal cutlery*
*Kettle*
*Metal and glass vacuum flasks*

*Cool box with mains or 12v power source*
*Inverter (12v to 240v)*
*Solar panel*
*Leisure battery and battery charging relay*
*USB and 12v "cigarette lighter" ports*
*Electrical hook-up and 240v sockets*
*Polarity adaptor and polarity analysing plug*
*Regional Plug adaptors*
*Laptops*
*External USB drives and cables*

*Fresh water container*
*Waste water container*

*Fold-up camping table*
*Fold-up canvas chairs*
*Fold-up step-stool*
*Fold-up trolley and bungee ropes*
*Pop-up shower tent*
*Bucket, sponge and trowel*
*Toilet paper*

*Emergency Road Kit (warning triangles, high-vis jackets, breathalysers[1] etc)*
*Fire extinguisher*
*Tool box*
*"Useful items box"*
*Cleaning products*
*"Mr Squirty"[2]*
*Bicycle repair and maintenance kit*
*Laminator and gels*

*Books*
*Games*
*CDs*
*Media Drive*
*Maps*
*Stationery bag and notebooks*

*Wash bags (mine containing a secret)*

*Dried food and drinks (in "cupboard of doom")*
*Perishable food and veg (in coolbox)*
*Sports nutrition in separate boxes*

*Camera, bag and accessories*
*Basic tripod*
*Microphones and accessories*
*Pop-up handheld reflector*

*Hybrid bicycle and accessories*
*Bike rack*

---

1    Disposable self-testing kits – mandatory in France.
2    Simply a one-litre plastic drinking bottle with a "sports" nozzle, so you can squirt out small amounts of water – very useful if you're rationing water whilst doing the dishes!

# Appendix III - Daily Nutrition

Below is a sample of what I ate during my 112 days of running (bar the occasional day off). The usual disclaimers apply – I am not a professional nutritionist and this is just a representative example of the sort of things I'd be eating each day. Another thing worth noting is my diet was largely, though not exclusively, vegetarian, with a high concentration of dairy and carbohydrates. Aradhna is vegetarian, although I am not. When we ate out sometimes, I would occasionally have red meat or chicken, but it did not form a staple part of my diet during the run.

*Breakfast*
    Granola with fresh fruit (200g)
    2 pains au chocolat (or other pastries)
    One fruit yoghurt
    One cup tea
    One cup coffee

*Snack*
    Dried fruit and mixed nuts

*Lunch*
    2 croissants with melted cheese
    Plate of cut fresh fruit and raw vegetables
    (i.e. grapes, melon, strawberries, cherry tomatoes,
    carrots, cucumber)
    2 boiled eggs with salt
    Several plain biscuits
    Fruit yoghurt
    Rice pudding
    Chocolate muffin
    One cup tea
    Chocolate milk
    Sports drink (i.e. Lucozade)

*Afternoon snack*
> Dried fruit and nuts
> Trail bar
> One energy gel

*Post-run snack*
> Fizzy drink (i.e. Irn Bru)
> Pastry
> Crisps
> One cup tea

*Dinner*
> Pasta with roast vegetables and tomato sauce
> Side salad
> Chocolate pudding
> 1 beer or glass of red wine
> Tablet or fudge
> One cup tea

*Throughout day:*
> 4 litres of water (2 plain, 2 containing two tablets of electrolyte)

Total Calories: approximately 6000

## Appendix IV – Please Don't Eat Me Mister Bear

For your delectation, here are the full, unexpurgated lyrics of the song I used to scare of any putative bears I might meet in the Romanian wilderness.

It can be sung to any melody you like, provided that it is performed a) cheerfully and b) LOUDLY.

PLEASE DON'T EAT ME MISTER BEAR
Please don't eat me, mister bear
I'm stringy and skinny and I taste of poo
Please don't eat me, mister bear
I really wouldn't bother, if I were you

I'll stay here, and you stay there
And please don't eat me, mister bear

Please don't eat me mister bear
I mean you no harm, I'm just running by
Please don't eat me, mister bear
And don't be alarmed by one such as I

Just keep on fishing, I really don't care
And please don't eat me, mister bear

Please don't eat me, mister bear
I'm coming round the corner and then I'll be gone
Please don't eat me mister bear
I don't want to stay where I don't belong

I'll be out of your woodland and out of your hair
So please don't eat me, mister bear